E. Henderson

The Book of the Prophet Ezekiel

Translated from the original Hebrew: with a commentary, critical, philological, and

exegetical

E. Henderson

The Book of the Prophet Ezekiel
Translated from the original Hebrew: with a commentary, critical, philological, and exegetical

ISBN/EAN: 9783337310950

Printed in Europe, USA, Canada, Australia, Japan

Cover: Foto ©Lupo / pixelio.de

More available books at **www.hansebooks.com**

THE BOOK

OF THE

PROPHET EZEKIEL,

TRANSLATED FROM THE ORIGINAL HEBREW.

WITH A

COMMENTARY,

CRITICAL, PHILOLOGICAL, AND EXEGETICAL.

BY

E. HENDERSON, D.D.

AUTHOR OF COMMENTARIES ON THE BOOK OF THE MINOR PROPHETS,
JEREMIAH AND LAMENTATIONS, ISAIAH, ETC.

Andover:
WARREN F. DRAPER, PUBLISHER.
MAIN STREET.
1870.

PREFACE.

In preparing the following work for the press the author has been greatly encouraged by the kind reception given to his previous labors on the Prophets by theological readers both in this country and America. It has been a satisfaction to him to find that the principles on which he has conducted his exegetical inquiries have been generally approved of by those most competent to judge. To these principles he still adheres; convinced that whatever there abounds of symbol, vision, enigma, and parable in the compositions of Ezekiel, there runs through them a vein of historical reality which serves as a safeguard against the vagaries of the mystical school of interpretation.

While the Biblical student is ever to be careful not to allow the divine meaning of Scripture to evaporate into thin air, he is equally to be solicitous not to load the inspired text with the cumbrous lucubrations of his own imagination. In fixing upon the sense to be brought out, he is not at liberty to force into the sacred word any preconceived notions of human invention; but, carefully weighing all the circumstances of the context, to give that interpretation which best harmonizes with them, and brings them into view. All far-fetched and arbitrary constructions he is utterly to repudiate. The literal and the figurative are to be allowed their respective claims, but never to be confounded, mixed up together, or substituted the one for the other. It behoves the interpreter, with his mind open to receive the truth of God, to maintain the attitude of young Samuel, and earnestly to give utterance to the beautiful prayer: " Speak Lord; for thy servant heareth."

In prosecuting his expository task the author has endeavored to avoid indulging in the discursive — confining himself to the matter in hand; making the text his leader; and condensing, within as small a compass as was compatible with due regard to perspicuity, what he had to offer in elucidation of the subjects treated of by the sacred writer.

Warned by the palpable failure of others who have staked their literary reputation on calculations relative to events still supposed to be future in the history of the church, he has not presumed to lift the veil which it hath pleased the Spirit of inspiration should be left to remain on certain portions of prophetic scripture. His province has not been to prophesy, but humbly and carefully to investigate the meaning of the prophecies dictated by the Holy Ghost, and recorded in the Divine word.

The charge of obscurity brought against Ezekiel is nothing new. Nor can it be denied that there are portions of his book which, at first sight, seem hard to be understood. It may fairly be questioned, however, whether the alleged want of perspicuity be not mainly attributable to the mists of false interpretation in which he has been involved, rather than to any impenetrable veil thrown over the prophecies by his own hand. To understand his pictures they must be surveyed as wholes, without the mind being distracted by dwelling upon the minor and accessory features of which they are made up. Minute attention to these (especially in studying the description of the temple), apart from a grand view of the whole, is one of the principal causes of the difficulty accompanying its interpretation.

While constrained to abide by the idea of a literal temple, the author sees no violation of the laws of sound exegesis in maintaining at the same time the symbolical import of the structure and its ordinances, just as we understand the typical character of the former temple erected by Solomon. Both adumbrated or shadowed forth the substantial blessings of the gospel dispensation; serving as στοιχεῖα, elements, or rudimental means of instruction, adapted to the then infantile state of the church, and leading the mind forward in anticipation of better things to come. See the Apostle's definition, Col. ii. 17; Heb. x. 1.

INTRODUCTION.

EZEKIEL first introduces himself to our notice on the banks of the Chebar, a river of upper Mesopotamia, whither he had been transported, along with the more distinguished of his countrymen, when Jehoiachin, having surrendered to Nebuchadnezzar (B.C. 599), was carried into exile in Babylon. He was in part contemporary with Jeremiah and Daniel, between the latter of whom and Ezekiel there are more points of resemblance than one, especially in the character of his visions and the grotesque cast of his images. Having, previously to his removal from Jerusalem, filled the sacerdotal office, he possessed an influence which must have been of great service to him in his intercourse with his fellow-captives, who were accustomed to assemble in his house at Tel-abib to consult him in reference to their future prospects.

Whether he had been married before he arrived in Chaldea does not appear; but while there he had the affliction to be suddenly deprived of the object of his conjugal affection, a circumstance in reference to which he was constituted a type of the calamity which was to befall the inhabitants of Jerusalem, xxiv. 15–25.

His field of labor embraced not merely his countrymen from Judea, but also, in all probability, the descendants of the ten tribes, who had partly been located in the same region when removed from their native land by Shalmanezer, king of Assyria, 2 Kings xviii. 9–12. In the remote province of Mesopotamia our prophet enjoyed a freedom of action, and consequently opportunities of usefulness, which might not have fallen to his lot if he had accompanied his captive sovereign to the metropolis of the empire. He was not only unmolested by the Chaldeans, but undisturbed by the plots and caballings to which his contemporary Jeremiah was exposed from the profligate courtiers of Judah.

Nor, in discharging the duties of his office, is there reason to believe that his labors were confined to his fellow exiles. Many of his discourses were addressed to the Jews who still remained in Jerusalem, with whom he might have held communication by letter or verbal messages. These, like most of those with whom he was brought into contact, were obstinately resolute in their determination to persist in their rebellious courses. Though suffering the punishment of their sins in a foreign country, the latter had too much idolatrous sympathy with their countrymen in Judea to lend a willing ear to the solemn calls to repentance and reformation tendered to them by the prophet. Still Ezekiel, strengthened with power from on high, pursued his course, unintimidated by their stubborn opposition, displaying throughout the utmost intrepidity and fidelity of character. We find him incessantly at work, exposing vice, urging to the observance of the divine commandments, and consoling the pious with the hopes of better times. While there is much in his book to arouse and alarm, and much that is calculated even to terrify, there are at the same time such aboundings of tender compassion, as cannot but administer consolation to the sorrowing spirit. Ezekiel was not only the denouncer of judgment: he was at the same time the publisher of glad tidings. While in the first part of his book his thoughts revolve round the calamitous circumstances of his ruined country, in the latter half he delights in holding out assurances that the Most High would receive back into favor and abundantly bless repentant Israel. Interspersed are gracious promises of the Messiah and the blessings of the dispensation which he should introduce. The Hebrews were not left to imagine that their return from Chaldea and the restoration of their civil and ecclesiastical polity were to exhaust the blessings which their covenant God had in store for them. Blessings of an infinitely higher order he teaches them to anticipate, and repeatedly gives them to understand that no failure on the part of the Divine Being should occasion the withdrawal of their enjoyment. He ever evinces a sacred regard to the best interests of those whom he addresses, which is admirably calculated to arrest the attention, and promote the edification of readers in every age. The ethical element pervades the whole; and no one can peruse the book in a proper spirit without having his mind impressed with a sense of the majesty, holiness, rectitude, and compassion of the Divine Being, who had selected the prophet to be his messenger to his guilty people. *"Thus saith the Lord Jehovah"* reverberates on every page; and hard must that heart be which is not penetrated by the sound.

It is worthy of notice that among the predictions which denounce judgments against the enemies of the covenant people we find none directed against Babylon. To what this is to be ascribed it is difficult to imagine, except it arose from a desire not to give unnecessary offence to the government under which the prophet lived.

With respect to style, Ezekiel may be said to hold a middle place between the high poetic and the depressed prosaic. Without, on the one hand, rising to the more elevated heights of prophetical composition, he pursues, on the other, his easy flow of diction, occasionally breaking out in passages that are rough and rugged in their aspect, in accordance with the nature of his theme. The language abounds more in the picturesque than any other biblical writing. The imagery is of the richest and boldest description. Allegory, symbol, and vision predominate.

Without trenching upon the claims of our prophet as an inspired writer by attributing to his human powers what was supplied from a higher source, we may regard him as an instrument singularly qualified for executing the task devolved upon him. In this point of view he appears before us as possessing a rich and gorgeous imagination, to which he gives the freest course, working everything out in adaptation to his subject, and laying everything under contribution that was calculated to impart dignity to his theme, and to produce a deep and salutary impression upon his hearers. Some parts of his book are truly magnificent in their sublimity, and others are affectingly awakening in their pointedness of appeal. He is most emphatic in his denunciations of the divine judgments.

One of the peculiar characteristics of our prophet is a proneness to indulge in amplification which scorns to be arrested in its course, and branches out into image after image and repetition after repetition, till nothing is left untouched that might be expected to impress the reader. In his objurgations he returns to the charge again and again, unwilling to let his guilty countrymen escape from the shafts of conviction. To the same cause is to be ascribed the minuteness with which every subject is treated. Not content with exhibiting his pictures in broad outlines, he embodies his ideas in microscopic forms, omitting no feature that may render them perfect in their presentation to view.

Attempts have been made to reduce the composition of Ezekiel to strict symmetrical verse, such as marks the structure and turn of sentences in other prophetical writers; but though there are parts of the book that may, after a fashion, be metrically disposed, such as the elegies on Tyre, chapters xxvii., xxviii., and those on Egypt, chapter xxix.–xxxi., yet as a whole the language is to be regarded as prose without rhythm or parallelism, only characterised by warmth of feeling such as became a writer deeply interested in the fates of his countrymen and the glory of his God. In presenting the text, therefore, to my readers, I have retained the ordinary cast of prose throughout.

It would appear from chapter xxix. 17, that the ministry of Ezekiel was continued till the twenty-seventh year of the exile; at least this is the latest date which we meet with in his book. According to tradition, he ended his days in Chaldea, having been put to death by one of the princes of his people, whom he had enraged by reproving him for having indulged in the worship of idols.

SELECT LITERATURE OF THE BOOK.

THE most important of the Jewish commentaries on Ezekiel is that of David Kimchi, justly esteemed on account of its strictly grammatical character. It is found in Buxtorf's Biblia Rabbinica (Amstelódami, 1724–1727, four volumes, folio).

The best works of the Fathers on the prophet are those of Theodoret and Jerome, who, for the most part, confine themselves to the literal interpretation of the text.

What was designed to be a first-rate work on Ezekiel is that of two Spanish Jesuits, Pradus and Villapandus, which, however, especially that portion written by the latter, is rather to be regarded as an ostentatious display of architectural learning, than as calculated to satisfy any reader seriously endeavoring to ascertain the true meaning of the word of God. It was published at Rome, 1596, in three huge folio volumes, with numerous plates designed to ilustrate the buildings of the temple. It is a book of extreme rarity, being scarcely ever found in any private library.

The earliest work of the Reformers on the prophet is that written by Oecolampadius (Basileæ, 1548, folio). Considering the age in which it was published, it is justly entitled to respect. It is to be regretted that Calvin did not carry his Commentary on Ezekiel further than the twentieth chapter, since from the exegetical tact which he has displayed it is manifest none was better qualified to do justice to the author.

The German Translation of the Old Testament by J. D. Michaelis, with Notes for the unlearned, Part x. (Göttingen, 1781), and Archbishop Newcome's Attempt towards an Improved Version of Ezekiel (London, 1785, 4to.), both furnish not unimportant contributions to the elucidation of the prophet; but neither of them scrupled to take unjustifiable liberties with the Hebrew text. Their labors in Hebrew literature have been superseded by those of later critics.

The Scholia in Vetus Testamentum, by the younger Rosenmüller (Leipzig, 1808–1810, 8vo.), will ever retain their value as a repertorium of materials for Biblical interpretation.

The Commentarius Criticus of Maurer (Leipzig, 1838, 8vo.) will be found exceedingly serviceable as a hand-book for the use of the exegetical student, if only he be on his guard lest he should occasionally be led astray by the rationalistic views of the author. The same caution is requsite in regard to studying the earlier editions of Rosenmüller.

Heinrich Ewald, in the Notes to his Propheten Des Alten Bundes, introduces a series of criticisms such as might be expected from a Hebrew grammarian of acknowledged merit. Not unfrequently, however, they will be found to fail in yielding satisfaction with respect to the true meaning of the text.

Commentar über den Propheten Ezekiel by Hävernick (Erlangen, 1843, 8vo). This work, together with that on Daniel, by the same author, formed quite an epoch in the theological literature of Germany. The author goes at great length into the exposition of the prophet, and is more fruitful and happy in philological investigation than any of his predecessors. He is characterized throughout by a spirit of earnest and warm-hearted piety.

Der Prophet Ezekiel, by Dr. Ferdinand Hitzig (Leipzig, 1847). This work, which is appropriately characterized by Fairbairn as *elastic*, though containing acute and ingenious remarks, carries Biblical criticism to such excess that it may be regarded as a specimen of literary trifling, rather than a sober exposition of the oracles of divine truth.

Umbreit's Praktischer Commentar über den Ezekiel (Hamburg, 1843) is chiefly valuable on account of his close and accurate translation of the Hebrew text. The Notes, however, which are rather sparse, contain choice elucidations of particular passages.

The latest English work on the prophet is from the pen of the Rev. Patrick Fairbairn (Edinburgh, 1851), who, in expounding the concluding chapters, follows pretty much in the track of Hävernick, for the most part merging the literal Israel and their institutes in what he regards as the higher Messianic element of the Christian church.

EZEKIEL.

CHAPTER I.

The prophet commences his book by detailing the circumstances connected with his call to the prophetic office. After specifying the time and place in which he received his commission, 1–3, he proceeds to describe the wonderful phenomena which were presented to his imagination in inspired vision, and which were designed to furnish him with an impressive symbolical representation of the formidable agencies by means of which Jehovah executes his purposes as the Ruler among the nations, 4–25; concluding with a description of the vision which he had of the divine glory, and the solemn effect which it produced upon his mind, 26–28.

1 Now it came to pass in the thirtieth year, in the fourth month, on the fifth day of the month, when I was among the captives by the river Chebar, the heavens were opened, and I saw visions

1. The formula וַיְהִי with the copula, is not unusual at the commencement of the sacred books of the Old Testament. See Joshua Judges, Ruth, Samuel, etc. It is designed to intimate the continuation of historical or prophetic records. Considerable difficulty has been found in determining what particular date is intended by *the thirtieth year* here specified. Setting aside the opinion, that it may indicate the age of the prophet, as being unusual in prophetic computations, or that it designates the number of years that had elapsed since the reformation effected in the eighteenth year of Josiah, as being destitute of any sufficient ground, the probable supposition is that advanced by Scaliger in his work De Emend. Temporum; according to which the date is taken from the commencement of the reign of Nabopolassar, which formed the era of the Babylonian empire, B.C. 625. As our prophet now lived under that monarchy is was natural for him here to adopt the chronology of the country, which he otherwise uses interchangeably with that of the captivity. See on chap. viii. 1. We find Daniel, and others of the prophets in like manner, employing the era of the people among whom they lived when out of their native country. כְּבָר, *Chebar*, the same as חָבוֹר, *Habor*, whither the ten tribes had been transported by Tiglath-pileser and Shalmanezer, 2 Kings xvii. 6. It was a considerable river of Mesopotamia, formed by the confluence of a number of smaller streams, and known among the Greeks by the names of Χαβώρας and Ἀβόῤῥας, and among the Arabs by that of خابور, *Khabour*. It takes its rise near the ruins of Ras-el-Ain, which lie in a south-westerly direction from the town of Merdin, and flows into the Euphrates at Carchemish or Circusium, about two hundred miles to the north of Babylon. Layard describes it as flowing

2 of God. On the fifth day of the month, which was the fifth
3 year of king Jehoiachin's captivity, the word of Jehovah came expressly to Ezekiel (the son of Buzi), the priest, in the land of the Chaldeans, by the river Chebar; and the hand of Jehovah was upon him there.
4 And I looked, and behold a whirlwind came out of the north, a great cloud, and a self-attracting fire, and a brightness round

through the richest pastures and meadows, its banks covered with flowers of every hue, and presenting the loveliest scene he had ever beheld. In this region the king of Babylon had planted a colony of Jews, among whom was our prophet, as he states, ver. 3. בָּרְאוֹת אֱלֹהִים, *visions of God*, do not mean representations of Deity exhibited to the bodily eyes of the prophet — such an idea could only have originated in the theoretical speculations of the Hutchinsonian school; but the sublime discoveries made to the mind of Ezekiel, and deposited in the present book. The phrase occurs again chaps. viii. 3; xl. 2. The revelations contained in them were such as had specially the glory of Jehovah for their object, including also such other objects as tended by symbolical representations to set forth to view the divine government of the world and the church.

2, 3. Comp. 2 Kings xxiv. 12; Jer. xxii. 24, 25; xxix. 2. Jerome is of opinion, that, as Jehoiachin voluntarily surrendered to Nebuchadnezzar, גָּלָה is not, as in the LXX., to be rendered αἰχμαλωσία, *captivitas*, but *transmigratio*. Ewald accounts for the change of person from the first to the third by the supposition that the prophet, on revising his book, inserted these two verses for the purpose of introducing the computation which dated from the commencement of the captivity, together with his own name, which occurs again only chap. xxiv. 24. This computation Ezekiel afterwards uses, chaps. viii. 1; xx. 1; xxiv. 1; xxvi. 1; xxxi. 1; xxxii. 1; xl. 1. The first person is immediately resumed, ver. 4, after the interruption of the narrative commenced ver. 1. According to Hebrew usage (see Zech. i. 1) the designation הַכֹּהֵן, *priest*, is in apposition with Ezekiel and not with Buzi. I agree with Maurer in thinking that the double form הָיֹה הָיָה, in which the idea of the verb is expressed twice over, is employed for the sake of intensity or emphasis, so that the infinitive is not redundant, as Rosenmüller would make it. Our translators, therefore, properly add *expressly*, וַתְּהִי עָלָיו, *the hand of Jehovah was upon*, is a formula frequently used to denote the exertion of supernatural and divine agency by which the prophets were prepared to receive and deliver divine communications. Comp. 2 Kings iii. 15; Isaiah viii. 11; Ezek. xxxiii. 22; xxxvii. 1; xl. 1. Instead of עָלָיו, *upon him*, eight MSS., primarily four more, and now one by correction, the LXX., Syr., and Arab. read עָלַי, *upon me;* but the variation has obviously arisen from the copyist not having adverted to the interruption occasioned by the change of person.

4. The formula רָאִיתִי וְהִנֵּה, *I looked, and behold,* is peculiar to the prophets Jeremiah, Ezekiel, Daniel, and Zechariah. רוּחַ סְעָרָה, the *whirlwind* or *tempest*, so called from the violence with which it rushes on, and agitates and scatters the objects with which it is brought into contact, was a fit emblem to represent the divine judgments. Comp. Isaiah xxix. 6; Jer. xxiii. 19; xxv. 32; Nahum i. 3. This tempest the prophet saw coming מִן־הַצָּפוֹן, *from the north,* by which is indicated, not the heathenish idea, that that was the quarter of the heaven where the gods had their abode,

5   about it, and from the midst of it as the appearance of polished brass from the midst of the fire. And from the midst of it was the resemblance of four living creatures, and this was their

as Rosenmüller and Maurer expound, but the country of Babylon, whence the Chaldeans, who were a northern people, should come to execute the divine indignation upon the Jews. Compare Jer. i. 14; iv. 6; vi. 1. The direction is taken, not from the position of the prophet at the time of the vision, for Babylon lay to the south of that, but in relation to Judea, against which the hostile power would come by taking a northerly course and entering it from that quarter. עָנָן גָּדוֹל, *a great cloud*, is introduced into the scene in order to enhance its magnificence and sublimity. The participle מִתְלַקַּחַת, rendered *infolding itself*, properly denotes reciprocal or reflexive action. The verb לָקַח, signifying *to take*, the Hithpael conjugation here used, conveys the idea of any thing taking hold of itself, or taking to itself; אֵשׁ מִתְלַקַּחַת will, therefore, mean *self-attracting fire*, and, by implication, consuming what it thus attracts. LXX. πῦρ ἐξαστράπτον; Sym. πῦρ ἐνειλούμενον; Aquil. συναναλαμβανόμενον; Vulg. *ignis involvens*. The idea is that of a fire which lays hold on whatever surrounds it, draws it into itself, and devours it. A truly fearful object. The same form and mode of expression occurs Exod. ix. 24, in reference to the union of fire with the hail. To enhance the idea of the fire, it is added, that "out of the midst of it" was as the appearance of חַשְׁמַל, a term which occurs again ver. 27, and in the feminine, chap. viii. 2, and respecting which there has been no small diversity of opinion. The most ancient interpretation is that given by the LXX. ἤλεκτρον; Vulg. *electrum*, a metal compounded of gold and silver, and distinguished for its brilliancy. Compare χαλκολιβάνον, *burnished metal*, Rev. i. 15. To render the word by *amber*, as our translators have done, is not so appropriate; since this substance, though reckoned among the phosphori, from the circumstance that by friction it is made to yield light copiously in the dark, does not possess the brilliancy which the word in this part of the description would seem to require. Bochart and some of the older critics adopt the derivation נְחֹשֶׁת, *brass*, and the Chaldee דְּהַבָא, *gold*; but the word is more probably compounded of נָחָשׁ for נְחֹשֶׁת, *brass*, the נ and the ת being removed by aphaeresis, and כָּלַל, softened into בַּל by the elision of the final ל, *to be smooth*, so that *polished brass* is most easily brought out as the signification. The idea of excessive splendor is evidently what it was intended to convey. See Gesenius in voc. and Stuart on Rev. i. 15, and compare ver. 7. Hitzig is of opinion that the word is composed of two Chaldee terms, in use in the country where Ezekiel was living. עַיִן does not signify *color*, as given in our common version after the Talmudic Hebrew, but *eye*, and hence by metonymy *look, appearance, aspect*, or the like. The repetition מִתּוֹכָהּ – כְּתוֹךְ הָאֵשׁ is equivalent to *from the midst of the fire*.

5. The prophet now comes to describe the extraordinary compound figures which he saw in vision. In treating of this subject I shall first examine the several details of the description, and then attempt to ascertain what the whole was designed to represent. In investigating the subject, it must all along be borne in mind, that the object described was purely ideal, and not anything actually existing in rerum natura. חַיּוֹת, *living creatures*, as the word is properly rendered here by our translators; but the corresponding term ζῶα, which John borrows from the LXX., they have as improperly rendered *beasts*, Rev. iv. 6. From the circumstance that they are

6 aspect, they had the appearance of a man. And every one had
7 four faces, and every one had four wings. And their feet were
straight feet; the sole of their feet was like the sole of a calf's
foot: and they sparkled like the appearance of polished brass.
8 And they had the hands of a man under their wings on their
four sides, and they four had their faces and their wings.
9 Their wings were joined one to another; they turned not when
10 they went; they went every one straight forward. And as for

emphatically called "the *living* creatures," it is manifest that the notion of life or vital energy must lie at the foundation of the idea. It is true that most of the animals were irrational creatures, but as one represented a human being there is an incongruity in designating them all by the term *beasts*. Man being the noblest in creation, his form is selected as the pattern after which they are represented. לְהֵנָּה as feminine agrees with חַיּוֹת; but, the objects not being real, the distinction of sex is not kept up — now the feminine, and now the masculine being employed. It is doubtless owing to inattention to this wellestablished rule of Hebrew syntax, that such a great number of various readings are found in the MSS. The point of comparison between the form of the living creatures and that of man would seem to be the erect posture of their bodies. To the number *four* our prophet appears to attach considerable importance, since he employs it so frequently in his description.

6. The most striking peculiarity connected with this cherubic representation is, that there were not only four distinct living creatures, but each of the four had four faces, the appearance of which is described at ver. 10. The aggregate, though not amounting to the number calculated by the Rabbins, amounted to not fewer than sixteen.

7. Since the soles of the feet resembled those of a calf, it is evident the feet could not have projected horizontally like human feet, but must have formed a continuation of the legs stretching down vertically. In Hebrew the term רַגְלֵיהֶם signifies, not the feet merely, but all the lower parts of the body. יְשָׁרָה, *straight*, therefore, must be intended to denote a perpendicular, and not a horizontal direction. The feet must have been two in number, like those of man; otherwise the number four would have been expressed, as it is with respect to the faces and the wings. נְחֹשֶׁת קָלָל, *polished brass*. קָלָל, from which the adjective is derived, must originally have had as one of its significations *to smoothe, polish*, though this signification is now only found in the Pilpel conjugation. Comp. Dan. x. 6.

8. Instead of וִידֵי, the Keri and a great number of MSS., and among these the best Spanish, with the Brixian and Soncinian editions, read correctly וִידֵי. The error of transcription has arisen from what has frequently taken place — the elongation of Yod into Vau. The hand is, in Hebrew, a very common symbol of power; on the ground, that it is principally through that member of the body that power is exerted. It consequently denotes active energy.

9. The living creatures had no occasion to turn when changing the direction in which they proceeded, for being four in number they had a face looking towards each of the four quarters of the heavens, and could move on without changing their posture. Hitzig regards חֹבְרֹת אִשָּׁה אֶל־אֲחוֹתָהּ as a gloss borrowed from ver. 11, where the mention of the junction of the wings by pairs occurs most appropriately; whereas here the impression left on the mind of the

the likeness of their faces, they four had the face of a man, and the face of a lion, on the right side; and they four had the face of a bull on the left side; they four also had the face of an eagle.

11 Thus were their faces, and their wings were parted upwards: two wings of every one were joined one to another, and two
12 covered their bodies. And they went every one straight forward; whither the spirit was to go, they went: and they turned not when they went.

13 As for the likeness of the living creatures, their appearance was like burning coals of fire, like the appearance of lamps; it went up and down among the living creatures; and the fire was

reader is, that all the four wings were joined together, which is not otherwise borne out by the description.

10. Either we are to conclude that the face of the man was in front and that of the eagle behind, or that both that of the man and the lion were on the right side, as the position of the words in the text would seem to intimate, and thus Castalio and Lowth interpret; but the two members of the first clause of the verse may be separated, and thus the former of these positions might be justified. In the Hebrew text this separation is actually made by the great distinctive accent Segolta, which shows the construction adopted by the Masoretes. Each of the other animals being the most distinguished of its kind, I have not scrupled to render שׁוֹר by *bull*, as he is the strongest and most ferocious of the beeve kind.

11. Two of the wings being designed for flying are represented as expanded upwards, and the other two were appropriated, for the sake of decency, to the covering of the bodies of the living creatures. The redundant form of the pronominal affix חָנָה in וּבִיוֹתֵיהֶנָה is not peculiar to this place; the prophet employs the masculine חֶמָּה in the same way, chap. xl. 16.

12. It has been matter of dispute, whether חָרוּחַ here is to be rendered *the spirit* or *the wind*. The term is susceptible of either rendering, according to the circumstances of the context in which it occurs. In favor of the latter it has been urged, that, as special mention is made of רוּחַ, *wind*, ver. 4, it is most natural to conclude that reference is here made to the same. On the other hand, from its being expressly stated, that the רוּחַ was that of the living creature, or *living creatures*, חַיָה being taken as a collective noun, and from the motion of the compound figure being attributed to the will of the רוּחַ (ver. 20), I consider it more appropriate to regard the term as expressive of the impulsive principle by which they were moved according to the divine pleasure. Comp. ver. 21, and chap. x. 17. Some regard רוּחַ חַיָה as equivalent to רוּחַ חַיִים, *the spirit of life*, but the latter formula alone is used in this sense.

13. The apparent tautology at the commencement of this verse may be relieved by remarking, that while דְּמוּת expresses the general form or figure, מַרְאֶה expresses the particular aspect or appearance of a thing. The conjecture of Cappellus, who, to render the text conformable to ἐν μέσῳ τῶν ζώων of the LXX., would substitute בְּתוֹךְ for דְּמוּת, cannot be approved. From the circumstance that the LXX. have not translated חיא, we are not to conclude that it did not originally stand in the text. It refers to אֵשׁ, going before. נֹגַהּ indicates the splendor or brightness produced by the fire which was rendered

14   bright; and out of the fire went forth lightning. And the living creatures ran and returned as the appearance of a flash of lightning.
15   And I beheld the living creatures, and behold there was one wheel
16   upon the earth by the living creatures, with its four faces. The appearance of the wheels and their work, was the color of Tarshish-stone; and they four had one likeness; and their appear-

intensely hot by the coals with which it was fed. בְּעָרִית is to be construed with גֶּחָלִּים, though differing in gender, the idea of sex not being involved in the object. See on ver. 5.

14. Hitzig proposes to read יָצוֹא instead of רָצוֹא, as Gen. viii. 7, but acknowledges his inability to reconcile the idea of going and returning with the description verses 19-21. The current reading is more suitable, since the idea of velocity which it expresses is quite in keeping both with that part of the description and with the symbol of the eagle. רָצוֹא וָשׁוֹב, the infinitive for the finite forms of the verbs, is not uncommon in Hebrew syntax. The root רָצָא, to run, which occurs nowhere else, is equivalent to the usual form רוּץ. The objection of Hitzig, that the idea of running and returning does not correspond with that of the equable motion of the wheels, is of no force, since the action predicated is not that of the living creatures, or of the wheels attached to them, but that of the fire shooting forth its flames. To cancel the whole verse, with this author, because it is omitted by the LXX., would be most unwarrantable. The conjectural change of בָּרָק into פֶּרֶק, is equally unjustifiable. The latter word, which occurs at the end of the preceding verse, is a general term for *lightning*, the former is designed to express its *coruscations* or *flashes*. Comp. the Arab. برق, *to throw out, send forth, to scatter, to sow*. Parchon explains the word by מִין הַבָּרָק, *species fulguris*. De Rossi's codices 60 and 637 have gallicè לְנִצִּירְלָא, *l'étincelle, scintilla*.

15-21. The prophet now proceeds to describe the wheels which conveyed the living creatures. They were four in number, and of the singular structure, that one wheel appeared transversely within another, so that the chariot might roll on without turning, to whichever quarter the four living creatures supporting it were to advance. Hitzig acknowledges a difficulty in פָּנָיו, *his faces*, and not finding any term corresponding to it in the LXX., at once cancels it. Rosenmüller refers it to *chariot* understood, but not expressed, which Maurer considers harsh; and both he and Hävernick prefer the reference to אוֹפַנִּים, *the wheels*, the singular affix ו, *his*, being used collectively; which seems, on the whole, the true exegesis. The observation that one of the wheels was בָּאָרֶץ, *in the earth*, intimates that only one of the transverse wheels appeared in contact with the ground at the same time, i.e. viewing the chariot from one of its sides, it being understood that the same was the case in regard to the corresponding wheel on the opposite side. אֶחָד, *one*, is regarded in relation to the wheel within a wheel, and not to the entire number. By מַעֲשֵׂה, *the work of the wheels*, is meant the material of the workmanship, not the fabrication of it. תַּרְשִׁישׁ, *gem* or *precious stone of Tarshish*; Aquil. χρυσολίθου; Sym. ὑακίνθου; the LXX. θαρσείς, which is merely the Hebrew name in Greek letters, on which the Scholiast remarks, τὸ θαρσείς χρυσόλιθόν φησιν, ἢ ὑάκινθον. Kimchi, נימה לעין תכלת. It is supposed to have meant the *topaz*, a gem still found in Spain, and known to the ancients by

ance and their work was as it were a wheel within a wheel.
17 When they went, they went upon their four sides; they turned
18 not when they went. And as for their felloes, and their height,
they were terrible, and their felloes were full of eyes round about
19 them four. And when the living creatures went, the wheels
went beside them, and when the living creatures were lifted up
20 from the earth, the wheels were lifted up. Whithersoever the
spirit was to go, they went, whither the spirit was to go; and
the wheels were lifted up along with them for the spirit of the
21 living creature was in the wheels. When those went, these went,
and when those stood, these stood; and when those were lifted up
from the earth, the wheels were lifted up along with them; for the
22 spirit of the living creature was in the wheels. And the likeness
of the firmament above the heads of the living creature was as the
color of the terrible crystal, stretched forth over their heads above.

the name of Tarshish, from the circumstance of its having been brought from Tartessus. It is smooth and brilliant in appearance. It formed one of the gems in the breastplate of the high-priest. Exod. xxviii. 20. Comp. Song v. 14; Ezek. xxviii. 13; Dan. x. 6; in all which passages it is rendered *beryl* in our authorized version. Ver. 17. The meaning of this verse is, that when the wheels moved, they moved according as each of the four quarters or sides of the square chariot fronted the direction in which the movement was made. When a new direction was taken, the wheels that were not to roll were suspended from the ground, so as to leave the others free to perform their revolutions. The גַּבִּים, rendered *rings* in the authorized version, were the felloes forming the rim or circumference of the wheels. They are described as so very high as to have been tremendous, ver. 18. Much as they were thus calculated to impress the mind of the spectator, I can discover nothing specially symbolical in the property here ascribed to them, except it be that, from their extreme height, as they rolled round, the eyes that were in them must be conceived of as commanding a complete view of whatever came within the scope of vision. In the sentence עַל אֲשֶׁר יִהְיֶה־שָּׁם הָרוּחַ לָלֶכֶת יֵלֵכוּ הָרוּחַ לָלֶכֶת, the latter part is not to be considered as a bare tautology, but is a repetition for the purpose of more forcibly impressing the idea upon the mind. לְעֻמָּתָם, *in correspondence*, or *conjunction*, *along with them*, vers. 20, 21. The adverb *over against* is less appropriate. By הָרוּחַ הַחַיָּה, *the spirit of the living creature* (put collectively for *creatures*) being in the wheels, is meant the impulsive influence by which they were put and kept in motion. See on ver. 12, and comp. chap. x. 17.

22. עַל here is not to be rendered *upon*, as if the firmament rested on the heads of the cherubim, but *above*, as distinct from them, and occupying an elevated position. See on ver. 26. קֶרַח primarily signifies *ice*, and secondarily *crystal*, from its resemblance to it. The combination הַקֶּרַח הַנּוֹרָא, *the terrible crystal*, expresses the effect produced upon a spectator by the view of a large mass of crystallization. It is so powerful when seen glistening in the sun, that the eye cannot sustain its lustre. Some have supposed that the *diamond* is meant, that gem being remarkable for its brilliance and hardness.

23 And under the firmament their wings were straight, one towards another; each had two which covered on this side, and each had
24 two which covered on that side, their bodies. And I heard the sound of their wings, like the sound of many waters, like the sound of the Almighty, when they went; the sound of a tumult, as the sound of a host; when they stood, they let down their wings.
25 And there was a sound from the expanse which was above their head when they stood and let down their wings.
26 And above the expanse that was over their head was the appearance of a sapphire-stone, the likeness of a throne: and upon the likeness of the throne, was the likeness as the appearance of a
27 man above upon it. And I saw as it were the appearance of

23. Between the representation here given and that which we find ver. 11, there is no positive contradiction. Although the two wings which were expanded upwards were specially designed for flying, yet till they reached the summit of the figure and were parted from each other, they necessarily covered the upper part of the body, while the other two were specially intended to cover the lower parts.

24. קוֹל־שַׁדַּי, *the voice of the Almighty*, means thunder. See Ps. xxix. קוֹל הֲמֻלָּה, occurring only here, and Jer. xi. 16, means *the sound of a tumult*, such as that of a multitude of warriors rushing on to the attack, as the prophet presently explains חָמַל does not occur as a root in Hebrew, but the corresponding Arab.

همل, *continuè pluit, liberè fluxit*, suggests the idea of impetuosity, or violent rushing, as of a heavy rain. The LXX. according to the Alexandrian copy have φωνὴ τοῦ λογοῦ, *the voice of the Logos*, which Jerome explains of the second person of the Trinity. They must have read קוֹל הַמִּלָּה.

25. As it would have been unbefitting in the living creatures to have continued moving on when the Almighty gave forth his voice, they are here represented as stopping in their course, and reverently letting their wings fall, while they listen in silence to the divine communication.

26. Ezekiel now advances to the highest point in the vision. Having mentioned the רָקִיעַ, *expanse*, in relation to the figures underneath it, his eye catches a glance of the throne of the Almighty, occupying a place above it, and the Divine Being himself as there enthroned in human form. This divine manifestation is one of the most remarkable Theophanies of the Old Testament. While, like other anthropomorphic appearances of the Deity, it was prelusive of the future incarnate state of the Logos, it distinctly and specially recognized the God-man Redeemer in his character as the inflicter of punishment upon his enemies. Comp. 2 Thess. i. 7-9; Rev. xix. 11-16. The throne is described as having the appearance of אֶבֶן־סַפִּיר, *a sapphire-stone*. By this is meant, not the lapis lazuli, as some have imagined, but the gem properly called sapphire; which is surpassed only by the diamond in hardness, lustre, and beauty. It is mostly of a blue color, but is of various shades, from the deepest azure to the purest white. In the description given of the vision of the God of Israel (Exod. xxiv. 10), he is said to have had under his feet as it were *a transparent work of sapphire*.

27. The description here given of the Son of God quite corresponds with that furnished, Dan. x. 5, 6; Rev. i. 14, 15. For חַשְׁמַל see on ver. 4. בְּרִית־לָהּ סָבִיב,

polished brass, the likeness of fire within it around, from the appearance of his loins and upwards, and from the appearance of his loins and downwards, I saw as it were the appearance of
18 fire, and it was surrounded with splendor. As the appearance of the bow which is in the cloud in the day of rain, so was the appearance of the surrounding splendor. This was the appearance of the likeness of the glory of Jehovah. And when I saw, then I fell upon my face, and I heard a voice of one that spake.

within it around, to indicate the intrinsic purity and terrible rectitude of the divine judgments. The appearance of the Divine Man being wholly invested with fire, likewise denoted his readiness to punish the wicked with awful destruction.

28. To intimate that however severe should be the divine judgments, still they would be accompanied with displays of faithfulness and mercy, the cheering appearance of a glorious rainbow is presented to the view of the prophet, who had fallen prostrate under an overwhelming sense of the majesty and glory of manifested Deity. וָאֶרְאֶה וָאֶפֹּל, lit. *and I saw and I fell.* The force of the conjunctive particle in this case, is simply to point out the relation of the two verbs to each other, the one indicating the cause, and the other the effect.

Respecting the import of the cherubim described in Scripture, and more especially those supposed to be described in the visions of Ezekiel, there has been much speculation. Various attempts have been made to harmonize the different passages in which they are presented to view, and very different have been the hypotheses which have been constructed in elucidation of them. I shall not, however, detain my readers with anything in the shape of a critical review of these hypotheses, adjusting their respective merits and demerits, or with any attempts to prove their inapplicability to the subject before us. I shall content myself with examining the various parts of the picture in their bearing upon the historical aspects of the times in which the prophet flourished, and the object which the Spirit of inspiration may be supposed to have had in view in suggesting the images to his mind.

At one time it was fashionable to endeavor to obtain light from the aids of etymology; but all Hebraists of note now acquiesce in the opinion, that the search in this quarter is fruitless, there being no certain data on which to rest, either in the Hebrew or in any of the cognate dialects.

The principal difficulty which has pressed upon all who have made the vision the subject of investigation, has consisted in their having attempted to construct an hypothesis that should reconcile all the phenomena of the different passages of scripture in which the cherubim are presented to view. Accordingly, though on some points their opinions might at first sight appear to satisfy the claims of certain passages, they are found more or less to clash with others; as I am satisfied every hypothesis must which lays it down as a first principle that the cherubim, wherever they occur in scripture, are symbolical of the same identical objects. Of the form or appearance of those stationed at the gate of Paradise, and of those placed on the mercy-seat in the tabernacle and the temple, we have no account; and all attempts to transfer to them any part or parts of the description in Ezekiel's vision proceed upon a gratuitous assumption.

It must be obvious to every attentive reader of the Bible that the symbols were not fixed and uniform, but varied according to circumstances. Proceeding upon this as a generally admitted fact, I shall now, without stopping to examine the import of the symbols in other passages, proceed to place before my readers what appears to me to be the symbolical teaching of the living creatures as described by Ezekiel. Regarding it as a first principle in hermeneutics, that the statements of a writer are to be interpreted in accordance with his position, or the circumstances in which he is placed, and the scope and tenor of his work, it is necessary that we inquire what were those circumstances in the history of our prophet or his times that may be supposed to throw light upon the subject. A portion of the Jewish people had been transported to the banks of the Chebar. Their city and temple still stood; but the greater number of the inhabitants that had been left behind still indulged in the grossest idolatrous practices. To punish them for their daring and obstinate rebellion against the God of their fathers, he had purposed to employ the power of the Chaldeans, whose army should invade Judea, invest Jerusalem, burn the city and the temple, exercise the greatest cruelties upon the inhabitants, and carry away the principal of them into captivity in Babylon. Now it was, I conceive, to represent symbolically this formidable hostile power that Ezekiel had presented to his view in sublime vision a colossal compound object, consisting of the resemblance of four living creatures, each of which had the face of a man, a lion, a bull, and an eagle. Add to which, wheels of tremendous size, and wings for flight, with hands for operation under their wings. Being all designated *living creatures*, and each of those specified being the most distinguished of his class, it is evident that life or vital energy in its highest visible creature form is intended to be represented. The properties at once suggested by the symbols are those of intelligence, strength, swiftness, and ferocity. And the combination of them all in one figure I regard as designed to set forth the truly appalling and destructive character of the agency to be employed for the punishment of the Jews. They are to be viewed not as abstract qualities, but as concrete in the person of Nebuchadnezzar as the head of the Babylonian empire. Though the elements of the vision are altogether unique in regard to their composite form, they are found either separately or partially combined, as symbols of royalty, both in scripture and in profane antiquity. "Throughout all Pagan mythology, the lion and the bull are the emblems, respectively, of royalty and of power, and these animals are consequently of frequent recurrence, either singly or in a form compounded of both animals, among almost all the ancient structures of Persia." — Vaux's Nineveh and Persepolis, p. 293.

In numerous passages of the Bible animals are employed to symbolize monarchs or royal personages, as heads of nations or leaders of armies. Thus the lion, as the most daring and powerful of all the carnivorous animals, the monarch of the forest, was selected as the symbol of the tribe of Judah (Gen. xlix. 9), in reference to which our Saviour, in his regal character, is styled "the lion of the tribe of Judah" (Rev. v. 5). This symbol was specially prominent in the fourteen lions which supported and adorned the throne of Solomon (1 Kings x. 19, 20). Under the same symbol the king and royal family of Nineveh are represented (Nah. ii. 11). The ox or bull, the principal animal of the beeve kind, distinguished for his strength and ferocity, is similarly employed as a symbol of the prince of Shechem (Gen. xlix. 6). In the same light we are doubtless to regard the colossal bull discovered by Layard among the sculptured ruins of Nineveh, and now in the British Museum. To the formidable and ferocious character of this animal, reference is made Ps. xxii. 12. With respect to the eagle, renowned as the king of the birds of prey, and remarkable for his farsightedness, velocity, and strength, he is employed as a symbol of the king of Babylon (Ezek. xvii. 3, 7), the swiftness of whose armies is compared to that of the eagle (Hab. i. 8). He is also spoken of as the most eminent of the birds of prey (Isa. xlvi. 11), to symbolize Cyrus, who was the first to use the figure of this bird on his military standard — a custom afterwards adopted by the Romans, and in modern times by the Austrians, Russians, and other continental nations, all of whom regard the eagle as the bird of victory. "It is remarkable that in the earliest Assyrian monuments, one of the most frequently met with is the eagle-headed human figure. In other cases the head of the bird occurs, united with the body of a lion." — Vaux, *ut sup.*, p. 32. If all the properties thus symbolized are united with the intelligence and skill of man, we have then one of the most terrific objects that can be presented to the human imagination. While the symbols must have powerfully impressed the mind of Ezekiel, and urged him as a faithful watchman to give his guilty people warning of their impending danger, there was in the rainbow, as the mild sign of the covenant, an assurance that the judgment of God's providence should be tempered with mercy, so that while the incorrigible should perish without remedy, Jehovah would treat the penitent with compassion, and make for them a way to escape. No introduction to his prophetic ministry could have been more appropriate.

Recollecting that there were no fewer than four such compound symbolical forms, we are furnished with a most imposing picture of the rapid, resistless, ferocious, and all-subduing conquests of the king of Babylon, powerfully calculated to inspire the Jews with terror, and induce them by timely repentance and the abandonment of their idolatrous and other wicked courses to avert the severe judgments with which they were threatened. The idea of a vast military apparatus, with lofty wheels, bearing down upon them, full of eyes from whose glance there could be no possibility of escape, accompanied with images of skill, velocity, invincibility, and cruelty, must have greatly increased their terror; and it is only by taking into consideration their deep-rooted aversion to their covenant-God, and their fixed determination to cleave to their idols, that we can account for their rejection of the prophetic messages which thus bore on their front such portentous intimations of approaching wrath.

In contemplating this sublime vision, special attention must be paid to what is exhibited in its two separate compartments — the living creatures with all their appurtenances, as significant of the providential execution of the divine purposes on earth; and the glory of Jehovah, enthroned in human form above the expanse. The former is represented as movable, — ready, without turning aside or back, to proceed withersoever it was the divine purpose it should go; the latter as stationary and permanent, exhibiting the Supreme Ruler on the throne of the universe, directing and controlling all things according to the pleasure of his own will; managing with perfect ease the vast concerns of his empire; making the wrath of man to praise him, and restraining the remainder of it. To intimate the future incarnate state of the Logos, in which were involved the all-important results of redemption, and with a view to which the covenant-people were to be preserved in spite of all the hostility that might be brought to bear upon them, the theophany exhibits humanity upon the throne, invested with all the glory of Deity.

CHAPTER II.

Ezekiel now receives his prophetic commission, 1-5. He is instructed not to be intimidated by the formidable opposition he should meet with from his infidel countrymen, but faithfully to deliver his message, 6-8; which is emblematically represented as being of a very mournful character, 9, 10.

1 AND he said to me, Son of man stand upon thy feet, and I will
2 speak to thee. And the Spirit entered into me when he spake with me, and set me on my feet; then I heard him that spake
3 with me. And he said unto me, Son of man, I send thee to the

1. בֶּן־אָדָם, *son of man.* This designation, by which Ezekiel is addressed upwards of a hundred times, is given to no other prophet except Daniel, who receives it only once, chapter viii. 17. Though Jerome, with whom Hävernick agrees, accounts for the singularity by the supposition, that our prophet was thus addressed to prevent his being elated with pride by the sublime visions with which he was favored, there does not appear to be more in the phrase than an Aramaic idiom, in common use in the country in which Ezekiel was living. In the Syriac New Testament it is of frequent occurrence as merely parallel with *man.* Thus, however strange it may sound in our ears, we read 1 Cor. xv. 45, "Adam the first *son of man;*" and again, ver. 47, "The first *son of man* was of the earth; the second *son of man* was the Lord from heaven." Traces of the same idiom occur in Hebrew, in which אָדָם, *man,* and בֶּן־אָדָם, *son of man,* are perfectly parallel, Numb. xxiii. 19; Job. xxv. 6; xxxv. 8; Ps. viii. 5. To encourage the prophet, he is commanded to rise from the prostrate position into which he had fallen, and standing on his feet, to receive his commission. אֹתָךְ instead of אֹתְךָ, as frequently in Jeremiah.

2. It has been made a question whether by רוּחַ here we are to understand *breath,* the *animal spirit,* or the *Holy Spirit of God* as imparted for invigorating the exhausted mind of the prophet. As the Queen of Sheba was so overcome by the sight of the splendor of Solomon's royal court, that it is said there was no more רוּחַ, *spirit* or *breath,* in her, 1 Kings x. 5, thus it has been maintained, Ezekiel was so completely overpowered by the transcendent splendor of the Lord's glory, presented to his view as narrated in the preceding chapter, that he had fallen exhausted to the earth, i. 28. The connecting of the entering of this *Ruach* with the address that was given to the prophet, might seem to argue that the term is to be taken in this inferior acceptation; but the effect of its entering into him being represented as making him to stand on his feet, decides the question in favor of the Spirit of God being intended. The speaker on this, as on other occasions, was the Logos, who commissioned the prophets, and revealed to them the divine will. The Dagesh forte in the Daleth of הַמְדַבֵּר, which the punctator appears to have placed, on the supposition that the word was the participle of Hithpael, affords no sense. It should be pointed מְדַבֵּר the participle of Piel, and this punctuation we find in some of the best Hebrew MSS.

3. Ezekiel is reminded of the fact, of which he must have had abundant proofs before he left Jerusalem, that the people among whom he was to exercise his prophetic ministry had all along been

children of Israel, to rebellious heathen, who have rebelled
against me, they and their fathers have sinned against me, unto
4 this very day. And as for the children, they are hard-faced and
stout-hearted. I send thee to them, and thou shalt say unto
5 them: Thus saith the Lord Jehovah. And as for them, whether
they will hear, or whether they will forbear (for they are a
rebellious house), they shall assuredly know that a prophet hath
6 been among them. And thou, son of man, be not afraid of them,
neither be afraid of their words, though briers and thorns be
with thee, and thou dwellest among scorpions; be not afraid of
their words, neither be dismayed at their looks, though they are
7 a rebellious house. And thou shalt speak my words unto them,
whether they will hear, or whether they will forbear; for they

notorious for their rebellious disposition towards their covenant-God. Though, instead of גוֹיִם, *nations, Gentiles, heathens,* one of De Rossi's MSS., the Syr., and the Targum read גּוֹי, *nation*, in the singular, yet the plural form seems to have been purposely chosen in order emphatically to express the *heathenish* character of the Jewish people, which they had acquired by adopting the idolatrous practices of the nations by whom they were surrounded. In like manner Isaiah identifies the people in his day with the inhabitants of Sodom and Gomorrah, i. 10. The position of Hitzig, that the plural, and not the singular, is employed, because the Hebrews, to whom the prophet was sent, were no longer a *nation*, but only separate portions of it, is by no means borne out by the signification of גּוֹיִם, *nations*, Deut. xxviii. 12, to which he refers.

4. הַבָּנִים, *the children*, is to be taken as a noun absolute, and is a resumption of הֵמָּה, *they*, in the preceding verse. It places the living generation in more aggravating apposition with אֲבוֹתָם, *their fathers*. קְשֵׁי פָנִים, *hard-faced*, impudent, shameless. Those whom the prophet had to address had put on a bold front, and were resolute in their determination to cleave to their abominations. Their very countenance was an index to their obstinacy of heart.

5. The form אִם – אִם, *if — if*, or *whether — whether*, puts two supposable, but uncertain cases. Were the former realized, there would be the exercise of pardoning mercy; in case there should be a desisting to hear, or a rejection of the prophet's message, the consequent infliction of the threatened punishment would be an irrefragable proof of his divine commission. The copulative וְ in וְיָדְעוּ is emphatic: *they shall certainly know*.

6, 7. The repetition of אַל־תִּירָא, *be not afraid*, gives peculiar emphasis to the sentence, and is not to be exchanged in the second instance for אַל־תֵּחַת, *be not dismayed*, as Hitzig proposes, to make the original correspond to chap. iii. 9, and to ἑκστῆς of the LXX. The very circumstance that אַל־תִּירָא וְאַל־תֵּחַת occur together immediately after renders it less probable that an error of transcription is to be suspected in the present instance. There is no variation in the MSS. Ezekiel was not to allow himself to be intimidated by the formidable opposition he should meet with from his countrymen. Because סָרָב in Chaldee signifies *to be refractory, rebellious*, Gesenius, Lee, and others, ascribe this signification to the Hebrew here, where the noun occurs as a ἅπαξ λεγ.; but from סָרָבִים occurring in immediate combination with סַלּוֹנִים, *thorns*, it appears

8   are most rebellious. But thou, son of man, hear what I say to
    thee: be not thou rebellious like the rebellious house; open
9   thy mouth and eat that which I give thee. And I looked, and
    behold a hand was extended to me, and behold there was in it
10 a roll of a book. And he spread it before me, and it was written
    on the face and the back; and there was written on it, LAMEN-
    TATIONS AND MOURNING AND WOE.

more natural to adopt the acceptation in which it is taken by the Rabbins, who render it by *briers* or *nettles*. Compare for the etymology קָדַד, קְדַד, קַד, to *burn*, סְרָפ, *nettle*, as the Latin *urtica* from *uro*, to burn, in reference to the burning sensation occasioned by the stinging of the nettle. Houbigant is of opinion that this signification of the term may be supported on the ground that it is parallel with *scorpions*, which occurs afterwards in the verse; עַקְרַבִּים occurs again in the singular, עַקְרָב, with the signification of *thorn*, chap. xxviii. 24. The noun is derived from סָקַב, *to raise*, *elevate*, hence used of the boughs and twigs of the palm-tree, and so of the thorns or prickles with which they are covered. Thus the Arab. سلاء, *spinæ in palmarum ramis*. עַקְרָב, *the scorpion*, is a formidable insect, the body of which terminates abruptly in a jointed tail, armed at the extremity with an acute spike. It lives in places exposed to the sun, and, hiding under stones or in crevices, runs rapidly when disturbed, with its tail curved over its back. The larger ones in tropical climes are from five to eight inches in length, and have a sting which is very much dreaded, as its poison frequently causes convulsions and death. In some places they are so numerous as to become a constant object of apprehension to the inhabitants. By the use of these metaphors, borrowed from the vegetable and animal kingdoms, Jehovah indicates to the prophet the annoying and dangerous character of those to whom he was sent. Instead of מְרִי, *rebellion*, in ver. 7, twenty MSS., the LXX., Syr., Arab., and Targ. read בֵּית מְרִי, *house of rebellion*, or, taking מְרִי adjectively, *rebellious house*. This reading, which is that in vers. 5, 6, and 8, and chap. iii. 26, 27, is also found in three of the earliest editions. The Chald. has עַם, *people*. On the ground, that abstract nouns are used to express intensity, our translators render מְרִי by *most rebellious*.

8–10. There was so much in the communications which Ezekiel had to make that was calculated to stir up the enmity of the hearts of his people against him, that he must naturally have shrunk back from the undertaking, or been tempted to modify or soften down the terms of his message. He is, therefore, warned not to imitate his countrymen in their refractory and disobedient disposition, but fully to possess himself of that message, carefully to digest it in his mind, and faithfully to deliver it to his hearers. To express the former of these ideas, the metaphor of eating food is employed, just as Jer. xv. 16; Ezek. iii. 1; Rev. x. 9, 10; which last-cited passage is exactly parallel with the language in our prophet. Of course the language is to be understood symbolically, and not of a real transaction; just as when we speak of *devouring* a book, the meaning is that we peruse it with the greatest avidity. Thus also the Latin, *devorare*, *deglutire*, *imbibere*. The books of the ancients were in the shape of rolls, and were usually written on what would be the inside when rolled up. When, however, the quantity of matter was too great to admit of its being contained within this space, the remainder was inscribed on the back. Hence the phrase פָּנִים וְאָחוֹר, *on the face, and the back*. The inside is called the *face*, because when unrolled it is that which presents itself to view. Large as the contents of the present roll were, their import is summed up in the three emphatic words קִינִים וָהֶגֶה וָהִי, *lamentations* and *mourning* and *woe*. הִי is formed, by aphæresis of נ, from נְהִי, a *ditty* or doleful song.

CHAPTER III.

This chapter begins with a resumption of the subject with which that preceding had concluded, somewhat amplifying it, and stating the prophet's compliance with the injunction given him, 1-3. He has again placed before him the obstinate character of those to whom he was sent, 4-7; but he is assured that he shall be enabled to confront them, 8-10. He is next carried in vision to a colony of Jews in the neighborhood, 11-15; where, after a period of seven days, he receives a fresh charge, 16-21. Having been removed to some distance, he is favored with a repetition of the vision of the Shechinah, that he might be further instructed how to proceed, and told what would be the result of his mission, 22, 23. He is then commanded to retire to his house, where he is to be restrained for a season from public duty, and afterwards to go forth and announce to the people that it was at their option whether they would obey or not, 24-27.

1 AND he said unto me, Son of man, eat that which thou findest, eat
2 this roll, and go, speak unto the house of Israel. Then I opened
3 my mouth, and he caused me to eat that roll. And he said unto me, Son of man, cause thy belly to eat, and fill thy bowels with this roll which I give thee. Then I ate it, and it was in my
4 mouth like honey for sweetness. And he said unto me, Son of man, come, go unto the house of Israel, and speak with my
5 words unto them. For thou art not sent unto a people deep of

1. Instead of בֵּית יִשְׂרָאֵל, *house of Israel*, the reading בְּנֵי יִשְׂרָאֵל, *children of Israel*, is found in eighteen of Kennicott and De Rossi's MSS.; it has originally been in four more, is now in one by emendation, and appears in the printed text of the Soncinian edition. It has the suffrages of the Syr., Vulg., and Chald. The present textual reading occurs ver. 4, without any variation in the MSS. and versions.

3. The prophet is again charged, in more particular terms, to appropriate the contents of the roll. The language is of the same metaphorical stamp as before. The delightful sensation which he experienced, notwithstanding the doleful character of the roll, was produced by the conviction, that the messages which it contained were instinct with glorious exhibitions of the divine holiness and the equity of the divine government — subjects which must ever afford refined pleasure to the renewed mind. Compare, as parallel in sentiment and phraseology, Rev. x. 8-11. Hitzig remarks, that the ה in וְאָכְלָה, is raphe, on account of the distinctive accent.

5, 6. עִמְקֵי שָׂפָה וְכִבְדֵי לָשׁוֹן, lit. *deep of lip and heavy of tongue:* phraseology formed with reference to a malformation of the organs of speech, by which the expression of ideas by articulate sounds is rendered difficult and unintelligible. It was natural for the Hebrews to use it

6 speech and heavy of tongue, but unto the house of Israel. Not
to many peoples of deep speech and heavy of tongue, whose
words thou shouldest not understand: surely if I had sent thee
7 unto them, they would have listened unto thee. But the house
of Israel will not listen unto thee, for they are not willing to
listen unto me: for all the house of Israel are of impudent fore-
8 head, and hard-hearted. Behold, I have made thy face strong
against their faces, and thy forehead strong against their fore-
9 heads. As an adamant, harder than flint, have I made thy forehead; be not afraid of them, neither be dismayed at their faces,
10 though they are a rebellious house. He said further unto me,
Son of man, all my words which I shall speak unto thee, receive
11 in thy heart and hear with thine ears. And come, go to the
captivity, to the children of thy people, and speak unto them,
and say unto them, Thus saith the Lord Jehovah, whether they
12 will hear, or whether they will forbear. Then the Spirit lifted
me up, and I heard behind me the sound of a great rushing,
13 *saying*, Blessed be the glory of Jehovah from his place. Also

when speaking of foreigners whose language they did not understand. To show more strikingly the unreasonableness of the Jewish people in rejecting the message of the prophet, he is told that if he had been sent to any of the barbarous nations with whose language he was unacquainted, they would nevertheless have at least listened, and not turned a deaf ear to him. None of the ancient versions have expressed לֹא after אִם in ver. 6. The only way of interpreting the two particles as here combined is to regard them as expressing a strong asseveration or obtestation. Comp. Job i. 11; ii. 5; xxii. 20; Isa. v. 9. They are therefore properly rendered *surely* in our Authorized Version; and the rendering of Newcome, who retains the negative sense, is to be rejected.

7. The Jews labored under no physical incapacity to understand the prophet, but were morally disinclined to listen to the divine message by whomsoever it might be delivered.

8, 9. Ezekiel was not to be discouraged or intimidated by the shameless treatment he had to expect from his countrymen. Strengthened by Him of whose message he was the bearer, he should be able to face them with all boldness, and unreservedly to make known to them the divine communications.

12, 13. By רוּחַ here we are not, with Hitzig and others, to understand *wind*, but the prophetic *Spirit* by whom Ezekiel was impelled to proceed on his mission. Comp. Acts viii. 39: Πνεῦμα Κυρίου ἥρπασε τὸν Φίλιππον. In neither case is a supernatural passage through the air to be imagined. The import of the sound of great rushing, which the prophet heard, was an ascription of praise to the divine glory which he had seen above the firmament, chap. i. 26-28. The manifestations of that glory had been at the temple of Jerusalem, but had now departed and been withdrawn to the immediate divine presence in heaven. In connection with the display of that glory which Ezekiel had witnessed, he now hears the sound of the cherubic apparatus as already on its way towards

the sound of the wings of the living creatures touching each other, and the sound of the wheels over against them, even the sound of a great rushing. And the Spirit lifted me up, and took me away. And I went in bitterness, in the heat of my spirit; and the hand of Jehovah was strong upon me. And I came to the captives at Tel-abib, who dwelt on the river Chebar, and I beheld them sitting there, and I sat there seven days, astonished, among them.

16 And it came to pass at the end of seven days, that the word of
17 Jehovah came unto me, saying: Son of man, I have appointed thee a watchman to the house of Israel; hear then the word
18 from my mouth, and warn them from me. When I say to the wicked, Thou shalt surely die, and thou warnest him not, nor speakest to warn the wicked from his wicked way, to make him live, that wicked man shall die in his iniquity, but his blood

Jerusalem. The קָדוֹשׁ, *place* of the divine glory, was that of its manifestation over the mercy-seat. As it indicated the peculiar presence of Jehovah, thither the special adoration of the Jews was directed. The מ prefixed is privative in signification, and expresses the removal of the Shechinah from the temple. See chap. ix. 3.

14. Partly alarmed by the sound, and partly discouraged by anticipating the fruitless results of his mission, the prophet proceeded with a heavy heart, but a powerful divine impulse urged him forwards.

15. תֵּל אָבִיב, *Tel-abib*, an accusative absolute, the name of a place in the neighborhood, most probably the principal location of the captive Jews. תֵּל signifies *an elevation, mound,* or *heap,* and is still incorporated with the names of ruined cities in the East. Michaelis supposes the town to be the same that is called *Thallaba* on the map of D'Anville, situated on the Chabour, between Resein and Obeidia. If the name was given to the place by the Jewish captives, it may have been intended to express their hopes of future restoration, אָבִיב signifying the *green ears* of corn which appeared in the month Nisan, the first of the civil months of the Jewish year. To וָאֵשֵׁב, as occurring first in this verse in many of the best MSS., and three of the early editions, and which the Keri, after the Chald., approves, וָאֲשֶׁר of the Textus Receptus is decidedly to be preferred, since the other reading makes no sense. The root of אֲשֶׁר is שׁוּר, *to look, behold,* and the punctuation should be אָשֻׁר, as אֶקְרָא, 1 Kings iii. 21. That חֵמָה is to be taken in the oblique case, Hitzig justifies by a reference to Jer. xlvi. 5, בַּהֲדוּךְ רְאִיתִי חֵמָה, and removes the zakeph katon from the preceding word. When the prophet arrived at Tel-abib, instead of finding the Jews engaged with different occupations, he beheld them sitting on the banks of the river, no doubt in the attitude of grief on account of their banishment from Jerusalem. Comp. Ps. cxxxvii. 1. Partly from a kindred feeling, and partly to show his sympathy with them, he took his place among them in the same attitude, disconsolate, for the space of seven days.

16–21. It is well remarked by Fairbairn, that Ezekiel alone of all the prophets is formally appointed to the office of watchman. In this interesting paragraph he is specially instructed respect-

19 will I require at thy hand. And thou, when thou warnest the wicked, and he turneth not from his wickedness and from his wicked way, he shall die in his wickedness, but thou hast deliv-
20 ered thy soul. And when a righteous man turneth from his righteousness, and committeth wickedness, and I put a stumbling-block before him he shall die ; because thou warnedst him not, he shall die in his sin, and his righteousnesses which he hath wrought shall not be remembered, but his blood I will
21 require at thy hand. But thou, when thou warnest a righteous man not to sin, and the righteous man sinneth not, he shall surely live, because he took warning, and thou hast delivered
22 thy soul. And the hand of Jehovah was there upon me, and he said unto me: Arise, go forth unto the valley, and there will
23 I speak unto thee. Then I arose, and went forth unto the valley, and behold, the glory of Jehovah was standing there, as the glory which I beheld by the river Chebar, and I fell upon
24 my face. Then the Spirit entered into me, and caused me to stand upon my feet, and he spake unto me, and said unto me :
25 Go, shut thyself up in the midst of thy house. But thou, son of man, behold, they will put cords upon thee, and bind thee
26 with them, and thou shalt not go forth among them. And I

ing the duties of his office, and shown the bearing of the discharge, or the neglect of them, both on his own interests and on the interests of those to whom he was sent. The awful responsibility of the public teachers of religion is here strikingly depicted.

20. מִכְשׁוֹל, a *stumbling-block*, or occasion of moral falling. It is thus the passage is to be understood ; for we cannot conceive of God's laying anything in the way of a moral agent that would necessarily cause him to sin. There may be an adaptation in the object to call forth the sinful propensities of the human heart, but there is no compulsory influence exerted in any way to affect the free-agency of the individual. For צִדְקָתוֹ in the singular the Keri has צִדְקֹתָיו in the plural, to agree with הֵנָּה.

22. For the purpose of producing a deeper impression upon the mind of the prophet, he receives an inspired charge to repair to a valley or plain in the neighborhood, that there, in a state of seclusion from his countrymen, he might obtain a fresh manifestation of the divine glory, and receive further communications from the Angel of the Covenant The בִּקְעָה is not further described, but it was in all probability, a *cleft* or *valley* between two mountains, running in the direction of the Chebar. As the vision here specified is restricted to the glory of the Lord, it is evident it did not include that of the cherubim.

24–27. Having been again raised by the power of the Divine Spirit from the ground, on which he had fallen, Ezekiel is charged to return and shut himself up in his house, with the intimation that he should be restrained for a time from discharging the duties of his prophetic office, after which he was to announce to the people that they had to make their

will make thy tongue cleave to the roof of thy mouth, and thou shalt be dumb, and shalt not be to them a reprover, for they 27 are a rebellious house. But when I speak unto thee, I will open thy mouth, and thou shalt say unto them, Thus saith the Lord Jehovah: He that heareth, let him hear; and he that forbeareth, let him forbear; for they are a rebellious house.

election, whether they would receive or reject the divine message. The binding of the prophet by the people is not to be understood literally, but is spoken allegorically of the influence which their rebellious conduct would exert upon his spirit, filling him with despondency, and thus disqualifying him from frankly and faithfully bearing his testimony against them. Nothing is more dispiriting to a minister than to see his people indisposed to profit by his labors. As a just judgment upon them, God threatens that he would render his servant incapable of ministering among them, than which we cannot imagine a worse state in which a people can be left.

CHAPTER IV.

Under the symbol of a siege the prophet is commanded to portray the investment of Jerusalem by the Chaldeans, 1-3; then to lie a certain number of days on his two sides alternately, as under a heavy burden, to serve as a type of the punishment to which the Hebrews of the two kingdoms were to be subjected for their sins, 4-6. To represent the extremities to which they were to be exposed during the siege, he was to prepare food made up of different kinds of grains, and bake it with the most nauseous fuel, and then from time to time to eat a small quantity, as well as to use a stinted quantity of water, 7-13. After being indulged with a modification in the article of fuel, he is furnished with a direct application of the symbol to the circumstances of the inhabitants of Jerusalem, 14-17.

1 AND thou, son of man, take thee a tile, and lay it before thee, and
2 portray upon it a city, even Jerusalem. And lay siege against it, and build a fort against it, and raise a mound against it, and

1. Hitzig fancifully concludes from the etymological signification of לְבֵנָה that it was a *lime-stone* the prophet was commanded to take; but *brick* was likewise so called, from the white clay of which it was frequently made, and which was either burned in the kiln or dried in the sun. Some of the latter kind acquired a sufficient degree of compactness to admit of inscriptions or impressions of various objects being represented on them. Such bricks abound in the ruins of Babylon and the remains of other ancient cities in the vicinity of the region in which Ezekiel was. They are frequently of two feet in length by one in breadth; consequently sufficiently large to allow of what is here described being portrayed upon them.

2. For דָּיֵק, *specula, watch-tower*, see on Jer. lii. 4. כְּ Hävernick plausibly interprets from the etymology (כּוּר, or כָּרָה, signifying *to dig* or *bore through*), and renders the term by *Durchbrecher*. So far as the derivation is concerned he certainly is correct, since the word, as

set camps against it, and place battering rams against it round
about. And thou, take to thee a pan of iron, and make it a
wall of iron between thee and the city, and direct thy face against
it, and it shall be in a state of siege, and thou shalt besiege it:
4 it is a sign to the house of Israel. And thou, lie upon thy left
side, and lay the iniquity of the house of Israel upon it; the
number of the days which thou shalt lie upon it, thou shalt bear
5 their iniquity. For I have appointed for thee the years of their
iniquity, according to the number of days, three hundred and
ninety days; and thou shalt bear the iniquity of the house of
6 Israel. And when thou hast finished these, then thou shalt lie a

a primitive noun, takes the signification of לָמָב, or the *pastures* where the lambs feed, and the transition from the idea of such a harmless creature to that of *ram* would seem too violent to be tolerated. There cannot be a doubt that the word is here to be taken in the signification of *arietes*, *a battering-ram*, or long log of wood, so called because one of the ends was armed with a mass of heavy metal in the shape of a ram's head. Such machines, either carried by soldiers or suspended by ropes or chains, were driven with force against the walls of a fortified city, so as to make a breach in them, or batter them down.

3. The מַחֲבַת, *frying-pan of iron*, from the rust which it contracted, was a fit symbol of the city of Jerusalem, the accumulated guilt of which was now to be punished. The better to represent the city, this pan was to be surrounded with a raised edge of iron in the shape of a wall. בֵּית יִשְׂרָאֵל, *house of Israel*, as occurring in this verse, is to be distinguished as to signification from the same phrase as used in the following verses. Here it is employed to denote the Hebrews generally; there, in contradistinction from בֵּית יְהוּדָה, *house of Judah*, to denote the ten tribes which separated in the time of Rehoboam.

4–6. The supposition, broached by Jarchi and adopted by Hitzig, that the left side was designed to be symbolical of the northern kingdom, and the right of the southern, because geographically the localities which they occupied lay in these directions, according to the Oriental mode of considering the east to be in front, is more fanciful than real. Little more tenable is the opinion of Grotius, that the sides were purposely chosen to point out the dignity of the two tribes of Judah and Benjamin as superior to those which formed the northern kingdom. I agree with the opinion of Steudlin and Hävernick, that no importance is to be attached to the selection.

There are some chronological difficulties attaching to a literal or historical computation of the periods here specified. The most tenable seem the calculations of Eichhorn, Michaelis, Scholz, Rosenmüller, Maurer, and others, who date, in the one case, from the separation of the ten tribes in the reign of Jeroboam, and in the other, from the reformation effected by Josiah, 390 and 40 being used as the nearest round numbers. It has indeed been objected that the prophet is here treating, not of the time during which the sins were committed, but that during which the people were bearing the punishment inflicted on account of them; but a designed correspondence between the term of punishment and the season of transgression is not infrequent in Scripture. See especially Numb. xiv. 34. As many years as the people had continued in idolatry, so many days the prophet was in symbolic action to bear

second time upon thy right side, and bear the iniquity of the house of Judah, forty days ; a day for a year have I appointed thee.
7 And thou shalt direct thy face towards the siege of Jerusalem, and thou shalt uncover thine arm and prophesy against it. And,
8 behold, I will lay cords upon thee, and thou shalt not turn thee from one side to another, until thou hast finished the days of thy
9 siege. And thou, take for thyself wheat, and barley, and beans, and lentiles, and millet, and spelt, and put them in one vessel, and make thee bread of them for the number of the days which thou shalt be lying upon thy side, three hundred and ninety

their chastisement. The opinion recently adopted by Hitzig, Ewald, and Fairbairn, and which was already entertained by the Rabbins in the time of Jerome, that the periods are to be considered analogically, as corresponding to the time in which the Israelitish people were absent from their own land, and suffered in Egypt and in the wilderness, is open to the objection that in order to make the periods tally, the number 40, which represents the years of wandering in the desert, needs to be also reckoned along with the 390 to make up the 430 years, mentioned in Exod. xii. 40, 41 ; in addition to which it must be remembered that a comparison of Gen. xv. 16, Exod. vi. 16-20, and Gal. iii. 17, leads to the idea that the 430 years so reckoned included the sojourn of the patriarchs in Canaan as well as the detention of their posterity in the house of bondage. The Hebrew phrase נָשָׂא עָוֹן, *to bear iniquity*, uniformly means, to suffer punishment on account of iniquity. Sin being conceived of by the Orientals as a burden, the idea of bearing it was naturally suggested ; and, being transferred to its punishment, it consequently acquired that of suffering it. By בִּשְׁנֵי עֲוֹנָם, ver. 5, we are to understand *the years of their punishment* on account of iniquity. There is no necessity to press the application of these arithmetical symbols to the exact duration of the punishment which they foreshadowed : all attempts to do so have proved futile. The very disproportionate inequality of the periods during which the punishment of the two divisions of the Hebrew people was to last must not be considered as suggesting the idea that the amount of guilt contracted by Judah was small compared with that contracted by Israel, which would be in flat contradiction of the representations made by the prophet, chap. xvi. 44-59 ; for though the ten tribes were much longer in a state of actual captivity than the two tribes of Judah and Benjamin, yet the sufferings of the latter were greatly aggravated by the hardships to which they had to submit during the siege of Jerusalem, and the cruelties exercised upon them by the Chaldeans after that event.

7. To set forth the certainty of the siege, and the preparedness of the enemy to conduct it, the prophet is commanded to direct his face against the city ; and, as the Orientals usually do when about to engage in any undertaking, to tuck up the sleeve of his right arm that he might be ready for action. In this attitude he was to deliver his prophecy. Comp. Isa. lii. 10.

8. Though the siege, specified verses 1-3, is to be taken literally of that of Jerusalem, yet it is here employed in a more extended signification, to denote the entire calamity that had befallen, and was yet to befall, the Hebrew people. To set forth their helpless condition, and the impossibility of their being able by any efforts of their own to recover them-

10 days thou shalt eat thereof. And thy food which thou shalt eat by weight, twenty shekels a day, from time to time thou
11 shalt eat it. Thou shalt also drink water by measure, the sixth
12 part of a hin, from time to time thou shalt drink. And thou shalt eat it as barley cakes, and with dung that cometh out of
13 man thou shalt bake it in their sight. And Jehovah said: Thus shall the children of Israel eat their polluted bread among the
14 heathen, whither I will drive them. Then I said, Ah, Lord Jehovah! behold, my soul hath not been polluted, nor have I eaten that which hath died of itself, or been torn in pieces, from my youth until now; neither hath there entered into my mouth

selves, the prophet is informed that he should be prevented, by a divine influence resting upon him, from moving from one side to the other during the periods of his symbolical punishment.

9–13. As the basis of the direction here given, compare Lev. xxvi. 26. Graphically as the circumstances of the inhabitants of Jerusalem during the siege may be considered as depicted in these verses, yet the description is obviously intended to include those of the captives, in which, absent from the holy and plenteous land, they should be reduced to want in the midst of the idolatrous pollutions of the heathen.

9. Ezekiel was to take six different kinds of grain, better and worse as it respects quality, and mixing them all together, to prepare bread of them. Instead of flour simply, which was used for baking more delicate cakes, Gen. xviii. 6, the Hebrews should have to content themselves with such coarse bread, as only the poorest would submit to eat. The *three hundred and ninety days* were doubtless, as the larger number, intended to include both periods, as we may infer from what is said, verses 16, 17; so that we are not, with Maurer, to conclude, that the omission of the *forty* was *per oblivionem*.

10, 11. When cities are reduced to straits by all supplies from without being cut off by the besieging army, it is customary to place the inhabitants upon short allowance. The quantity both of bread and water here specified was the smallest conceivable for the bare sustenance of life. The shekel being only the weight of about ten ounces, and the sixth part of a hin, a pint and a half English measure, the pressure must have been extreme. The scarcity would be so great that the utmost management would be required in order to make the stinted quantity of provisions hold out.

12, 13. To express the aggravation of the miserable circumstances of the Hebrews, they are represented as reduced to the necessity of using human excrements as fuel for the purpose of baking their bread. It is customary with the Arabs and Tatars to this day, as it is in some parts of Europe where there is a destitution of wood or turf, to make use of the dried dung of cattle for this purpose, but we can only conceive of the case here resorted to as one of the most extreme necessity. The very allusion was calculated to produce feelings of the utmost disgust, which we find the command actually did produce in the mind of Ezekiel, ver. 14. As the design of the command only had for its object the production of these nauseous feelings, and was not intended to be actually complied with, all ground for the objection of the infidel is removed.

14. Ezekiel having been a priest had been accustomed to the strictest absti-

15 abominable flesh. Then he said unto me: Behold, I have appointed thee cow's dung instead of man's dung, and thou shalt bake thy bread therewith.
16 And he said unto me: Son of man, behold, I will break the staff of bread in Jerusalem, and they shall eat bread by weight and with carefulness, and water by measure and with astonishment
17 they shall drink. To the end that they may lack bread and water, and be astonished one with another, and pine away in their iniquity.

nence from everything inconsistent with the legal enactments relative to external purity. To this circumstance he here appeals as an argument why he should be relieved from the disagreeable necessity that had been imposed upon him. Compare the striking parallel, Acts x. 13, 14. Neither the prophet nor the apostle could reconcile the mandate with the express prohibitions of the ceremonial law. By בָּשָׂר פִּגּוּל, *abominable flesh*, is meant meat that stank from putridity. Flesh of animals that had been killed three days was strictly prohibited by the law to be eaten (Lev. vii. 17, 18; xix. 6, 7). LXX. κρέας ἕωλον.

15. The concession made to relieve the feelings of the prophet indicated the divine disposition to mitigate the punishment of the captive Hebrews. The ashes of animal excrements in which bread has been baked having been carefully removed, and the external crust only having been brought into contact with them, the interior is left entirely free from everything disagreeable to the taste. Dr. Robinson, describing a scene on his journey to Nâbulus, says: "The men were baking a large, round, flat cake of bread, in the embers of a fire of camel's and cow dung. Taking it out when done, they brushed off the ashes, and divided it among the party, offering us also a portion. I tasted it, and found it quite as good as the common bread of the country" (Researches, vol. iii. p. 76). The teaching of the passage is, that in wrath God remembers mercy; that those to whom afflictions are sanctified, and who turn to him with their whole heart, shall obtain mercy, and be delivered out of all their troubles.

16, 17. The prophet is here furnished with a further illustration of the necessitous condition to which their sins should reduce his countrymen.

CHAPTER V.

Ezekiel is commanded to cut off the hair of his head and beard, 1; to burn a third part of it with fire, to cut another third part with a sword, and to scatter the remaining third to the winds of heaven, 2; of this last portion, however, he was to reserve a small quantity in his girdle, but even of it he was to cast part into the fire, 3, 4. The import of these symbolical actions is next pointed out, and the reasons are assigned why the Jews were to be so severely dealt with, 5-11. A further explanation of the symbols is given, 12; together with a description of the heavy calamities of which they were significant, 13-17.

1 MOREOVER thou, son of man, take thee a sharp knife, a barber's razor let there be taken to thee, and cause it to pass upon thy

head, and upon thy beard, and take to thee weighing scales and divide the *hair*. A third part thou shalt cause to pass through the fire in the midst of the city, when the days of the siege are fulfilled: then thou shalt take a third part, and smite about it with a knife, and a third part thou shalt scatter to the wind, and I will draw out a sword after them. Thou shalt also take a few of them in number, and bind them in thy skirts. Then take of them again, and cast them into the midst of the fire, and burn them in the fire; from it shall fire go forth into all the house of Israel. Thus saith the Lord Jehovah: This is Jerusalem: I have placed her in the midst of the nations and of the

1. חֶרֶב is used in the Hebrew Scriptures not only to denote the *sword*, but also any other sharp-edged instrument for cutting with, just as תַּעַר is used both of a penknife and a razor. Though with great propriety the latter is mentioned in reference to the shaving of the hair, there is an equal propriety in employing the term sword in reference to the use of that weapon by the Chaldeans. That both are here identified, seems the most natural construction of the sense. To indicate the just discrimination to be employed by Jehovah in the punishment of his rebellious people, the prophet is further commanded to weigh out the hair into several portions. The priests having been prohibited from shaving, (Lev. xxi. 5), the command given to Ezekiel on the present occasion must have appeared peculiarly severe; but he was thereby taught, and the people through him, that the ceremonial must give place to the moral. That Ezekiel here represented the Hebrew people there cannot be a doubt, but Hitzig refines too much when he interprets his head of Jerusalem, as the capital. The suffix in חֻלְקֹתָם refers to the hairs, understood.

2. When the prophet had completed the term of his symbolical siege he was to burn a third part of the hair which he had cut off, in the midst of the pan employed as a symbol of the siege. By this was intimated that a portion of the inhabitants should be destroyed by fire and famine during that awful calamity. Comp. ver. 12. Those who were cut off by the Chaldeans around the city are next described, and then the hopeless condition of the fugitives is depicted.

3, 4. יֶשׁ is used loosely for מְעַט. The few here referred to were not reserved to be saved from punishment, as the words might at first sight seem to indicate, but to have that punishment inflicted upon them. They were to undergo a further fiery trial. The calamity was to be total. It was to extend to the whole posterity of Jacob.

5, 6. A definite application of the symbol. A more favorable situation as the centre of religious unity and moral influence could not have been selected than Jerusalem. Like a central sun, she was destined to radiate the light of true religion over three continents. But instead of being faithful to her vocation, she adopted the idolatrous practices of the surrounding nations, and thereby incurred the displeasure of her covenant God. וַתֶּמֶר is to be regarded as the future apocopated of מָרָה, *to rebel*. Compare וַיֵּרֶד, Judges xv. 4; וַיֵּפֶן, Ps. cv. 24. מָרָה אֶת, *to rebel against*, affords a sense equally pregnant with that derived by Jarchi, De Wette, and others from מוּר, *to change*. Compare מָרָה אֶת־פִּי יְהֹוָה, *to rebel against the command of Jehovah*, 1 Sam. xii. 15. The preposition in לְרִשְׁעָה indicates quality, state, or condition. The He-

6 countries round about her. But she hath wickedly rebelled against my judgments more than the heathen, and my statutes more than the countries which are around her; for they have despised my judgments, and as for my statutes they have not
7 walked in them. Therefore thus saith the Lord Jehovah: Because ye have been more outrageous than the heathen which are round about you; ye have not walked in my statutes, and my judgments ye have not practised, but have done according to the judgments of the heathen that are round about you:
8 Therefore thus saith the Lord Jehovah: Behold, I, even I, am against thee, and will execute judgments in the midst of thee
9 in the sight of the nations. And I will do in thee what I have not done, nor will I do the like any more, on account of all
10 thine abominations. Therefore the fathers shall eat the children in the midst of thee, and the children shall eat their fathers, and

brews had plunged themselves, by their rebellions against the laws of Jehovah, into circumstances of wickedness more aggravated than those of their surrounding neighbors in Syria, Egypt, or Babylon. The nominative to כְּאָסֹף and הֲלֹא is not the heathen, spoken of immediately before, but the inhabitants of Jerusalem, understood.

7. הֲמָנְכֶם is not, after Aquil., the Peshito Syriac, and Ewald, to be read as if pointed הִמָּנְכֶם, the Niphal of מָנָה, *to number* — the meaning, *because ye were numbered among the heathen*, not being suitable to the connection; but is to be taken as an anomalous form for הֲמָנְכֶם, the Infinitive in Kal of הָמָה, *to tumultuate, rage, be enraged, outrageous*. The word is here used in this last signification, to denote the mad and unbridled riotousness with which the Jewish people ran after their idols. They set no bounds to the exorbitancies which they committed, and surpassed in crime the heathen around them. לֹא, before עֲשִׂיתֶם, at the end of the verse is omitted in thirty of Kennicott and De Rossi's MSS., primarily in five more, in the Soncin. and Brixian editions, in the Syriac, and in twenty-four codices of the Vulg.; and appears to have originated with some copyist who supposed that the negative expressed just before was to be repeated here. The retention of it would make the Lord declare what was contrary to fact and to what is expressly declared chap. xi. 12. Supposing, with Rosenmüller and Hävernick, the negative to have been the original reading, the only tolerable interpretation would be, that the Jews had not remained faithful to their covenant God as the pagans around them had been to their idols.

9. What is here threatened cannot be absolutely explained of the divine dealings with the Jews in the time of the prophet, since there is every reason to believe that the sufferings of the inhabitants of Jerusalem when besieged by Titus were still more dreadful than those inflicted by Nebuchadnezzar, but is to be interpreted of them as compared with other nations. They were treated with a severity such as no other people, either before or after, has experienced. As they had been unparalleled in wickedness, so they should be in punishment. Hävernick's attempt to combine both destructions is very unsatisfactory.

10. Compare Lev. xxvi. 29; Deut. xxviii. 53. To these passages in the

I will execute judgments in thee, and scatter the whole remnant
11 of thee to every wind. Wherefore, as I live, saith the Lord
Jehovah: Surely because thou hast polluted my sanctuary with
all thy detestable things, and with all thine abominations, therefore I also will cut thee off, neither will mine eye spare, nor
12 will I have pity. A third part of thee shall die with the pestilence, and with the famine they shall be consumed in the midst
of thee; and a third part shall fall by the sword round about
thee; and a third part I will scatter to every wind, and I will
13 draw out the sword after them. Thus shall mine anger be
spent, and I will cause my fury to rest on them, and comfort
myself; and they shall know that I, Jehovah, have spoken in
14 my jealousy, when I have spent my fury on them. Moreover
I will deliver thee over to desolation and reproach among the
nations that are round about thee, in the sight of every one that
15 passeth by. And it shall be for a reproach and a reviling, an
example and an astonishment to the nations that are round
about thee, when I execute judgments in thee in anger and in

Pentateuch there is here an obvious reference, with the aggravating addition of the sons eating their fathers.

11. חַי־אָנִי, *as I live,* is a formula of swearing employed by Jehovah when about to introduce a declaration of peculiar solemnity or importance. It pledges the existence of the ever-living God for the certainty of the event. Than the life of God, which includes his necessary and eternal self-existence, it is impossible to conceive of a more sublime or powerfully influential idea. The culminating point of the daring wickedness of the Jews was their desecration of the holy habitation of Jehovah by introducing idolatrous worship into it. The idols which they thus introduced are designated שִׁקּוּצִים, *detestable objects,* from שָׁקַץ, *to be filthy, polluted, abominable,* and תּוֹעֵבוֹת, the same. Instead of אֶגְרַע, *I will withdraw or diminish,* the reading אֶגְדַּע, *I will cut down, cut off,* is found in six MSS., it has originally been the reading of five more, and is that of one by correction. It is supported by all the ancient versions, better

suits the following connection, and has more emphasis.

12. God now declares in plain terms what was intended by the symbolical treatment of the hair. A third part of the inhabitants of Jerusalem were to perish by pestilence and famine during the siege, another third part were to be cut off by the Chaldean army in the surrounding country while attempting to escape, and the remaining third were to be scattered in every direction by the armed foe. Wherever they fled they should find their enemies in possession, and not be able to escape their sword.

13. The Jews should experience no relief or alleviation with respect to the punishments to be inflicted upon them. וְהִנֶּחָמְתִּי, for הִתְנֶחָמְתִּי, in Hithpael.

14. לְחֶרְבָּה וּלְחֶרְפָּה form an onomatopœia. The surrounding idolaters, whose practices they had adopted, instead of affording them any comfort or aid, would only exult at their calamities. For לַגּוֹיִם, *to the nations,* ver. 15, fourteen MSS., primarily five more, and the Complutensian Text read בַּגּוֹיִם, *among*

19 fury, even in furious rebukes; I, Jehovah, have spoken it: When I shall send among them the evil arrows of famine which shall be for destruction, which I will send to destroy you, for famine I will accumulate upon you, and will break the staff of your
17 bread: I will both send upon you famine and evil beasts, and they shall bereave thee; and pestilence and blood shall pass through thee; and I will bring the sword upon thee; I, Jehovah, have spoken it.

the nations, as in ver. 14, and thus the Vulg. and Arab. Instead of הָיָה, the third person, at the beginning of ver. 15, all the ancient versions have read הָיָה, the second, which is required by the connection. מוּסָר, properly *an instructive example*, from יָסַר, *to chastise, correct, instruct by punishment;* an example held out for the warning of others.

16. חִצֵּי הָרָעָב, *arrows of famine*, Grotius interprets of lightning, storms, locusts, etc., which are prejudicial to corn, and thus superinduce famine; but the phrase seems rather to describe the famine itself, with reference to the acute pain occasioned by hunger.

17. A third repetition of the threatening of famine, aggravated by the addition of other calamities usually consequent on war. That חַיָּה רָעָה, a collective for *evil beasts*, is to be taken literally, and not interpreted of the king of Babylon and his armies, would seem more suitable in the connection. שָׁכֵל, properly means *to be bereaved of children;* in Piel, as here, to destroy children, and thus render barren or desolate. In order more deeply to impress the minds of the Jews with alarming apprehensions of the divine judgments which were to be inflicted upon them, the language is repetitiously and variously charged.

CHAPTER VI.

The prophet is directed to address himself to the inhabitants of the whole country, and denounce the destruction at once of the idols and the idol-worshippers, 1-7. A promise is then given for the comfort of those who, in the midst of their calamities, should repent and turn from their idolatrous practices, 8-10. By most significant actions it is indicated that the threatened punishment would assuredly be inflicted to the utmost, 11-14.

1 AND the word of Jehovah came unto me, saying: Son of man, set
2 thy face against the mountains of Israel, and prophesy against
3 them, and say: Ye mountains of Israel, hear ye the word of the Lord Jehovah: Thus saith the Lord Jehovah to the mountains

1-3. By "the mountains of Israel," etc., we are not to understand those of Ephraim exclusively, but those of the country of Palestine generally, in which idolatry had abounded. They are personified in order to give greater effect to the discourse. Although the Babylonians were themselves idolaters, and there was in many respects an affinity between their idol-worship and that of the Hebrews who had borrowed it from them, yet such should be the strength of

and to the hills, to the channels and to the valleys, Behold, I,
even I, bring a sword against you, and I will destroy your high
4 places. And your altars shall be desolate, and your images
shall be broken, and I will cast down your slain before your
5 idols. And I will lay the carcases of the children of Israel
before their idols, and will scatter your bones round about your
6 altars. In all your dwelling-places the cities shall be laid waste
and the high places shall be desolate, in order that your altars
may be laid waste and made desolate, and your dung-gods may
be broken and cease, and your solar images may be cut down,
7 and your works destroyed. And the slain shall fall in the midst
8 of you, and ye shall know that I am Jehovah. Yet will I reserve
a remnant, that ye may have those who escape the sword among
9 the nations, when ye shall be scattered in the countries. And
those of you that escape shall remember me in the nations
whither they shall be carried captives, when I break their whorish heart, which hath departed from me, and their eyes which

hostile feeling by which the invading army would be actuated, and such their cupidity for the gold and silver with which the wooden idols were covered, that they would hew them down, and involve them and their worshippers in one common destruction. The אֲפִיקִים were *channels*, running through and fertilizing the valleys, which abounded in groves favorable for the worship of Astarte. The term is parallel with גֵּאָיוֹת, and has pretty much the same signification. The two terms correspond, just as the preceding הֶהָרִים and גְּבָעוֹת do. They are combined, as synonymes frequently are in Hebrew, for the sake of emphasis. The collocation הִנְנִי אָנִי מֵבִיא־אֲנִי is unusual. The proper form is וַהֲנִי מֵבִיא־אֲנִי, but הִנְנִי אֲנִי מֵבִיא is also admissible.

4. For חַמָּנֵיכֶם, *your solar pillars*, see on Isa. xvii. 8; and compare 2 Chron. xxxiv. 4, 7. To expose the filthy character of the idols, and excite a loathing of them, they are called גִּלּוּלִים, *dung gods*. Compare the reading Βεελζεβούλ, Matt. xii. 24. The term is frequently used by Ezekiel, but it occurs also in the Pentateuch and other Historical Books. Hävernick's rendering, *stone-masses*, is not sustained by his attempt to establish another derivation.

5. To express the futility of all idol-confidences, and the ruin in which they would involve those who cherished them, the bones of the idolaters are represented as scattered around their altars.

6. The destruction that was to overtake the places of idol-worship was to be complete. The idols are here said to be the "works" of the Hebrews, because they were fabricated by their hands.

8–10. Those who might escape the destructive havoc effected by the invading foe, and be preserved as captives among the nations, should there be brought to repentance and self-abhorrence, when they reflected upon the way in which they had provoked their covenant God.

9. וְנִשְׁבַּרְתִּי is not here passive, but reflexive in signification: when I have broken, or when I shall have broken for myself, — when I have produced such a change in their idolatrous dispositions as shall induce them to renounce their idols and return to my worship and service. Though at first sight it may seem less appropriate to speak of break-

have gone a whoring after their dung-gods, and they shall loathe themselves in their own sight for the evils which they have
10 committed in all their abominations. And they shall know that I am Jehovah: it is not in vain I have said that I would inflict
11 this calamity upon them. Thus saith the Lord Jehovah: Smite with thy hand, and stamp with thy foot, and say: Alas, for all the evil abominations of the house of Israel, for they shall fall
12 by the sword, by the famine, and by the pestilence. He that is far off shall die of the pestilence, and he that is near shall fall by the sword, and he that is left and is besieged shall die by
13 the famine, and I will exhaust my fury on them. And they shall know that I am Jehovah, when their slain shall be in the midst of their dung-gods round about their altars, on every high hill, on all the tops of the mountains, and under every green tree, and under every thick oak, in the place where they offered

ing the "eyes" than of breaking the heart, yet when we consider the stubborn looks of the Hebrews, and that the same verb is applied to the destruction of pride (Lev. xxvi. 19), there is nothing incongruous in such construction. וְנָקֹטּוּ is, according to the punctuation, the Niphal of קָטַט, as נְסֹבּוּ of סָבַב; but as this root occurs nowhere else in the Hebrew Bible, it is better to reject the Dagesh forte, and refer the verb to קוּט which is frequently used in the sense of *loathing*, or regarding anything with disgust. בִּפְנֵיהֶם is construed by some with אֱלִילֵיהָ preceding, and the prophet is supposed to mean that the Jews should loathe themselves in the very presence of their idols; but as the same form occurs chaps. xx. 43, xxxvi. 31, it is rather to be taken as designed to give force to the expression of self-abhorrence, the idea of which was conveyed by קוּט. They should have a vivid perception of their wickedness; the abhorrent image of themselves, as the perpetrators of it, should stare them in the very face. In the passages just quoted our translators, considering the phrase to be equivalent to בְּעֵינֵיכֶם render: *in your own sight*. אֶל־הָרָעוֹת is equivalent to עַל־הָרָעוֹת, *on account of* the evils.

10. יָדַע here, as frequently, signifies to know by experience.

11. It was not uncommon for the prophets to employ violent gesticulations while announcing alarming declarations of the divine will. אָח, *ah! alas!* an onomatopoetic, like the corresponding Arabic آح, used by the Orientals to express deep emotions of grief. The prophet, foreseeing the awful judgments which were coming upon his people in punishment of their atrocious wickedness, was thus to give expression to the keen feelings which were pent up in his breast, in order more powerfully to work upon the minds of his hearers. What he exhibited was emblematical of the light in which they were regarded by Jehovah. Compare xxi. 12, 14.

12. וְהַנִּשְׁאָר וְהַנָּצוּר is descriptive of those Jews who were not carried away into captivity, or who had not made their escape into the country, but were left to suffer all the calamities of the siege. For נָצוּר, in the sense of *besieged*, see my comment on Isa. i. 8. I cannot find, with Hävernick, that the term derives any light from the ancient proverbial expression: צוּר וְקָדִים.

14. לְיִדְבָּה וּבִלְשִׂמָה, a beautiful paro-

14 sweet incense to all their dung-gods. And I will stretch forth my hand against them, and will make the land more waste and desolate than the desert of Diblah in all their dwelling-places; and they shall know that I am Jehovah.

nomasia, from the same root עָשֵׁם, *to be laid waste*. It is in frequent use by our prophet. I agree with Hävernick and Maurer, that דִּבְלָתָה, *Diblathah*, is not, with Kimchi, Michaelis, Gesenius, and Hitzig, to be exchanged for רִבְלָתָה, *Riblathah*. Such conjecture is unsupported either by MS. authority or by that of any of the ancient versions. That the wilderness of Arabia Deserta, to the east and south of the Dead Sea, so well known, and so well fitted to be employed for comparison, is here intended, appears most probable, in which case we may suppose that דִּבְלָה, *Diblah*, is only another form for the Dual דִּבְלָתַיִם, *Diblathaim*, the name of a city in the country of Moab (Numb. xxxiii. 46; Jer. xlviii. 22). That Diblah should be a noun common, and not a proper name, seems less likely. I am surprised that Hävernick should adopt the opposite view, and rendering the term by *destruction*, suppose Babylon to be meant. What idea could the Jews possibly attach to the words with such a reference? The prepositive מִ in מִדִּבְלָתָה I take to be comparative, as it is properly rendered in our common version.

CHAPTER VII.

The prophet announces the speedy ruin of the Jewish state, 1-15; the penitent reformation of a remnant, 16-19; the destruction of the temple, which the Jews had polluted with their idols, 20-22. He is commanded to make a chain, thereby symbolizing the captivity that should follow the utter destruction of the city and the theocratic establishment, 23-27.
In the former half of the chapter the language is marked by an abruptness and a repetitiousness which strongly indicate the suddenness and certainty of the approaching calamity.

1 And the word of Jehovah came unto me saying: And thou, son
2 of man, thus saith the Lord Jehovah: There is an end to the land of Israel; the end is come, upon the four corners of the
3 land. Now the end is upon thee, and I will send mine anger upon thee, and I will judge thee according to thy ways, and
4 will lay upon thee all thine abominations. And mine eye shall not spare thee, neither will I have pity, but will recompense thy ways upon thee, and thine abominations shall be in the midst of

2, 3. קֵץ is properly separated from what follows by Athnach. The prophet is first to express himself indefinitely with respect to the termination of the Jewish state, and then by prefixing the article to the word (הַקֵּץ), to mark the event as that which had been determined in the divine counsel, and definitely predicted by the prophets.

4. תּוֹעֲבֹת, *abominations*, by meton-

5 thee, and ye shall know that I am Jehovah. Thus saith the
Lord Jehovah: A calamity, an only calamity; behold, it is
6 come. An end is come, the end is come; it waketh up against
7 thee; behold it is come. The crown is come against thee, O
inhabitant of the land; the time is come; the day of tumult is
8 come, and not the joyous shout of the mountains. Now speedily
will I pour out my fury upon thee, and exhaust mine anger on
thee, and judge thee according to thy ways; yea, I will render
9 unto thee all thine abominations. And mine eye shall not
spare, neither will I have pity; according to thy ways I will
render unto thee; and thine abominations shall be in the midst
of thee, and ye shall know that I am Jehovah that smiteth.
10 Behold the day, behold, it is come, the crown is gone forth, the

ymy of the cause for the effect, the punishments inflicted on account of the abominable idolatries in which the Jews had indulged. In these punishments, the idolatries in all their hateful forms might be regarded as presenting themselves to the view of those who had been guilty of them.

5. The threatened calamity is announced as אֶחָת, *one, only, singular*, the only one of its kind, because of its unexampled severity. Comp. Song vi. 9, and the Arab. يَوْمُ الْوَاحِدِ, *the only day*, a time distinguished on account of its unusual calamity. אַחַר, *after*, though the reading of upwards of twenty-three MSS. and adopted in nine printed editions, is less entitled to regard.

6. A repetition of the language employed ver. 3. The addition of הִנֵּה, *behold*, in this and the preceding verse, gives emphasis to the announcements.

7. The prophet commences this verse with בָּאָה, the verb with which he had concluded the last. Its frequent repetition was calculated to strike terror into the minds of the Jews. Various interpretations have been given of צְפִירָה. Our translators appear to have adopted the idea of *morning* from the Syriac and Chaldee, and from the strikingly parallel passage Joel ii. 2, where, however, the Hebrew is שַׁחַר. Gesenius, Maurer, and others: *the circle comes to thee;* meaning, it is now thy *turn* to be punished. From the fact, that the same word, written without the Yod, occurs as parallel with מַטֶּה, *sceptre*, ver. 10, I regard the signification to be *crown*, i.e. *the crowned one* = Nebuchadnezzar. The powerful and victorious monarch had already come forth from his residence, and would speedily inflict the predicted judgments on the Jews. For this signification of the term see my Comment. on Isa. xxviii. 5. The idea of conqueror inheres in the cognate Arab. ظَفِرَ, *vicit, superavit, victoriam reportavit.* הַיּוֹם מְהוּמָה should, according to rule, have been יוֹם מְהוּמָה or simply יוֹם הַמְּהוּמָה but the awful period of judgment was so prominently in the mind of the prophet that more emphatically to mark it, he places the article before the former of the two nouns. הֵד is a contracted form of הֵדָד, which is otherwise used of the joyous shout of the vintagers, but here of that of idolatrous feasts, celebrated on the mountains in honor of the false gods. Instead, nothing was to be heard but the sounds of tumult and confusion occasioned by the fury of the enemy.

8, 9. A repetition of verses 3 and 4.

10. Here, as observed on ver. 7, צְפִירָה, *crown*, and מַטֶּה, *rod* or *sceptre*, are parallel, and designate the king of Babylon.

11 sceptre flourisheth, pride hath budded. Violence hath risen up for a rod of wickedness; there shall be none of them, neither of their multitude, nor of their substance; neither shall there be any
12 wailing for them. The time is come, the day hath approached; let not the buyer rejoice, and let not the seller grieve, for fury
13 shall be to all her multitude. For the seller shall not return to that which is sold, though they were yet alive; for the vision is for the whole multitude of her; one shall not return, nor shall
14 any man strengthen his life by his iniquity. Blow ye with a blast, and make all ready; yet none goeth to the battle, for my

As the latter term signifies the *rod* or instrument of punishment, as well as the badge of royalty, it has singular force in this connection. Compare Isa. x. 5. The blossoming and budding are to be referred to the imposing and insolent bearing of the conqueror and his army. That זָדוֹן, *pride*, is to be referred to the king of Babylon, compare Jer. l. 31, 32. This construction is more suitable to the connection than that adopted by Jerome and others, which would refer the term to the pride of the Jews.

11. By מַטֵּה־רֶשַׁע is meant the rod for the punishment of wickedness, i.e. of the idolatry of the Jews. Compare Zech. v. 8. That rod was invested with irresistible power, and should come down upon them with awful violence. Considerable obscurity attaches to the following striking paronomasia: לֹא מֵהֶם וְלֹא מֵהֲמוֹנָם וְלֹא נֹהַּ בָּהֶם. The most probable rendering is that given by Gesenius: There shall remain *nothing of them, neither of their multitude, nor of their wealth,* taking הֵם or הָם in the last word to be an unusual form, equivalent to הֲמוֹן, and adopted for the sake of the paronomasia. לֹא is used as مِنْ, the negative absolute in Arabic, in the sense of *nothing of*. נֹהַּ, as interpreted by Gesenius to signify *something splendid,* winds up the description very tamely. I prefer the sense of *wailing* as given in our common version from the Jewish interpreters, who derive the noun from the root נָהָה,

to bewail, lament. The prophet was to announce the universally sweeping consequences of the Chaldean conquest of Jerusalem. There should be none left to bewail the slain and the captives. Compare Jer. xvi. 4-7.

12, 13. A complete change was to take place in the affairs of life. The buyer of a portion of land should have no ground for self-congratulation on account of the bargain he had made, nor the seller for regret on account of what he had parted with; they were to be deprived of all their property, or removed to a distant country, and thus be denied the privilege of recovering their possessions in the year of jubilee (Lev. xxv. 13). Though they might be spared in life till the return of that year, it would avail them nothing. Nor was any one to imagine that while he emboldened himself in his iniquity, he could possibly prosper. Instead of חָרוֹן, *wrath*, ver. 12, we have חָזוֹן, *vision*, forming a paronomasia with it, ver. 13. Since the former word occurs again in the same sentence repeated ver. 14, there is less reason to suspect an error of transcription, however much the words resemble each other.

14. So completely disheartened should be the inhabitants of Judea, that none should be found with sufficient courage to obey the summons to encounter the Chaldeans. The words תָּקְעוּ בַתָּקוֹעַ so correspond to בְּתָקוֹעַ תִּקְעוּ Jer. vi. 1, that some have supposed that Ezekiel

15 wrath is against all her multitude. The sword is without, and the pestilence and the famine within; he that is in the field shall die by the sword, and him that is in the city the pestilence and the
16 famine shall devour. But those of them that escape shall escape, and be upon the mountains as doves of the valleys, all of them
17 mourning, every one for his iniquity. All hands shall be feeble,
18 and all knees shall flow like water. And they shall gird themselves with sackcloth, and horror shall cover them, and shame
19 shall be upon all faces, and baldness upon all their heads. They shall cast away their silver into the streets, and their gold shall be removed; their silver and their gold shall not be able to deliver them in the day of Jehovah's indignation: they shall not satisfy their souls nor fill their bowels, because it was the stum-
20 bling-block of their iniquity. And as to their beautiful ornament, it was placed for glory, but they set up their abominations

borrowed them from his brother prophet. Whatever there may be in this, it is doubtful whether תְּקוֹעַ is, as there, to be taken as the name of a place, or whether it is not rather to be regarded as the infinitive used substantively, denoting *a blast*. I incline to the latter construction.

15. No security should anywhere be found. Whether in the open country, or in the fortified city, the Jews should be equally exposed to disaster. There is a striking analogy between the description here given of the circumstances of the Jews at the time of the Chaldean invasion, and that given by our Lord of the invasion by the Romans (Matt. xxiv. 16-18).

16. However universal the havoc made by the enemy might be, as predicted in the preceding verses, a few would escape to the clefts of the mountains, and there find safety. Timid as doves frightened from their peaceful valleys (compare Ps. xi. 1), and having time for reflection, they should sincerely repent of the sins which had brought such calamities upon their city and nation, each one specially filled with sorrow on account of his own guilt.

17-19. The comparison to water has reference to its gentle flow, without any power of resistance. It is emblematical of extreme weakness (Josh. vii. 5; Ps. xxii. 15). The כ of comparison is elliptically omitted. The prophet here reverts to his countrymen generally, and depicts their disconsolate and bewildered condition when attacked by the Chaldeans. To express this more forcibly, they are described as appearing with such tokens of mourning as were customary on occasion of great national calamities as well as of private losses, and casting their silver and gold-bedecked idols into the streets to satisfy the cupidity of the enemy, and thus divert his attention from themselves and their houses. That these idols, and not gold and silver simply considered, are meant, appears from its being added that they were the stumbling-block of their iniquity. Their worship of these objects, instead of adhering to the service of the true God, was the cause of their ruin. What silver or gold they might otherwise have had, could procure them no sustenance, for this was not to be had at any price.

20-22. Most modern commentators explain צְבִי עֶדְיוֹ, *his beautiful ornament*, of the costly ornaments of the Jews, con-

and their abhorrent idols in it; wherefore I have delivered it
21 to them for removal. Yea, I have delivered it into the hand of the barbarians for a spoil, and to the wicked of the earth for a
22 prey, and they shall profane it. And I will turn away my face from them, and they shall profane my secret place; yea, tyrants shall enter into it and pollute it.
23 Make the chain, for the land is filled with blood-guiltiness, and the city is filled with violence.
24 And I will bring the worst of the heathen, and they shall possess their houses, and I will make the pomp of the strong to cease,
25 and they shall profane their holy places. Destruction cometh,
26 and they shall seek for peace, but there shall be none. Calamity upon calamity cometh, and report shall follow report; and they shall seek a vision from the prophet, but the law shall perish

sidering the prophet to be merely enlarging on their personal privations, of which he had been treating; but I agree with Hengstenberg and Fairbairn that the temple is meant. The term צְבִי is indeed frequently applied to the land of the Hebrews (Dan. viii. 9; xi. 16, 41; Ezek. xx. 6, 15; Jer. iii. 19); but as the temple was the most magnificent object in the country, the term may specially be regarded as applicable to that splendid edifice. גָּאוֹן, *pride*, in a good sense: *majesty, glory*. The temple, which was designed to be the residence of the Divine Majesty, the Jews had polluted by setting up and worshipping idols in it. אֹתָהּ, used impersonally, is best rendered in English by the passive. תּוֹעֲבֹתָם שִׁקּוּצֵיהֶם, *their detestations, their abominations*, i.e. their most abhorrent idols. These they had had the audacity to establish as rivals of Jehovah in his own sacred temple. See chap. viii. 3–17. What confirms this view of the prophet's meaning is the mention made, ver. 22, of the צְפוּנִי יְהֹוָה, *secret place* of Jehovah, the holy of holies, entrance to which was interdicted to all except the high priest, who was only allowed to go into it once a year, on the great day of atonement. The pronominal affix ה in בָּהּ is by enallage to be

referred to צְבִי. The Chaldeans would profane the temple by entering its most sacred recess, and destroying and robbing its treasures. לָהֶם, ver. 20, *to them*, the Chaldeans characterized as חַיֵּי הָאָרֶץ, *the barbarians*, in the following verse.

23. The prophet is directed to make a chain, which was a fit symbol of the captivity; it having been customary in ancient times to lead away the captives in a row, with a chain passed on from the neck of one to that of another; as may be seen on the plates in Wilkinson's *Manners of the Ancient Egyptians*. Compare Jer. xxvii. 2. הָרַתּוֹק, with the Art., *the* well-known chain employed on such occasions (Jarchi, שַׁלְשֶׁלֶת). The word is derived from רָתַק, Arab.

رتق, *to bind, put in fitters*.

24. רָעֵי גוֹיִם, the genitive of comparison, *the wicked of nations*, for the most wicked, the worst. מִקְדָּשֵׁיהֶם should be pointed מִקְדְּשֵׁיהֶם, *their sanctuaries*, i.e. the sacred compartments of the temple, and other places set apart for devotion. Comp. chap. xxi. 7.

25–27. קְפָדָה, *horrible destruction*. The idea is taken from the appearance of the hedgehog (קִפֹּד), which, rolling itself up into a ball, presents a phalanx of

27 from the priest and counsel from the elders. As for the king, he shall mourn, and the prince shall be clothed with astonishment, and the hands of the people of the land shall shake; because of their way I will deal with them, and according to their deserts I will judge them; and they shall know that I am Jehovah.

spears that renders the attack of most animals fruitless. In the accumulation of calamities which should come upon the people, they would gladly receive instruction from those who had been their spiritual guides, compare Isa. xxvi. 9; but these should not have it in their power to afford them any counsel. The ecclesiastical estate should be entirely broken up. They should go to the priests, not penitently to present an atonement for their sins, but merely to see whether they, as learned men, would be able to suggest any means by which they might be delivered from the calamities that had come upon them. זְקֵנִים, *elders*, the official ecclesiastical rulers of the people.

27. The consternation and perplexity should be general, extending to all ranks of the people. עַם הָאָרֶץ, *the people of the land* or *country*, i.e. the common people as contrasted with the classes just mentioned. The בְּ in כְּדַרְכָּם expresses the ground or cause of the threatened calamities. For וּבְמִשְׁפְּטֵיהֶם, seventeen MSS., perhaps one originally, and the Vulg. read וּכְמִשְׁפְּטֵיהֶם.

CHAPTER VIII.

This chapter contains the account of a trance in which Ezekiel was in his house on the Chebar, 1, 2; his conveyance in this state to Jerusalem, where, within the precincts of the temple, he had a renewed manifestation of the divine glory which he had seen in the first vision, 3, 4; a vision of different forms of idolatry practised in the temple: the Syrian 5, 6; the Egyptian, 7-12; the Phœnician, 13, 14; and the Persian, 15, 16; on which an appeal is made in reference to these atrocious abominations, and a denunciation of the unsparing punishment with which they were to be visited, 17, 18.
Rosenmüller, Hävernick, and Hitzig, regard this chapter, together with the three following, as forming a separate and distinct portion of the book. Fairbairn treats the viii. by itself, and the ix. x. and xi. as a connected portion.

1 AND it came to pass in the sixth year, in the sixth *month*, on the fifth of the month, I was sitting in my house, and the elders of Judah were sitting before me, and the hand of the Lord Jehovah

1. The *sixth year* here assigned as the date of the vision is doubtless that of the captivity of Jehoiachin, the fifth of which is specified chap. i. 2; the seventh, chap. xx. 1; the ninth, chap. xxiv. 1; the tenth, chap. xxix. 1; the eleventh, chaps. xxvi. 1, xxxi. 1; the twelfth, chaps. xxxii. 1, xxxiii. 21; the twenty-fifth, chap. xl. 1; the twenty-seventh, chap. xxix. 17. That captivity was an event so fresh in the memory of the exiles and so determinative of their fate, that it must, in their estimation, have had an unparalleled degree of importance attached to it. The reason why the elders were sitting before Ezekiel is not stated;

2 descended upon me there. And I looked, and behold, a form like the appearance of a man ; from the appearance of his loins and downwards there was fire, and from his loins and upwards there was as the appearance of splendor, as the appearance of
3 polished brass. And he put forth the form of a hand, and laid hold of me by a lock of my head, and the Spirit raised me up between the earth and the heaven, and brought me to Jerusalem, in the visions of God, to the door of the inner gate that looketh northward, where was a pedestal, the image of jealousy, which
4 caused jealousy. And behold, there the glory of the God of

but most probably it was that they might listen to any further communications which he might have been commissioned to make to them in reference to their captivity. That they otherwise were present as witnesses of the sublime scene, as Hävernick supposes, I cannot find. For the phrase הָיְתָה יָד, see on chap. i. 3.

2. Instead of אֵשׁ, *fire*, the LXX. according to the Complut. and Aldine editions, have read אִישׁ, *a man*, which, though only one of Kennicott's MSS. has read thus originally, commends itself as the true reading by the reference made in the immediate connection to the loins and hand of a man, and by the circumstance of אִישׁ occurring in the following clause. This conjecture is approved by Houbigant, Secker, Newcome, Rosenmüller, Ewald, and Hitzig. The appearance of this human form was distinguished by a brilliancy such as the prophet had seen in his first vision, chap. i. 4 ; and the person referred to was doubtless the Angel of the Covenant. חַשְׁמַלָה, the feminine of חַשְׁמַל in the passage just quoted, which see.

3. The hand taking the prophet by a lock of his hair, and his being lifted up by the Spirit, are not, of course, to be taken literally, but are parts of the scenic representation. Ἐπιστῆσαι δεῖ, ὅτι ἐν ὁράσει Θεοῦ ταῦτα ὁ προφήτης ἐφὴ ἑωρακέναι. Οὐ τοίνυν σωματικὴ ἦν μετάθεσις, οὐδὲ τῶν τῆς σαρκὸς ὀφθαλμῶν ἡ θεωρία, ἀλλ' ἐν τῷ οἴκῳ καθήμενος μεταξὺ τῶν πρεσβυτέρων Ἰούδα ταύτην ἅπασαν τὴν ὀπτασίαν ἑώρα, Theodoret. Transported in spirit to Jerusalem, the prophet was set down at the north gate, which was that facing the direction in which he is supposed to have been conducted from his residence on the Chebar. Within this gate, which opened into the outer court of the temple, was another, הַפְּנִימִי, *the inner*, leading to the court of the priests, in which stood the altar of burnt-offering, where the ordinary worship was presented. Here was the מוֹשָׁב, *pedestal*, on which had stood the statue or image of Astarte, which Manasseh had had the audacious effrontery to erect in the temple of Jehovah (2 Kings xxi. 7). This idol, arresting the attention of all who came to worship in the temple just as they entered it, claimed, as the rival of Jehovah, their adoration, on which account it is called סֵמֶל הַקִּנְאָה *the image of jealousy*. The worship of this idol, consecrated by the Syrians to Venus, was accompanied with licentious rites, and must have been peculiarly offensive to the Holy One of Israel. See my Comment. on Isa. xvii. 8.

4. Great as had been the provocation given by the worship of this idol, Jehovah is represented as not yet having removed his presence from the temple. The symbol of that presence — the glorious effulgence of Him who dwelt between the cherubim — met the eye of the prophet. See chap. x. 4. It is added that there was a correspondence between

5 Israel, as the appearance which I saw in the valley. And he
said unto me: Son of man, lift up now thine eyes in the way
towards the north. So I lifted up mine eyes in the way towards
the north, and behold, on the north, at the gate of the altar,
6 this image of jealousy at the entrance. And he said unto me:
Son of man, seest thou what they are doing? the great abominations which the house of Israel are committing here, to cause
me to go far off from my sanctuary? but turn yet again, and
7 thou shalt see greater abominations. And he brought me to the
door of the court, and I looked, and behold, a hole in the wall.
8 Then he said unto me; Son of man, dig now in the wall; and
9 I digged in the wall, and behold, a door. And he said unto me;
Go in, and see the wicked abominations which they are commit-
10 ting here. So I went in, and saw, and behold, every form of
creeping things and abominable beasts, and all the dung-gods

this display of the divine glory, and that which he had seen in the plain, chaps. i. 26-28; iii. 12, 22, 23.

5. Ezekiel is now supposed to be within the court of the priests; and, facing the north, he has his attention specially directed to the idolatrous statue which had been placed beside the gate leading to the altar of burnt-offering. From what is here stated, it is to be inferred that the prophet saw the idol in vision, though it may actually have been removed by Josiah when he purified the temple. The object of the vision was to represent the different forms of idolatry in which the Jews had indulged within the precincts of the sacred edifice, and which drew down upon them the punishment of the captivity.

6. מָה הֵם, a contracted form of מָה הֵם, as בַּלְּבָב for בַּמֶּה־לְּבָב, Isa. iii. 15. In לְרָחֳקָה, the ה is paragogic and emphatic. It has been questioned to whom this Infinitive is to be referred as its object, whether to Jehovah or to the Jews. In my opinion, it is more natural to refer it to the former, the removal of whose glory from the temple was the immediate precursor and signal of its being abandoned to destruction.

7-12. The framework of the temple consisted of massive stone, wainscoted with cedar-wood. The hole in the wall marked the entrance which led into the chambers of imagery. It had, however, been blocked up in the time of the reformation effected by Josiah, and required to be re-opened in order to afford access. This operation the prophet is commanded to perform, on which the door of the idolatrous adytum presented itself to his view. He now found himself surrounded by monuments of Egyptian idolatry depicted on the walls of the chambers. That it was customary for the Egyptians to adorn their chambers with hieroglyphics, appears from the testimony of Diodorus Siculus, who states, (i. p. 59, ed. Wess.) that "round the room at Thebes, where the body of king Osymanduas was buried, a multitude of chambers was built, which had elegant paintings of the animals held sacred in Egypt." Thus also Ammianus Marcellinus (lib. xxii.): Sunt et Syringes subterranei quidam et flexuosi secessus, quos, ut fertur, periti rituum vetustorum ..... penitus operosis digestos fodinis per loca diversa struxerunt, et excisis parietibus, volucrum ferarumque genera multa sculpserunt, quas hieroglyphicas literas appellarunt. The hieroglyphics,

of the house of Israel, portrayed upon the wall round about.
11 And there stood before them seventy men of the ancients of the house of Israel, and in the midst of them stood Jaazaniah, the son of Shaphan, every man with his censer in his hand; and a
12 thick cloud of incense was ascending. Then he said unto me: Seest thou, son of man, what the ancients of the house of Israel are doing in the dark, every man in the chambers of his imagery? for they say: Jehovah seeth us not; Jehovah hath forsaken the
13 earth. He said also unto me: Turn yet again; thou shalt see

which were pictured signs of outward objects, in general abounded in those of all kinds of animals, and were symbolical of the degrading objects of Egyptian worship:

" The wildest images, unheard of, strange,
That ever puzzled antiquarians' brains;
Genii with heads of birds, hawks, ibes, drakes,
Of lions, foxes, cats, fish, frogs, and snakes,
Bulls, rams, and monkeys; hippopotami
With knife in paw, suspended from the sky;
Gods germinating men, and men turned gods,
Seated in honor, with gilt crooks and rods;
Vast scarabæi, globes by hands upheld,
From chaos springing, 'mid an endless field
Of forms grotesque, the sphinx, the crocodile,
And other reptiles from the slime of Nile."

To these the Jews, insatiate with idolatry, had added pictured representations of all the other fictitious deities to whose worship they were addicted. The chambers formed a complete Pantheon. To aggravate the evil, it is represented as committed by the members of the Sanhedrim, who, from their judicial character, were bound to suppress all acts of idolatry. Instead of fulfilling their duty in discountenancing whatever was opposed to the holy service of Jehovah, they were not only ringleaders in the scenes of wickedness, but went so far as to deny the omniscience and omnipresence of the Most High. The seventy elders were originally a select body taken from the oldest and most judicious of the people (Numb. xi. 16, 17, 24, 25). If the Shaphan here mentioned is to be conceived of as the scribe who read to Josiah the book of the law which was found in the temple, we cannot imagine that he would neglect to communicate to his family all that transpired on the occasion: the circumstance will enhance the guilt of his son Jaazaniah, who rendered himself conspicuously prominent in the act of idolatrous worship. When it is said each of the seventy had his censer in his hand, it is not implied that they were priests belonging to the temple, and that the censers were necessarily those which had been therein used, but simply that they were all engaged in burning incense before and in honor of the idols. If, indeed, they prostituted the sacred utensils for this purpose, their character must have appeared to Ezekiel in a still more odious light. Degrees of guilt are to be estimated according to the circumstances in which that guilt is contracted.

13, 14. The next scene to which the prophet is introduced, was one of Phœnician idolatry.

" Thammuz came next behind,
Whose annual wound in Lebanon allured
The Syrian damsels to lament his fate
In amorous ditties all a summer's day;
While smooth Adonis from his native rock
Ran purple to the sea, supposed with blood
Of Thammuz yearly wounded: the love tale
Infected Sion's daughters with like heat,
Whose wanton passions, in the sacred porch,
Ezekiel saw, when by the vision led,
His eye surveyed the dark idolatries
Of alienated Judah."

The position occupied by the Jewish females here described, was just inside the outer court, or that of the women, on the north side of the temple. Instead of bewailing their own sins, and those of their people, they are represented as celebrating the feast of Adonis, whose

14 greater abominations which they are doing. Then he brought
me to the door of the gate of the house of Jehovah, which was
towards the north, and behold, there sat women weeping for
15 Tammuz. And he said unto me: Hast thou seen this, O son
of man? turn yet again; thou shalt see greater abominations
16 than these. And he brought me into the inner court of the
house of Jehovah, and behold, at the door of the temple of Jehovah, between the porch and the altar, were about five and twenty
men with their backs towards the temple of Jehovah, and their
faces towards the east, and they were worshipping the sun tow-

---

name the Vulgate here substitutes for Tammuz. This Adonis, according to the ancient mythology, was a beautiful youth, who lived in one of the most enchanting regions of Lebanon, where the river has its spring which is called by his name. Having, while engaged in a hunt, been killed by a wild boar, he was bitterly lamented by Venus, who had been enamored of him. Owing to her influence, as the myth goes, Proserpina permitted him to spend one half of the year with Venus upon earth, but he was obliged to spend the other half in the lower world. Annually as the time of his death came round, a feast in honor of it was celebrated at Byblos, where the river Adonis, red with blood, descended into the sea, on which occasion the Syrian females, in frenzied grief, cut off their hair, or else yielded their bodies for prostitution, the money they earned by which being consecrated to Venus. This feast was succeeded by several days of rejoicing on account of the return of Adonis to the upper world. To the former feast the name of ἀφανισμὸς Ἀδώνιδος, *the disappearance of Adonis*, was given, and to the latter εὕρεσις Ἀδώνιδος, *the finding of Adonis*. The same festival was celebrated in Egypt in honor of Osiris, with respect to whom the fabulous story somewhat varied. The worship is otherwise supposed to have been symbolical of the course of the sun and his influence on the earth. The celebration of this festival falling in our June or July, the name of Tammuz was given to this month in the Jewish calendar. Etymology may be said to have exhausted its powers in endeavoring to obtain a suitable derivation for תַּמּוּז. That proposed by Hävernick is as probable as any. He considers the root to have been יָמַז, equivalent to כָּסַס, *to fail, melt, flow down*, and the form to be contracted for הַתַּמּוּז, just as הַמָּרוּר is derived from מָרַר. The idea thus suggested will equally apply to the fabulous account of Adonis, to the river so called, and to the diminution of the solar influence. The Article in הַתַּמּוּז appears to be used with reference to the appellative signification of the term. Hävernick aptly remarks, that the prophet could not have used the name Adonis, owing to the appropriated use of אֲדוֹן to Jehovah. The Jewish females are represented as *sitting*, which was the posture of mourners (Job ii. 13; Isa. iii. 26; xlvii. 1).

15, 16. The most aggravated form of idolatry here described as witnessed by Ezekiel was that commonly known by the name of the Persian, which we find recognized as existing so early as the time of Job (chap. xxxi. 26). It was afterwards reformed by Zoroaster, and consisted chiefly in the worship of the sun, which the ancient Persians considered to be the eye of Ormuzd, their principal deity. The heinousness of the crime presented to the view of Ezekiel consisted in the contempt cast on the

17 ards the east. Then he said unto me: Hast thou seen this, O son of man? Is it a light thing to the house of Judah that they commit the abominations which they are committing here? for they have filled the land with violence, and have turned back to provoke me to anger; and behold, they put the branch to
18 their nose. Therefore I also will deal in fury; mine eye shall not spare, neither will I have pity, and though they may cry in mine ears with a loud voice, yet I will not hear them.

God of Israel, by the worshippers turning their backs upon him, as dwelling between the cherubim over the altar of burnt-offering, directly in front of the eastern entrance of the temple; and facing the east, paying their adorations to the rising sun. What added to the greatness of the crime was the relation in which the worshippers are supposed officially to have stood to Jehovah. That these worshippers were the priests, has justly been inferred, both from the place in which they appeared, which was that where the Jewish priests were accustomed to perform the principal duties of their office, and from the circumstance that, as Lightfoot perceived, the number corresponds to that of the twenty-four prefects of the courses into which David had distributed the priests, with the high priest at their head, making the twenty-fifth. מְשַׁלְחִים is so manifestly an error of the copyist, that it is surprising how Hävernick and Fairbairn should have attempted to vindicate the position so uncritically adopted by Lightfoot, that the word was originally written in this corrupt form, and designedly employed to indicate the corrupt worship which it describes. מְזַמְּרִים is the reading of eight MSS., and has been that of seven more originally. Among these codices are two Spanish, ancient and good.

17. The scene concludes with a pointed appeal in reference to the abominations which had been described; and in the following verse with an announcement of Jehovah's inexorable threatening of condign punishment. וְהִנָּם שֹׁלְחִים אֶת־הַזְּמוֹרָה אֶל־אַפָּם, "And behold, they put the branch to their nose." That by זְמוֹרָה here we are to understand a *twig* or *branch* (compare for this signification chap. xv. 2), and not a *song*, seems best to agree with the context, and to have reference to a ceremony practised by the sun-worshippers, who, on the rising of that luminary in the eastern horizon, celebrate the event with a hymn, during the singing of which they hold before their face a bundle of branches, taken from the pomegranate tree, the tamarisk, or the pine. To this collection of branches they give the name of *Barsom*. Strabo thus describes the custom: Τὰς ἐπῳδὰς ποιοῦνται πολὺν χρόνον ῥάβδων μυρικίνων λεπτῶν δέσμην κατέχοντες. Compare Hyde, Hist. Relig. Veter. Persar. lib. i. cap. xxvii. and Kleuker's Zendavesta, vol. iii. p. 204. Hävernick takes much pains to set aside this interpretation, and to establish a reference to lamentations for Adonis; but in my opinion unsuccessfully. All the MSS. read אַפָּם, *their nose*, none אַפִּי, *my nose*. The prophet was so much disgusted at the profanity which he had witnessed in the temple, that he could not close his description without adverting to this further indication of an idolatrous preference of the creature to the Creator.

CHAPTER IX.

The vision in this chapter embraces the instruments to be employed by Jehovah in taking vengeance on the guilty inhabitants of Jerusalem, 1, 2; his merciful regard to his true worshippers, 3, 4; the unsparing punishment of the incorrigible, 5-7; and the refusal of the prophet's intercession on behalf of the city, 8-11.

1 THEN he cried in mine ears with a loud voice, saying: Cause them that are in charge of the city to draw near quickly, even
2 every one with his weapon of destruction in his hand. And behold six men came from the way of the upper gate which faced the north, and every one with his deadly weapon in his hand, and one man among them clothed in linen, with a writer's inkhorn by his side, and they went in and stood beside the

1. Ezekiel is still in a state of trance in the temple, where he hears the charge given to the executioners of the divine indignation to approach, prepared for the onslaught. These executioners are designated פְּקֻדּוֹת הָעִיר, which may either be taken as an elliptical form for אַנְשֵׁי פְקֻדּוֹת, *men of the punishments of the city*, i.e. the men appointed to inflict these punishments; or, פְּקֻדּוֹת may be regarded as a concrete feminine, such as is frequently used to designate persons in office. See Isa. lx. 17. The term will thus characterize those who were in charge of the city, not indeed its usual guardians, but those who were appointed to destroy it. These were now to draw near and commence their work of destruction. קָרַב, as here used in Piel, is intensive, to intimate that their operations were to begin speedily.

2. Some, after Jerome, have supposed that the six men were angels; but I agree with those who think they were representatives of the Chaldean generals who led on the hostile army against Jerusalem. What confirms this view is the circumstance, that they are exhibited as coming from the north, the direction from which the attack would be made. דֶּרֶךְ שַׁעַר הָעֶלְיוֹן, *the way of the higher gate*, i.e. the way leading to it. This gate was in all probability that of Ephraim, situated much about where the present gate of Damascus is. כְּלִי מַפָּץ, *a maul, war-hammer*, or *club*, consisting of a heavy piece of wood, effectively used as an offensive weapon by the ancients. Root נָפַץ, *to dash in pieces*. It is the same that is called כְּלִי מַשְׁחִית, *a destroying weapon*, in the preceding verse. The man who appeared among the six military leaders, though classed along with them, had a very different office assigned him. He was a messenger of mercy, having been appointed to mark the pious, to prevent any punishment from being inflicted upon them. His being dressed in a linen garment implies that he was a priest, such being specially the sacerdotal attire (Exod. xxviii. 42); and, comparing the present passage with Dan. x. 5; xii. 6, we may infer that he was designed to represent the Angel of the Covenant, in his priestly character, mediating in behalf of his people. His having a writer's inkhorn by his side indicates his being prepared to perform the task devolved upon him at the time. He had his implements at hand, as the oriental scribes in the present day, who suspend their inkhorn in the girdle at their side.

3. The cherubic figure here mentioned

3 brazen altar. And the glory of the God of Israel was gone up from above the cherub, over which he had been, to the threshold of the house. And he cried to the man who was clothed in
4 linen, who had the writer's inkhorn by his side. And Jehovah said unto him: Go through the midst of the city, through the midst of Jerusalem, and set a mark upon the foreheads of the men that are sighing and crying on account of all the abominations which are wrought in the midst of it.

differed from the composite figure seen by Ezekiel at the Chebar, and was that which overshadowed the mercy-seat in the holy of holies. There the symbol of the divine presence had resided, (2 Sam. vi. 2; Ps. lxxx. 1; but it had now departed in token of the abandonment of the temple to destruction.

4. בְּתוֹךְ וִירוּשָׁלָ͏ִם, *through the midst of Jerusalem*, is added to בְּתוֹךְ הָעִיר, *through the midst of the city*, for the purpose of emphatically marking it as the locality in which the divine judgments were to be inflicted. The priestly messenger was commissioned to distinguish, by a mark on their foreheads, those inhabitants of the city, who, deeply affected by the sight of abounding idolatry, gave unequivocal signs of fidelity to Jehovah. הַנֶּאֱנָחִים וְהַנֶּאֱנָקִים form a beautiful paronomasia, and express with great force the pungent feelings of holy grief of which the individuals were the subjects. They not only groaned inwardly (אָנַח), but they were in such anguish that they almost choked themselves by endeavoring to give utterance to their feelings (אָנַק). These feelings were too intense to admit of their being embodied in articulate speech. Compare the στεναγμοὶ ἀλάλητοι of the apostle, Rom. viii. 26. Because תָּו, *Tav*, the last letter in the Hebrew alphabet, had originally, as may be seen on the Phœnician monuments, the shape of a cross, or a post with a transverse beam, it has been maintained, that the mark which the messenger was to imprint on the foreheads of the pious was specifically that of the cross, and have consequently given it a Christian significance. Even Hitzig renders *zeichne ein kreuz*. But, though the Arabs give the name of توي to a mark in the shape of a cross burnt into the neck or thighs of horses and camels, it cannot hence be inferred that the word employed in our prophet is to be so interpreted, or that there is any reference whatever to a letter of the alphabet. The Arabic here has علامة, *a mark* or *sign*. The text is simply וְהִתְוִיתָ תָּו; LXX. δὸς σημεῖον; Syr. ܘܪܫܘܡ ܪܘܫܡܐ, *mark a mark*. The noun is derived from the verb, and takes the same general signification. This verb occurs only here in Hithpael, and but once besides in Piel (1 Sam. xxi. 13), where it is used in reference to the marks which David scrawled on the doors at Gath. It was customary with the ancients to impress a characteristic mark upon the foreheads of servants, and the worshippers of particular deities were in like manner thus distinguished. Compare Rev. vii. 3; xiii. 16; xiv. 1, 9. The object of the marking, in the present instance, was to insure the safety of those who remained faithful to Jehovah amidst the abounding abominations. The pious may ever count on the protecting care of their heavenly Father, and feel assured, that how severe soever may be the trials through which they may have to pass, they shall work together for their good (Ps. xxvii. 3–6; 2 Peter ii. 6–9; Isa. xliii. 2). No doubt provision was made for the escape of

5 And to those he said in my ears: Go through the city after him,
6 and smite; let not your eye spare, neither have pity. Slay utterly old and young, both maids and little children and women, but come not near any man upon whom is the mark; and begin at my sanctuary. Then they began at the ancient
7 men who were before the house. And he said unto them: Defile the house, and fill the courts with the slain: go ye forth.
8 And they went forth, and slew in the city. And it came to pass as they were slaying them, that I was left, and I fell upon my face: and I cried and said: Ah, Lord Jehovah, wilt thou destroy all the remainder of Israel in thy pouring out of thy
9 fury upon Jerusalem? Then he said unto me: The iniquity of the house of Israel and Judah is exceedingly great, and the land is full of blood, and the city is full of perverseness; for they say; "Jehovah hath forsaken the earth," and "Jehovah
10 seeth not." And as for me also, mine eye shall not spare, neither will I have pity; I will recompense their way upon their head.

these distinguished servants of God, compare Jer. xv. 11 ; xxxix. 11-18, just as afterwards, at the destruction of Jerusalem by the Romans, the Christians made their escape to Pella, beyond Jordan.

5–7. It seems passing strange that Hävernick should attempt a defence of the reading עַל, which is so obviously an orthographical mistake for אֶל, the pronunciation being the same. אֶל is found in very many of Kennicott and De Rossi's MSS., and in several of the earlier printed editions. The pious having been placed in safety, the Chaldeans were let loose upon the city, and an indiscriminate slaughter ensued. The destruction was to commence where the greatest abominations had been committed, and punishment inflicted upon those who had been ringleaders in idolatry. Compare 1 Peter iv. 17, 18. The temple in which only the blood of sacrificial victims had been poured out, was now to be desecrated by the dead bodies of the slain. Having executed exemplary punishment in the sanctuary upon those who had been the foremost in crime, the enemies were to go into the city and slay all whom they fell in with.

8–10. The anomalous form נַאְשַׁאַר has doubtless arisen, as Gesenius observes, from the mingling of the participial form נִשְׁאַר with that of the future אֶשָּׁאֵר. The reading of the MSS. varies, some omitting the א, and others the נ. The emphatic addition of the pronoun אֲנִי, I, would seem to express the idea, that Ezekiel conceived himself to be a solitary exception to the universal slaughter in the temple. The introduction of the prophet's intercession was designed to afford occasion for the further declaration of the divine abhorrence of the flagrant crimes of the Hebrew people. Though deeply convinced that they richly deserved the judgments that were inflicted upon them, Ezekiel could not witness the murderous scene which was being enacted, without feelings of commiseration. The double form בִּמְאֹד מְאֹד, *very, very, exceedingly*, ver. 9, is superlatively expressive ; LXX. σφόδρα σφόδρα. See Gen. xvii. 2, 6 ; Ezek. xvi.

11 And behold, the man clothed in linen, with the inkhorn by his side, reported the matter, saying: I have done according as thou commandedst me.

13. קָשָׁה, properly the participle of Hophal, from נָטָה, *to stretch out, turn away.* Hence the phrase הִטָּה מִשְׁפָּט, *to turn aside, wrest justice,* and here קָשָׁה, moral distortion, *perverseness*.

11. The messenger, having accomplished his task, is represented as reporting the fact, to intimate the certainty of the awful event.

CHAPTER X.

Further to indicate the dreadful character of the approaching catastrophe to be effected by the Chaldean power, Ezekiel has a repetition of the vision described, chap. i. Some of the minor features vary, but the grand outlines are identical. His attention is first arrested by a luminous display of the divine throne, 1; when he hears an order given to the sacerdotal messenger described in the preceding chapter to inflict the judgments on the city, 2; after which he sees the visible symbol of the presence of Jehovah remove to the threshold of the temple, 3–7. Thence, to the end of the chapter, follows the description of the cherubim.

1 Then I looked, and behold, in the expanse that was above the head of the cherubim, there appeared over them as it were a
2 sapphire-stone, as the appearance of the form of a throne. And he spake unto the man clothed in linen, and said: Go in between the wheels under the cherub, and fill thy hand with coals of fire from between the cherubim, and scatter them over the city,

1. The prophet has again presented to his view a manifestation of the glorious throne of Jehovah, to indicate that, whatever inferior agents might be employed for the punishment of the Jews, they were under His supreme direction. See chap. i. 26.

2. The nominative to וַיֹּאמֶר is Jehovah, understood. The messenger of mercy is now transformed into a messenger of judgment. He is commissioned to procure coals of fire from the cherubim, and scatter them over the city—not, as some contend, for the purpose of purifying, but as a symbol of destruction. Comp. Rev. viii. 5. The destructive energy of the Babylonian power was to be called into fearful operation. גַּלְגַּל, *galgal,* the name here given to the wheels, derived from גָּלַל, *to roll,* is, from its peculiar form, expressive of their quick circular motion, and thus differs from אוֹפָן, *ophan,* which merely conveys the idea of their revolving, from אָפַן, *to turn.* Compare chapters xxiii. 24; xxvi. 10. כְּרֻב, *cherub,* is used collectively for כְּרֻבִים, *cherubim.* Thus the LXX. χερουβίμ. The plural follows immediately after in this and the following verse.

3. That the cherubim here referred to were those which Ezekiel had seen in the first vision, and not those which overshadowed the mercy-seat, is evident

3   And he went in in my sight. Now the cherubim stood on the right side of the house, when the man went in, and the cloud filled the inner court.
4   Then the glory of Jehovah went up above the cherub at the threshold of the house; and the house was filled with the cloud, and the court was filled with the brightness of Jehovah's glory.
5   And the sound of the wings of the cherubim was heard even to the outer court, as the voice of Almighty God when he speaketh
6   And it came to pass, when he had commanded the man clothed in linen, saying: Take fire from between the wheel, from between the cherubim; then he entered and stood beside the
7   wheel. And the cherub stretched forth his hand from between the cherubim to the fire that was between the cherubim, and he took it up, and put it into the hands of him that was clothed in
8   linen, who took it and went out. And there appeared in the
9   cherubim the form of a man's hand under their wings. I also saw, and behold, four wheels beside the cherubim, one wheel beside one cherub, and one wheel beside another cherub; and the appearance of the wheels was as the color of Tarshish-stone.
10 And as for their appearances, they four had one likeness, as it
11 were a wheel within a wheel. When they went, they went upon their four sides; they turned not when they went; but to the place whither the head looked, thither they followed it; they
12 turned not when they went; even their whole body, and their backs, and their hands, and their wings: and as for the wheels,

from their being stationed on the right side of the house, and not in the holy of holies, as well as from their having had wheels, which was not the case with the latter. That the symbol of the Chaldean power should be thus represented as occupying a position on the right, which was the *south* side of the temple, and not on the north, from which direction it had come from Babylon, is to be accounted for by the circumstance that by this time it is contemplated as having so far done its work by filling the temple with the dead bodies of those who had been slain in it, and was now ready to destroy the city, which lay to the south and west.

4. The עָנָן, *cloud*, instead of the כָּבוֹד, *glory*, now filled the inner court as a symbol of the holy displeasure with which God regarded the place where his worship had been performed.

5. The rustling made by the wings of the cherubim as they moved was loud, like thunder, reverberating in the outer court of the temple. All was prognostic of the awful change which was to take place in Jerusalem.

6–8. The going in and out has reference, not to the temple, but to the cherubic appearance here specified. When within, the messenger was enclosed by wheels on every side. Having received the fire from the hand of one of the living creatures, he immediately came out to scatter it over the city.

9–12. See on chap. i. 16–21.

13. With special reference to the

they were full of eyes round about; to them four were their wheels. To the wheels one was crying in mine ears: O wheel.
14 And there were four faces to each: the face of the one was the face of a cherub; and the face of the second was the face of a man; and the third was the face of a lion; and the fourth the
15 face of an eagle. And the cherubim were lifted up; it was the
16 living creature which I had seen by the river Chebar. And when the cherubim went, the wheels went beside them; and when the cherubim lifted up their wings to mount up from the
17 earth, the same wheels also turned not from beside them. When they stood, these stood; and when they were lifted up, these were lifted up also; for the spirit of the living creature was in
18 them. And the glory of Jehovah went forth from off the thresh-
19 old of the house, and stood above the cherubim. And the cherubim lifted up their wings, and mounted up from the earth in my sight, when they went forth: and the wheels were beside them, and they stood at the door of the east gate of the house of Jehovah; and the glory of the God of Israel was over them
20 above. It was the living creature which I had seen under the God of Israel at the river Chebar; and I knew that they were
21 cherubim. To each one were four faces, and four wings to one,
22 and the form of a man's hand under their wings. And as to the form of their faces, they were the faces which I had seen by the river Chebar: their appearances and themselves, they went each straightforward.

signification of גַּלְגַּל, the term used in application to the wheels, ver. 2, it is addressed to them as possessing the force of an imperative, *roll, roll*, i.e. with the utmost celerity, for the accomplishment of the divine decree.

14. Compare chap. i. 10. As to the use of כְּרוּב, *cherub*, here, instead of שׁוֹר, *bull*, in the corresponding description, we may adopt the language of Maurer: ratio non est in promptu.

15, 20, 22. Ezekiel distinctly recognized this cherubic vision as identical with that which he had of the living creatures at the Chebar. His repeated declaration to this effect shows the importance that was to be attached to the visions, and was calculated to secure deeper attention to the significance of the symbols.

16, 17. Compare chap. i. 21.

18, 19. The symbol of the divine presence now entirely departed from the temple; and the cherubic figure proceeded to execute the work of destruction in the city.

21, 22. Compare chap i. 8, 9.

CHAPTER XI.

This chapter contains a further vision of unbelieving presumption before the prophet left the precincts of the desecrated edifice, 1-3; the sin and judgment of the scoffers, 4-12; the intercession of the prophet, 13; a prediction of the recovery of the Hebrews from idolatry, and the ultimate destruction of the incorrigible, 14-21; and concludes with a final glimpse of the Divine glory, the cessation of the vision, and the return of the prophet in a trance to his captive countrymen in Chaldea, to whom he communicates all the circumstances of the visions, 22-25.

1 MOREOVER the Spirit took me up, and brought me to the east gate of the house of Jehovah, that faceth the east; and behold, in the door of the gate five and twenty men, and I beheld among them Jaazaniah the son of Azur, and Pelatiah the son of Ben‑
2 aiah, princes of the people. Then he said unto me: Son of man, these are the men that devise iniquity and counsel wicked‑
3 ness in this city, that say: It is not near; to the building of

1, 2. From the circumstance that the number of twenty-five coincides with that of the sun-worshippers, chap. viii. 16, it has been supposed by Jarchi, Hävernick, and Fairbairn, that the persons here described were the priests, whose idolatrous conduct is there reprobated, and that the present vision is designed to teach that the sacerdotal order, of which they were the representatives, was henceforth to cease from ministering in the temple, and to suffer in the general calamity. However natural this interpretation may at first sight appear, there is an insuperable objection to it in the designation, שָׂרֵי הָעָם, *princes of the people*, a designation nowhere given to the priests. When called princes in this acceptation, it is either in the form שָׂרֵי קֹדֶשׁ, *princes or rulers of the sanctuary*, as Isa. xliii. 28, or in that of שָׂרֵי הַכֹּהֲנִים, *princes of the priests*, as 2 Chron. xxxvi. 14. The conjecture of Fairbairn, that they are called princes of the people somewhat ironically, because they were their ringleaders in wickedness, is not satisfactory. I rather take them to have been the civil officers elected by the suffrages of the people, who used their influence with Zedekiah, and persuaded him not to submit to the king of Babylon, in flat contradiction of the message which Jehovah had commissioned Jeremiah to deliver to the king. See Jer. xxxviii. 4. They are characterized, ver. 2, as "the men that devise mischief, and give wicked counsel." The prophet sees them assembled outside the portico, or vestibule, commonly called Solomon's porch, at the east end of the temple, and forming the principal entrance into it. They are doubtless to be contemplated as met in counsel to devise the wicked advice which they gave to Zedekiah.

3. The force of their wicked counsel, which here assumes a proverbial aspect, appears to be this: "A long period will elapse before our city shall be taken; we may therefore furnish ourselves with every accommodation, and shall receive no essential damage from the enemy, any more than the flesh that is being boiled does from the fire that is burning around the pot. Let the flames of war burn around us; we are perfectly secure; and should matters at last come to the worst, it will be time enough then to think about the measures to be adopted for our safety." לֹא בְקָרוֹב בְּנוֹת בָּתִּים, Go‑

4 houses; it is the caldron, and we are the flesh. Therefore
5 prophesy against them, prophesy, son of man. And the Spirit of Jehovah fell upon me, and he said unto me: Speak, Thus saith Jehovah; Thus ye have spoken, O house of Israel: for as for the things that come into your mind, I know each one of
6 them. Ye have multiplied your slain in this city, and have filled
7 the streets thereof with slain. Therefore, thus saith the Lord Jehovah: Your slain which ye have placed in the midst thereof, they are the flesh, and she is the caldron; but as for you, get
8 you out of the midst of her. Of a sword ye have been afraid, and a sword I will bring upon you, saith the Lord Jehovah.
9 And I will cause you to go forth from the midst of her, and will deliver you into the hand of strangers, and execute judgments
10 upon you. By the sword ye shall fall; at the boundary of Israel I will judge you, and ye shall know that I am Jehovah.
11 It shall not be to you for a caldron, and ye shall not be in the midst of it for flesh: at the boundary of Israel I will judge you.
12 And ye shall know that I am Jehovah, in whose statutes ye have not walked, and whose judgments ye have not executed, but have acted according to the judgments of the nations that were around you.

---

senius and Ewald, after the LXX., render interrogatively: "is it not near, the building of houses?" and interpret the words of the rebuilding of the houses ruined in the seige. This construction, however, affords no appropriate sense, even were it conceded that לֹא stands for הֲלֹא, which Hitzig considers to be inadmissible. I prefer, therefore, to divide the sentence, and to take לֹא as an absolute negative. בְקָרוֹב, near, is used of time — the period of destruction being understood as prominently in the mind of the speakers. The objection of Maurer to the rendering of בְּנוֹת בָּתִּים, *let us build houses*, that it would require the Infinitive absolute, is grammatically just; but, if we take the construct form as expressing what the minds of the evil counsellors were intensely fixed on — *the building of houses*, it will be sufficiently accurate in a proverbial statement. There may be here an implied reference to Jer. xxix. 5. "The prophet contemplates us in a state of captivity in Babylon, and advises us to prepare for a long residence in that land by building houses for our accommodation; but we will make ourselves comfortable where we are; it will be long enough before such captivity be realized."

4. To give emphatic earnestness to the command, הִנָּבֵא is repeated.

5. The Searcher of hearts asserts his perfect knowledge of the secret machinations of the princes.

6, 7. They had advised those measures which brought destruction upon the city and its inhabitants, who, in allusion to their own figure, were to be regarded as the flesh that had been killed and was lying in the streets. As for themselves, they might escape destruction in the city, but they should not escape punishment from the Chaldeans, who should execute it upon them at the frontier. See ver. 10.

8–12. An amplification of the predic-

13 And it came to pass, as I prophesied, that Pelatiah the son of Benaiah died; then I fell upon my face and cried with a loud voice and said: Alas, O Lord Jehovah! thou art making an end of the
14 remnant of Israel! Then the word of Jehovah came unto me,
15 saying: Son of man, thy brethren, thy brethren, the men of thy relationship, and the whole house of Israel, concerning whom the inhabitants of Jerusalem are saying: 'keep at a distance from
16 Jehovah; the land is given to us for an inheritance. Nevertheless speak: Thus saith the Lord Jehovah: though I have removed them far off among the nations, and though I have scattered them among the countries, yet I will be for a little a
17 sanctuary to them in the countries whither they come. Where-

tion delivered in verses 7 and 8, accompanied with a direct contradiction of their proverbial utterance with respect to safety. For הוֹצִיא, ver. 7, the finite form אוֹצִיא is found in thirty-nine MSS., in two early editions, and is so translated in all the ancient versions; but the reading of the received text appears better to suit the connection. On ver. 12 compare chap. v. 6.

13. Scarcely had the doom of the wicked rulers been pronounced, when one of them was struck dead on the spot, as an earnest that the prophecy should assuredly be fulfilled. Regarding him as a representative of the people, the prophet breaks out in a pathetic exclamation, and asks whether Jehovah would effect a complete extermination of his people.

14, 15. The inhabitants of Jerusalem, full of arrogant self-confidence, despised their brethren who had been carried into captivity, and contemptuously bade them be satisfied with their new abode, at a distance from the land of their fathers and the residence of their covenant God, for they had no longer any part or lot in the national theocracy. That establishment with all its advantages belonged now exclusively to those who had been left in the land. They alone were in possession, and would admit of no competitors. With those who were thus despised, and expelled not only by the Chaldeans, but by their own fellow-citizens, Ezekiel was to consider himself as in the closest alliance. These, viewed as recovered from idolatry, he was to regard as, in a higher sense, his brethren and near relatives; and not those only who had been carried away with him under Jehoiachin, but also the subjects of the former captivity. אַחֶיךָ is repeated to give force to the relationship. These whom he was thus specially to regard as his brethren, אַנְשֵׁי גְאֻלָּתֶךָ, *his kinsmen*, and the whole house of Israel, are in apposition. They were all repudiated by the proud Jews in Jerusalem. It does not appear that the persons here referred to were related to Ezekiel as belonging to the priesthood, but are understood in a wider sense as his countrymen, endeared to him the more by their sufferings, and their reformation in the land of captivity. גְאֻלָּה primarily signifies blood-relationship, including all whose blood, shed in murder, such relatives were bound to avenge, and whose right of inheritance they were bound to vindicate. The connection shows that all the fellow-captives of the prophet were to be regarded by him as standing in such a near relationship.

16. Ezekiel might well extend to them this regard, for though cast far off among the heathen, they were the objects of compassionate regard on the part of Jehovah himself. Though they had no

fore say: Thus saith the Lord Jehovah: I will yet gather you from the peoples and assemble you from the countries whither ye have been scattered, and I will give you the land of Israel. 18 And they shall come thither, and remove all its detestable things 19 and all its abominations. And I will give them one heart, and will put within you a new spirit, and take away the heart of 20 stone out of their flesh, and grant to them a heart of flesh: In order that they may walk in my statutes and observe my judgments and do them; and they shall be my people, and I will

longer any access to the sanctuary at Jerusalem, he promises to be a sanctuary to them in the lands of their captivity. Although, unquestionably, the term מִקְדָּשׁ is to be taken here, as in Isa. viii. 14, in the sense of *asylum*, and the privilege of security is promised in contrast with the material temple at Jerusalem, in which the inhabitants trusted, but which, instead of affording them any protection, was itself to be destroyed by the Chaldeans, — the Jews were at the same time taught, that the Divine presence was not confined to any earthly spot, but that in every place true worship would be acceptable to him. Having free access to their covenant God in the lands of their enemies, they should find in him an omnipotent defence against all evil. If they had learned their lesson well, they would have been prepared to welcome the new dispensation, the privileges of which were not to be restricted to their nation and country alone, but to be extended to all spiritual worshippers throughout the world. Mal. i. 11; John iv. 21-24. It was, however, a lesson hard for a Jew to learn; and it required a second destruction of the material temple, by the Romans, to wean them in any degree from their restricted and narrow conceptions. מְעַט is here an Adverb of time, signifying *a little while*, *for a little*, or the like. To express the idea of *little*, in the sense of small, the adjective קָטֹן would have been required, but it would ill have suited the connection. How long soever the captivity might appear, they should experience it to be short, in the enjoyment of such a privilege as having Jehovah for their Protector and Friend.

17, 18. Though exiled in punishment of their national sins, the Jews were assuredly to be restored to their own land, when they should remove thence every vestige of idol-worship and serve Jehovah alone. Their absence was only to be temporary.

19, 20. To prepare them for such a result, Jehovah promises to produce in them a spirit of devoted piety. Their heart was no longer to be divided between Jehovah and false gods, but was to be solely devoted to his service. לֵב אֶחָד, *one heart*. Compare the parallel promise, Jer. xxxii. 39. Hitzig lamely endeavors to defend the reading לֵב בַּ אַחֵר, *another heart*, which is countenanced by the LXX. but is found in no Hebrew MS. This "one heart" is that of flesh — tender, sensitive, and easily impressible by Divine truth, which is promised in the latter part of the verse: in contrast with that of stone, under the influence of which the Jews had obstinately resisted all the expostulations of the prophets, and stubbornly persevered in idolatrous practices, without feeling any compunctions relentings, or any desire to return to the service of Jehovah. Such a heart might well be called רוּחַ חֲדָשָׁה, *a new spirit*, i.e. a new disposition, inclining its possessor to hate the sinful abominations in which he had formerly indulged, and to find delight in the right ways of the Lord. Compare Ps. li. 10. This change in all its completeness, involves the καινὴ

21 be their God. But as for those whose heart goeth after the heart of their detestable things and their abominations, I will
22 bring their way upon their head, saith the Lord Jehovah. And the cherubim lifted up their wings, and the wheels along with them ; and the glory of the God of Israel was over them above.
23 And the glory of Jehovah ascended out of the midst of the city, and stood upon the mountain which was to the east of the city.
24 Then the Spirit bore me up and brought me to Chaldea to the captives, in a vision through the Spirit of God ; and the vision
25 which I had seen went up from me. And I told the captives all the things of Jehovah, which he had showed me.

κτίσις of the New Testament, a renovation of the entire inner man, 2 Cor. v. 17. Whether a change so radical and thorough-going was realized in the experience of the great body of the Jews before their return from Babylon, may fairly be questioned ; but that they experienced more or less of its subordinate stages, sufficiently powerful to induce them to abandon the worship of idols, and addict themselves exclusively to that of Jehovah, the exigency of the present passage in our prophet clearly demands. And this was sufficient to restore them to their outward relation as a people to God, while there was, as there has been in every age, "a remnant according to the election of grace," who realized the change in all its fulness. The passage unquestionably traces all that is good in man to Divine influence, to whatever extent or for whatever purpose that good is effected.

21. A threatening denounced against the impenitent and incorrigible.

22, 23. The Shechinah, which had moved from within the temple and taken its station at the east gate, chap. x. 4, 19, now removed to the Mount of Olives, as it were lingering and unwilling to abandon the devoted city, a commanding view of which was afforded by that elevation. Compare Zech. xiv. 4.

24, 25. Here closes the description of these wonderful visions. The prophet is conducted back to the Chebar in the same manner in which he had been conveyed to Jerusalem. No change had taken place in his relation to the outward world ; but, while sitting quietly in his house, chap. viii. 1, his inner eye was supernaturally opened to behold the things contained in the intermediate chapters. He now communicated for the benefit of his fellow-captives what had been revealed to him. How calculated was the record to fill their minds with adoring views of the Divine Majesty, and an utter abhorrence of every form of idolatry !

CHAPTER XII.

Still more to affect the minds of his countrymen on the banks of the Chebar, and through them all in Judea with whom they might be in communication, Ezekiel is, in this chapter, ordered to exhibit himself as a symbolical representation of persons going into captivity.
After a description of the obstinate rebelliousness of the Jewish people, 1, 2, he typically predicts the approaching total captivity of the inhabitants of Judea, 3-7; then plainly foretells the flight, capture, and sufferings of Zedekiah and his adherents, 8-16; portrays the consternation and desolation of his countrymen, 17-20; and concludes with an exposure and refutation of the objections to his predictions by unbelieving scoffers, 21-28.

1 And the word of Jehovah came unto me, saying: Son of man,
2 thou dwellest in the midst of the rebellious house, who have eyes to see, but see not; they have ears to hear, but hear not;
3 for they are a rebellious house. Thou, therefore, O Son of man, prepare thee articles for removal, and remove by day in their sight; yea, remove from thy place to another place in their sight; perhaps they may consider, though they are a rebellious
4 house. And carry forth thy stuff by day in their sight, as stuff for removal; and thou shalt go forth in the evening as captives
5 go forth. Dig thee a hole in the wall in their sight, and go out
6 through it. In their sight thou shalt carry it on thy shoulder in the dark: thou shalt carry it forth: thou shalt cover thy face, and shalt not see the ground; for I have made thee a sign to
7 the house of Israel. And I did as I was commanded: my stuff I took out as stuff of captives by day, and in the evening I dug me a hole in the wall with the hand: in the dark I conveyed it

1, 2. The period to which this chapter belongs being only the sixth year of the captivity on the banks of the Chebar, the change of circumstances had only had time to operate partially on those who composed it. Too many of them sympathized with the refractory spirit of their brethren in Jerusalem; and like them, indulging the hope that the city would not be taken, and that they would speedily be restored to their own land, they rejected the prophetic messages. They were naturally qualified, by the faculties with which God had endowed them, to form a judgment from the begun accomplishment of the Divine predictions in their own experience, respecting their further accomplishment in the future, so that their rebellious disposition was without excuse. Ezekiel was to class together all such, both in and out of Judea, and viewing himself as in the midst of them, to discharge his prophetic office. For בֵּית מְרִי, compare chaps. ii. 5, 6; iii. 27; and for בֵּית הַמֶּרִי, chap. ii. 8.

3-7. The simple announcements of the prophet having proved ineffectual, he was commanded symbolically to furnish his countrymen with an ocular demonstration of the removal of those who had been left behind in Judea, in order, if possible, to lead them to reflection. He was to furnish himself with כְּלֵי גוֹלָה, *articles for exile*, such as persons in the East select when migrating from one

8 forth: I bore it on my shoulder in their sight. And the word
9 of Jehovah came to me in the morning, saying: Son of man, do
    not the house of Israel, the rebellious house, say to thee: What
10 art thou doing? Say unto them: Thus saith the Lord Jehovah:
    This oracle is the prince in Jerusalem, and all the house of
11 Israel who are in the midst of them. Say: I am your sign; as
    I have done, so shall it be done to them; they shall go into
12 exile, into captivity. And the prince who is in the midst of
    them shall carry on his shoulder in the dark, and shall go forth;
    they shall dig a hole in the wall to remove out through it; he
    shall cover his face, so that he shall not see the country with his

country to another, as a staff, victuals, water, cooking-utensils, clothing, coverlets, etc. There is no contradiction between the injunctions here laid upon Ezekiel; first, that the transactions should take place by day, and then that they should be effected by night. Respect is had to the preparation which he was to make for departure, by collecting the articles together by day, and then to his actual departure by night. כְּמוֹצָאֵי הַגּוֹלָה, *as the outgoings of captives* — הַגּוֹלָה, the absolute singular, being used for the concrete in the plural. I cannot agree with Hävernick and Fairbairn, that מוֹצָא denotes the time of going forth. I do not find it thus used anywhere in the Hebrew Bible. The passages Dan. ix. 25 and Micah v. 1, to which Hävernick appeals, give no countenance to such construction. In both places the *act*, not the *time*, of going forth, is expressed. The term עֲלָטָה occurs only in verses 6, 7, 12, and Gen. xv. 17; but there is no doubt that it denotes *darkness*. Arab. غَلَظَ, *crassus est*: by transposition غَصَلَ, *nubibus obductum fuit cœlum*. The prophet was to make his exit in the darkness of the night, with his face muffled, so that he should not see the country through which, or into which, he was passing.

8–12. The actions of the prophet are supposed to have been productive of effect; they had excited attention on the part of his fellow-captives. The typical representation of Ezekiel had a special reference to king Zedekiah. In the paronomasia חֲמִשְׁרָא הַמִּשְׁרָא, this is tersely expressed. The oracular saying had the monarch and his idolatrous subjects for its theme. "This is" for "this betokens," as Matt. xxvi. 26. Though the king is not named, there could be no mistake as to who was meant. For the literal fulfilment of the prediction, see 2 Kings xxv. 1–7; Jer. lii. 1–11. The eyes of that monarch having been put out by the king of Babylon, he was deprived of the power of seeing the land whither he was carried into captivity. מוֹפֵת, LXX. τέρας, a sign, wonder, portent, prodigy, an object foretokening good or ill. Compare chap. xxiv. 27; Zech. iii. 8. Such Ezekiel was constituted, in the latter acceptation; and it was impossible seriously to contemplate his instructive conduct without foreboding the calamity to which it pointed. According to a tradition in Josephus, Antiq. lib. x. c. 7, the prophet sent a copy of his prediction to Zedekiah, who, imagining that he found a contradiction in this prophecy of Ezekiel to that of Jeremiah (xxiv. 8), resolved to believe neither; but what truth there may be in it must be left undetermined. I see no sufficient reason to induce the conclusion that what is here recorded was done in vision, and not in real life. אֲנָשִׁים, ver. 14, corresponds to כְּאֵלֶּה,

13 eyes. And I will spread my net over him, and he shall be taken in my snare, and I will bring him unto Babylon, the land of the Chaldeans, yet he shall not see it; but he shall die there.
14 And all his auxiliaries that are around him, and the wings of his army I will scatter to every wind; and will draw out a
15 sword after them. And they shall know that I am Jehovah, when I scatter them among the nations and disperse them among
16 the countries. Yet I will leave of them those who shall be few in number, from the sword, from famine, and from pestilence, in order that they may declare all their abominations among the nations whither they shall come; and they shall know that I am Jehovah.

17 And the word of the Lord came unto me, saying: Son of man, thou
18 shalt eat thy bread with trembling and drink thy water with
19 trepidation and solicitude. And thou shalt say to the people of the land: Thus saith the Lord Jehovah to the inhabitants of Jerusalem, to the land of Israel: They shall eat their bread with solicitude; and drink their water with astonishment, that her land may be despoiled of its fulness by reason of the violence of
20 all who dwell in it. And the cities that are inhabited shall be laid waste, and the land become a desolation; and ye shall know that I am Jehovah.

21 And the word of Jehovah came unto me, saying: Son of man,
22 what proverb is this of yours respecting the land of Israel, say-
23 ing: The days are prolonged and every vision faileth? Therefore say unto them: Thus saith the Lord Jehovah: I will make this proverb to cease, and they shall no more use it as a proverb in Israel; but say to them: The days draw near, and the matter

---

Isa. viii. 8, and denotes the *wings* of an army, for the army itself. Compare chap. xxxviii. 6.

16. The scattering of the Jews among the heathen was intended, not merely to cure themselves of their propensity to idolatry, but also to afford them opportunities of bearing testimony against that evil as practised by those among whom they lived. Compare Zech. viii. 13; Isa. xliii. 8–13. They would trace all the evils that had come upon them to their true source — the adoption and practice of abominable idolatries.

17–20. With the view of deepening the impression of the miserable results of the Chaldean invasion, Ezekiel was to partake of his nourishment with signs of anxiety and trepidation. He thus served anew as a sign to the people.

22. The infidel objection contained in the end of this verse, had assumed the form of מָשָׁל, *a proverbial saying* in the mouth of the rebellious Jews. It was bandied about from one to another, the contagion spreading as it circulated, to the distress of the minds of the pious, while the ungodly were confirmed in their unbelief of the Divine messages. As day after day passed by, the scoffers

24 of every vision. For there shall no more be any vain vision or
25 smooth divination in the midst of the children of Israel. For I,
Jehovah, will speak the word which I shall speak, and it shall be
performed: it shall not be deferred; for in your days O rebellious house, I will speak a word and perform it, saith the Lord
26 Jehovah. And the word of Jehovah came unto me, saying:
27 Son of man, behold the house of Israel are saying: The vision
which he seeth is for many days, and he prophesieth for distant
28 times; Therefore say unto them: Thus saith the Lord Jehovah:
None of my words shall any longer be deferred; when I speak
a word, it shall be performed, saith the Lord Jehovah.

argued that the things seen in prophetic visions would never be realized. Compare 2 Pet. iii. 3, 4. Thus it hath been in every age, and in none more than the present.

24. There is here a reference to the false prophets against whom Ezekiel is specially commissioned to prophesy in the following chapter. בְּקָסֶם, *divination*, from קָסַם, to practice divination by dividing by lot. The terms are used of false prophets, both among the heathen and the Hebrews. Those whom the prophet specially had in his eye were such as flattered his fellow-captives with the vain hope of a speedy return to their own land. Instead of בֵּית יִשְׂרָאֵל, *house* of Israel, we have בְּנֵי יִשְׂרָאֵל, *children of Israel*, in eleven codices, one in the margin and one at first hand; the edition of Manasseh ben Israel, Amsterdam, 1630; with the Venetian editions and all the versions.

26-28. A repetition, for the sake of effect, of the matter contained in the preceding verse. Those to whom the prophet was to address himself were to be assured that the calamity, however apparently delayed, should most certainly be speedily inflicted. Jerusalem was taken within five years after the prophecy was delivered.

CHAPTER XIII.

Ezekiel is instructed specially to denounce the false prophets whom he had introduced to view towards the close of the preceding chapter, 1, 2; he describes their character, 3-9; points out the futility of their pretended vaticinations, and the destruction in which they would involve both themselves and the people, 10-16; he then denounces false prophetesses, who in like manner deceived the people, 17-23.

1 And the word of Jehovah came unto me, saying: Son of man,
2 prophesy against the prophets of Israel that prophesy; and say
thou to those who prophesy out of their own heart: Hear ye

2. The designation נָבִיא, *prophet*, is applied in Scripture both to the true and the pretended prophets. When used in reference to the latter, there is always, as in the present verse, something added, which sufficiently marks the futility of

3 the word of Jehovah. Thus saith the Lord Jehovah: Woe to the foolish prophets who are following their own spirit, and have
4 seen nothing. Thy prophets, O Israel, are like foxes in des-
5 olated places. Ye have not gone up into the breaches, nor have ye built a wall about the children of Israel to stand in the battle
6 in the day of Jehovah. They have seen vanity and lying divination who say, "The oracle of Jehovah," though Jehovah hath not sent them; yet they have made men to hope that they would
7 confirm the word. Is it not a vain vision which ye have seen, and a lying divination ye have spoken? Yet ye are saying,
8 "The oracle of Jehovah," though I have not spoken. Wherefore thus saith the Lord Jehovah: Because ye have spoken vanity, and have seen lies, therefore, behold I am against you, is the
9 oracle of the Lord Jehovah. And my hand shall be against the prophets who see vanity and divine lies; they shall not be in the assembly of my people, and in the register of the house of Israel they shall not be registered; neither shall they enter the land of Israel: and ye shall know that I am the Lord Jehovah.

their claims. While the genuine messengers of Jehovah had unmistakingly their subjects communicated to them from without, and spoke as they were moved by the Holy Ghost (2 Pet. i. 21), the false prophets merely gave utterance to what had originated in their own minds.

3. The vaticinations of these hollow pretenders had no higher origin than רוּחָם, their own corrupt disposition: 'the wish was father to the thought.' Their visions were purely imaginary.

4. The pretended prophets are compared to foxes; not, as Bochart and some others interpret, because of their burrowing and undermining the walls of vineyards, but because of their crafty and voracious disposition. The animal had long been proverbial for these qualities. Nor could any creature more aptly symbolize those insidious and greedy upstarts who deceived the Jewish people. They appear, from the prophecies of Jeremiah, to have abounded at the time both in Judea and among the exiles. See chaps. xxvii. 9, 10; xxviii. 1; xxix. 8, 9, 15–32.

5–7. Instead of giving such counsel as might have tended to promote the true interests of the theocracy, and undo the mischief which had already overtaken it, they flattered the people with false hopes of security in Jerusalem. Unauthorized by Jehovah, they had had the temerity to utter falsehoods in his name. יִחֵלוּ, *they have made others to hope.* This verb is not used in Kal, but in Piel, with a transitive and causative signification, as in Hiphil.

9. As a just judgment upon them for their presumption, they are threatened, not only with exclusion from all hope of ever occupying an honorable position in the government of the nation, but of having an existence under it as citizens. They should not even be ever after permitted to enter the land of their fathers. סוֹד, a *council* of judges and others, assembled to consult on the national affairs. כְּתָב, a *register*, in which the names of the citizens were inscribed, and which was annually revised, when those who had died during the year had their names erased. Michaëlis thinks the reference is rather to the genealogies; and that the

10 Because, even because they have seduced my people saying, "Peace," and there is no peace, and one buildeth up a wall and
11 others plaster it with falsehood: Say to them that plaster with falsehood: It shall fall: there shall be a pouring rain and ye, O
12 great hailstones, shall fall, and a storm-wind shall rend it. And behold, the wall shall fall. Shall it not be said unto you, Where
13 is the plaster with which ye have plastered it? Wherefore, thus saith the Lord Jehovah: I will even rend it with a storm-wind in my fury, and there shall be a pouring rain in mine
14 anger, and great hailstones in wrath to consume it. And I will break down the wall which ye have plastered with falsehood, and I will bring it down to the ground, and its foundation shall be laid bare, and it shall fall; and ye shall perish in the midst of
15 it; and ye shall know that I am Jehovah. And I will spend my wrath upon the wall, and upon them that have plastered it with falsehood, and will say unto you: The wall is no more, and
16 they that plastered it are no more,— the prophets of Israel, who prophesy to Jerusalem, and who see for her a vision of peace,

threatening implies, that the persons against whom it is denounced, should have no descendants.

10. יַעַן וּבְיַעַן emphatically: *because, even because.* The pronoun הֵם is to be taken collectively of the class of persons spoken of in the immediately preceding context, and not without some tinge of contempt. Compare 2 Chron. xxviii. 22. Agreeably to this the pronominal suffix in הֵם is to be similarly regarded as designating others of the false prophets. They were not satisfied with individual effort, but co-operated in their endeavors to delude the people. Alas! how much of this has been realized in the professing church of Christ, as well as in the ancient church of Israel. While one party was busily engaged in building a wall, another was as busily occupied in whitening it with whitewash, in order to give it a pleasing and imposing appearance. Compare Matt. xxiii. 29; Acts xxiii. 3. תָּפֵל, *lime, plaster*, or *whitewash;* טוּחַ, *to cover over* with such material.

11-16. The wall, with its builders and plasterers, should be involved in one un- distinguishable mass of destruction. A severe hailstorm is one of the severest calamities with which Palestine is visited, and is employed figuratively to denote severe judgments Isa. xxviii. 2; xxx. 30; Rev. xvi. 21. אֶלְגָּבִישׁ is properly the Arab. الكبش, retaining the form of the Article: LXX. λίθους πετροβόλους. רוּחַ סְעָרוֹת, lit. *a wind of storms*, a violent, tempestuous wind, which bears down all before it. גֶּשֶׁם שֹׁטֵף, a *pouring, inundating rain* is equally destructive to buildings. While the hailstones break in pieces what they come in contact with, the rain, suddenly collected in rushing masses, washes away the foundations, and occasions the fall of the buildings. There is a singular force in personifying the hailstones, considering that sometimes they fall in size larger than an inch, and with a velocity of seventy feet a second, or about fifty miles an hour, acquiring by this means a momentum which renders them awfully destructive. Compare Job xxxviii. 22, 23.

17. Ezekiel is now commanded to

17 and there is no peace, saith the Lord Jehovah. Likewise, thou son of man, set thy face against the daughters of thy people who prophesy out of their own heart; and prophesy against
18 them, and say: Thus saith the Lord Jehovah: Woe to the women that sew pillows for all elbows, and make cushions for the head of every stature, to lie in wait eagerly for souls: Will ye lie in wait eagerly for the souls of my people? and will ye
19 save alive the souls that come unto you? And will ye pollute me among my people for handfuls of barley, and morsels of bread, to put to death the souls that should not die, and to preserve the souls that should not live, by your lying to my people
20 who hear lies? Therefore thus saith the Lord Jehovah: Behold, I am against your cushions with which ye there eagerly lie in wait for the souls to make them fly, and I will tear them from off your arms, and will set free the souls for which ye eagerly

direct his oracular denunciation against the false prophetesses, who lent their aid in helping forward the delusions of the people. True female prophetesses were more rare among the Hebrews. The only instances in which they occur in the history of that people, are those of Miriam, Deborah, and Huldah. So impudent were these female pretenders to inspiration, that Ezekiel was required to put on a stern countenance (שִׂים פָּנֶיךָ), while he denounced the pernicious influence which they exerted over the people.

18. כְּסָתוֹת occurs only here and ver. 20, but there can be no doubt that it signifies *pillows*, or cushions, covered with ornamental work, from כָּסָה, *to cover*. That these are intended, and not coverlets, appears from their being connected with אַצִּילֵי יָדַי, *arm-joints*, or elbows. These, indeed, Gesenius interprets to mean knuckles; but their being referred to the יָדַיִם, *arms*, ver. 20, favors the opinion that joints higher up the arms are meant. The LXX. supposing bolsters for the head to be intended, render προσκεφάλαια; Vulg. *pulvillos*. יְדֵי is used by syncope for יָדַיִם, and syncedochically for יָדָיו. מִסְפָּחוֹת, LXX. ἐπιβόλαια, I take to mean *coverlets* or quilts, from סָפַח, *to spread*, which, equally with cushions, form an essential part of oriental luxury. These were made to suit the קוֹמָה, *height* or *size* of the different persons who were to use them. LXX. ἡλικία. The females in question not only employed flattering words to decoy the souls of the unwary, but, by their seductive speeches, lulled them as effectually as if they had literally prepared articles of luxury for their bodily repose. צדד, the Pilpel of צוּד, Arab. صَادَ, *to hunt, catch, lay snares* for taking wild animals. This conjugation, being reduplicate in form, is expressive of intensity, and thus indicates the eager and untiring efforts which the false prophetesses employed in endeavoring to effect their purpose. So far should they be from preserving those who listened to them, that they should be instrumental in bringing about their destruction.

19. The sordid, self-interested character of these prophetesses is here distinctly set forth — a character by which false teachers in every age have been distinguished.

20. לְפֹרְחוֹת, *to cause to fly*, is borrowed from the practice of fowlers, who

21 lie in wait, the souls to make them fly. And I will tear your cushions and rescue my people from your hand, and they shall no more be in your hand for a prey; and ye shall know that I
22 am Jehovah. Because with falsehood ye have made sad the heart of the righteous, which I have not made sad, and strengthened the hands of the wicked, that he should not turn from his
23 wicked way to be preserved alive: Therefore ye shall not see vanity nor divine divination any more; for I will rescue my people from your hand; and ye shall know that I am Jehovah.

disturb a covey of birds, not that they may fray them away, but that they may make them fly into the gins that they have set for them. LXX. εἰς διασκορπισμόν.

21. בְּיֶדְכֶן, *in your hand*, i.e. in your power — exposed to your influence.

22. כָּאָה signifies to be *dejected*, have the mind filled with despondency, and is synonymous with כָּאַב. To witness the alluring arts of false teachers, and listen to their seductive doctrine, cannot but be a source of grief to every pious mind. While such teachers rob the people of God of that consolation which he hath purposed they should enjoy, they confirm the wicked in their rebellious practices by holding out to them hopes of immunity from punishment.

23. The Divine judgments should overtake these impudent pretenders to revelation, and thus put an end to their nefarious artifices, and their bad influence over the people.

CHAPTER XIV.

A company of official persons present themselves before Ezekiel under the hypocritical mask of religious inquirers, 1; their character is described and their punishment threatened, 2-5; they are called to repentance, and the sentence of their doom, if they should continue incorrigible, is repeated, 6-8; the punishment to be inflicted on the false prophets is described, 9, 10; and its result, the recovery of the Jews to the service of the true God, 11; the unavailing intercession of the most eminent saints of God on behalf of the impenitent is strongly and repeatedly asserted, 12-21; still a remnant should be left, who, recovered from idolatry, should testify to the rectitude of the Divine conduct, and experience the returning favor of their God, 22, 23.

1   And there came to me men of the elders of Israel, and they sat

1. The syntax of וַיָּבוֹא in the singular with אֲנָשִׁים in the plural is not abhorrent in Hebrew practice — the number of the noun not necessarily having been determined, when the simple idea expressed by the verb first occurs to the mind. Some MSS., however, read וַיָּבֹאוּ, which is the more correct orthography.

יִשְׂרָאֵל, *Israel*, is here and throughout the chapter to be taken, not as designating the captivity of the ten tribes, but that of the Hebrews generally, with special reference to those Jews who were located on the Chebar. The זְקֵנִים, *elders*, were civil officers, who retained their office though in a state of exile, —

2 before me. And the word of Jehovah came to me, saying:
3 Son of man, these men have set up their idols in their heart, and they have placed the stumbling-block of their iniquity before
4 their face: Should I at all be inquired of by them? Wherefore address them, and say unto them: Thus saith the Lord Jehovah; Every man of the house of Israel who setteth up his idols in his heart, and who placeth the stumbling-block of his iniquity before his face, and cometh to the prophet, I, Jehovah, myself will answer him that cometh, according to the multitude of his
5 idols: In order to take the house of Israel in their own heart, because they are all of them alienated from me through their

the Jews still submitting to their authority. What they wished to learn from the prophet, we are not informed; most probably it related to the duration of the captivity, or to the fate of Jerusalem. That they were not actuated by any purely religious motive is manifest from the following verses.

3. Whatever appearances these elders might have assumed when they came to Ezekiel, he is divinely informed that they were purely hypocritical. Not only had the love of idolatry not been eradicated from their hearts; they had not so much as put away their idols from their presence; a striking type of their countrymen who still remained in Judea. הַאִדָּרֹשׁ, a form of the Infinitive Absolute, with the interrogative הֲ adopted to avoid the cacophony that would have been occasioned by writing הֲהִדָּרֹשׁ, which would have been the regular from of the Infinite.

4. With such dissemblers Jehovah could have no fellowship, but, on the contrary, must spurn them from his presence with holy indignation. Compare Ps. lxvi. 18. נַעֲנָה in Niphal differs here little from the signification in Kal, excepting that it conveys the idea of the action being more immediately performed by God himself, and so far retaining the reflexive force of that conjugation, as *I myself*, or the like. Instead of furnishing an answer by his prophet, he would himself give one by the actual infliction of the merited punishment. For בָּה some propose to point בָּם, and consider it to be anticipative of בְּרֹב following, as is common in the Aramaic dialects; but to this construction it is objected, that there is a want of agreement in gender, — רֹב being masculine, whereas בָּה is feminine. To obviate this objection, Hitzig unsatisfactorily proposes to point בָּה in the masculine. I abide by the Keri which proposes בָּא, *him that cometh*. This reading, adopted by our translators, is found in the text of nine Heb. MSS. and has originally been in seven more. The only difference lies in the exchange of ה for א. The proposed reading בָּה is without any authority.

5. The meaning is, that Jehovah would come upon them while indulging in the idolatries on which their hearts where set. תָּפֹשׂ בְּלֵב, *to take in the heart*, is otherwise an unusual mode of expression, but there seems no solid ground for the construction put upon it by Hävernick, as if it referred to the working of a change in the dispositions of the Jews. All that it expresses is the certainty of the calamity overtaking them while they were going on in their trespasses.

6. The only way in which the Jews could expect the calamity to be averted or removed was by an entire renunciation of idols, and a sincere return to the service of the true God. In שׁוּבוּ וְהָשִׁיבוּ there is a combination of the Kal and

6 idols. Wherefore say unto the house of Israel: Thus saith the
Lord Jehovah: Turn ye thoroughly from your idols and turn
7 away your faces from all your abominations. For every man
of the house of Israel, and of the stranger who sojourneth in
Israel, and is alienated from me, and setteth up his idols in his
heart, and placeth the stumbling-block of his iniquity before his
face, and cometh to the prophet to inquire of me for himself, I,
8 Jehovah, myself will answer him. And I will set my face,
against that man, and will make him a sign and proverbs, and
will cut him off from the midst of my people, and ye shall know
9 that I am Jehovah. And as for the prophet who alloweth
himself to be deceived, and uttereth a speech, I, Jehovah, have
deceived that prophet, and I will stretch forth my hand against
10 him, and destroy him from among my people Israel. And they
shall bear the punishment of their iniquity; according to the
punishment of him that inquireth shall be the punishment of the

Hiphil conjugations for the sake of emphasis. Return unreservedly from your abominable idolatries. Be no longer estranged from me either in heart or practice. They were neither to hanker after in desire, nor look towards the accursed thing.

7. The same judgment should overtake the proselyte as the native Jew who indulged in idolatry, and hypocritically applied to a prophet for counsel. Compare ver. 4. Strangers were only legally tolerated in the land of the Hebrews on the condition that they worshipped no god, but Jehovah alone. Lev. xvii. 8, 9. בִּי, at the end of the verse, is emphatic, *by myself*, and may be regarded as an ellipsis of בִּי נִשְׁבַּעְתִּי, *by myself have I sworn*, as Gen. xxii. 16. The signification, *obsecro, quæso*, for which Gesenius contends, however it may suit other passages, is not at all apt here. The occurrence of בִּי in the phrase בִּי דָרַשׁ, *to inquire of me*, in the preceding sentence, naturally leads to the construction which I have suggested. לוֹ refers to the applicant, not to הַנָּבִיא, the prophet: who comes to a prophet for himself, for his own satisfaction, to inquire of me. The ל marks here the Dat. commodi.

8. The signal punishment to be inflicted, as denounced at the close of the previous verse. Instead of וַהֲשִׁמֹתִיהוּ, *I will destroy him*, which is the current reading of the printed text, I prefer וְהָשִׂמֹתִיו, *I will set*, or place *him*, which is that of Bomberg's edition of 1525. It may be regarded, indeed, as a mere conjectural emendation, but it is supported by all the ancient versions, and is more suitable to Hebrew usage.

9. If matters should turn out differently from what the prophet expected and foretold, I have so ordered them in the course of my providence as to issue in such a result. It is the prerogative of Deity to control the sinful operations of created minds, without interfering with free-agency. Οὐ τοίνυν κατ' ἐνέργειαν — ἀλλὰ κατὰ συγχώρησιν (Theodoret). See on Jer. iv. 10. The prophet here referred to was a false, not a true prophet.

10. עֲוֹנָם, *their iniquity*, i.e. *the punishment of their iniquity*, as chap. iv. 4–6. The term is properly so rendered here in our common version.

11. The result of such severe punishment would be the recovery of the Israelites from their addictedness to idolatry, to be again a holy people to

11 prophet; That the house of Israel may no more go astray from me, and that they may no more defile themselves with all their transgressions, but may be my people and I may be their God, saith the Lord Jehovah.

12 And the word of Jehovah came to me, saying: Son of man, when
13 a land hath sinned against me by committing a grievous transgression, and I stretch forth my hand against it, and break its staff of bread, and send famine into it, and cut off man and beast
14 from it; And though these three men were in the midst of it, Noah, Daniel, and Job, they should deliver their own souls by
15 their righteousness, saith the Lord Jehovah. Should I cause wild beasts to pass through a land, and it is bereaved and becomes desolate, so that no one passeth through it because of the wild
16 beasts; Though these three men were in the midst of it, as I live, saith the Lord Jehovah, they should deliver neither sons nor daughters; they alone should be delivered, but the land

Jehovah, who would then renew his ancient relationship to them as their God.

12–21. בְּמַעֲלָם מַעַל, *to trespass a trespass;* i.e. to commit an enormous trespass. With manifest reference to Jer. xv. 1, the prophet is repeatedly instructed in these verses, that not only should the powerful intercessions of such eminent men as Moses and Samuel prove of no avail on behalf of the Jewish people, but that those of such righteous men as Noah, Daniel, and Job should prove equally fruitless. Highly as the personal righteousness of these three illustrious individuals was held in estimation by the Most High, there was no merit in it transferable to any of the guilty inhabitants of the land. Even Noah, on account of whose righteous character his family were saved along with him in the ark, should not now, were he alive upon the earth, be able to deliver either sons or daughters, if they were found to have joined the rebellions. Every one should be treated on the ground of his own individual character. The prophet multiplies instances in order to work a conviction in the minds of his countrymen of the enormity of their crimes. Daniel having been fourteen years in Babylon at the time here referred to, must have been well known by fame to the Jews of the captivity. His historical existence, as well as that of Job, is taken for granted, and can with no show of argument be denied any more than that of Noah. The chronological order of the names presents no difficulty. A similar inversion occurs Heb. xi. 32. Besides, as Hävernick observes, there is a climax in the introduction of Job's name last, none of his sons or daughters having been saved for his sake, as appears so manifestly on the very face of the narrative, chap. i. Four of the greatest calamities that can befal a people are hypothetically threatened — famine (ver. 13), wild beasts (ver. 15), war (ver. 17), and the plague (ver. 19), חַיָּה, *wild beasts*, is used collectively.

15. For שִׁכְּלָתָה two of Kennicott's MSS. read שִׁכַּלְתִּיהָ, in the first person. Thus also the LXX. τιμωρήσομαι αὐτήν.

16. אִם, *if,* an elliptical formula of swearing in Hebrew, having all the force of a negative. Compare Ps. xcv. 11.

19. בְּדָם is not to be rendered *on account of blood,* as Rosenmüller proposes,

[Chap. XIV. 19-23.]   EZEKIEL.   75

17 should be desolate. Or if I should bring a sword against that
    land, and should say, Sword, go through the land, and I should
18 cut off man and beast from it; And these three men were in the
    midst of it, as I live, saith the Lord Jehovah, they should deliver
    neither sons nor daughters, but they by themselves should be
19 delivered. Or if I send a pestilence against that land, and pour
    out my fury upon it in blood, to cut off man and beast from it;
20 And Noah, Daniel, and Job were in the midst of it, as I live,
    saith the Lord Jehovah, they should deliver neither son nor
    daughter; they by their righteousness should deliver their own
21 souls. For thus saith the Lord Jehovah: How much more
    when I send against Jerusalem my four calamitous judgments,
    the sword, and the famine, and the wild beasts, and the pesti-
22 lence, to cut off from her man and beast! Yet behold, there
    shall be left in her those that escape, who shall be brought out,
    sons and daughters: behold, they shall go forth to you, and ye
    shall see their way and their doings, and ye shall be comforted
    concerning the evil which I have brought upon Jerusalem, all
23 that I have brought upon it. And they shall comfort you, when
    ye shall see their way and their doings; and ye shall know that
    it is not for nothing that I have done all that I have done in it,
    saith the Lord Jehovah

but *in blood:* the judgment was to consist in the shedding of blood by war.

21. אַף כִּי, *quanto magis*, is strongly affirmative of a proceeding on the part of Jehovah, in accordance with the instances cited in the preceding verses.

22, 23. הַמּוּצָאִים, *those who shall be brought out,* made to escape the entire destruction of the city. The participle is not to be read actively הַמּוֹצִיאִים, as Houbigant proposes and Newcome adopts. I cannot find, with Calvin, Hävernick, and Fairbairn, that these verses contain a threatening, and not a promise. Whenever a remnant is spoken of as being left, in antithesis with what goes before, it is always in mercy, never in judgment. The persons spoken of, were reformed Jews, upon whom the capture of Jerusalem had produced a beneficial moral effect. "Their ways and their doings" were not those by which they had provoked the Lord to punish the nation, but the fruits of righteousness — the good works to the practice of which they had been recovered by the severe discipline through the course of which they had been brought. While they justified God in all the calamities which he had inflicted upon them, their being spared was a proof of his great mercy, and a pledge that, if their brethren in the captivity followed their example, by renouncing idolatry, they also should be dealt with in mercy.

CHAPTER XV.

The object of this short chapter, which is evidently introductory to the following, is to set forth the worthlessness and, by implication, the wickedness of the Jewish people. It consists of two parts, — the parable, 1-5, and its application, 6-8.

1 AND the word of Jehovah came to me, saying: Son of man, what
2 is the wood of the vine more than any other wood? the shoot
3 that is among the trees of the forest? Shall wood of it be taken to make any work? Will men take a peg of it to hang any
4 vessel on? Behold, it is cast into the fire for fuel; the fire devoureth both the ends of it, the midst of it also is burned.
5 Should it be fit for any work? Behold, when it was whole it was not made into any work: how much less when fire hath devoured it, and it is burned, should it be made into any work?
6 Wherefore thus saith the Lord Jehovah: As the wood of the vine is among the trees of the forest, which I have appointed to the fire for fuel, so have I appointed the inhabitants of Jeru-
7 salem. Yea, I have set my face against them: they shall go out of one fire, but another fire shall consume them; and ye shall know that I am Jehovah, when I set my face against them.

1-3. Teaching by similes drawn from nature, when judiciously conducted, possesses great beauty and force. The instance before us is eminently clear, simple, and appropriate. The point of comparison does not lie in the fruit, but simply in the wood of the vine. Although sometimes of considerable girth at the stem, yet generally the vine is small, and its branches consist of soft and brittle tendrils, carried along the face of a wall, or left to trail on the ground. They are, as here represented, totally unfit to be formed into any kind of instrument, or appropriated to useful purposes, as the wood of other trees may be. הַזְּמוֹרָה is in apposition with עֵץ. The question is understood to be repeated: What is the shoot more than that of any other tree in the forest? יָתֵד, a large wooden peg or pin, which the Orientals fix inside the walls of their houses for the purpose of hanging upon it household articles in constant use.

See on Isa. xxii. 23-25. The fire naturally attacks the ends of a piece of wood first, and then advances to the middle, burning till the whole be consumed. If unfit for any purpose before it was cast into the fire, how much more so when consumed? אַף כִּי, *quanto minus*, here, in a negative proposition. It is questionable whether the two ends are to be pressed, and made to symbolize the extremities of the Hebrew people — the northern kingdom carried into captivity by Tiglath-pileser, and the southern by Nebuchadnezzar, — the middle marking out Jerusalem.

6-8. After a brief repetition of the comparison, the parable is directly applied to the inhabitants of Jerusalem, or the Jewish state, represented by that city. עֵץ is to be taken as a collective noun. Three MSS. read בְּעֵצֵי, in the plural; and thus all the ancient versions. הָאֵשׁ ... הָאֵשׁ, *the fire and the fire*, is properly translated "one fire and another

8   I will also make the land desolate, because they have committed
a grievous transgression saith the Lord Jehovah.

fire." The Jews having utterly failed to answer the Divine purpose in selecting them to be witnesses for Jehovah in the midst of the heathen, they were to be completely broken up as a nation, and punished by severe and fiery trials in succession, till the dross of their idolatry was purged away. When a professing people act unworthily of their calling, they are only fit to be rejected. Compare Matt. iii. 10; v. 13.

CHAPTER XVI.

In an allegory of great length and minute detail, the prophet is commissioned to exhibit the positive side of the picture, which he had negatively held up to view in the previous chapter. In a striking poetical prosopopœia, Jerusalem is introduced as a new-born female exposed at her birth, 1-5; but mercifully taken by Jehovah under his protection, and, when grown up to womanhood, joined to him by a matrimonial covenant, and provided with everything that might set off her beauty, and minister to her comfort, 6-14. She afterwards becomes an adultress, and indulges in the grossest pollutions, 15-34. Merited punishment is then denounced against her, 35-43; in aggravation of the monstrous character of her lewdness, it is portrayed as incomparably greater than that of any of her neighbors, 44-59. The allegory concludes with a gracious promise of restoration, 60-63. How abhorrent or indelicate soever certain parts of the imagery may be to our more refined feelings, they are admirably adapted to the subject, and quite in keeping with the greater freedom in modes of speech which have always obtained among natives of the East. The pious mind will instinctively recoil from dwelling upon any improper ideas which they may be supposed to suggest.

1   AGAIN the word of the Lord came unto me, saying: Son of man,
2   cause Jerusalem to know her abominations, And say: Thus saith
3   the Lord Jehovah unto Jerusalem: Thy origin and thy nativity
were of the land of the Canaanite; thy father was an Amorite,

2, 3. Jerusalem is the symbolical representative of the Jewish people, or the kingdom of Judah. In order to prepare the minds of the Jews for the very humiliating picture about to be exhibited of their national degradation, they are first of all reminded of their Canaanitish origin. It is, however, rather the character of the inhabitants of Canaan than the country itself that is meant. Compare Zeph. i. 11; Zech. xiv. 21. As neither Abraham nor Sarah was descended from the tribes here specified, but were Aramæans, it is evident the reference must be to Jerusalem as originally inhabited by the Jebusites, who were more or less mixed up with the neighboring Amorites and Hittites. Comp. Numb. xiii. 29. In idolatry they were one; and in this respect furnished appropriate types of the Jewish inhabitants in after times, when they had apostatized from the worship of the true God. The iniquity of the Amorites is specially marked, Gen. xv. 16; and the family of Heth is likewise mentioned with disapprobation, chap. xxvii. 46. The difference between מְכֹרָה and מֹלֶדֶת is scarcely perceptible. They are merely synonymes expressive of *nativity* or *birth*.

78 EZEKIEL. [CHAP. XVI. 3–6.

4 and thy mother a Hittite. And as for thy birth, in the day when thou wast born, thy navel was not cut, neither wast thou washed with water for purification, nor rubbed at all with salt,
5 neither swaddled at all. No eye pitied thee to do any of these things unto thee, to compassionate thee, but thou wast cast out into the open field in the loathing of thy person on the day when

The prefix מ is not necessarily indicative of locality, which is the idea adopted by Gesenius and some other Hebraists, but is a simple formative, as in מִיָּם, כָּבֵד, כָּשׁוֹל, and the like. The distinction made by Hävernick, who interprets כְּבֵירָה by *Zeugungsort*, and מִילֶדֶת by *Geburtsort*, is quite an unnecessary refinement. The plural form in both cases is against the interpretation. That the former noun, however, is derived from כּוּר, *to dig*, seems the best established etymology.

4. Reverting to the earliest history of Jerusalem, the city being put for the inhabitants, the prophet exhibits her as a female infant cruelly neglected with respect to the performance of those offices which it requires on first coming into the world. הוּלֶּדֶת אֹתָךְ, the passive is here, as usual, construed with the accusative. Comp. Gen. xl. 20; Hos. ii. 5. The historical circumstances allegorically alluded to are those of the Hebrews in Egypt, where they were exposed to every species of cruelty. Γέννησιν δὲ αὐτῆς καλεῖ τὴν ἐξ Αἰγύπτου ἔξοδον (Theodoret). שָׁרֵר, the *umbilical cord* or navel-string, which requires to be cut at the birth of the infant. Root שָׁרַר, *to bind, twist*, etc. This, with the other terms here employed, presupposes some acquaintance with the obstetric art in the age of our prophet. The next circumstance adverted to is the washing with water, for the purpose of removing all impurities attaching to the surface of the body. לְמִשְׁעִי, *for purification*.

Comp. for derivation the Arab. صَبَغَ, v. conjug. *removit a se noxam vel potius corporis inquinamentum*, and the Syr.

ܡܨܲܡܚܳܐ, *splendidum faciens*. The LXX. must have understood the word in this light, since they have left it altogether untranslated, supposing that the idea was sufficiently expressed by ἐλούσθης, by which they had rendered רֻחַצְתְּ. The Targum, as read by Abulwalid, לְאִתְחֲזָאָה, *ad mundandum*; by Jarchi, לְצַחְצוּחַ, *for brightness*. This derivation seems preferable to that adopted by Gesenius, who refers the word to the root שָׁעָה, *to look, view*, and supposes the meaning to have respect to the presentation of a new-born infant, when washed, to the parents or others. This interpretation, however applicable to the circumstances of the case, and however it may seem to relieve the etymological difficulty, is less natural than that above suggested. For the form and punctuation, compare לְבִרְיָה. That it was customary in ancient times to rub the bodies of new-born children with salt, for the purpose of hardening the skin, appears from Galen, De Sanit. i. 7: Sale modico insperso cutis infantis densior solidiorque redditur.

5. The infant is supposed to have been entirely neglected, and pitilessly thrown down in the open field, exposed to the elements or to wild beasts. The exposure of infants was a practice very common in ancient times. בְּגֹעַל נַפְשֵׁךְ, *in the loathing of thy person*, is to be taken objectively, with reference to the abhorrent aspect of the infant thus exposed to view. Such was the primitive condition of the Hebrew people when in Egypt.

6. Jehovah here represents himself as a traveller who, on passing by, discovers the unsightly and pitiable object which

6 thou wast born. Then I passed by thee, and saw thee sprawling in thy blood, and I said to thee in thy blood, Live; yea I said to
7 thee in thy blood, Live. I made thee to increase by thousands as the sproutings of the field, and thou didst increase and become great, and camest with most splendid ornaments; thy breasts were formed, and thy hair was grown, whereas thou hadst been
8 naked and bare. And I passed by thee, and saw thee, and, behold, thy time was a time of love; and I spread my skirt over thee, 'and covered thy nakedness, and sware unto thee, and entered into a covenant with thee, saith the Lord Jehovah, and

had just been described, and interposes for its rescue. Notwithstanding its pollution, he takes compassion upon it, and saves its life. מִתְבּוֹסֶסֶת may most appropriately be rendered by *sprawling*, as expressive of the convulsive struggles and contortions of a child endeavoring to move from a disagreeable situation. The word is derived from בּוּס, *to trample, stamp* with the feet, *kick*. The form in Hithpael, is active and reflexive — not passive, as Gesenius interprets. In this miserable and helpless condition Jehovah found the Hebrews in the land of bondage. Extending the principle involved in the figure beyond the direct teaching of the text, it is strikingly descriptive of the condition of sinners previous to conversion. As Calvin observes, till they feel this to be the state to which they are reduced, they will never appreciate the provisions of mercy. Houbigant rejects the last clause of the verse, on the ground of its having been omitted in the LXX., Syr., and Arab.; but there is a singular force in the repetition, of which even Hitzig approves.

7. This verse describes the change which took place in consequence of the Divine interposition. Instead of being left to pine away and become extinct in Egypt, the Hebrews grew and increased in number, and were made to appear beauteous in their civil and religious polity. Instead of שָׁדַיִם, *breasts*, one of Kennicott's MSS. and another originally read שָׁדַיִךְ, *thy breasts*, and thus the LXX., the Peshito Syr., the Hexap.

Syr., the Arab, and the Vulgate. רְבָבָה, *a myriad, ten thousand*; often used for any great indefinite number. I made thee to increase by thousands, as the productions of the field. צֶמַח is used as a collective. Root צָמַח, *to sprout*, spring up. The metaphor is still continued, representing the infant growing up to womanhood, and exhibiting unmistakeable signs of puberty. בַּעֲדִי עֲדָיִים, taking the former of the two words collectively, *ornaments of ornaments*, i.e. as a superlative of intensity, *most splendid ornaments*. The constructions put upon עֲדִי by Grotius, Hävernick, and Hitzig are complete failures. The LXX. πόλεων, as if they had read עָרֵי עֲרָיִם. בּוֹא בְּ, *to come with* anything. I cannot agree with Fairbairn that וְעֶרְיָה וְעֶרְיָה, *naked and bare*, is to be regarded as contemporaneous with the prosperous condition just described. Our translators very properly place the states in contrast, rendering וְ by "whereas." Compare Hos. ii. 3. In עֶרֹם וְעֶרְיָה we have the abstract for the concrete, in order to give greater force to the language. עֶרְיָה, though derived from the same root as עֶרְוָה, yet here simply signifies *nude, bare*, whereas the latter has always the superadded idea of obscenity, or shame. It is not unusual for female children among the Bedowins to grow up without wearing any clothing; and, being common, it is not accompanied with any feeling of impropriety.

8. A resumption of the declaration made at the commencement of verse 6.

9 thou becamest mine. Then I washed thee with water, and thoroughly cleansed thy blood from thee, and anointed thee with
10 oil. And I clothed thee with embroidered cloth, and shod thee with shoes of seal-skin, and bound thee round with a turban of
11 byssus, and covered thee with silk. And I made thee most beautiful, and put bracelets on thy arms, and a chain on thy neck,

The same act is referred to. Unsightly and loathsome as the Hebrew people were in themselves, and thus calculated to excite disgust rather than to attract, they nevertheless were the objects of the Divine love, which regarded them as those whom it was the purpose of Jehovah to deliver, beautify and foster. Deut. iv. 37; vii. 9–13; x. 15; Hos. xi. 1. עֵת דֹּדִים, *a time of loves*, i.e. not, when thou wast marriageable, as Rosenmüller and Gesenius interpret, but, when thou wast an object of affection. There was nothing in Israel that was lovely. It was all pure affection on the part of Jehovah. The advance in the allegory is now to that of the espousals. To betoken this פָּרַשׂ כָּנָף, *the spreading of the skirt* or flap of the coverlet is introduced. That this is the meaning, with reference to matrimonial cohabitation, is evident from Ruth iii. 9. Similar phraseology with like reference occurs in the Greek classics, as quoted by Rosenmüller. Thus Theocritus, Idyll. xviii. 19:

Ζανός τοι θυγάτηρ ὑπὸ τὰν μίαν ᾤχετο χλαῖναν.

and Euripides:

Ὅταν ὑπ᾽ ἀνδρὸς χλαῖναν εὐγενοῦς πέσης.

Reference to simple protection, alleging in proof Deut. xxxiii. 12, as some have done, is out of the question. All that the Orientals wear over them at night is a quilt or coverlet, or, when travelling, the cloak which they have worn during the day. Hence, in the language of the Hebrews, to uncover the nakedness of a person means to throw back such a coverlet with a view to unlawful or incestuous union, Lev. xviii. There is in this verse an obvious reference to the solemn transactions at Sinai, when Jehovah entered into covenant with the Hebrews, thereby contracting as it were a conjugal relation, by which he pledged himself to love, provide for, and protect them; while they came under an obligation to love, worship, and obey Him to the exclusion of every rival god. Hence, as it follows in the sequel, and so frequently in the Old Testament, idolatry is represented as spiritual adultery, the nation thereby being guilty of a breach of the marriage covenant.

9. There seems here to be reference to a custom prevalent in the East of washing the bride in the bath, anointing her with oil, and adorning her with ornaments, previous to the celebration of the marriage ceremony (Esther ii. 9–12). The דָּמִים, *blood*, here mentioned is not that of the menstrual discharge, as Rosenmüller interprets, but that mentioned verse 6. The Israelites underwent a thorough purification before they entered into the covenant, Exod. xix. 14. Compare Jer. ii. 2, 3. They were designed to be a holy people to the Lord.

10. רִקְמָה, *embroidered cloth*, compare רִקְמָתִים, Ps. xlv. 15, and the Arab. رقم, by which is meant cloth of versicolor, richly intersticed with threads of gold. תַּחַשׁ, a kind of skin, used by the Hebrews to make an over-covering to the tabernacle, Exod. xxvi. 14, and, as appears from the present verse, used also for shoes; but of what particular animal, has been disputed. The most probable opinion is, that the seal is intended. See Gesenius in voc., and Winer's Realwörterbuch, ii. 595. שֵׁשׁ, *byssus*, fine cotton cloth, such as was anciently prepared in Egypt. מֶשִׁי, *silk*, garments prepared of this material.

12   and I put a ring in thy nose, and rings in thine ears, and a crown
13   of beauty on thy head. And thou wast adorned with gold and
     silver, and thy garments were of byssus and silk and embroidery;
     thou didst eat flour and honey and oil; and thou wast exceedingly
14   beautiful, and didst prosper into a kingdom. And thy fame went
     forth among the nations on account of thy beauty, for it was
     perfect through my splendor which I put upon thee, saith the
     Lord Jehovah.
15   But thou trustedst in thy beauty, and didst commit lewdness
     through thy fame, and didst pour out thy lewdness to every one

11, 12. For most of these female ornaments, see my Comment on Isa. iii. 18–23. It must appear strange that our translators should have rendered נֶזֶם עַל־אַפֵּךְ, *a jewel on thy forehead*. נֶזֶם properly means a *ring*, and denotes either such as was worn in the nose, which is still common in the East, or such as is worn in the ears. The addition of אַפֵּךְ, *thy nose*, shows that the former is meant in the present instance; — the term, אַף, though sometimes used for the countenance or face in general, is never employed to denote the forehead, but is strictly and properly *the nose*. What has lead to the mistake, has been the too close adherence to the common signification of עַל, *upon*, whereas it also admits in certain instances of being rendered *in*. בְּגִילִים, *rings*, so called from their circular form, from גִּיל, *to turn round, be round* (Numb. xxxi. 50).

13, 14. Through the Divine goodness the Hebrew people were most abundantly supplied with everything requisite both for use and ornament. Their riches and splendor far surpassed those of any other nation. As a kingdom theirs was distinguishingly flourishing in the days of David and Solomon, the former of which monarchs greatly extended its boundaries, and enriched it with the spoils of his victories. The theocracy then reached its highest point of glory, and was of great celebrity among the surrounding nations (1 Kings x). Still they are reminded that their prosperity and glory were not owing to any merit of their own. It was a "comeliness" which Jehovah, their covenant God, had put upon them. To his unmerited bounty they owed all that they enjoyed. The Yod in שָׂמְתִּי and אֲשֶׁר־שַׂמְתִּי is redundant, and is therefore left unpointed.

15. Beauty often proves a snare to those who possess it. Listening to flattery, they are easily drawn into the trap that is laid for them. The Jews were proud of their endowments, and forgetting Him by whom these had been bestowed, they transferred their affections to other gods, and thus became guilty of conjugal infidelity. עַל־שְׁמֵךְ, rendered by some after the Vulgate: *contra nomen tuum*, supposing the meaning to be, that as a wife is called by the name of her husband, and that as adultery is an act committed against him whose name she bears, so the idolatries of the Hebrews were to be viewed in reference to the sacred name of Jehovah their God. Since, however, שֵׁם is often used in the acceptation *fame, renown, celebrity*, it seems more natural to take it in this sense here, and to render עַל, *propter, on account of*; teaching, that the Jews had employed the renown which through the Divine goodness they had acquired, as a means of seducing neighboring nations to commit spiritual fornication. The proposed rendering of Manger, "notwithstanding thy renown," is not to be approved. The term תַּזְנוּת, *lewdness, fornication*, used of idol-worship, is pecu-

16 that passed by; his it was. And thou didst take of thy garments and make for thyself patched high places, and thou committedst lewdness upon them, such as never had been and never shall be.
17 Yea, thou didst take of thy beautiful jewels of my gold and my silver, which I had given thee, and didst make for thyself images
18 of men, and committedst lewdness with them. And didst take the garments of thine embroidery, and didst cover them; and
19 my oil and my incense thou didst place before them. Yea, my meat which I gave thee, the flour and oil and honey with which I fed thee, thou didst place before them for a sweet odor: and
20 it took place, saith the Lord Jehovah. And thou didst take thy sons and thy daughters, which thou didst bear unto me,
21 and didst sacrifice them to them for food. Were thy lewdnesses a small matter, that thou didst sacrifice my children, and deliver
22 them up to cause them to pass through the fire to them? And with all thine abominations and thy lewdnesses, thou rememberedst not the days of thy youth, when thou wast naked and bare,

---

liar to Ezekiel. יָפְיֵךְ, thy beauty, though somewhat distant, is unquestionably the nominative to וַיְהִי־לוֹ, his it was.

16. בָּמוֹת טְלֻאוֹת, patched high places, spoken contemptuously of the temples erected in honor of Astarte, for adorning which the Jewish females wove hangings, 2 Kings xxiii. 7. LXX. εἴδωλα ῥαπτά. יִהְיֶה לֹא בָאֵי לֹא elliptically for יִהְיֶה לֹא בָאֵי לֹא כָאֵלֶּה, the like things have not come, nor shall there be. So atrocious was the conduct of God's ancient people when they apostatized from him. It was altogether unparalleled in the past, as it should be in the future.

17–21. Jehovah asserts his propriety in all the objects which apostate Judah employed in the service of idols. He had bestowed them upon her to be appropriated for his glory, but she had wickedly prostituted them to his dishonor. By צֶלֶם זָכָר, images of men, Scholz and Hävernick understand what were worshipped in the idolatrous service of phallus, or the membrum virile, which the Egyptians regarded as the emblem of fecundity, and which is still licentiously worshipped by the Hindoos under the name of lingam. If such be the meaning, as probably it is, this is the only passage in which any allusion is made to such abomination in the Bible.

Compare the Arab. كَرّ, membrum genitale maris, penis, veretrum, Kamoos. Not only the superfluities of luxury, but the productions of nature necessary for the sustenance of life, and the very children, were devoted to the idols. Such practices, common in the pagan world, were equally in vogue among the Jews in the worst periods of their history. For the burning of children in honor of Moloch, see Deut. xviii. 10; Ps. cvi. 37; Jer. vii. 31; xix. 5. That the phrase הֶעֱבִיר בָּאֵשׁ, to cause to pass through the fire, actually means to burn, and not, as the Rabbins would have it, that the Jews merely made the children to pass through the fire, uninjured, as an act of lustration, see Gesenius, Heb. Lex. Artic. עָבַר, Hiph. 4. To such an extreme of cruelty will men, from a consciousness of guilt, proceed, with the view of propitiating the Deity. Comp. Micah vi. 7. The barbarous and most unnatural practice of sacrificing children to

23 sprawling in thy blood. And it came to pass after all thy wick-
24 edness — woe, woe to thee, saith the Lord Jehovah — Thou
    didst build a brothel and make for thyself a high place in every
25 street. At the head of every road thou didst build thy high
    place, and cause thy beauty to be abhorred, and didst open thy
    feet to every one that passed by, and multiply thy lewdnesses.
26 Thou didst also commit lewdness with the Egyptians thy neigh-
    bors, great of flesh, and multiply thy lewdness to provoke me
27 to anger. And behold, I stretched my hand over thee, and
    withheld thine allowance, and delivered thee to the will of them
    that hated thee, the daughters of the Philistines who were
28 ashamed at thy atrocious way. And thou didst commit lewd-
    ness with the sons of Assyria, because thou wast insatiable, yea,
    thou didst commit lewdness with them, but wast not satisfied.
29 Thou didst also multiply thy lewdness with the land of Canaan,
30 unto Chaldea, yet even with this thou wast not satisfied. How
    withered is thine heart, saith the Lord Jehovah, since thou doest

idols was specially prevalent among the Phœnicians. The more aggravated forms of idolatry are here charged upon the elect but apostate nation.

22-27. When the Jews knew God, they glorified him not as God, neither were thankful, and in this respect resembled other idolaters (Rom. i. 21). Forgetfulness of God and his benefits is the source of all other sins. The Jews became most inordinate in idolatrous indulgences. They set no bounds to their lust. גַב (verse 24), LXX. οἴκημα πορνικόν, a fornix, vault, brothel, place of prostitution: used tropically for an idol-temple. So shameless did they become that their beauty, instead of attracting paramours, filled them with disgust. רָמָה, an elevated place, equivalent to בָּמָה, so often used in reference to places of idolatrous worship. פְּדֻלֵּי רַגְלָיִךְ (ver. 26), an euphemism to express the enormity of Egyptian idolatry. The idolatries of the Egyptians were of the grossest and most multifarious kinds. Compare chap. xxiii. 20. I cannot agree with Calvin and Fairbairn that political alliances, and not idolatries, are here intended. The connection is decidedly against such a construction. They were indeed much mixed up with each other, and the one naturally led to the other, but the grosser of the two evils is here specifically referred to. בְּנוֹת פְּלִשְׁתִּים, daughters of the Philistines, their descendants, or the inhabitants of the country of the Philistines, who were ever the indomitable enemies of the Jews. Even these, idolatrous though they were, could not endure the licentiousness of the Jewish nation. They were contented with their own idols, and not adopting, like the Jews, those of every other country, consequently despised that people for their exorbitancy.

28, 29. Not satisfied with adopting the idolatries of Egypt, the Jews practised those of the more distant Assyrians and Babylonians. They were perfectly insatiable in their lust. Their idolatry was an amalgamation of all the different forms which obtained in the countries around them.

30. The influence of sin on the soul is to render it morally impotent. Though it may not deprive it of the powers which are requisite to constitute man a responsible agent, it weakens his princi-

31 all these things — the work of a self-willed adultress. In that thou buildest thy brothel at the head of every road, and constructest thy high place in every street, and wast not as a harlot,
32 scorning hire. An adultress under her husband, thou didst re-
33 ceive strangers. They give a present to all whores, but thou givest thy gifts to all thy lovers, and hirest them to come to thee
34 from every side to thy lewdnesses. And there was in thee the contrary of women in thy lewdnesses, in that none followed thee and in that thou gavest a present, and no present was given to thee: in this thou wast contrary.
35 Wherefore, O harlot, hear the word of Jehovah. Thus saith the
36 Lord Jehovah: Because thy copper is poured out, and thy nakedness is discovered, through thy lewdnesses with thy lovers, and with all thine abominable idols, and through the blood of thy
37 children which thou didst give to them; Therefore, behold, I will collect all thy lovers to whom thou hast been pleasant, and all them whom thou hast loved, in addition to all whom thou hatedst, I will even collect them round about thee, and expose thy nakedness to them, and they shall see all thy naked-

ples of action, takes possession of those powers, and forms itself into habits which the individual allows to grow upon him, so that he becomes at last insensible to the operation of the strongest moral motives. אֶזְרָח, *willard*, the Pahul Participle in Kal; more commonly the Pulal אֶזְרָח is employed. There is no necessity, with Hitzig, to point, מַה־לְּךָ אֶזְרָח בַּת, and render: *what hope is there for thy daughter?* בַּת־אֶזְרָח, *self-willed, domineering*, imperious, impudent. Compare the Arab. سَلَطَة, *femina clamosa*. Theodor. παῤῥησιαζομένης.

31. A repetition of verse 24. The idolatries of the Jews were not practised for the love of gain, but solely for the sake of the gratification which they found in them. To sin for the mere love of sin argues the highest degree of depravity. קָלַס, *to scoff, deride*, with reference to the custom of prostitutes, who pretend to despise what is offered them as the price of whoredom, in order that it may be raised. Vulg. *fastidio augens pretium*. For an instance of bar-

gaining in such cases, see Gen. xxxviii. 16. The לְ in קָלַס, is not to be connected with זוֹנָה, but with הָיָה immediately preceding.

32. אֵשֶׁת אִישׁ, to be under a man, as a married woman, in subjection to her husband.

33, 34. To aggravate the guilt of the Jews, they are forcibly represented as acting contrary to other prostitutes, by hiring their paramours, instead of being hired by them. In בְּתַזְנוּתַיִךְ, the preposition בְּ indicates purpose or intention. נֵדֶה, the word here used for *gift*, or the price of prostitution, occurs nowhere else in the Hebrew Bible. The ־ in the plural נְדָנֶיךָ following, is epenthetic. Root נָדָה, *to be liberal*. Arab. نَدِيَ, *dispersus, liberalis fuit*. Conjug. v. *liberalem monstravit se*. نَدَ, fem. نَدِيَّة, *munificus*. The conjunction וְ in וַתְּהִי־לָךְ, is inferential.

35—43. Now follow denunciations of judgment against the Jews on account of their flagitious conduct. I see no

38 ness. And I will judge thee as those who commit adultery and shed blood are judged, and I will render to thee the blood of
39 anger and of jealousy. And I will deliver thee into their hand, and they shall demolish thy brothel, and break down thy high places, and strip thee of thy garments, and take thy splendid
40 jewels, and leave thee naked and bare. And they shall bring up against thee a company, and stone thee with stones, and cut thee
41 in pieces with their swords. And they shall burn thy houses with fire, and execute judgments in thee in the sight of many women, and cause thee to cease from whoredom, and thou also
42 shalt give no hire any more. And I will cause mine anger against thee to cease, and my jealousy shall turn away from thee,
43 and I will be at rest and not be angry any more. Because thou didst not remember the days of thy youth, but hast provoked me to anger with all these, therefore, behold I also will recompense thy way upon thine own head, saith the Lord Jehovah, and thou shalt not practise this wickedness in adition to all thine abom-

occasion to seek for any other signification of נְחֻשָׁה (verse 36) than the ordinary one of *brass*, or money consisting of brass or copper, in allusion to the lavish expenditure of gifts as the wages of idolatrous prostitution (verses 31, 33, 34); LXX. τὸν χαλκόν ; Vulg. *aes*. Our Translators appear to have obtained that of *filthiness* from the verdigris or green crust which it contracts. By those whom the Jews hated (ver. 37), are meant the Edomites, Moabites, and Ammonites, between whom and them there existed an implacable enmity. It would seem, from the threatening to expose the nakedness of the Jews, that an allusion is made to one of the modes of punishing prostitutes in ancient times. וּנְתַתִּיךְ דַּם חֵמָה וְקִנְאָה (ver. 38), *and I will give thee the blood of fury and jealousy*, i.e. I will furiously shed thy blood, as an enraged husband does that of his unfaithful wife when his jealousy is roused. In ver. 40, the two kinds of capital punishment authorized by the Mosaic law are introduced; stoning, and killing with the sword. Here, and in the following verse, the invasion and destruction of Jerusalem by the Chaldeans are predicted.

בָּתַק, in Piel בִּתֵּק, a ἅπαξ λεγ. *to hew or cut in pieces*. הָא, Chaldee (ver. 43), the same as the Heb. הֵן, *behold!* used once besides, Gen. xlvii. 23. The last clause of this verse is very obscure, but the idea which seems to be conveyed by it is, that, corrected and reformed by the judgments which were inflicted upon the Jews, they should not any more perpetrate the atrocious wickedness described in the preceding part of the chapter. עַל I take in the acceptation of *in addition to*. Moral evils of all kinds were prevalent among them, but it was principally on account of idolatry — emphatically אֶל־הַזִּמָּה (compare Zech. v. 8, זֹאת הָרִשְׁעָה, *this is wickedness*) — that they were punished. The Targum, Jarchi, Kimchi, and Rosenmueller interpret זִמָּה, *plan* or *purpose*, in a good sense, and suppose the meaning to be, that the Jewish people did not form the design to repent of all their wickedness. It is true, זִמָּה, occuring simply by itself, may be taken in a good sense, as it appears to be Job xvii. 11, but the phrase עָשָׂה זִמָּה, here used, is never employed in any other sense than that of committing flagrant wickedness. The inter-

44   inations. Behold every one who gives utterance to proverbs shall utter a proverb against thee, saying: As is the mother, so is
45   her daughter. Thou art the daughter of thy mother who loathed her husband and her children; and thou art the sister of thy sisters who loathed their husbands and their children; your

pretation of Michaëlis and Hävernick, adopted by Fairbairn, appears to me to be exceedingly forced: viz. that עִשָּׂה is to be pointed עָשְׂתָה, and referred to Jehovah, on the supposition, that he declares he would not act the part of the reckless parent who encouraged his daughter to prostitute herself (Lev. xix. 29).

43. בְּאִשׁ is used elliptically for בֶּאֱשָׁה, which is supplied in three MSS. at first hand, and by the LXX., Syriac, and Vulgate. Between this verse and that preceding there is no contradiction. There is merely a resumption of the threatened judgment, with a statement relative to its happy result. The Jews were no longer to add to their guilt by indulging in the crime of idolatry.

44. The Mashal, or derisive proverb, here introduced is the most sententious and expressive of any used in the Bible. In Hebrew it consists only of two short words, the former of which is a compound: כְּאִמָּהּ בִּתָּהּ, as the mother, her daughter; כְּ, so, the corresponding particle of comparison, is, as often, omitted for the sake of brevity. The meaning is, that Jerusalem had fully proved herself to be of Canaanitish origin, as had been stated, verse 3.

45, 46. How Samaria and Sodom can be said to have loathed their husbands and their children, does not clearly appear. By the Sinaïtic covenant Jehovah was the husband of Samaria — the representative of the ten tribes, just as much as he was of Jerusalem — the representative of those of Judah and Benjamin; but he never stood in any such relation to Sodom. Still, though we have no historical account of defection to idolatry on the part of the inhabitants of that city previous to its destruction, yet as that sin in all probability was indulged in by them, their abandonment of the worship of the true God might be regarded as essentially analogous to that of the covenant people. It was a violation of those sacred engagements which, as his professing worshippers, they had come under. Or, if we view Sodom and her daughter-towns as representatives of the Moabites and Ammonites on the east of the Jordan and the Dead Sea, among whom a similar defection must have taken place, it will amount to the same thing. Connected as these peoples were by collateral descent with the father of the faithful, there can be little doubt that in the patriarchal age they were worshippers of the true God, though they afterwards apostatized to the worship of Baal-peor, Chemosh, and Moloch. In the same sense we are to regard the Canaanites to whom the origin of Jerusalem is traced. On the principle, now generally admitted, that monotheism was prior to polytheism, they must originally have been worshippers of the true God. Melchizedek, king of Salem, was priest of the Most High God (Gen. xiv. 18). Jehovah, as entitled to their supreme love, had inalienable claims upon them, which they disowned when they fell away to idolatry. By abandoning his service, they obviously proved that they had rejected him. גָּעַל signifies *to abhor, cast off*, reject with loathing. It argues the highest pitch of reckless depravity to abhor the character of the Infinitely pure. Compare θεοστυγεῖς, Rom. i. 30. The circumstance that the names of the father and mother of Jerusalem occur here in the inverse order of that in which they are presented in ver. 3, is not to be pressed.

46. Samaria is called the greater

46 mother was a Hittite and your father an Amorite. And thy elder sister is Samaria, who dwelleth at thy left hand, she and her daughters; and thy younger sister, who dwelleth at thy right
47 hand, is Sodom and her daughters. Yet thou didst not walk in their ways, nor act according to their abominations; it was only a small matter; but thou hast acted more corruptly than they in
48 all thy ways. As I live, saith the Lord Jehovah, Sodom thy sister hath not done, she nor her daughters, as thou hast done,
49 thou and thy daughters. Behold, this was the iniquity of thy sister Sodom: pride, fulness of bread, and quiet security she and her daughters had, but she strengthened not the hand of the poor
50 and needy; But were haughty and committed abomination be-
51 fore me; therefore I removed them according as I saw. Neither had Samaria committed the half of thy sins, but thou hast multiplied thine abominations more than they, and hast justified thy

הַגְּדוֹלָה or *elder* sister of Jerusalem, not with respect to age, for Jerusalem existed long prior to her; but in regard to the worship of the two golden calves established by Jeroboam in that city. As, in determining the points of the heavens, or, as we should say, the compass, the Orientals regarded the East as the principal, they always spoke of it as being קָדִים or קֶדֶם, *in front* or *before*, consequently שְׂמֹאל, *the left*, would designate the North, just as יָמִין, *the right*, would designate the South, the direction in which Sodom had lain. This last-named city is said to have been הַקְּטַנָּה, the *smaller* or younger sister of Jerusalem, principally in the same moral point of view: her guilt, great as it was, not being to be compared, in point of aggravation, with that contracted by Jerusalem. The kingdom, too, of which it was the capital, was small compared with that of Judah. The "daughters" of cities, is a term used idiomatically in Hebrew, to denote either their inhabitants, or smaller cities and villages connected with, or dependent upon them. Thus Num. xxi. 25 בְּחֶשְׁבּוֹן וּבְכָל־בְּנוֹתֶיהָ in *Heshbon and in all her daughters*, rendered by our translators "in *all her villages*."

47. Enormous as were the sins of those cities, they were not in point of guilt to be compared with those of Jerusalem, which were proportionally enhanced by the distinguished spiritual advantages that her inhabitants had enjoyed. In Jerusalem were the temple, the legal sacrifices, the priests, and the law. Before it was polluted by idolatry Jehovah was worshipped there in the beauties of holiness. קַק רַק בְּרַק, I adopt the signification of *only*, as attaching to רַק, which was proposed by Schultens, after the Arab. لاً, *duntaxat*.

48–50. The two representative cities are now taken up singly. First Sodom, depicted in such dark characters in the O. T. history. Worldly prosperity often proves dangerous to the interests of virtue. It easily inflates its possessors with pride; and, leading them to abandon active habits of life, superinduces indulgence in those of idleness, than which universal experience proves that nothing can furnish greater occasions to the commission of sin. שַׁלְוַת הַשְׁקֵט, *careless idleness*. The latter word is the Infinitive in Hiphil used substantively. Root שָׁקַט, *to rest, recline, be inactive, idle*.

51. בְּהֵנָּה, *more than they*, i.e. the inhabitants of Samaria understood, as im-

52 sisters in all thine abominations which thou hast done. Do thou also bear thy reproach, which hast judged thy sisters in thy sins that thou hast committed more abominably than they: they are more righteous than thou: be ashamed then, also thou, and bear
53 thy reproach, in that thou hast justified thy sisters. And I will reverse their captivity, the captivity of Sodom and her daughters, and the captivity of Samaria and her daughters, and the cap-
54 tivity of thy captivities in the midst of them: In order that thou mayest bear thy reproach, and be ashamed of all that thou hast
55 done, when thou comfortest them. And thy sisters, Sodom and her daughters, shall return to their former estate; and Samaria and her daughters shall return to their former estate; and thou
56 and thy daughters shall return to your former estate. And thy sister Sodom was not a report in thy mouth in the day of thy

plied in the name of the city. Two MSS. read מִמֵּךְ, *than she, the city.* Instead of אֲחוֹתֵךְ, *thy sisters,* sixty-four MSS., among these many Spanish, originally three more, and six by correction, read אֲחוֹתֵךְ, *thy sister,* which would appear better to harmonize with the context. The Keri in many MSS., as well as not a few printed editions, reads the word in the plural, which has also the support of the ancient versions. "To justify the crimes of others" is a Hebrew mode of speech, denoting, to make them appear comparatively innocent by the side of others, accompanied with much more aggravating circumstances.

53–55. Here a most unexpected change in the scene takes place. Instead of expatiating further on the calamities to be inflicted upon the guilty, all at once a gracious promise of restoration is introduced. שׁוּב שְׁבוּת, *to reverse a captivity,* signifies to restore captives and other sufferers to liberty and prosperity; see Job. xlii. 10. If the interpretation given of the three cities, Jerusalem, Samaria, and Sodom, be correct, namely that they are to be viewed as symbolical of the surrounding people whose centre they formed, or with whom they stood connected, no difficulty will arise relative to the restoration of Sodom. If we regard her as the representative of the Ammonites and Moabites, the descendants of Lot, we shall here have only a parallel prediction to Jer. xlviii. 47; xlix. 6. However obscure the lights of history relative either to the captivity or the restoration of the nations beyond the Dead Sea, there can be little doubt that they participated more or less in the fate of the Jews, to whose country they lay contiguous. It was a source of consolation to the other apostates that, their guilt not being so aggravated as that of Jerusalem, the punishment inflicted upon them would not be so severe (verse 54). That most of the ten tribes, of which Samaria had been the capital, were restored under Cyrus, is now generally admitted. The restoration of all the three classes of people is here predicted to take place at the same time.

56. So haughtily did the Jews carry themselves during the period of their national prosperity, that they did not deign even to mention the name of Sodom as a warning example. שְׁמוּעָה, *a report,* anything heard, and supposed, from its importance, to be repeated by those who hear it.

57. By "the reproach" of the cities of Syria, was not meant anything derogatory to the character of those cities

57 pride. Before thy wickedness was revealed, as at the time of the reproach of the daughters of Aram and all that were round about her, the daughters of the Philistines that despised thee round about.
58 Thou hast borne thy lewdness and thine abominations, saith
59 Jehovah. For thus saith the Lord Jehovah: I also will act towards thee as thou hast acted, because thou hast despised the
60 oath, breaking the covenant. Yet I will remember my covenant with thee in the days of thy youth, and I will establish for thee
61 an everlasting covenant. And thou shalt remember thy ways and be ashamed, when thou receivest thine elder sisters in addition to those who were younger than thou; and I will give them
62 to thee for daughters, but not by thy covenant. And I will establish my covenant with thee, and thou shalt know that I am

nationally considered, but the indignity offered by the Syrians to the Jews, when, under Rezin, they invaded the land of Judah (2 Kings xv. 37; Isa. vii. 1-9). That this is the construction to be put upon the words is evident from the parallelism, in the corresponding member of which the manner in which the Jews had been treated by the Philistines is mentioned. Compare for the insults offered by both Isa. ix. 11, 12.

58, 59. נְשָׂא זִמָּה וְתֹעֲבוֹת, *to bear lewdness and abominations*, means to suffer the punishment due to them. All the sufferings inflicted by the neighboring nations were retributively imposed upon them on account of their violation of the sacred engagements of the national covenant. Jehovah employed the nations as his instruments in punishing them.

60, 61. Though the Jews had acted most perfidiously towards their covenant God, and he might justly have cast them off for ever, yet in remembrance of his ancient covenant with them, ratified at Sinai, when he solemnly pledged himself to be their God, he promises still to have compassion upon them. They were again to be restored to their own land, but it was not so much that they might enjoy the temporal advantages of the old covenant, as that he might confer upon them the spiritual blessings of the new, to be ratified, while they were in that restored condition, by the death of Messiah. That this is the covenant elsewhere called "the everlasting covenant," see 2 Sam. xxiii. 5; Isa. lv. 3; Ezek. xxxvii. 26, and which, as here, is contrasted with the Sinaitic (Jer. xxxi. 31-34). Those who were to share with Jerusalem the spiritual benefits of the new covenant were to be brought into relation to her — not in virtue of any principles involved in that established at Sinai, but solely in virtue of those belonging to the Messianic. בְּרִיתֵךְ, *thy covenant*, is the Genitive of object, the covenant made with thee, for thy benefit — the national covenant. The New Jerusalem was henceforth to be the mother of all believers, whether Jews or Gentiles (Gal. iv. 26); and the calling of the last-named division of the human family is virtually here included. I must demur to the statements of Calvin, adopted by Hävernick and Fairbairn, who represent the old covenant to be the fountain-head of the new, and that they were well-nigh the same in substance, though different in form. So far indeed as the typical aspects of the former dispensation are concerned, they unquestionably had respect to the bless-

63. Jehovah. That thou mayest remember, and be ashamed, and there shall be no more to thee an opening of the mouth on account of thy shame, when I am reconciled to thee in reference to all that thou hast done, saith the Lord Jehovah.

ings of the gospel. But these aspects did not essentially belong to that covenant. They were merely a corollary or appendage, introduced into it for the purpose of illustrating the promise given in the Abrahamic covenant, which still remained, and ran parallel with the law, unaffected by its introduction four hundred and thirty years afterwards (Gal. iii. 17). The new dispensation, therefore, had a more ancient origin than that of Moses, and was established on better promises. Along with the old covenant, the language of which was: "Do this, and thou shalt live," there existed another, the language of which, illustrated by the legal sacrifices pointing forward to the all-perfect atonement of our Saviour, was: "Believe, and thou shalt be saved." It was this arrangement of mercy, distinct from, though incorporated with, the ancient economy, which secured the eternal happiness of believers previous to the advent of Messiah.

63. Nothing can be conceived of more calculated to produce feelings of deep penitential shame and sorrow, than the superabounding mercy of the Most High manifested towards his rebellious and guilty creatures. Contrasting the baseness of their conduct with His infinite compassion and love, their former self-boasting is cut off, and, lying low in the dust before Him, they can open their lips only in celebration of the riches of His grace.

CHAPTER XVII.

This chapter contains a parable of two eagles and a vine, 1-10; the explanation of the parable with application to the kings of Babylon and Egypt, and the fate of the kingdom of Judah in reference to them, 11-21; and concludes with a parabolic representation of the Messiah, and of the origin, universality, and prosperity of his kingdom, in language borrowed from the preceding, 22-24.
"From the beauty of its images, the elegance of its composition, the perspicuity of its language, the rich variety of its matter, and the easy transition from one part of the subject to another, this chapter forms one of the most beautiful and perfect pieces of its kind that can possibly be conceived in so small a compass." — Smith on the Prophets.
The place in point of time assignable to this prophecy lies between the sixth month of the sixth year of the reign of Zedekiah, and the fifth month of the seventh year after the carrying away of Jehoiachin to Babylon; consequently five years before the destruction of Jerusalem by the Chaldeans.

1 AND the word of Jehovah came unto me, saying: Son of man,
2 propose a riddle, and use a simile to the house of Israel;

2. חוּד חִידָה, *propose an enigma.* Comp. Judges xiv. 12, 13, 14; 1 Kings x. 1; Psalm xlix. 5; lxxviii. 2; and the Arab. حَدّ, *acuit, acutus fuit;* 2d Conj. تَحْديل, *acutum reddidit, exacuit.*

Agreeably to this etymology, enigmas are sharp, pointed, and penetrating; they are powerfully calculated to excite attention, whet the intellect of the hearer or reader, and more fixedly secure the investigation of the subject. They are

3 And say: Thus saith the Lord Jehovah: The great eagle, great
   of wings, long of pinion, full of feathers of various colors, came
4 to Lebanon and took the foliage of the cedar. He broke off the
   topmost branch, and brought it to the land of merchants; he

artificial and obscure, and express things in a sense different from that which the words, taken in their literal acceptation, would imply. Among other figures of speech by which they are distinguished, prosopopœia predominates. They are likewise marked by ingeniousness of thought and aptitude of expression. The truths or facts to which they relate, lie not upon, but under the surface. Scripture-enigmas differ from fable, inasmuch as they teach not fictions, but real facts. They are not, like ordinary riddles, designed to puzzle and perplex, but to instruct.

In the instance before us, as likewise in Prov. i. 6; Ps. xlix. 5; lxxviii. 2, חִידָה and מָשָׁל are classed together as synonymous. The only shade of difference in meaning between them is, that while the former has respect to the obscurity, the latter regards the figurative traits by which the composition is characterized, and the impression which its diversified imagery is calculated to produce on the mind.

3, 4. The eagle was an apposite symbol of royalty — that bird being the king of all the feathered tribes, distinguished for its majestic size, its great perspicacity, its indomitable courage, the rapidity of its motion, and its resistless powers of attack. It had been employed by Jeremiah with reference to the king of Babylon, chaps. xlviii. 40; xlix. 22; and Daniel gives the wings of the eagle to the body of the lion when symbolically portraying the same power, chap. vii. 4. Compare Comment. on Ezek. i. From the predominance of the head and wings of the eagle as symbolical of kingly power in the Assyrian monuments lately discovered at Nineveh, it is evident the Jewish captives must have been familiar with the symbol; and considering the history of the times, they could have been at little loss to perceive to whom the symbol was designed specifically to apply. The "wings," described as "great and long," characterized the extent of monarchical power, including the army; and the "divers colors," the various nations, tribes, and languages over which that power was extended. The spread of the eagle's wings is sometimes not less than seven feet six inches. "Lebanon," being one of the most remarkable mountains of Palestine, is used symbolically to denote the whole country, and especially Jerusalem as the capital. The "cedar" for which that mountain has long been distinguished, was symbolical of kingly majesty, grandeur, and power, (see on chap. xxxi. 3, and Dan. iv. 10–12). The "highest branch" betokens the royal or reigning family, and צַמֶּרֶת, "the top of the young twigs," the youngest and most tender member of that family. צַמֶּרֶת, is a word peculiar to Ezekiel, who, besides the present passage, employs it in ver. 22; and chap. xxxi. 3, 10, 14. It is derived from צָמַר, *to cut off*, as wool in sheepshearing; hence it came to signify *the fleece*, and transferred to trees, the curly, fleecy, or woolly part of the branches. Jehoiachin, to whom reference is here symbolically made, was only eighteen years of age, when he assumed the reins of government (2 Kings xxiv. 8). Not only was the country of Babylon famous for its transport-traffic by means of the Euphrates, but the city itself was celebrated for its manufacturing and mercantile establishments. From the connection of Babylon with the Persian Gulf, the commerce carried on between that city and India must have been immense. The term כְּנַעַן, is here to be understood according to the explanation

5 placed it in a trafficking city. And he took of the seed of the land, and set it in a field of seed; he took it beside great waters,
6 he set it as a willow. And it sprouted and became a spreading vine, of low stature; its branches turned towards him, and its roots were under him; and it became a vine, and produced branches, and shot forth beautiful twigs.
7 And there was another great eagle with great wings and much plumage; and behold, this vine bent her roots towards him, and shot forth her branches towards him from the terraces of her
8 plantation, that he might water her. She was planted in a good soil by great waters, that she might produce branches and bear
9 fruit, to become a goodly vine. Say: Thus saith the Lord Jehovah: Shall she prosper? Shall he not pluck up her roots, and cut off her fruit, that she may wither, that all her fresh foliage may wither? yet not with great power, nor with much

which follows of the country and metropolis of the Babylonians.

5. זֶרַע הָאָרֶץ, *the seed of the land*, means what we should call "a son of the soil," as distinguished from a foreigner. On the removal of Jehoiachin, the king of Babylon did not choose a Chaldean or other foreign general to succeed him as stadtholder, but his uncle Zedekiah of the royal Davidic family. קָח with Kamets to distinguish it from קַח, the Imperative, and abbreviated for לָקַח, *he took*. הִצְפָצָה occurs only here, and is designated by Winer: *perobscurum*. Judging from the form הִצְפָצָה, derived from חוּל, it is most natural to refer the word to צוּף, *to flow, overflow*, and to regard it as designating some plant or tree noted for its fondness for water. The Rabbinical interpretation *willow*, derives confirmation from the Arabic صفصاف, *salix* (see Kitto, Art. TZAPHTZAPHA. In poetic style כְּ, *like*, is frequently omitted. The comparison of Zedekiah to a willow is anything but honorable to him. Though there were no מַיִם רַבִּים in Palestine to be compared with those of the Euphrates, yet the language may also be applied to that country in consideration of the abundance of water with which it was supplied.

Compare Deut. viii. 7, and ὕδατα πολλά, John iii. 23. There is no departure from the propriety of the figure in representing the vine as growing in low watery places. It is not uncommon in France and Italy to plant vines in such a situation, in which they trail or creep along the surface of the ground, and of course quite contrast with those which grow up along walls or are supported by trees. The vine was also cultivated in Egypt in the low lands covered with the mud of the Nile. The subjection of Zedekiah to Nebuchadnezzar is significantly expressed by his being turned towards him; while he continued faithful as his vassal, though he never rose to any elevation, yet the affairs of the kingdom went on peaceably, and the subjects increased rather than diminished.

7. The other symbolical eagle, to whose description the parable now proceeds, was Pharaoh, king of Egypt. He was also a monarch of great power, and ruled over many different nations. Tired of subjection to the king of Babylon, Zedekiah applied to Pharaoh in the hope that he would send an army to establish the independence of his throne.

8-10. If Zedekiah had maintained his fidelity to Nebuchadnezzar, there was

10　people to carry her away from her roots. And, behold, being planted, shall she prosper? Shall she not, when the east wind toucheth her, utterly wither? in the terraces of her plantation she
11　shall wither. And the word of Jehovah came unto me, saying:
12　Say now to the rebellious house: Know ye not what these things mean? Say: Behold, the king of Babylon came against Jerusalem, and captured her king and her princes, and conveyed
13　them to himself to Babylon. And he took of the seed royal, and made a covenant with him, and caused him to enter into an
14　oath; and he took away the mighty men of the land, that the kingdom might become depressed, and not raise itself up, but

nothing to threaten a reverse in the affairs of his government, but, on the contrary, the prospect of increasing prosperity. By his perfidy, however, the hopes of the nation were entirely blasted, and its destruction effected. Michaelis, supposing that the king of Babylon must have brought a large army against Jerusalem when he captured it in the time of Zedekiah, suspects the negative לֹא in the sentence וְלֹא־בִזְרוֹעַ גְּדוֹלָה וּבְקָהָל רָב (ver. 9), but finding his conjecture not substantiated by any MS. authority, he translates agreeably to the printed Hebrew text. Hävernick appears to have stumbled at the same difficulty, and endeavors to get over it by referring the agent to Pharaoh, and not to Nebuchadnezzar. To this construction, however, which is forced and unnatural, we are not necessitated, since there is nothing in the shape of historical evidence to show that any great military demonstration was made at the final taking of Jerusalem by the eastern conqueror. In all probability, a division of the Chaldean army which had raised the siege of Jerusalem, remained on the frontiers of Egypt to watch the movements of the Egyptian troops, while those who returned found it no difficult task to gain the victory over the disappointed and helpless inhabitants of the Jewish metropolis. See Jer. xxxvii. לְמַשְׂאִית, the Infinitive in Kal, with the performative מ after the Chaldee manner, and וֹת, agreeably to the ending of verbs לה. The רוּחַ קָדִים, *east wind*, proving noxious to vegetation in Palestine, is here fitly employed as a symbol of the Chaldean army, which came from that quarter. It was only necessary to bring that army into contact with the Jewish state, in order to effect its ruin. The interrogatory repetition in ver. 10 of the declaration made in ver. 9 is singularly forcible.

11. The prophet is instructed to furnish an explanation of the preceding parable, that the refractory Jews might be without excuse if they persevered in their course of disobedience against the clearly revealed will of Jehovah.

12-14. The Jews are here reminded of the plain matter of fact, that Nebuchadnezzar, represented by the former of the two eagles, had taken away Jehoiachin and his princes captives to Babylon, and having made Zedekiah swear fealty to him, placed him as his vassal on the Jewish throne, in the room of his nephew. He had thereby evinced how completely the Jews who remained in the land were in his power, but at the same time also his disposition to preserve their existence as a state, however humbled, if only they remained faithful to the contract (2 Chron. xxxvi. 10-13).

15 Though, as Scholz remarks, we have no account of this mission to the king of Egypt anywhere else in the Jewish records, we may rest satisfied with the testimony of Ezekiel, who was a con-

15 that it might keep his covenant and stand. But he rebelled against him, and sent his ambassadors to Egypt, that they might grant him horses and much people. Shall he prosper? shall he be delivered who doeth these things? yea, shall the breaker of
16 a covenant be delivered? As I live, saith the Lord Jehovah, surely in the place of the king who made him king, whose oath he despised, and whose covenant he brake, he shall die with him
17 in the midst of Babylon. Neither shall Pharaoh with his great army and great company act with him in the war, when the mounts are thrown up, and the towers built, to cut off many
18 persons: Because he despised the oath by breaking the covenant, though, behold, he had given his hand and done all these
19 things, he shall not escape. Therefore thus saith the Lord Jehovah: As I live, surely mine oath that he hath despised and my covenant that he hath broken, even it I will recompense
20 upon his own head. And I will spread my net over him, and he shall be taken in my snare, and I will bring him to Babylon, and will plead with him there for his trespass which he hath trespassed against me:
21 And all his fugitives in all his wings shall fall by the sword, and those who remain shall be scattered to every quarter; and ye shall know that I Jehovah have spoken it.

temporary. Here again the use of the interrogative gives force to the style of the prophet. Egypt was celebrated in ancient times for its breed of horses. According to Diod. Sic. (i. 45), the whole region from Thebes to Memphis was filled with royal stalls, and such was the abundance of horses, that no fewer than twenty thousand chariots, each having two, could be furnished in time of war. It was, therefore, natural for Zedekiah to turn to that quarter for aid, and, considering the hostile attitude of the two great empires, he might reasonably expect that his application would not be made in vain.

17. The Pharaoh here referred to was Pharaoh-Hophra, known to the Greeks by the name of Apries or Vaphres, and supposed to be Psamatik III. of the Egyptian monuments. He was the successor of Pharaoh-Necho. See Comment. on Jer. xliv. 30.

18–21. נָתַן יָד, *to give the hand*, was, as it still is in the East, and among ourselves, a pledge of agreement or fidelity (2 Kings x. 15; Ezra x. 19; Jer. l. 15). Zedekiah is charged with having proved faithless to the oath and covenant of Jehovah; because in pledging his fealty to the king of Babylon he did it by a solemn appeal to the God of the Jews (2 Chron. xxxvi. 13). The threatening denounced against him was fulfilled five years afterwards by his being carried away captive to Babylon, where he died in prison. Jer. lii. 8–11. Instead of מִבְרָחָיו or מְבָרָחָיו, *his fugitives*, the Syr. and Chald. appear to have read מִבְחָרָיו, *his choice ones*, i.e. his nobles or generals. The accomplishment of this threatening would furnish an indubitable proof of the divine authority of the prophet.

22–24. In striking contrast with the Lord's dealing with Zedekiah in the way of judgment, which was calculated to sink the hopes of the church to the very lowest ebb, is here unexpectedly intro-

22 Thus saith the Lord Jehovah: 'I will also take of the highest branch of the lofty cedar, and will set it; from the top of its young twigs I will cut off a tender one, and will plant it upon a mountain high and eminent;
23 In a lofty mountain of Israel will I plant it, and it shall produce boughs, and bear fruit, and become a magnificent cedar, and under it shall dwell every bird of every wing; in the shadow of its branches shall they dwell.
24 And all the trees of the field shall know that I Jehovah have laid low the high tree, have raised on high the low tree; have dried up the green tree, and have made the dry tree to flourish. I Jehovah have spoken, and will do it.

duced a parabolic prophecy relating to the Messiah, and to the universality and prosperity of his kingdom. That this prophecy is strictly Messianic, Hitzig, Ewald, and other free-thinking expositors have been compelled to acknowledge. Indeed the language of the parable is so plain, that there was no necessity, as there was in regard to the preceding, to add any explanation. It is passing strange that Grotius should have adopted the idea advanced by some of the Rabbins, that Zerubbabel is the person intended. He never reigned as king, but was merely the Persian stadtholder. Nor could the prophecy by any possibility apply to the Asmonean princes, for they were of the tribe of Levi, and not of the family of David, which is here recognized. The Rabbins, Jarchi, Abendana, and Abarbanel, expressly declare in favor of the Messianic interpretation.

22. By הָאֶרֶז הָרָמָה, *the lofty cedar*, is meant the Davidic family, which, however treated with indignity, and trampled in the dust by Nebuchadnezzar, occupied a high place in the divine counsels, and was destined to rise to greater dignity than any mere earthly power. As the highest branch was the furthest from the roots, the reference is to the remote descendants of the royal family, and the *tender one* beautifully symbolizes the Messiah as the חֹטֶר, *shoot*, and the נֵצֶר, *sprout*, predicted Isa. xi. 1. The " high and eminent mountain " was Zion, Ps. ii. 6. It is here described as the mountain of the height of Israel, as at chap. xx. 40, in reference to Jerusalem, which at the time of the Messiah's advent was to be what it had been, the centre of all the tribes, who, restored to their land, would go up again to the festivals, as they had done before the revolt. It derived its chief glory, however, from its being destined to become the spot where the spiritual kingdom was to be established, and whence it was to extend its blessings throughout the whole world. The imagery in this parable is borrowed from what the prophet had employed in reference to the cedar of Lebanon (ver. 3). How despicable soever the kingdom of Christ may appear to a worldly mind, and however small it was at its commencement, it is truly prolific; and, while all the glory of earthly kingdoms fades and perishes, it affords refuge and nourishment to men of every color and every clime. Universal history proves that it is Jehovah who ruleth in the kingdom of men, and giveth it to whomsoever he will, debasing the proud and exalting the humble, agreeably to the predictions uttered by his servants the prophets. עֵץ, *tree*, is used here, as in chap. xxi. 15, figuratively of a prince or ruler.

CHAPTER XVIII.

This chapter contains a vindication of the rectitude of the divine government against an impious imputation to the contrary alleged by the unbelieving Jews. Jehovah begins by quoting a proverbial maxim current among them, to the effect, that they were suffering not on account of their own sins, but of those of their fathers, 1-4; the impartiality of the divine conduct is then illustrated by supposing a variety of instances: the first, that of a righteous father, 5-9; the second, that of a wicked son of a righteous father, 10-13; the third, that of a righteous son of a wicked father, 14-18; the fourth, that of a wicked son who repents, 19-23; and the fifth, that of a righteous man who deflects from a course of rectitude, 24. The chapter concludes with a summing up of the argument, 25-29, and an application of the whole to the case of the Jews individually — earnestly urging upon them the necessity of personal repentance as the only means of securing immunity from punishment, 30-32.
The whole is a noble piece of just reasoning on a subject of immense importance in relation to God's moral government.

1 AND the word of Jehovah came unto me, saying: Wherefore do
2 you use this proverb respecting the land of Israel, saying: The fathers have eaten sour grapes, and the teeth of the children are

1. This chapter connects intimately with the preceding. The happy state of things under the reign of Messiah had just been touched upon, and here it is convincingly shown that in punishing the Jewish nation Jehovah was acting on the strictest principles of rectitude, and that without individual repentance no hope could be entertained of participating in the blessings of the new dispensation.

2. From this verse, and from chap. xii. 22, 23, it appears that in the days of the prophet the Jews were accustomed to wrap up their infidel objections in sententious sayings, which they bandied about from one to another. The import of the proverb before us is, that the teeth of the fathers who ate the sour grapes should have been set on edge, and not those of their children who had not partaken of them; in other words, that while the guilty had been suffered to escape, the punishment had fallen upon the innocent. There is, in fact, couched in the language, the same spirit of self-righteousness for which, notwithstanding their national and personal guilt, the Jews were ever distinguished, with the additional aggravation of impiously charging God with injustice in punishing them.

There might have been some appearance of validity in the objection of those who made it, had they never been chargeable with idolatry and other sins therewith connected, or if they had repented of and forsaken their wicked courses; but it was urged with the worst possible grace by those who were to the full as wicked as their ancestors, or even worse, as they are represented Jer. xvi. 11, 12. If they had listened to the warning voice of the prophets, and abandoned the service of idols, they would have averted the calamities which they had brought upon the nation; or if they had at all been sensible of the enormous evil of sin, as committed against a holy God, instead of criminating, they would have justified him in the judgments which he had inflicted upon them. Those who truly feared Jehovah, so far from bringing any charge of injustice against him, would have been forward to acknowledge that he had punished them less than their iniquities deserved (Ezra ix. 13).

If the captivity did not take place in the days of their fathers, it was to be ascribed to the divine long-suffering, by

3 set on edge? As I live, saith the Lord Jehovah, ye shall no
4 longer use this proverb in Israel. Behold, all souls are mine;
  as the soul of the father, so the soul of the son is mine: the soul
5 that sinneth, it shall die. When now a man shall be just, and
6 practise judgment and justice, Hath not eaten upon the mountains, nor lifted up his eyes towards the idols of the house of
  Israel, nor defiled his neighbor's wife, nor approached a men-
7 struous woman, And hath not oppressed any, hath restored his
  pledge, hath not taken the spoil, hath given his bread to the
8 hungry, and hath covered the naked with a garment; Hath not
  lent on usury, nor taken interest, hath withholden his hand
  from wickedness, and hath executed the judgment of truth

which time was afforded them for repentance. That it happened when it did, was a demonstration to the living generation, that their sins could not go unpunished, but that verily there was a God that judgeth in the earth.

We read frequently in the Old Testament of God's visiting the iniquities of the fathers upon the children, but it is always with the proviso, expressed or understood, that the descendants persevered in the sins of their ancestors (Exod. xx. 5; Matt. xxiii. 30–32).

3. When Jerusalem was about to be destroyed, measures were adopted under the divine administration to secure the escape of the righteous, chap. ix. 1–4; and when the captivity in Babylon had worked out its intended result in recovering the Jews from their idolatrous practices, they were restored to circumstances of prosperity in their native land. In the whole of Jehovah's conduct to them, he made it evident, that he did not act with partiality or capriciously, but that he dealt with every one according to his works. He here employs the most solemn oath to confirm this fact, and to silence the daring of the infidel.

4. In this verse God asserts his universal propriety in his rational creation. כָּל־הַנְּפָשׁוֹת, all the souls, i.e. persons — the noblest part of the constituent elements of the human subject being put for the whole. He had created them all, and having endowed them with those powers and faculties which are necessary to constitute them subjects of moral government, he had a sovereign and indisputable right to deal with them in equity according to their deserts. In punishing the guilty, he acts without respect of persons. The individual culprit is dealt with on the ground of his own personal deserts. מוּת, to die, is here, as elsewhere, used in the enlarged sense of being subject to penal infliction; to suffer the punishment due to transgression; to become the subject of misery as the effect of retributive justice. Without any attempt at proof, Michaëlis asserts that Ezekiel adopted this acceptation of the term from the language of the Chaldeans among whom he lived.

5. In illustration of the proposition so emphatically laid down, the prophet proceeds with an induction of particular cases, arising out of the different characters, and relations of men. The first is that of an individual of irreproachable moral character.

6–9. Most of the vices here specified were expressly condemned in the law of Moses, and, having in all probability been rampant among the Jews in the days of Ezekiel, their enumeration furnished scope for the consciences of his contemporaries to operate in the way of conviction. "Eating upon the mountains," connected as the language here is with the worship

9 between man and man; Hath walked in my statutes, and kept
my judgments to practise truth; he is righteous, he shall surely
10 live, saith the Lord Jehovah. But if he beget a son who
is a robber, a shedder of blood, and doeth the like of one of
11 these things, But doeth none of those; but hath eaten upon
12 the mountains, and hath defiled his neighbor's wife: Hath
oppressed the poor and needy, hath taken away the spoil, hath
not restored the pledge, and hath lifted up his eyes to the idols,
13 hath wrought abomination; Hath given upon usury, and taken
interest: should he then live? he shall not live: he hath done
all these abominations; he shall surely die; his blood shall be
14 upon him. And, behold, he begetteth a son, who seeth all the
sins which his father hath committed, and feareth, and doeth
15 not like them, Hath not eaten upon the mountains, nor lifted
up his eyes to the idols of the house of Israel; nor defiled his
16 neighbor's wife; Hath oppressed none, hath not taken a pledge,
nor taken the prey, hath given his bread to the hungry, and

of idols, doubtless refers to idolatrous feasts celebrated in the "high places" where such worship was performed. That אֶל is used for עַל there can be little doubt. These prepositions are not infrequently interchanged in our prophet. For the sins of impurity here specified, see Lev. xx. 10, 18. So far was the individual referred to from being guilty of any acts of oppression, that he was distinguished for acts of benevolence. חֹב חֲבֹלָתוֹ, lit. *the debt of his pledge:* the meaning is, what is pledged with him for the payment of a debt. The Jewish law had many wise and benevolent enactments on the subject of pledges, Exod. xxii. 26, 27; Deut. xxiv. 6, 10, 11. נֶשֶׁךְ, the term used for usnry is very expressive. It literally signifies *biting*, and must have originated in the practice of taking exorbitant interest. The law of Moses absolutely prohibited the Jews from taking any interest from their brethren, but permitted them to do so from a foreigner, Exod. xxii. 25; Deut. xxiii. 19, 20. תַּרְבִּית, *increase*, from רָבָה, *to multiply, increase wealth*, is another term expressive of interest or usury, denoting riches obtained by lending money at high interest, or by making exorbitant charges on the natural productions of the soil. The man who was blameless with respect to all the points here specified was accounted צַדִּיק, *righteous* in the eye of the law, and was entitled to enjoy the life which the law secured.

10–13. The second case instanced by the prophet is that of an impious son, who, instead of following the good example of his pious parent, adopts a course directly the reverse, and unscrupulously indulges in crimes condemned by the law. Upon him an unmitigated sentence is pronounced. In the language of the Orientals the blood which a murderer has shed is said to be upon him, till it be avenged by his punishment.

14–18. The third case is likewise that of a son, not, like the former, of a righteous man, but of the unrighteous person whose character had just been depicted. This son is supposed to be shocked at the sight of his father's depravity, and to be influenced by a due regard to the consequences, to avoid the sins which his parent had committed. It is expressly declared that he should not be punished

17 clothed the naked with a garment; Hath turned back his
hand from the afflicted; hath not taken usury, nor increase,
hath executed my judgments, and walked in my statutes, he
shall not die for the iniquity of his father; he shall surely live.
18 His father, because he hath grievously oppressed, spoiled his
brother by violence, and hath not done that which is good in the
19 midst of his people, behold, now he shall die in his iniquity. Yet
ye say; Why? doth not the son bear the iniquity of the father?
When the son hath done that which is just and right, hath kept
20 all my statutes, and done them, he shall surely live. The soul
that sinneth, it shall die; the son shall not bear the iniquity of
the father, neither shall the father bear the iniquity of the son:
the righteousness of the righteous shall be upon him, and the
21 wickedness of the wicked shall be upon him. And the wicked,
when he shall turn from all his sins which he hath committed,
and shall keep all my statutes, and do that which is just and
22 right, he shall surely live, he shall not die. All his transgressions which he hath committed, shall not be remembered against
him; in his righteousness which he hath done, he shall live.
23 Have I any pleasure at all that the wicked should die? saith the
Lord Jehovah, and not that he should turn from his ways and
24 live? And when a righteous man turneth from his righteousness, and committeth iniquity, and doeth according to all the
abominations which the wicked man doeth, should he then live?
All his righteousness which he hath done shall not be remembered; in his trespass which he hath committed, and his sin in

for the crimes of his father, but that the father only, being the guilty party, should suffer. Instead of וירא taken by the Masoretes as a repetition of וַיַּרְא immediately preceding, and by them directed to be read וְיִרְאֶה, the full form of the future of the same verb, the LXX. have read יִירָא, καὶ φοβηθῇ, *and was afraid*, which is followed by the Vulg. and Arab. Considering that the difference does not amount to more than the change of a vowel-point, and that it better suits the connection, I have without hesitation adopted the latter reading. הֵשִׁיב יָד בְּיָד is to be understood in a good sense — to turn back the hand, i.e. from oppressing the poor. Comp. chap. xx. 22, to withdraw the hand from punishing.

19-24. Finding the unbelievers still disposed to indulge in their impudent criminations, notwithstanding the convincing declarations to the contrary just alleged, Jehovah condescends to adduce two other instances which equally go to prove the equity of his government. The former is that of a repentant sinner, who is dealt with, not on the score of his past transgressions, but on the ground of his new obedience: the Most High thereby testifying that he hath pleasure in rewarding right-doing rather than in punishing sin. The latter instance is that of a righteous man who abandons the righteous course which he had been pursuing, and indulges in sin. In his case, none of the righteous acts that he

25 which he hath sinned, he shall die in them. Nevertheless ye say: The way of the Lord is not equal. Hearken now, O house of Israel: is not my way equal? are not your ways unequal?
26 When a righteous man turneth from his righteousness and committeth iniquity, and dieth in them, for his iniquity that he hath
27 done, shall he die. And when a wicked man turneth from his wickedness which he hath done, and doeth that which is just and
28 right, he shall preserve his soul alive. Because he considereth, and turneth from all his sins which he hath committed, he shall
29 surely live; he shall not die. Yet the house of Israel saith: The way of the Lord is not equal. Are not my ways equal, O house
30 of Israel? are not your ways unequal? Wherefore I will judge you, O house of Israel, each according to his own ways, saith the Lord Jehovah: turn ye, and return from all your transgressions,

had performed should be taken into the account, but he should be punished for the sinful course which he had preferred to that of virtue (Heb. x. 38, 39; 2 Pet. ii. 20–22). Thus Jehovah equally evinced his abhorrence of sin, and his love of righteousness.

25. Jehovah here justly retorts the censure employed by the Jews, and appeals to their discriminative faculty for a judgment as to the impartiality of his proceedings, and of self-condemnation on themselves.

26–28. The two preceding instances reversed are again brought forward in justification of the divine conduct.

29. A repetition of the retort employed ver. 25, which pointedly throws back the objection upon the Jews themselves.

30. This verse contains a personal application of the argument, asserting Jehovah's determination to deal with the Jews individually according to their deserts, and calling upon them, in the prospect of his judgment, to sincere repentance and thorough reformation. If these did not ensue, they had nothing in prospect but utter destruction. שׁוּבוּ וְהָשִׁיבוּ, turn ye and return.

31. Many persons who have perplexed themselves with metaphysical speculations relating to human inability, have sadly stumbled at the call here given to the Jews to make to themselves a new heart and a new spirit. Strictly speaking, however, it is nothing more than a declaration of the duty of sinners to be otherwise minded towards God and holiness than they are. It does not require them to create within themselves any new faculties — that were a physical impossibility; but to exercise in the right direction the faculties with which, as moral and responsible agents, their Maker has endowed them. These faculties are as capable of being exercised in reference to good as they are in reference to evil; nay, they may be said to be more so, inasmuch as their original destination proceeded in that direction. Unhappily the mind of the unrenewed is under the influence of a corrupt bias and a disinclination to choose the right and the good; and while this is the case, their natural reluctance to holiness will prove an effectual barrier to their submission to the will of God. But, so to exhibit to their view the injurious consequences of a course of wrong-doing as to fill them with alarm, and induce them to give a patient hearing to the claims of rectitude, and finally effect their true conversion to God, is perfectly conceivable. The discovery of a superior good may prevail over their choice of evil so as to superinduce the contrary choice without in the

31 that iniquity may not be the cause of your ruin. Cast away from you all your sins in which ye have sinned, and make for yourselves a new heart and a new spirit; for why will ye die,
32 O house of Israel? For I have no pleasure in the death of him that dieth, saith the Lord Jehovah: turn ye, and live.

least trenching on the freedom of moral agency. In this view of the case, there is ample room left for the doctrine repeatedly and clearly taught in Scripture, that it is the divine prerogative to work a saving change in the hearts of sinners.

32. Completely to silence the cavils of unbelievers, what had been urged interrogatively, ver. 23, is here unequivocally declared, — that when Jehovah punishes it is not from any delight which he takes in the infliction of punishment. The very reverse is implied: hence the call to repent and live with which the chapter concludes.

CHAPTER XIX.

An elegy over the fall of the Davidic house and the Jewish state, set forth in the form of two parables: the former of the two, that of a lioness and her whelps, 1-9; and the latter, that of a fruitful vine, plucked up, and planted in a barren desert after its best branches had been burned with fire, 10-14.

1 AND thou, take up a lamentation for the princes of Israel;
2 And say:
What is thy mother? A lioness: she lay down among the lions,

1. קִינָה, LXX. θρῆνος, *a dirge, a lamentation, elegy;* a species of Hebrew poetry characteristic of the melancholy fate of those who are the subject of it, and the doleful feelings to which it gives utterance. Sometimes, as in that over Saul and Jonathan, it is exquisitely tender and pathetic. The royal personages here referred to, designated נְשִׂיאֵי יִשְׂרָאֵל, *princes of Israel,* were in reality those of the kingdom of Judah. They are so called because they were the only legitimate rulers of the Hebrew people. Those who had reigned over the ten tribes were, so far as the theocracy is concerned, merely usurpers. The LXX., of whose reading Houbigant approves, have τὸν ἄρχοντα in the singular; but, as Rosenmüller remarks, though the pronominal affix in אִמְּךָ, *thy mother,* is in the singular number, with special reference to Jehoahaz, then in captivity in Egypt, yet, there being more than one king referred to in the elegy, the plural expressed in the Hebrew text is sufficiently justified. לְבִיָּא, *lioness,* is certainly, as to form, masculine if pointed לָבִיא, for which Bochart contends; but the sense obviously required by the context justifies the Masoretic punctuation, which gives the feminine, however contrary to analogy according to that author, or savoring of grammatical artifice according to Gesenius. The latter otherwise approves of this construction, principally on the ground that many names of female animals have masculine terminations. Arab. لبيةَ, لبوةَ, *leaena.* The lion being a symbol of kingly power, the state, to which the monarch owed his birth and which nour-

3   in the midst of young lions she nourished her whelps; And
    she brought up one of her whelps, he became a young lion, and
4   learned to catch the prey; he devoured men. And the nations
    heard of him; he was taken in their pit, and they brought him
5   in chains into the land of Egypt. Now when she saw that de-
    layed, perished, was her hope, she took another of her whelps,
6   and made him a young lion. And he went up and down among
    the lions; he became a young lion, and learned to catch the prey:
7   he devoured men. And he destroyed their palaces, and laid
    waste their cities; and the land was desolate, and the fulness

ished and supported him, might appropriately be represented as his mother. Comp. 2 Chron. xxxvi. 1. The concluding portion of the verse describes the position of the Jewish state in relation to the surrounding monarchies. רִבְצָה, her *lying down*, is expressive of the feelings of false security which she cherished in that position. Comp. Gen. xlix. 9; Num. xxiii. 24; xxiv. 9.

3, 4. וַיַּעַל is the apocopated future of Hiphil, and is distinguishable from the future of Kal only by the connection. כְּפִיר, *the young lion* here spoken of, was Jehoahaz, the son of Josiah, who affected to be a brave warrior, but, having provoked the jealousy of Pharaoh-Necho was taken prisoner at Riblah in Syria, and carried captive into Egypt, 2 Kings xxiii. 33. שַׁחַת, *pit*, is elsewhere used of artificial pitfalls for catching wild beasts. See my Comment. on Isa. xxiv. 17. The term may here be taken as signifying a stratagem of war. חַחִים, were properly *hooks* or *rings* fastened in the noses of wild beasts, in which a chain or cord was fastened in order to drag them about. It is here most appropriately applied in reference to the young lion.

5. How long the Jews waited for the restoration of their king from Egypt, we know not; but either having heard of his death, or despairing of such restoration, they proceeded to elect another: namely Jehoiachin, the whelp here referred to. This prince, it would appear, gave early indications of a warlike disposition, which caused Nebuchadnezzar to send and con-

vey him captive to Babylon, 2 Chron. xxxvi. 10. The words וַתֵּרֶא כִּי נוֹחֲלָה אָבְדָה תִּקְוָתָהּ have occasioned some diversity of interpretation; but little difficulty will remain, if we take תִּקְוָתָהּ, *her hope*, to be the nominative to both the verbs, and render: *and she saw that delayed, perished, was her hope*. While circumstances seemed to hold out some promise of the restoration of Jehoahaz, the Jewish people cherished some hope, but having been disappointed, their hope at last expired. נוֹחֲלָה the Niphal of יָחַל. Comp. Gen. viii. 12. That only these two princes should be exhibited in the parable, may be accounted for on the principle, that the others, such as Jehoiachim and Zedekiah, were placed upon the throne, one by the king of Egypt, and the other by the king of Babylon, and only held it as vassals, whereas Jehoahaz was raised to it by the choice of the people, and Jehoiachin reigned in the right of succession.

6–9. There is nothing in the historical narratives to throw light on this part of the parable. In all probability the lions spoken of were the petty kings of the neighboring states. That אַלְמְנוֹתָיו signify *palaces*, see on Isa. xiii. 22. This is confirmed by עָרֵיהֶם, *their cities*, immediately following. What has originated the idea of *widows* has been the use of the verb יָדַע, *to know*, which has been supposed to be used here in the euphemistic sense of having carnal intercourse with. This, however, seems harsh, and I am inclined, with Houbigant, Dathe,

8 thereof by the noise of his roaring. Then the nations set against him on every side from the provinces, and spread their
9 net over him; he was taken in their pit. And they put him in ward in chains, and brought him to the king of Babylon; they brought him into holds, that his voice might no more be heard upon the mountains of Israel.
10 Thy mother was like a vine in thy quietude, planted by the waters; she was fruitful, and full of branches, by reason of many waters;
11 And she had strong rods for the sceptres of rulers, and her stature was exalted among the thick branches and she appeared in her
12 height in the multitude of her branches. But she was plucked up in fury, she was cast down to the ground, and the east wind dried up her fruit; her strong rods were broken and withered;
13 the fire consumed them. And now she is planted in the wilder-

and others, to suppose that the reading must originally have been יֻבַּשׁ, though all the Hebrew MSS. have ד and not ר. LXX. ἰνέμετο; Targ. וְאַבְדֵּי, et diruit, deriving the verb from the root רָדַד, to break in pieces. Jehoiachin was carried captive to Babylon, where, though a prisoner, he was treated with kindness by Evil-merodach, 2 Kings xxv. 27–30.

10. Now follows the second parabolic representation of the kingdom of Judah under the symbol of a vine. It is parallel in language and meaning with chap. xvii. 5–10. The same figure had been beautifully employed in Ps. lxxx. בְּדָמְךָ, rendered by some in thy blood, affords no suitable sense. "In thy likeness," the rendering of Kimchi, taking דָם to be equivalent to דְּמוּת, resemblance, is likewise without any appropriate meaning. The LXX. have ὡς ἄνθος ἐν ῥοᾷ, as if they had read כְּרִמֹּן. The reading כַּרְמְךָ, thy vineyard, which is found in one of Kennicott's and in one of De Rossi's MSS., and approved by Gesenius, who renders: כְּגֶפֶן כַּרְמְךָ, like a vine of thy vineyard, must also be considered as insufficiently supported. On the whole, I must acquiesce in the interpretation of Piscator, adopted by Hävernick, in silentio tuo, from דָּמַם, Arab. ‌‌ﻗﻠﻮ, to be quiet, still, understanding

thereby the period of the Jewish history previous to the troubles and disasters which that people had brought upon themselves in punishment of their idolatries. At that time all was quiet and prosperous. Comp. Isa. xxxviii. 10.

11. בַּמֹּתֶיהָ שָׁרִים, strong rods, i.e. princes of the royal house. In her prosperous state, the Jewish kingdom so far from resembling one of those vines which creep upon the ground, was comparable to one trained up by the side of a wall, or supported by a tree. Some of these are carried to a great height, such as that mentioned by Schulz, the stem of which was a foot and a half in diameter, and about thirty feet high, while its branches formed a tent of upwards of fifty feet square. See Kitto, article VINE. עַל־בֵּין, a kind of compound adverb, the עַל expressing the elevated position of the vine, to which the affix ו in קוֹמָתוֹ is to be referred, though masculine in form, on the ground that no distinct recognition of sex is imaginable.

12, 13. With the formerly prosperous condition of the Jewish people, the prophet here contrasts the deplorable circumstances to which they were reduced in the captivity.

14. Hävernick appropriately calls attention to the circumstance, that the fire is said to proceed from a rod of her

14 ness, in a dry and thirsty land. And fire is gone out of a rod of her branches; it hath devoured her fruit; and she hath no strong rod, a sceptre to rule. It is a lamentation, and shall be for a lamentation.

branches, which he properly interprets as symbolising Zedekiah, which Cocceius had done before him. It was his revolt from Nebuchadnezzar which caused that monarch to march his army into Judea, take Jerusalem, and carry the Jews captive to Babylon. Thus an end was put to the vine and its branches — a consummation which every Jewish patriot must deeply have bewailed.

Resuming the word קִינָה, *a lament*, with which he had commenced the section, the prophet energetically concludes: קִינָה הִיא וְתְהִי לְקִינָה, *It is a lamentation, and shall be for a lamentation*. Part of the dirge had received its accomplishment, and was matter of history; the concluding part, relating to Zedekiah, belonged still to unfulfilled prophecy. As the former had been fulfilled in the melancholy experience of the nation, so the latter should be, within a brief period.

CHAPTER XX.

Certain of the elders of Israel having come to the prophet to consult him respecting the issue of events, 1, he is instructed not to give them any direct answer, but to exhibit to their view the guilt which, as a people, they had contracted in Egypt, 2-9, and afterwards in the wilderness, 10-26, and in the land of Canaan, 27-32. Jehovah then promises that after he shall have punished them in Babylon, and thereby purged away their idolatrous impurities, he will restore them to their ancient inheritance, 43-34.

1 AND it came to pass in the seventh year, in the fifth month, on the tenth of the month, that certain men of the elders of Israel came
2 to consult Jehovah, and they sat before me. And the word of Jehovah came unto me saying; Son of man, speak to the elders of Israel, and say to them: Thus speaketh the Lord Jehovah: Are ye come to consult me? As I live, I will not be consulted

1. The epoch from which the computation is here made is that of the deportation of Jechoniah to Babylon (chap. i. 2; viii. 1.) We are not told what was the subject on which the elders came to obtain information, but there can be no doubt that it had respect to the termination of the captivity which had recently commenced. A similar deputation had on a former occasion, as now, taken their position before the prophet (chap. xiv. 1).

2-4. Instead of holding out any hopes to them at the outset, the prophet is charged to pronounce upon the people the judgments which their rebellious conduct had merited. Jehovah declares, in the most solemn manner, that he will not hearken to the application made by the elders, which sufficiently shows that their sufferings had not yet effected any real reformation in their conduct. Comp. Ps. lxvi. 18. Instead of אִדָּרֵשׁ, ver. 3, upwards of thirty MSS. read אִם אִדָּרֵשׁ, which reading is also found in an early printed Heb. Bible. The ה in the dupli-

4 by you, saith the Lord Jehovah. Wilt thou judge them, wilt
thou judge; O son of man? Cause them to know the abomina-
5 tions of their fathers. And say to them: Thus saith the Lord
Jehovah: In the day when I chose Israel, then I lifted up my
hand to the seed of the house of Jacob, and I made myself
known to them in the land of Egypt; yea, I lifted up my hand
6 to them, saying: I, Jehovah, am your God In the day that I
lifted up my hand to them to bring them out of the land of
Egypt into a land which I had searched out for them, flowing
7 with milk and honey; it was the glory of all lands: Then I said
to them: Cast ye away each one the detestable objects of his
eyes, and defile not yourselves with the idols of Egypt: I,
8 Jehovah, am your God. But they rebelled against me, and would
not hearken to me; they cast not away each one the detestable
objects of his eyes, and did not forsake the idols of Egypt.
Then I threatened to pour out my wrath upon them, to exhaust
mine anger upon them, in the midst of the land of Egypt.
9 Nevertheless, I wrought for my name's sake, not to profane it
in the eyes of the nations in whose midst they were, to whom I
made myself known in their sight by bringing them out of the

cate form of the question ver. 4, strongly implies the affirmative. It was what the prophet could not but do. The case was so self-evidently flagrant, that he must at once have been prompted to execute his commission. In holding up to the view of the living generation the rebellious conduct of their fathers, he would furnish them with a portraiture of their own. שָׁפַט signifies not merely *to judge*, but also frequently, as here, to conduct a cause before a tribunal by adducing or hearing such evidence as bears upon it, and shall lead to the delivery of a righteous sentence.

5, 6. The threefold repetition of the lifting of the hand is designed to prove the earnestness of the gracious purpose of God to effect the deliverance of his people from Egyptian bondage. Such an action, accompanying the taking of an oath, betokened a solemn appeal to the Deity, and is here used anthropomorphically in reference to God.

7–9. Though Moses gives us no account of the practice of idolatry by the Hebrews while in Egypt, yet it is expressly stated, Josh. xxiv. 14; and indeed, it is scarcely conceivable that they could have escaped the contagion, surrounded as they were on every hand with idols and idol worship, and as yet but imperfectly acquainted with the character and will of the only living and true God. It is also implied in the history of the golden calf, Exod. xxxii. that they had still in their hearts a hankering after the gods of Egypt. See also ver. 24 of the present chapter. גִּלּוּלִים and שִׁקּוּצִים are two of the strongest words in the Hebrew language by which to express the abhorent character of idols. The idea of *polluted, filthy*, is inherent in them. Not only the miserable circumstances of their external condition, but still more the state of spiritual degradation into which the Hebrews had sunk, infinitely magnified the divine mercy which interposed for their deliverance. "Where sin abounded,

10 land of Egypt. And I led them out of the land of Egypt, and
11 brought them into the desert. And I gave them my statutes,
and made known to them my judgments, which if a man do, he
12 shall live by them. I also gave them my sabbaths to be a sign
between me and them, that they might know that I, Jehovah, am
13 their sanctifier. But the house of Israel rebelled against me in
the desert; they walked not in my statutes, but loathed my
judgments, which if a man do he shall live by them, and they profaned my sabbaths exceedingly: then I threatened to pour out
14 my wrath upon them in the desert to consume them. Nevertheless, I wrought for my name's sake, not to pollute it in the
sight of the nations in whose sight I had brought them forth.
15 And I also lifted up my hand unto them in the desert, not to
bring them into the land which I had granted, flowing with milk
16 and honey; it was the glory of all lands: Because they loathed
my judgments and did not walk in my statues, but profaned my
17 sabbaths; for their heart walked after their idols. But mine
eyes took pity upon them not to destroy them; and I did not
18 consume them in the desert. And I said to their children in the
desert: Walk ye not in the statutes of your fathers, neither
observe their judgments, nor defile yourselves with their idols.

grace did much more abound." The glory of this, as well as of the other attributes of Jehovah, was the ultimate end which he had in view in bringing them forth from the house of bondage. This is described, ver. 9, as his שֵׁם, *name*, i.e. the sum-total of his known perfections. See Rom. ix. 17; 2 Sam. vii. 23; Isa. lxiii. 12. The preservation of that name from desecration is repeatedly spoken of in this chapter; see verses 14, 22, 39.

10, 11. Having rescued the Hebrews from the tyranny of Pharaoh, and led them into the wilderness of Sinai, the Lord delivered to them the law by the hand of Moses. Obedience to the law would secure happiness.

12. It would appear from this verse, as well as from the wording of the fourth commandment, that the rest of the Sabbath had been intermitted in Egypt. אוֹת signifies a *sign, token, memorial*, here a proof or demonstration of the relation subsisting between Jehovah and the Hebrew people, and which, as enjoined upon them, was specially designed to keep up the remembrance of their deliverance from Egypt, Exod. xxxi. 13-17; Deut. v. 15. Though instituted at the creation of the world, and consequently binding upon all mankind, the day of rest was enforced with fresh obligations upon the Hebrews. Its observance or desecration will always be a demonstration of the state of religion among any people. The practical result of its sanctification will be an experimental acquaintance with the holy character of God, whose immediate object in enjoining it is to promote the holiness and happiness of his creatures. The seventh-day Sabbath was such by way of eminence, and its enactment formed part of the moral code. The other Jewish festivals, so called, were more ceremonial in their character.

13-24. Here the contrast between the divine character and that of the Israel-

19 I, Jehovah, am your God; walk in my statutes and observe my
20 judgments and do them: And ye shall sanctify my sabbaths,
that they may be a sign between me and you, that ye may know
21 that I, Jehovah, am your God. But the children rebelled
against me; they walked not in my statutes, and observed not
my judgments to do them, which if a man do he shall even live
by them; they profaned my sabbaths; then I threatened to pour
out my wrath upon them, to exhaust mine anger on them in the
22 desert. But I held back my hand, and wrought for my name's
sake, not to profane it in the sight of the nations in whose sight
23 I had brought them out. I also lifted up my hand to them in
the desert to scatter them among the nations, and to disperse
24 them among the countries: Because they did not execute my
judgments, but loathed my statutes and polluted my sabbaths,
25 and their eyes were towards the idols of their fathers: Wherefore also I gave them statutes that were not good, and judg-
26 ments by which they should not live. And I polluted them
in their own gifts, in their causing to pass through the fire
all that openeth the womb, that I might destroy them, that they

ites in the wilderness stands out most prominently. Though so recently delivered from Egyptian slavery, and with the prospect of the promised land before them, they nevertheless proved refractory and rebellious. Had it not been for the divine longsuffering, they must have perished in the wilderness.

25. Various attempts have been made to get rid of the apparent incongruity of the language here employed by the Divine Being. Taken absolutely it would be flatly contradictory of the purity and rectitude of his character, as well as of that of the laws which he actually gave to the Israelites. See Deut. iv. 8; Neh. ix. 13; Rom. vii. 12. The solution of the difficulty proposed by Manasseh Ben-Israel, that the words should be read interrogatively, is altogether unsupported by the structure of the sentence, and is otherwise not borne out by Hebrew usage. I agree with those interpreters who are of opinion, that the reference is to the idolatrous enactments of the heathen, and that the language may be best illustrated by comparison with Ps. lxxxi. 12; Hos. viii. 11; Acts vii. 42; Rom. i. 24; 2 Thess. ii. 11. Because the Hebrews cherished a propensity to indulge in idolatrous practices, God, in his holy providence, brought them into circumstances in which this propensity might be fully gratified, without his in any way imposing upon them the statutes of the Pagan ritual. On the contrary, he did all that was calculated in the way of moral influence to deter them from idolatry. Preferring, however, the rites and ceremonies of the heathen to his holy and righteous ordinances, they experienced not only that they were not good, but as the language, by meiosis, imports, that they were most pernicious.

26. The language of this verse is quite in accordance with that of the preceding. The Holy One did not actually pollute the people; he only permitted them to pollute themselves, and pronounced them polluted when they had rendered themselves such. In the language of the Hebrews, and of the Orientals in general, God is frequently said to do that which

27 might know that I am Jehovah. Therefore, speak to the house of Israel. O son of man, and say to them: Thus saith the Lord Jehovah: Thus further did your fathers dishonour me, in that
28 they grievously trespassed against me. When I brought them into the land, which I had lifted up my hand to give it to them, then they saw every high hill, and all the thick trees, and there they offered their sacrifices, and there they presented the provocation of their offering, and there they placed their sweet odors,
29 and there they poured out their drink-offerings. Then I said to them: What is the high place to which ye come? And they
30 called its name Bamah (*high place*) unto this day. Wherefore speak to the house of Israel; Thus saith the Lord Jehovah: Are ye polluted after the manner of your fathers? and, Do ye

he permits to be done. Comp. Storrii Observatt. ad. Analog. et Syntax. Hebr. p. 25, etc., and Hackspan in Nott. Philologico-Theolog. in varia SS. loca, P. ii. p. 897, etc. הַהֲבִיר elliptically for הַהֲבִיר בָּאֵשׁ, to cause to pass through the fire, i.e. as sacrifices to Moloch, Deut. xviii. 10; 2 Kings xvi. 3; xxiii. 10; Ezek. xx. 31. In this case, the sin was signally its own punishment; for what could have been more harrowing to the feelings of a parent's heart than thus to put his first-born infant-offspring to exquisite torture in honor of a grim idol? אָשֵׁם, to fail in duty, contract guilt, suffer punishment. LXX. ἀφανίζω.

27–32. After once more adducing the rebellious conduct of their fathers, even after they had been introduced into the land of Canaan, the prophet roundly charges the Jews of his own time with having committed the same sins, and therefore shows that they had no reason to expect exemption from deserved punishment.

27. עוֹד, *yet, still*, is emphatic. Instead of being moved by a sense of gratitude for the divine goodness manifested in the fulfilment of the solemn promises which God had made to the Hebrews, to induce them to return to his service from that of idols, the ancient Israelites persisted in the practice of idolatry. In זֹאת is an ellipsis of בְּ.

28. The וְ in וַיִּרְאוּ is simply continuative, and is in this connection unsusceptible of the construction which Hävernick puts upon it, as if it were designed to express the idea that the Hebrews joined the worship of idols to that of the true God. It merely unites the two clauses.

29. Michaëlis is of opinion that בָּמָה is equivalent to בָּמָה, and renders: *renit nescio ad quid;* but this appears far fetched. There does not appear to be anything more than a paronomasia in the words הַבָּמָה and הַבָּאִים, just as there is in בָּה and בָּמָה. There is no reason to believe that the ancient Hebrews attached any other etymological idea to בָּמָה than their descendants who applied it to places of idolatrous worship erected on mountains or other eminences. Root בָּמָה, *to be high;* equivalent to רָמָה. LXX. τί ἐστιν ἀβαμά. Owing to the idolatrous purposes to which the heathen prostituted such high places, Moses interdicted the use of them even for the worship of the true God, Deut. xii. 1–5. The exceptions, which we meet with in the Jewish history, of David and other pious men sacrificing on eminences, took place under peculiar circumstances, mostly before the altar was set up on Moriah.

30. The interrogations in this verse strongly imply the affirmative. The

31 commit whoredom after their abominations? For when ye offer your gifts in causing your children to pass through the fire ye pollute yourselves with all your idols unto this day: and should I be consulted by you, O house of Israel? As I live, saith the
32 Lord Jehovah, I will not be consulted by you. And that which cometh up in your mind shall by no means happen, which ye say : We will be as the nations, as the families of the countries
33 to serve wood and stone. As I live, saith the Lord Jehovah, surely with a strong hand, and with an outstretched arm, and
34 with fury poured out, I will rule over you. And I will bring you out from the peoples, and gather you from the countries in which ye have been scattered, with a strong hand, and with an
35 outstretched arm, and with fury poured out. And I will bring you into the desert of the peoples, and contend with you there
36 face to face. As I contended with your fathers in the desert of the land of Egypt so will I contend with you, saith the Lord
37 Jehovah. And I will cause you to pass under the rod, and
38 will cause you to enter into the bond of the covenant. And I will separate from among you the rebellious, and those who sin against me ; I will cause them to go forth from the land of their sojournings, but they shall not come into the land of Israel,

Jews addressed were equally guilty with their fathers.

31. Between such characters and the holy God of Israel, there could be no communion. The application, therefore, referred to, ver. 3, was utterly fruitless.

32. The Jews flattered themselves that none of the heavy judgments with which the prophets had threatened them would come upon them, and that they should be allowed unmolested to indulge their idolatrous propensities.

33. This verse and those which follow strongly contrast with that which goes before. The Jews had imagined that their dispersion would not extend beyond the neighboring countries; but Jehovah declares that he would punish them severely, until he had thoroughly corrected the evils which had prevailed among them, and then he would restore them to Jerusalem.

35–39. בְּדְבַּר הָעַמִּים, *the desert of the peoples,* a phrase apparently selected, partly with reference to the vast tracts of desert country which lay between Judea and Babylon and in other parts of that empire, and partly as parallel with the wilderness of Arabia, to direct the thoughts of the Jews back to the punishments which were there inflicted upon their fathers. Jehovah threatens to deal with them as in open court, by clearing those who had repented of their wickedness, and punishing the obstinate, as he had done their fathers of old.

37. All attempts to derive כָּסְרָה in the phrase מָסֹרֶת הַבְּרִית, *the bond of the covenant,* from any other root than אָסַר, *to bind,* have proved unsatisfactory. The Jews should be brought, by means of the severe discipline which they should undergo, to a due sense of their obligations to obey the divine law. By the ancient covenant they should again be bound to the service of Jehovah. See for the accomplishment of the prophecy, Neh. ix., x.

39 and ye shall know that I am Jehovah. And ye, O house of Israel, thus saith the Lord Jehovah: Go ye, serve ye every one his idols, and afterwards, since ye will not hearken unto me, profane not my holy name any more with your gifts and with
40 your idols. For upon my holy mountain, upon the mountain of the height of Israel, saith the Lord Jehovah, there shall all the house of Israel serve me, all of them in the land; there will I be favorable to them, and there will I require your heave-offerings, and the first-fruits of your oblations in all your holy
41 things. With a sweet savor I will accept you, when I bring you out from the peoples, and gather you from the countries in which I scattered you, and I will be sanctified among you in the
42 sight of the nations. And ye shall know that I am Jehovah, when I bring you into the land of Israel, to the land which I
43 lifted up my hand to give it to your fathers. And ye shall remember there your ways, and all your doings by which ye are polluted, and ye shall be loathsome in your own sight for all

38. The language here implies that the great body of the nation should be recovered from idolatry, and return to their native land, and that only a portion would continue in a state of rebellion against Jehovah, and consequently remain in exile. בָּרַר has been suggested by בָּרַר, with which the preceding verse concludes, and with it forms a paronomasia. בָּרַר is here to be taken, not in the sense of morally cleansing the persons spoken of, but in that of *separating* them from regenerated Israel, as dross is from purified metal.

39. Jehovah here utterly disowns all relationship with the rebels. He would have idolatrous worship severed from all connection with his name. The tone in which they are addressed is one of the keenest irony. Comp. Rev. xxii. 11. It is as much as to say: Well, since you will not listen to me and return to my service, you may take your own course, we henceforth part company. וְאַחַר, *and afterwards*, is intended to give emphasis to the address, and anticipates the continued apostasy of the rebels.

40. By "the mountain of the height of Israel" we are to understand mount Moriah. In the preceding verse the rebellious portion of the people are called "the house of Israel," because they retained the character by which that people had been notoriously distinguished. In this verse the designation is given to the nation in a good sense, as restored to the practice of true religion. They should no longer repair with their offerings to the high places throughout the land, but should all congregate at the appointed festivals, as of old, at Jerusalem and there present acceptable worship to their covenant God.

41, 42. The restoration of the Hebrews from the captivity, and the re-establishment of their religious services, would have the double effect of procuring honor to Jehovah from the surrounding nations, and attesting in their own experience the happiness springing out of the true knowledge of the divine character.

43, 44. Contrasting their renewed condition with their former abominations, they would be filled with self-abhorrence on account of all their wicked ways. Genuine and deep contrition always accompanies true conversion. See Neh.

44 your evils which ye have committed. And ye shall know that I am Jehovah, when I deal with you for my name's sake; not according to your wicked ways, and according to your corrupt doings, O house of Israel, saith the Lord Jehovah.

ix. Nothing tends so much to deepen this contrition as the view which is obtained of the forbearing and forgiving mercy of God, who, when he might have justly inflicted unmitigated wrath, remembers unmerited mercy.

Here the chapter properly concludes in the Hebrew Bible, and in several of the versions. The following five verses so evidently belong to the following chapter, that they ought never to have been separated.

CHAPTER XXI.

This chapter, to which the five concluding verses of that preceding are introductory, relates to the conquest of Judea and Jerusalem by the Chaldeans; and was delivered about five years before that event. The prophet begins by delivering a parable of a forest on fire, 1-5 (chap. xx. 45-49). He then changes the figure employed in the parable to that of an unsheathed sword drawn against the guilty land of Israel, 6-10; and, to denote the greatness of the catastrophe, uses signs of vehement grief, 11-12. He next resumes the figure of the drawn sword, and enlarges upon it, in order more forcibly to set forth the calamities of the war, 13-22; after which the king of Babylon is introduced into the scene, divining by arrows in order to determine which of the two capitals he should attack first, Rabbah or Jerusalem, 23-29. Zedekiah, the last king of the Jews, is now pointedly addressed; and, after a prediction of the total overthrow of the Jewish affairs, the advent of the Messiah is promised, 30-32. The last five verses form a distinct prophecy against the Ammonites, 33-37.

Most interpreters have grievously complained of the obscurity which rests over this section of our prophet, and the unsettled state of the text, to which, in part, it is attributable. Still, with all the difficulties, the general import may easily be determined. In some portions the language is smooth and easy; in others, it is abrupt and rugged, resembling, as Hävernick suggests, the struggle of a war-song, and is thus in perfect keeping with the subject to which it refers.

1 AND the word of Jehovah came unto me, saying: Son of man,
2 set thy face towards the south, and drop thy word towards the south, and prophesy towards the forest of the field of the south,

2. There are three words in the Hebrew text of this verse to express *south*: תֵּימָן, דָּרוֹם, and נֶגֶב. They are merely used as synonymes for the sake of varying the expression. The first is derived from יָמִין, *to be on the right*, borrowed with reference to the position of the quarter of the heavens when facing the east: hence also יָמִין, signifying both the *right hand*, and the *south*. דָּרוֹם is of less frequent occurrence, and besides in our prophet, and once in the Pentateuch, is found only in Job and Ecclesiastes. The derivation, as Fürst remarks, is still *ἐν αἰνίγμασι*. נֶגֶב, נֶגֶב in the Samar., Chald., and Syr. dialects, signifies *to be dry, dried up*: hence the south, where the heat of the sun is most severely felt. The LXX. retain the original terms θαιμάν, δαρόμ, ναγέβ. The Vulg. has Austri, Africum, and Meridiani. All the three terms specially apply here to the

3 And say to the forest of the south: Hear the word of Jehovah: Thus saith the Lord Jehovah: Behold, I will kindle a fire in thee, and it shall devour every green tree in thee, and every withered tree; the flaming flame shall not be quenched, and all faces shall be scorched therein, from the south to the north.
4 And all flesh shall see that I, Jehovah, have kindled it: it shall
5 not be quenched. Then I said: Ah, Lord Jehovah! they say
6 of me: Doth he not speak parables? Then the word of Jehovah
7 came to me, saying: Son of man, set thy face towards Jerusalem, and drop thy word towards the holy places, and prophesy
8 against the land of Israel. And say to the land of Israel: Thus saith Jehovah: Behold, I am against thee, and will draw my sword out of its scabbard, and will cut off from thee the right-

southern division of the Holy Land, of which at the time Jerusalem was the capital. Whether the words are designed to suggest the direction in reference to the position of the prophet in Babylon, as some suppose, may fairly be questioned. הַשָּׂדֶה נֶגֶב, instead of הַנֶּגֶב, as it stands ver. 3. The Article occupies its present position, contrary to rule, by attraction to the preceding יַעַר, which it was designed to render specially definite.

By "the forest" is meant the densely populated country of Judea, trees being understood figuratively to denote the inhabitants. הַטֵּף, drop, a term borrowed from the falling of rain, or the dropping of honey, and generally employed to denote gentle, flowing, and pleasing discourse; but here used of what the prophet was sternly to deliver in the way of commination. It is often used of prophesying.

3. The forest, apostrophised, is here declared to be set on fire by Jehovah, and consumed by an universal conflagration. In לֶהָבָה שַׁלְהֶבֶת is a paronomasia. To express the fearful character of the conflagration, the prophet employs this peculiar phrase, compounded of two forms of the same word, the latter of which is taken from the Shaphel conjugation in Aramaic. Their common root is לָהַב, Arab. لهب, Eth. ΛUΠ to

burn, inflame. צָרַב, Arab. ضرب, percussit, punxit, to scorch, burn. From the use of כָּל־בָּשָׂר, ver. 9, it is evident, that כָּל־פָּנִים is to be taken in the sense of *all faces* or *persons*, and not extended so as to denote all parts of the country — the whole superfices — as Rosenmüller, Maurer, and Hitzig interpret.

5. Desirous of shifting off the application of the prophecy to themselves, the Jews pretend not to understand it. They accuse Ezekiel of employing a high parabolic style.

6, 7. The prophet is now instructed to address himself directly against the city which had been specially consecrated to Jehovah, but which the Jews had polluted with their idolatries. מִקְדָּשִׁים, *sanctuaries*, include not only the temple with its holy places, but also the other edifices appropriated in purer times to divine worship, and afterwards called synagogues. Ps. lxxiii. 17. Instead of מְקֻדָּשִׁים however, three MSS. read מִקְדָּשָׁם, *their sanctuary*, which reading is supported by the Syr., but the LXX., Vulg., and Arab. exhibit the plural.

8. The symbol of fire is here exchanged for that of sword, which afterwards, with much force, occupies so prominent a place in the chapter. The Jews were not yet to be told in plain language what was to befall them. What had

9 eous and the wicked. Because I will cut off from thee the righteous and the wicked, therefore my sword shall go forth out
10 of its scabbard against all flesh from the south to the north. And all flesh shall know that I, Jehovah, have drawn my sword out
11 of its scabbard: it shall not return any more. And thou, son of man, groan with the breaking of thy loins, and with bitterness
12 groan in their sight. And it shall be when they shall say unto thee: Why groanest thou? then thou shalt say: For the report, because it cometh: and every heart shall melt, and all hands shall be feeble, and every spirit shall faint, and all knees shall flow as water; behold, it cometh, and shall take effect, saith the Lord Jehovah.
13 Again the word of Jehovah came unto me, saying: Son of man,
14 prophesy and say: Thus saith Jehovah: Say, a sword! a sword!

been told them was intelligible enough to those who were inclined to receive instruction. Tanchum interprets צַדִּיק, *righteous*, of those who regarded themselves as such, though they were not such in reality. The term would rather seem to be here used antithetically with רָשָׁע, *wicked*, for the purpose of indicating the universality of the destruction which was coming upon the country. It is as much as to say, that all should be involved in the common calamity. What is thus declared is quite in accordance with what we daily witness in the history of our race. Afflictions are the common lot of all. In national calamities, so far as suffering viewed simply in itself is concerned, no outward distinction is made between the good and the bad. Both appear to be treated substantially alike. There is no real contradiction, however, between the doctrine taught in this passage, and that vindicated chap. xviii. Though removed from their native land along with the wicked, inasmuch as they were nationally connected with them, yet the righteous were to be regarded only as the subjects of corrective discipline, whereas to the idolatrous Jews the sufferings were unmitigated punishment. The LXX., unable to reconcile the text with their conceptions of the Divine government have rendered צַדִּיק וְרָשָׁע by ἄνομον καὶ ἄδικον, *the lawless and unrighteous*. מִנֶּגֶב צָפוֹן, ver. 9, wants the local ה at the end of the latter word, which is expressed מִנֶּגֶב צָפוֹנָה, ver. 3. "From south to north," takes in the whole extent of the country.

11. The more deeply to affect his countrymen with a sense of the dire calamities which were soon to overtake them, the prophet is commanded openly to assume the appearance of a person in deep distress; clasping his loins with his hands, as sadly bruised, and giving utterance to piteous groans in the bitterness of his spirit, he was to present himself before them.

12. The import of the prophetic signs is here expressly declared. As they saw the prophet, so should it be universally throughout the land.

14. The prophet now proceeds to enlarge upon the symbol of the sword, which he had introduced, ver. 8. All is now ready for the onslaught. The repetition in חֶרֶב חֶרֶב, *a sword, a sword*, is not without effect — definitely pointing to the destructive weapon to be employed in the war. To augment the terror which the announcement was calculated to inspire, the sword is described as הוּחַדָּה, *sharpened*, prepared to do exe-

15 both sharpened and polished! It is sharpened, that slaying, it may slay; it is polished, that it may glitter: should we make
16 mirth? the rod of my son contemneth every tree. And he gave it to be polished, that it might be handled; it is a sharpened sword, and it is polished, to give it into the hand of the slayer.
17 Cry out and howl, O son of man, for it shall be against my people, against all the princes of Israel, they are delivered to the sword together with my people, therefore smite upon thy
18 thigh. Surely it is tried; and what, if indeed the rod despise!

cution, and also מְרוּטָה, *polished*. Root מָרַט, *to smooth, polish*, particularly the head by plucking out the hair: here transferred to the sword. מְרוּטָה, the Pahul participle of Kal; מֹרָטָּה, in the following verses, a contracted form of מְמֹרָטָה, the participle of Pual. The Dagesh is euphonic, but is omitted in several MSS. The glittering of a brightly polished sword, wielded in the sun, is truly terrific. Comp. Deut. xxxii. 41; Job xx. 25.

15. The sword was one of the deadliest weapons of ancient warfare; hence the frequent reference to it, when wars, of which it is considered as the appropriate symbol, are spoken of in the Old Test. אוֹ נָשִׂישׂ is abruptly introduced, and has much perplexed interpreters. The best sense appears to be that brought out in our common version, in which נָשִׂישׂ is taken as the first person plural of the future in Kal of the root שׂוּשׂ or שִׂישׂ, *to rejoice, be glad, merry*, or the like. There is thus no occasion for any conjectural emendation. The only difficulty, with such construction, lies in the particle אוֹ, which I consider to be used simply as an interrogative conjunction. Reproving his countrymen for their indulgence in levity and mirth, when such dire calamity was staring them in the face, he asks: *should we make mirth?* — implying that nothing could be worse-timed under such circumstances. Compare for the sentiment Isa. v. 11, 12; Amos vi. 5. The sword of Nebuchadnezzar would no more spare Judah than any other nation. It is represented as setting at nought the Jewish power equally with that of every other people. None had been able to withstand the universal conqueror. שֵׁבֶט, *rod*, is here used of the instrument of correction or punishment, and the Genitive in שֵׁבֶט בְּנִי, *the rod of my son*, is that of object: i.e. the instrument employed in punishing my son, as חֲמַס אָחִיךָ, *the violence of thy brother*, means, the violence done to thy brother. בְּנִי, *my son*, designates the Jewish people, as in Hos. xi. 1. מֹאֶסֶת is the regular feminine participle of מָאָס, *to despise*, connected with שֵׁבֶט an epicoene noun. עֵץ, *tree*, is used figuratively to denote a prince or ruler, as in chap. xvii. 24.

16. וַיִּתֵּן, *And he hath given*, used impersonally for *and it is given*, according to an idiom common in Hebrew. The instrument of destruction was quite prepared, and only required to be employed by Jehovah against his apostate people.

17. The object of the Chaldean expedition is here definitely pointed out. The Jews were not to delude themselves with the idea that it was Egypt, or any other neighboring nation, that was to be attacked. The punishment was to be inflicted indiscriminately upon themselves. The prophet is on this account again charged to exhibit tokens of extreme sorrow. מְגוּרֵי אֶל חֶרֶב אֶת־עַמִּי, *delivered up to the sword together with my people*.

18. כִּי is here used, not as a particle marking cause or reason, but, as frequently at the beginning of sentences, expressing certainty. בֹּחַן is the Pual of בָּחַן, *to try, prove*. Comp. בֹּחַן אֶבֶן, Isa.

19   it shall not be, saith the Lord Jehovah. And thou, son of man,
     prophesy, and smite *thine* hands together, and let the sword be
     doubled a third time, the sword of the slain; it is the sword of
20   the great slaughter, which besiegeth them. That the heart may
     melt, and the fallen be numerous in all their gates, I have made
     bare the sword; alas! it is made to glitter, it is drawn to slay.
21   Be united, strike on the right, *attack* on the left, whither thy face
22   is appointed. And I also will smite my hands together, and

xxviii. 16. The nominative is שֵׁבֶט, *the rod*, i. e. of chastisement, the Babylonian power. בְּ gives emphasis to it, and may here be rendered, *indeed*. If Nebuchadnezzar should really despise the resistance made by the Jewish state, which he did (comp. ver. 15), what was to be expected as the consequence? That state must necessarily come to an end. לֹא יִהְיֶה, *it shall not be*. Such I regard as the meaning of this most difficult verse.

19. The words וְהִכָּפֵל חֶרֶב שְׁלִישִׁתָה, however apparently obscure, are properly susceptible of no other rendering than that given in the common version: *and let the sword be doubled a third time*. They seem designed to express the tremendous size and power of the sword to be employed. It was no ordinary foe that was to attack the Jews. All hopes of escape were vain. It was a sword that had been well tried; and proved successful in many a battle. חֶרֶב חֲלָלִים, *the sword of the slain*. Numerous were the victims who had perished by it. חָלָל I take to be a noun signifying *slaughter*. Comp. קְטֶל from קָטַל, and שֶׁבֶר from שָׁבַר. חֶרֶב חָלָל הַגָּדוֹל, *the sword of the great slaughter*. There may be a reference to the great battle at Charchemish, in which the king of Babylon had been victorious over his powerful rival. הַחֹדֶרֶת לָהֶם, *which besieges them, encircles them*. with reference to an army of swordsmen surrounding a city in a state of siege.

20, 21. אִבְחַת־חָרֶב, *the naked sword*, being spoken of in connection with the gates of the city, confirms the interpretation given of חֹדֶרֶת in the preceding verse in regard to the besieging of a city.

Numerous derivations have been proposed for אִבְחָה, but give little satisfaction. That of Schnurrer, from the Arabic بَاح *apertum, in omnium conspectu positum esse*, seems preferable to any other. The *nakedness of a sword* for *a naked sword*. הָבְחָה, Arab. مَعِ, viii. أَمْتَعَ, and مَعْطَ, *eduxit e vagina gladium*. Not only was the sword made bright, and thus ready for use, but, further, it was *drawn*, and just about to be used. Nebuchadnezzar had gone forth from Babylon, and was on the point of invading Judea. By a bold apostrophe, the sword in its threefold character, is summoned to unite its powers הִתְאַחֲדִי, and advance to the onslaught. The Chaldean army, in one collected body, was to proceed onward to Judea, taking whatever route came first, whether the southern or the northern. It was not to turn in any other direction than that in which it was appointed to move. מְעָדוֹת, the Fem. plur. participle in Pual of יָעַד, *to fix, set, appoint*.

22. By a strong anthropopathy Jehovah declares he will do what he had commanded the prophet to do, ver. 19. כַּף אֶל־כָּף, *hand to hand*, is expressive of the act of clasping the hands together as an indication of violent grief. By causing the divine fury to rest, is meant, not the forbearing to pour it out in judgment, but the full and permanent infliction of it.

In whatever obscurity this remarkable prophecy may be involved, the glittering sword flashes vividly through the whole.

23 cause my fury to rest. I Jehovah have spoken it. And the word
24 of Jehovah came unto me, saying: And thou, son of man, appoint thee two ways, for the sword of the king of Babylon to come; from one land they shall both go forth; and cut a hand at
25 the head of the way, cut a city. Thou shalt appoint a way for the sword to come: Rabbah of the sons of Ammon, and Judah in
26 Jerusalem, the fortified city. For the king of Babylon shall stand at the mother of the way, at the head of the two ways, to practise divination; he shall shake arrows, he shall consult

24. The "one land" whence the two ways proceeded was that of Babylon, and the ways ran in a westerly direction; the more northerly by Riblah in Syria; and the more southerly by Tadmor, or Palmyra, in the desert. The former was that usually taken from Babylon to Jerusalem; the latter from the same city to Rabbah on the east of the Jordan. The prophet is directed to cut out a *hand* (יָד), or a sign, pointing to the direction in which the Chaldean army was to proceed. This he was to place בְּרֹאשׁ־דֶּרֶךְ, *at the head* or commencement *of the way* where the two roads separated, each taking its own course; while we are necessarily to understand its being made to point toward that which the king of Babylon was to select, as we are taught in ver. 26. בָּרָא and בָּרָא signify *to cut*, or fashion by cutting into any shape or form whatever. בָּרָה, the cognate verb, also signifies *to cut*, and then, as a secondary signification, *to choose, select*. This last idea our authorized translators have adopted. That the hand is not supposed to have been formed by sculpture, would appear from the circumstance that, in case it had been so, the verb עָשָׂה or פָּסַל would have been employed. It may have been made of wood, just like our finger-posts, with the representation of a city cut in it. The word עִיר, *city*, is purposely indefinite, the Article being left to be supplied by the consciences of those whom the prophet addressed.

25. It may at first sight appear inappropriate, that Rabbah, the metropolis of the country of the Ammonites, should be mentioned before Jerusalem, the guilty city against which the prophet was specially commissioned to denounce the divine judgments; but, considering to what an extent the Jews had adopted the idols of the Ammonites, there was a singular propriety in first taking up the heathen city, to intimate that as the Jews had participated in its crimes so they might expect to share in its punishment. רַבַּת בְּנֵי־עַמּוֹן, *Rabbah of the children of Ammon*, so called to distinguish it from a city of the name of רַבָּה in the tribe of Judah. It was built on the banks of the river *Moiet-Amman*, which empties itself into the Jabbok. See more respecting this city, on chap. xxv. 1–7. Instead of simply expressing the name of Jerusalem, the other metropolis, that of the inhabitants is prefixed, to mark them as the guilty objects of the divine indignation. The reason why Jerusalem is here said to be בְצוּרָה, *defenced* would seem to be, to intimate the vain confidence which the Jews reposed in their fortifications.

26. Nebuchadnezzar is supposed to have marched his army to a certain point to the west of Babylon, where the road branched off into the two referred to, ver. 24. אֵם הַדֶּרֶךְ, *the mother of the way*, so called, not as is generally supposed, because there the road divided, for that is immediately afterwards described, as רֹאשׁ שְׁנֵי הַדְּרָכִים, *the head of the two ways*, but because it was the principal road. Comp. the Arab. ام الطريق, *via magna regia*. Here the monarch is

27 his family-gods, he shall inspect the liver. In his right hand shall be the divination of Jerusalem, to place the battering rams, to open the mouth with the war-cry, to raise the voice with shouting, to place battering-rams at the gates, to throw up walls,
28 to erect a watch-tower. Yet it is to them as a vain divination in their sight; they are under the most solemn oaths, but he will cause the perfidy to be remembered, that they may be taken.

represented as having been at a loss to determine which of the routes he should take; and, in order to decide, as having recourse to divination. Of this as practised by the ancients there were different kinds, some of which are here mentioned. קִלְקַל בַּחִצִּים, he shook the arrows, i.e. the helmet, quiver, or whatever else they were put into. קִלְקֵל, the Pilpel of קָלַל, to be light, swift. Arab. قلقل, Eth. አዕፋፍአ commovit, concussit. It is most probable that he caused the name JERUSALEM to be inscribed on one arrow, and RABBAH on another, and mixing them with others, determined to march against the city whose name was first drawn out. This mode of divining by arrows was practised by the Arabs till the time of Mohammed, who strictly prohibited it in the Koran, Sur. iii. 39; v. 4, 94. The art, as practised by the Greeks, was known by the name of βελομαντεία. Another species of divination to which the king of Babylon had recourse, was that of looking into the liver or the entrails of a newly-killed sacrifice, and judging that any undertaking would be prosperous or otherwise according as they were found in a healthy or unhealthy state. This art was called by the Greeks ἱεροσκοπία, Hieroscopy, and is mentioned by Diodorus (chap. ii. 29) as practised among the Chaldeans. Not satisfied with the use of these two species of divination Nebuchadnezzar consulted the תְּרָפִים, Teraphim, which appear to have been penates or family gods, from whom it was thought possible to obtain information relative to future events. See Gen. xxxi. 19, 34; Judges xvii. 5; xviii. 14.

27. The arrow with JERUSALEM upon it was, on being drawn, held by the king in his right hand, and exhibited to animate his army to prosecute its march against that city. Now follows the adoption of the measures requisite for besieging the city. רֶצַח and הְרוּעָה are parallel with each other. Connected as the former term here is with the opening of the mouth, it cannot well be taken in its usual signification of murder, but must be understood, as Gesenius explains, as an outbreak of the voice: both terms thus energetically expressing the horible war-shout of the Chaldean soldiers when commencing the attack. For כָּרִים and דָּיֵק see on chap iv. 2.

28. קְסָם. The Vau is marked by the Masoretes as יתיר, redundant. The prophet now represents the light in which the Jews were disposed to view the indications of the advance of the Chaldean army. Though prone themselves to believe in divination, they affect to despise it when it tells against them. That the Jews and not the Babylonians are intended, the connection convincingly shows. To the Jews, moreover, the second לָהֶם, to them, may be understood to refer, as the Jews had come under solemn engagements to be subject to the Babylonians, but those engagements they had violated; and for this, as well as their other sins, they were now to be punished. שְׁבֻעֵי שְׁבֻעוֹת, oaths of oaths, meaning the most solemn oaths. The construction proposed by Ewald, "weeks upon weeks," is less suitable. There is nothing corresponding to the words, either in the version of the LXX. or the Syr. The oaths were those the Jews

29 Wherefore thus saith the Lord Jehovah: Because ye are put in remembrance of your iniquity, in your rebellions being revealed, in the manifestation of your sins in all your doings; because ye are put in remembrance, with the hand ye shall be taken.
30 And thou, profane wicked prince of Israel, whose day is come, at
31 the time of the iniquity of the end: Thus saith the Lord Jehovah: Remove the tiara, and take away the crown; this shall not be this; exalt him that is low, and lay low him that is
32 high. Subversion, subversion, subversion, I will make it; this also shall not be, till he come whose is the right, and I will give

had taken to the king of Babylon. הוּא, *he*, refers to Nebuchadnezzar, to whom the Jews had proved faithless, and who now should recall to their mind the crime of perjury, of which they had been guilty.

29. The Jews are now directly addressed by the prophet, who expressly teaches them, that the judgment to be inflicted upon them was to be regarded, not merely as a punishment of their infidelity to the king of Babylon, but of all the sins which they had committed, in connection with idolatry, against their covenant God. Their acts of disobedience were so notorious, and they had become so universally depraved in their conduct, that no course was left but for punishment to be inflicted upon them.

30. The prophet now pointedly singles out Zedekiah. Though Hävernick and Fairbairn contend for " pierced through " as the signification of חָלָל here, as at ver. 19, I rather agree with the rendering of our common version, *profane*, which is supported by the LXX., Vulg., and Syr., and approved by Winer, Gesenius, and Lee. That חָלַל signifies not merely to pierce through, slay with the sword, but also *to make common*, or *profane, to pollute, defile*, is so fully admitted as to require no proof. That monarch, by his wickedness, had desecrated his character as the Lord's anointed, and the period of his punishment had now arrived. His reign and wickedness were to terminate together. By עֲוֹן קֵץ, *the iniquity of the end*, is meant the treachery of Zedekiah towards Nebuchadnezzar, by which he brought destruction upon the Jewish state. Comp. ver. 31 and chap. xxxv. 5.

31, 32. Since מִצְנֶפֶת is frequently used in the Pentateuch of the *turban* or *tiara* of the high priest, it has been supposed by some, after the Targum: אֲמַר נְבִיָּא מֹשֶׁה כַּהֲנָא רַבָּא נִיבוּל דָּא וּצְדְקִיָּה מַלְכָּא, that the same application of the term is intended in the present case, and that the design of the prophecy is to show that from this time forth both the sacerdotal and regal offices were to cease till the advent of Messiah, in whose mediatorial undertaking they should be restored and united. As, however, it is the king, and not the high priest, that is here expressly addressed and as עֲטָרָה, a derivative from same root with מִצְנֶפֶת, is used of the head-dress both of the one dignitary and the other, Isa. lxii. 3; Zech. iii. 5, the latter term may without violence be regarded as applicable to the royal diadem of Zedekiah. Winer, Gesenius, and Lee concur in this view of the passage. The use of the two terms, to express nearly the same thing, forms no objection, since it was no doubt the object of the prophet most emphatically to foretell the fact of the complete cessation of the royal rule in Judah. The words זֹאת לֹא־זֹאת, *this not this*, or with the substantive verb תִּהְיֶה, understood, *this shall not be this*, however enigmatically it may sound, is very expressive. Taking the Feminine as a Neuter, the meaning is: The present state of things shall cease. A complete revolution in Jewish

33 it him. And thou, son of man, prophesy and say: Thus saith the Lord Jehovah concerning the Ammonites and concerning their reproach, thou shalt even say: A sword! a naked sword! it is polished for slaughter, to consume because of the glittering.

affairs was at hand. That the last clause of the verse is not to be taken as the enunciation of a general truth, frequently taught elsewhere in Scripture, that God depresses the proud but exalts the lowly, but that it is to be understood specifically of the Messiah and of Zedekiah, appears from the direct reference to the former in the following verse. The two are here placed in the strongest contrast: the root out of the dry ground, Isa. liii. 2, whom the prophet sees in the future, and the haughty monarch immediately present to his view upon the royal Jewish throne. The commands given in this verse are a strong mode of declaring prophetically that the things should be done.

עַוָּה עַוָּה עַוָּה, *subversion, subversion, subversion*. The threefold repetition is intensive. Hengstenberg ingeniously supposes that this word was purposely chosen with reference to יָוֹן, verses 28 and 29. Indeed the LXX. and Vulgate have manifestly mistaken the words for each other, rendering ἀδικίαν, ἀδικίαν, ἀδικίαν: *iniquitatem, iniquitatem, iniquitatem*. The ה in אֲשֶׁר־הָ I would refer to מְלוּכָה, the *kingdom* or *royal dignity*, understood from the connection. The like reference lies in זֹאת, *this*, in the phrase גַּם־זֹאת לֹא הָיָה, *yea, this shall not be*: the kingdom should cease till the time specified immediately after. The words עַד־בֹּא אֲשֶׁר־לוֹ הַמִּשְׁפָּט וּנְתַתִּיו, *until the coming of him whose is the right, and I will give it him*, point so obviously to the Messiah, that it cannot but appear strange that ever they should have been applied to any other person. Some of the Rabbins and Schnurrer interpret them of Nebuchadnezzar, who was to exercise מִשְׁפָּט upon the Jews. Grotius, as usual, applies it to his favorite Zerubbabel. By Abarbanel and Abendana,

however, the passage is without scruple applied to the Messiah, as it is expressly by Ewald. To him belonged הַמִּשְׁפָּט, by which is meant, not הַצְּדָקָה, the *righteousness* which otherwise is represented as inherent in the promised deliverer, and which was to form the distinguishing feature of the dispensation that he was to introduce, but *the just claim* which he had to occupy the throne of his father David. That מִשְׁפָּט is used to signify *right* in the sense of claim or prerogative, see Deut. xviii. 3; 1 Sam. viii. 9, 11; x. 25; Jer. xxxii. 7.

Between this passage and Gen. xlix. 10, is a remarkable coincidence, so much so that some have supposed that our prophet had the latter in his eye when he delivered it. It has been maintained indeed that אֲשֶׁר־לוֹ is merely expressing in full the abbreviated form שִׁילֹה; but not to insist upon the fact, that the reading of many MSS. is שִׁילֹה, *Shiloh*, as in the Masoretic text, and not שֶׁלֹּה, it cannot be shown that this abbreviation of the relative pronoun, which certainly occurs in the writings of Solomon, was in use in the time of Moses. In the only passage to which an appeal in favor of such usage has been made, Gen. vi. 3, בְּשַׁגָּם, the rendering now most approved is, *because of their wandering*, or transgression, from שָׁגַג, *to err, go astray*. The strict parallelism between Gen. xlix. 10, and Ezek. xxi. 32, consists in what is common to both passages — the perpetuation of the regal authority of the tribe of Judah, in the person and reign of the promised Messiah.

33. Lest it should be supposed that because Nebuchadnezzar had taken the route to Jerusalem, and not that to Rabbah, therefore the Ammonites should escape being invaded by his army, the prophet is instructed to denounce judg-

34　They have seen falsehood for thee, they have divined for thee a lie, to deliver thee to the necks of the slain wicked, whose day
35　is come, at the time of the iniquity of the end. Shall it be made to return into its sheath? in the place where thou wast created,
36　in the land of thy nativity, I will judge thee. And I will pour out my indignation upon thee, I will blow upon thee with the fire of my wrath, and deliver thee into the hand of brutish men,
37　skilled in destroying. Thou shalt be to the fire for consumption: thy blood shall be in the midst of the land, thou shalt not be remembered, for I Jehovah have spoken it.

ment against them also. חֶרֶב, *a sword*, is repeated חֶרֶב חֶרֶב, as at ver. 14, and the same participal form מְרוּטָה is employed as there, הָכֵל, which some improperly refer to כּוּל, signifying *to be able*, is simply the infinitive in Hiphil of אָכַל, *to devour*, the א quiescing in Kamets. See Gesenius's Lehrgebäude, p. 333. לְפִי אֶרֶץ is to be connected with מְרוּטָה in sense. The חֶרְפָּה, *reproach*, with which the Ammonites are here charged, was their opprobrious and insulting treatment of the Hebrews at different periods of their history, and especially when Jerusalem was taken by the Chaldeans. See on chap. xxv. 3, 6; Amos i. 13–15.

34. רָוָה and בָּקַשׁ are historical Infinitives. The Ammonites also had those who practised divination, and flattered them with assurances of safety; but Ezekiel declares that they should prove fallacious. The feminine affixes in לָךְ and אֹתָךְ refer to אֶרֶץ, the *country* of the Ammonites, which is to be understood of its inhabitants. They were to be added to the number of the slain Jews whose wickedness had finally, in the providence of God, brought the Chaldean army from Babylon. Both were to share the same fate. Schnurrer remarks that the phrase: צַוְּארֵי חֲלָלִים, *the necks of the slain*, is used poetically for the slain themselves, whose headless trunks are represented as stretched on the ground.

35–37. These verses are by some referred to the Chaldeans, but I am rather inclined to regard them as a continuation of the threatening against the Ammonites. They were not to be carried away captives, like the Jews to Babylon, but were to perish in their own land. While the Jews were to be restored after the captivity had cured them of idolatry, the Ammonitish kingdom was to cease for ever. The prophecy was fulfilled five years after the destruction of Jerusalem. בֹּעֲרִים, *brutish*, not in the sense of stupid, unintelligent, but ferocious. LXX. βαρβάρων. The question, Whether God should cause the hostile operations of the Chaldeans to cease when they had destroyed the Jewish polity, is to be answered in the negative; as it in effect is in the following denouncement of judgment upon the children of Ammon.

CHAPTER XXII.

The prophet, having in the preceding chapter exhausted what has not improperly been called the prophecy of the sword, resumes the subject of the enormous guilt of the Jewish nation, on which he had historically expatiated in chapter twentieth. He begins by reciting the enormous crimes of which the inhabitants of Jerusalem were guilty, 1-12. He then, in an episode, predicts the punishment which was about to be inflicted upon them, partly in plain terms, and partly in imagery borrowed from metallurgy, 13-22. The third section of the chapter comprises a review of their moral corruption, as pervading the different orders of society, and bringing down upon the nation the righteous indignation of Jehovah, 23-31.

1 MOREOVER the word of Jehovah came unto me, saying: And thou,
2 son of man, wilt thou judge, wilt thou judge the bloody city?
3 cause her then to know all her abominations. And say: Thus saith the Lord Jehovah: The city sheddeth blood in the midst of her that her time may come, and maketh idols within her to
4 defile her. Through thy blood which thou hast shed, thou art guilty, and through thine idols which thou hast made, thou art polluted; therefore thou causest thy days to approach, and art come to thy years: therefore have I rendered thee a reproach to
5 the nations, and a scorn to all lands. Those that are near, and those that are distant from thee, shall mock thee, thou polluted
6 of name, and very tumultuous! Behold, the princes of Israel, each according to his power, were in thee that they might shed

2, 3. Compare chap. xx. 4. On account of the murders committed in Jerusalem, and the offering of children in sacrifice to Moloch, she might well be denominated עִיר הַדָּמִים, *the city of bloods*, or *the bloody city*, comp. vers. 3, 4, 6, 9; xxiv. 6, 9. In this respect she rivalled Nineveh, Nah. iii. 1, and might justly anticipate the same doom. לְ in לָבֹא is, as Rosenmüller observes, *Lamed eventuale*, pointing out the result of the sins of the people, in the catastrophe which they brought upon them. Instead of deriving any advantage from their idolatries, they were only involved thereby in ruin.

4. For בֹּא two MSS. read בַּע which is expressed in all the ancient versions. The Jewish commentators distinguish between the "days" and the "years" here mentioned, interpreting the former of the siege and destruction of Jerusalem, and the latter of the captivity in Babylon. For הַבֹּא we should have expected הַבֹּאָה in the feminine to agree with עִיר, but regarding עַם, *people*, as understood, the discrepancy in point of gender is removed.

5. טְמֵאַת הַשֵּׁם, lit. *the polluted of name*, not inaptly rendered in our common version, *infamous*. LXX. ἀκάθαρτος ἡ ὀνομαστή. Formerly Jerusalem had been renowned as עִיר הַקֹּדֶשׁ, *the holy city*. Now it had been defiled by every kind of crime. רַבַּת הַמְּהוּמָה, *great of confusion*, tumultuous, from the seditions and violence which obtained among the inhabitants. To all, both far and near, the Jewish metropolis was to be an object of derision.

6. Instead of reigning according to law and justice, the princes of Judah, acted in the most despotic manner, crushing by the strong arm of power all

7 blood. They treated lightly father and mother in thee; they oppressed the stranger in the midst of thee; they maltreated
8 the orphan and the widow in thee. Thou hast despised my
9 sanctuaries, and thou hast profaned my sabbaths; Tale-bearers were in thee in order to shed blood; they ate on the mountains in thee; they have committed atrocious wickedness in thee:
10 A father's nakedness was uncovered in thee; her that was
11 removed for the menses they humbled in thee. And one committed abomination with his neighbor's wife, and another hath atrociously defiled his own daughter-in-law; and another
12 in thee hath humbled his sister, his father's daughter. They took a bribe in thee in order to shed blood. Thou tookest usury and increase, and hast done violence to thy neighbor by oppression, and hast forgotten me, saith the Lord Jehovah.
13 Therefore, behold, I have smitten my hand at thine unjust gain which thou hast acquired, and at thy blood which hath been in
14 the midst of thee. Shall thy heart endure, or thy hands be strong, in the days when I shall deal with thee? I Jehovah
15 have spoken, and will do it. Yea, I will disperse thee among the nations, and scatter thee among the countries, and consume
16 thine impurity out of thee. And thou shalt be polluted in thyself in the sight of the nations, and thou shalt know that I am
17 Jehovah. And the word of Jehovah came unto me, saying:

who were the objects of their personal displeasure. זְרוֹעַ, *arm*, metaphorically *power, strength*.

7–12. An enumeration of sins expressly forbidden in the law of Moses, which were rampant in Jerusalem. אַנְשֵׁי, רְכִיל, lit. *men of traffic*, ver. 9, those who went about for purposes of trade, pedlars; and, as such generally propagated reports, the phrase came to be used in the sense of *tale-bearers*. Those here referred to appear to have been what in the present day we call *informers*. נִדָּה טֻמְאָה, ver. 10; the rendering of the common version, *set apart for pollution*, suggests the idea of a female devoted to prostitution, whereas all that the Hebrew expresses is one that is unclean by reason of the menstrual discharge. The character of the Jews, as here described, is aptly given by Tacitus:

"projectissima ad libidinem gens, alienarum concubitu abstinent, inter se nihil illicitum." (Hist. lib. v. cap. 5). The crowning sin with which the Jews are charged, and that which is strictly speaking the source of all sin, is forgetfulness of God, ver. 12. It is only as God is kept out of view as the omnipresent, omniscient, holy, and righteous Governor of the world that sin can be indulged in.

13. "Smiting with the hand" was a gesture expressive of displeasure and grief.

14. However sinners may brave the divine threatenings, their courage and imaginary strength must fail when God executeth his judgments upon them.

15, 16. The object to be attained by the dispersion of the Jews was their recovery from idolatry and from the

18 Son of man, the house of Israel are become dross to me; all of them are brass, and tin, and iron, and lead, in the midst of
19 the furnace; they are dross of silver. Therefore thus saith the Lord Jehovah: Because ye are all become dross, therefore,
20 behold, I will collect you into the midst of Jerusalem. As men collect silver, and brass, and iron, and lead, and tin, in the midst of the furnace, to blow the fire upon it to melt it, so will I collect you in mine anger and in my fury, and will leave you, and
21 melt you; I will even gather you, and blow upon you in the
22 fire of mine indignation, and melt you in the midst thereof. As the melting of silver in the midst of the furnace, so shall ye be melted in the midst thereof, and ye shall know that I Jehovah
23 have poured out my fury upon you. And the word of Jehovah
24 came unto me, saying: Son of man, say to her, Thou art a land not cleared, nor rained upon in the day of indignation.
25 There is a conspiracy of her prophets in the midst of her, as a roaring lion tearing the prey; they devour souls, they take away treasure and precious things; her widows they multiplied

polluting influences which followed in its train. בָּךְ נִחַלְתְּ. The only translation of these words, which suits the connection, is that given in the margin of the common version: *and thou shalt be profaned in thyself.* The verb is the regular Niphal form of חָלַל, *to pierce, make common, profane, pollute;* and the meaning appears to be: thou shalt be inwardly conscious of thy polluted condition, and shalt loathe thyself on account of thy sins. There, among the heathen, thou shalt learn to appreciate my character as a God of holiness, righteousness, and truth.

18–22. In imagery borrowed from the art of smelting metals, the inhabitants of Judea are represented as a mass of the baser metals intermixed with the impure residue of silver. They had altogether become a compound of wickedness, and were to be gathered together in Jerusalem, as into a furnace, and there smolten in the fire of the divine indignation. Compare Jer. vi. 29, 30. פַּחַת, ver. 20, is the infinitive of נָפַח, *to blow.*

23. The prophet, having given a recital of the sins which prevailed in Judah, and described the punishment to be inflicted on account of them, is now charged to expose to view the wickedness of those who held office in the land, but who, instead of setting a good example to the people, were ringleaders in sin.

24. The early and latter rain having been withheld, the land had become unproductive, and the fields not having been cleared or cultivated, all was a scene of wildness and desolation — a fit emblem of the moral state of the nation.

25. For this and the two following verses, compare Zeph. iii. 3, 4. The false prophets are first singled out, on account of the greater influence which they exerted in seducing the people by their impious teachings. Not satisfied with each propagating error within his own sphere, they had formed a complot to oppose the messages of the servants of the Lord. Thus forming a powerful body, they resembled a roaring lion, tearing in pieces his prey. Unconcerned

26 in the midst of her. Her priests did violence to my law, and profaned my sanctuaries; they made no distinction between the holy and the unclean: and they distinguished not the unclean from the pure, and hid their eyes from my sabbaths, and I was
27 polluted in their midst. Her princes in her midst were as wolves tearing the prey, shedding blood, destroying souls for the
28 sake of unjust gain. And her prophets plaster them over with lime, seeing falsehood, and divining for them a lie, saying: Thus saith the Lord Jehovah; and Jehovah hath not spoken.
29 As for the people of the land, they exercise violence, and indulge in rapine: they maltreat the poor and the needy, and
30 oppress the stranger with injustice. And I sought of them a man to build up the wall, and to stand in the breach before me on behalf of the land, that I might not destroy it; but none did

about the welfare of the souls of whom they professedly had the care, and intent only upon their own gain, they had occasioned the death of those who perished in the war with the Chaldeans, and thus increased the number of widows.

26. The priests, whose lips should have kept knowledge, Mal. ii. 7, חָמְסוּ, *did violence* to the law by wresting its words from their natural signification and putting a false construction upon the doctrines taught in it. They likewise profaned the ordinances of the Lord's house by admitting persons indiscriminately to participate in the observance of them, and made no distinction between the Sabbath and other days of the week, giving license to sinful indulgences on that sacred day. How deteriorating such conduct must have been in its influence upon the morality and piety of a nation, may easily be conceived.

27. The שָׂרֶיהָ, *princes*, instead of employing the influence which their elevated position supplied, for promoting the welfare of the people, had nothing in view but the gratification of their own avarice, which they sought to obtain in the most unscrupulous manner, not sticking at murder and fraud. The wolf is an animal noted for its fierceness, cruelty, and rapacity.

28. The false prophets, by flatly contradicting the messages sent by Jehovah, and assuring the princes that the king of Babylon would not take Jerusalem, flattered their prejudices, and encouraged them in their resolution not to submit. Comp. chap. xiii. 10; Jer. xxiii. 16, 17; xxvii. 9, 10.

29. By עַם הָאָרֶץ, *the people of the land*, as placed here immediately after the classification of persons holding office, we are to understand the inhabitants generally, without distinction of rank or office. Corruption had spread downwards through the whole mass of the community (Jer. v. 1–4) The words are to be taken as the nominative absolute, and not, with some, as the accusative. גֵּר, *the stranger*, is rendered by the LXX. προσήλυτον. So far from encouraging, by their kindness and their holy example, those foreigners who sojourned among them to devote themselves in spirit and truth to the service of Jehovah, the Jews did everything that was calculated to alienate them from his worship. As all oppression is unjust, it may at first sight strike a reader as strange, that the prophet should add בְּלֹא מִשְׁפָּט, *unjustly*; but the phrase is used merely for the sake of enhancing the aggravation of the crime.

31 I find. Therefore will I pour mine indignation upon them; in the fire of my wrath I will consume them; I will render their way upon their own head, saith the Lord Jehovah.

30, 31. This is strong language, to express the universality of the defection from Jehovah.

CHAPTER XXIII.

Under the allegory of two sisters, the cities of Samaria and Jerusalem are presented to view for the purpose of reprobating the idolatries of the kingdoms of Israel and Judah; each being the metropolis of its respective kingdom. The same strong metaphorical language is employed as in chapter xvi., for the purpose of more powerfully exciting feelings of disgust at foreign alliances and the abominations of idolatry.

1 AND the word of Jehovah came unto me, saying: Son of
2 man, there were two women, daughters of one mother:
3 And they committed lewdness in Egypt: they were lewd in their youth: there men pressed their breasts, and there they
4 pressed the paps of their virginity. And their names were: Aholah, the elder, and Aholibah, her sister: and they were mine, and they begat sons and daughters; and their names

2. These two cities had a common mother — the Hebrew people; regard being had to what they had become in the possession of that people.

3. The object of the representation in this verse is not to teach that the two kingdoms existed as such in the time of the sojourn in Egypt, but to trace back the idolatry of those who afterwards composed them to that early period in the history of the Hebrews. Compare chap. xx. 6, 7, 8. רָעַךְ, Arab. كَسَعَ, fricuit, here press, compress. The Egyptians are understood as the nominative to עִשּׂוּ the corresponding verb in the parallelism. עִשָּׂה occurs in Piel only here and in verse 8, and is expressive of the acting of eager or intense desire. The last clause of the verse is rendered in the LXX. ἐκεῖ διεπαρθενεύθησαν.

4. The force of the distinctive use of the two names אָהֳלָה, Aholah, and אָהֳלִיבָה, Aholibah, lies in the circumstance, that the former, signifying her or her own tent, intimates that the worship celebrated at Samaria was self-invented; it had never received the sanction of Jehovah, but, on the contrary, had always been marked as an object of his abhorrence; whereas the latter signifying my tent is in her, is expressive of the appropriation of Jerusalem and the temple-worship by Jehovah, as having his divine and gracious warrant. וַתִּהְיֶינָה לִּי, and they were mine. Previous to the apostasy under Jeroboam, Samaria, equally with Jerusalem, worshipped the true God. Their inhabitants were sons and daughters of the Lord Almighty. He never renounced his right to the Israelites as subjects of the theocracy, but sent prophets to declare his will to them and warn them against idolatry. The northern kingdom was the sphere of the special labors of Elijah and Elisha. Thus תַּחְתָּי, ver. 5, under me, i.e. when subject to me as their lawful husband. Samaria is said to be the elder, or the greater, הַגְּדוֹלָה, not in

5 were, — Samaria, Aholah; and Jerusalem, Aholibah. And Aholah committed lewdness under me, and indulged in lust with
6 her lovers, with the Assyrians, her neighbors. Clothed in purple, governors and captains, desirable young men, all of them,
7 cavaliers riding on horses. And she bestowed her lewdness upon them, all of them the choicest sons of Assyria, and she was defiled with all with whom she indulged in lust and with
8 all their idols. Neither did she abandon her lewdnesses from the Egyptians: for they lay with her in her youth: they also pressed the paps of her virginity, and poured their lewdness upon
9 her. Wherefore I delivered her into the hand of her lovers, into
10 the hand of the Assyrians upon whom she doted. These uncovered her nakedness; they took away her sons and her daughters, and slew her with the sword, and she became a name

point of age, for Jerusalem had the priority in this respect, but with respect to defection from the pure worship of Jehovah.

5. From this verse to the tenth the subject treated of is Samaria, or the kingdom of the ten tribes. The adulterous connection of the Israelites with the Assyrians is metaphorically descriptive of the alliance which Menahem their king formed with Pul the king of Assyria, whose favor he purchased with a large sum of money (2 Kings xv. 19, 20). Not only, however, did this transaction involve a transfer of the confidence they had placed in Jehovah as the king of Israel, but opened the door for the entrance of idolatry. עגב is a verb of rare occurrence, being found only once in Jeremiah, and six times in Ezekiel, and the punctuation עָגְבָה is altogether unique; but its signification is well established by the passages in which it is used as well as by that of the cognate Arabic عجب, *miratus, admirationne affectus fuit.* The preposition עַל following the verb, adds to the force of the signification. The Assyrians might be called קְרוֹבִים, *neighbors* of the Israelites, because their country bordered on that of the latter, which at the time here referred to extended as far eastward as the Euphrates.

6. The only difference of signification between פַּחוֹת and סְגָנִים seems to be that the former denoted civil, and the latter military governors of provinces. See Jer. li. 57, where סְגָנִים and פַּחוֹת are closely connected; LXX. ἡγουμένους καὶ στρατηγούς. Their gorgeous, splendid apparel and youthful appearance attracted the libidinous Israelites.

7. From the reference to idols at the end of this verse, it is manifest that the alliances with the Assyrians were not merely of a political nature.

8. The Egyptian idolatries here referred to were the worship of the idol-calves, to which the Hebrews had been addicted while resident in that country, and which Jeroboam established among the ten tribes.

9, 10. The northern kingdom was punished for its idolatry by being invaded by Shalmaneser, who took Samaria, and carried the Israelites captive into Assyria, Media, and the adjacent countries of the East. וַתְּהִי־שֵׁם לַנָּשִׁים, *and she became a name to women,* she was rendered as notorious by her punishment as she had been by her crimes. She was made an example to which an appeal could be made by other states.

11. The prophet now turns to *Aholibah,* or Jerusalem, as the metropolis and representative of the southern kingdom. Though her inhabitants witnessed the

11 to women, and they executed judgments upon her. And her sister Aholibah saw it, and acted more corruptly in lust than she, and her lewdnesses were grosser than those of her sister.
12 To the sons of Assyria she extended her lust, governors and captains, her neighbors, clothed in perfection, cavaliers riding
13 on horses, all of them desirable young men. And I saw that
14 she was defiled; there was one way to them both. And she added to her lewdnesses, when she saw men portrayed upon
15 the wall, images of Chaldeans portrayed with vermilion, Girded with girdles on their loins, and dyed tiaras upon their heads, all of them in appearance military commanders, like the sons of
16 Babylon, whose native country was Chaldea. And she indulged in lust with them when she saw them, and sent messengers

destruction of the kingdom of Israel, instead of taking warning from it, they not only persisted in idolatrous practices, but carried their indulgence in them to still greater lengths.

12. The reference here, as Jarchi rightly interprets, is to the application made by Ahaz to Tiglath-pileser for his assistance against the Syrians and Israelites, recorded 2 Kings xvi. 7-9, which led to the idolatrous transaction at Damascus, and the introduction of the Syrian idolatry into Jerusalem, ibid. 10-16; 2 Chron. xxviii. 16-25. קְרֹבִים בְּכָלוּל some consider to mean, clad in complete armor — the latter term being considered as equivalent to πανοπλία. Regarding it, however, as designed to qualify the dress of the military leaders, it seems better to retain the idea of *perfection*, which it, as well as מִכְלָל, expresses, and interpret it of the splendidness or gorgeous appearance of their apparel. The costume of the Assyrian cavalry may be seen in the sculptures brought by Layard from Nineveh, which display all the magnificence of Oriental finery.

13. דֶּרֶךְ אֶחָד, *one way*. Both alike renounced their confidence in their covenant God, and adopted the idolatrous practices of the heathen.

14-16. It has been questioned where the Jews could have seen the pictures here described. That they were in Jerusalem would appear from what is stated ver. 16, that when they saw them they sent to Chaldea for the originals. In all probability these images had been imported along with the objects of idolatrous worship, which were pictured on the inside of the walls of the temple. See chap. viii. 10. The language מְחֻקֶּה עַל־הַקִּיר, *portrayed upon the wall*, is common to both passages. For שָׁשַׁר, *vermilion*, see on Jer. xxii. 14. Struck with the gallant appearance of these military leaders, the Jews could not rest satisfied without entering into an alliance with the Chaldean power, then established at Babylon. On what occasion the embassy here referred to took place, does not appear from the page of sacred history, but most probably it was when apprehensions were entertained of an attack on the part of Egypt. For the Chaldeans, see on Isa. xxiii. 13. Though now possessors of Babylon, the land of their nativity lay between the Black and Caspian seas. טְבוּלִים, *dyed turbans*. That these were of a large size, appears from the use of סְרוּחִים put in the construct סְרוּחֵי, from the root סָרַח, *to be ample, redundant*. Herodotus describes the Babylonians as having τὰς κεφαλὰς μίτρῃσι ἀναδέονται, i. 195. שָׁלִישִׁים, a first-rate class of military men, so called because they occupied chariots by *threes*, one of whom

17 to them to Chaldea. And the sons of Babylon came to
her into the bed of love, and defiled her with their lewdness,
and she was defiled by them, and her soul was alienated from
18 them. Then her lewdness was revealed, and her nakedness
uncovered, and my soul became alienated from her, as my
19 soul had become alienated from her sister. And she multiplied
her lewdnesses, recollecting the days of her youth, when she
20 committed lewdness in Egypt. And she indulged in lust with
her paramours, whose flesh was as the flesh of asses, and their
21 issue as the issue of horses. Thus didst thou call to remembrance
the crime of thy youth, when they of Egypt pressed thy paps, for
22 the sake of the breasts of thy youth. Therefore, O Aholibah,
thus saith the Lord Jehovah: Behold, I will raise up thy lovers
against thee, from whom thy soul is alienated, and will bring them

guided the horses, while the other two engaged in battle with the enemy. I do not know a better phrase in our language by which to express the Hebrew than *chariotcers*; German *Wagenkämpfer*.

17. Fond as the Jews were of this illegitimate alliance with the Chaldeans, they soon found that it cost them dear, and their love was exchanged for hatred, as is sooner or later the case with all illicit love. Compare 2 Sam. xiii. 15. Jehoiakim proved unfaithful to his pledge, which incensed Nebuchadnezzar, and first brought the Chaldean army as enemies against Jerusalem. The cognate verbs עָקַר and נָקַע employed in this and the following verse, Arab. عَقَّ, *excidit, se se oldulit*, signify *to rend away, turn from*; here, to be alienated from another in affection, and implies the disgust which follows in consequence. LXX. καὶ ἀπέστη ἡ ψυχὴ αὐτῆς ἀπ' αὐτῶν.

18-21. When the divine displeasure was manifested against Judah by the first invasion on the part of Nebuchadnezzar, instead of rejecting her false confidences, abandoning her idolatries, and returning to the worship and service of her covenant God, she indulged the gratification of her lustful propensities in the most open and shameless manner — having recourse anew to the grossest idolatries of the Egyptians which she had cherished at the earliest period of her history. פְּקֹד, *calling to remembrance*, I would refer to Jerusalem, the subject of discourse, and not, with some, to Jehovah. The use of פִּלַגְשִׁים in the masculine is singular, occuring only in this place. The word has been supposed by some to have been of Greek derivation, from πάλλαξ; but it is just as probable that the Greek was derived from the Hebrew, or some other of the Semitic dialects. The pronominal affix הֶם, *their*, in פִּלַגְשֵׁיהֶם, refers to the Egyptians. פָּקַד, Jerusalem may be said to have *visited* her early lewdness when she renewed her intercourse with the idols of Egypt, conciliating the political favor of the Egyptians by conforming to their religion. The ל prefixed in לְמִצְרַיִם, Maurer takes to be the לְ partitive; but I agree with Hävernick, that it is to be regarded as marking the agents by whom the actions were performed. עָשָׂה is here used in Kal in the same sense as it was in Piel, ver. 3 and 8.

22, 23. Jehovah here threatens to excite against the Jews the Babylonians of whom they had formerly been enamored, but who were now become the objects of their disgust. The instru-

23 against thee round about. The sons of Babylon and all the Chaldeans, Pekod, and Shoa, and Koa, all sons of Assyria, choice young men, governors and commanders, military officers.
24 and celebrated riders on horses, all of them: They shall even come against thee, strong in chariots and wagons and a multitude of peoples: buckler and shield and helmet they shall place against thee round about; and I will set judgment before them,
25 and they shall judge thee with their judgments. And I will set my jealousy against thee, and they shall deal with thee in fury; they shall remove thy nose and thine ears, and thy remnant shall fall by the sword. They shall take away thy sons and thy daughters, and thy remnant shall be devoured with fire.
26 And they shall strip thee of thy garments, and take away thy
27 splendid jewels. And I will make thy wickedness to cease from thee, and thy lewdness from the land of Egypt, and thou shalt not lift up thine eyes to them, and thou shalt remember Egypt

ments of their sin were now to be made the instruments of their chastisement. The force of the Babylonian empire was to be brought to bear upon them in punishment of their sins. From the circumstance, that the words פְּקוֹד וְשׁוֹעַ וְקוֹעַ, *Pekod, and Shoa, and Koa*, occur in immediate connection with the Babylonians, the Chaldeans, and Assyrians, and further, that פְּקוֹד, *Pekod*, is used by Jeremiah, chap. l. 21, as a descriptive name of Babylon, it may be inferred that all three are to be so interpreted in this place. No such geographical names as *Shoa* and *Koa* occur either in sacred or profane writers. The former, however, signifying *wealth*, or *opulence*, and the latter, *princely, noble*, are aptly descriptive of the state of Babylon in the days of her prosperity, as פָּקוֹד, *Pekod*, is of her anticipated punishment. קְרוּאִים, *called, celebrated, renowned* as warriors, and therefore, as might be expected, well fitted to execute the task devolved upon them.

24. בְּ, *with*, is understood before the words הֹצֶן רֶכֶב וְגַלְגַּל. Of the first of these terms the signification *strong* is that best supported, and which best suits the connection. The גַּלְגַּלִּים, *wheels* of oriental wagons being unusually high, and consequently very conspicuous, there was a propriety in introducing them here. Comp. chap. i. 16-20. Not only should the most select military men, armed with all the necessary implements of war, come against Jerusalem, but a multitude of people should accompany them to render them all the assistance they might require. When it is said that the Chaldeans were to judge the Jews, בְּמִשְׁפְּטֵיהֶם, *with their judgments*, it is implied that from such a barbarous people they had nothing to expect but the most severe punishments, as it follows in the next verse.

25, 26. Punishment by cutting off the nose and ears was inflicted for adultery, not only among the Chaldeans, but also among the Egyptians, Greeks, and Romans. It was therefore most appropriate, to represent that which adulterous Judah was to suffer under the image of such ignominious and cruel treatment. They were also to be stripped of what lewd females set most value upon — their rich dresses and costly jewels, by which they attract the notice of their paramours (chap. xvi. 39).

27. The effect of the punishment which

28 no more. For thus saith the Lord Jehovah: Behold, I will deliver thee unto the hand of those whom thou hatest, unto the
29 hand of those from whom thy soul is alienated. And they deal with thee hatefully, and take away thy earnings, and leave thee naked and bare, so that the shame of thy lewdnesses and
30 wickedness and whoredoms may appear. I will do these things unto thee, because thou hast gone a whoring after the nations, because thou hast defiled thyself with their abominations.
31 Thou walkedst in the way of thy sister, and I have given her
32 cup into thine hand. Thus saith the Lord Jehovah: Thou shalt drink of the cup of thy sister, deep and large; thou shalt be an
33 object of scorn and derision; it containeth much. Thou shalt be full of drunkenness and sorrow: a cup of desolation and
34 astonishment is the cup of thy sister Samaria. And thou shalt drink it, and suck it to the dregs, and craunch the shreds of it, and cut off thy breasts; for I have spoken it, saith the Lord
35 Jehovah. Wherefore thus saith the Lord Jehovah: Because thou hast forgotten me and didst cast me behind thy back, therefore thou also shalt bear thy wickedness and thine adulteries.
36 And Jehovah spake unto me. Son of man, wilt thou judge Aholah and Aholibah? show them, then, their abominations.
37 For they have committed adultery, and blood is in their hands; yea, they have committed adultery with their idols, and have even caused their children which they bore unto me to pass

the Chaldeans would inflict should be the entire cessation of idolatry among the covenant people. They should no more think of applying to the king of Egypt for help, and they should renounce all connection with idols.

28. See verses 17, 18.

30. עָשֹׂה is the historical Infinitive, standing for the future.

31–35. By a change of metaphor the judgments to be inflicted upon Judah are represented as the contents of a cup which she was to drink. This metaphor is of frequent occurrence both in the Old and New Testaments. See especially Ps. lxxv. 8; Jer. xxv. 15; Rev. xiv. 10; xvi. 19; xviii. 6. The force of the metaphor lies in the idea that the ingredients were nauseous and deleterious. Judah was to be treated as Israel had been, only more severely in proportion to the greater guilt she had contracted. Verse 34 expresses most forcibly the desperation to which the Jews should be reduced, when compelled to undergo the extreme infliction of their punishment. By a bold hyperbole, not satisfied with having sucked out the last drop that was in the cup, they are represented as craunching the very shreds of it with their teeth, and tearing their breasts, which they had prostituted in adultery. גָּרַם, Arab. جرم, *resecuit, abstulit, sustulit*, denotes *to break off, cut or gnaw* as a bone with the teeth (Num. xxiv. 8). The ו in וַיְגָרֵם, ver. 35, is used inferentially for the purpose of assigning the cause of the punishment described.

36. From this verse to the 44th wo

38 through the fire for food to them. Further, this they did to me; they polluted my sanctuary on that day, and desecrated my
39 sabbaths. And when they slaughtered their children to their idols, then they came on the same day into my sanctuary to profane it: and behold, they did this in the midst of my house.
40 Yea, they sent to men who came from far, to whom a messenger had been sent; and behold they came; for them thou didst bathe thyself, powder thine eyelids, and deck thyself with orna-
41 ments. And thou didst sit on a magnificent bed, before which a table was prepared, and upon it thou didst place my incense
42 and my oil. And there was the noise of a careless multitude in her, and to men of the common sort drunkards were brought from the desert, and they put bracelets on their hands and a
43 splendid crown upon their heads. Then I said respecting the
44 old adultress, Will they now commit lewdnesses with her, and she with them? They went in unto her, as they go in unto a whorish woman: thus they went in unto Aholah, and to Aholi-
45 bah, the profligate women. And righteous men shall judge them with the judgment of adultresses, and the judgment of those who shed blood; for they are adultresses, and blood is in their hands.

have a brief anacephalosis, or summing up of the wickedness of the two sisters, special prominence being given to that of Jerusalem.

37. Here first נָאַף, the verb signifying *to commit adultery*, occurs in the chapter.

38, 39. So callous and daring were the Jews in their idolatry, that on the very day on which they had burned their children to Moloch in the valley of Gehenna, they hypocritically presented themselves as worshippers in the temple of Jehovah. Comp. Jer. vii. 9, 10.

40. Comp. ver. 16. כָּחַלְתְּ, a ἅπαξ λεγ. Arab. كَحَلَ, illevit collyrio, pec. stibio *oculos suos*. Freytag; to spread fine paint of a black color on the eyelids so as to produce a black margin, and thus make the white of the eye look more beautiful and seducing. It is a custom still practised by Oriental females. See Kitto, Art. Eye. Jerusalem is represented as so doing to entice her lovers.

She left nothing untried by which this might be effected.

41. In aggravation of her guilt she is charged with impiously devoting to their gratification the offerings which belonged to Jehovah.

42. Instead of receiving the warnings given them by the prophets, and humbling themselves on account of their idolatries, the inhabitants of Jerusalem indulged in rioting and drunkenness — bringing even the vulgar Arabs from the desert to keep them company. סֹבָאִים, *drunkards*, and not סָבָאִים which the Keri exhibits, would seem to be the preferable reading, since the Sabæans in Ethiopia do not appear ever to have been confederate with the Jews. To mark these drunkards with disgrace, the feminine pronominal affixes are employed in יְדֵיהֶן and רָאשֵׁיהֶן. That bracelets were worn by males as well as females, see the authorities in Rosenmüller.

43, 44. Disgusting as was her character as an old adultress, Jerusalem

46 For thus saith the Lord Jehovah: I will bring up a company
47 against them, and deliver them to oppression and spoil. And a
multitude shall stone them with stones, and cut them with their
swords; they shall slay their sons and their daughters, and burn
48 up their houses with fire. And I will cause profligacy to cease
from the land, and all wives shall receive instruction and shall
49 not do according to your profligacy. And they shall lay your
profligacy upon you, and the sins of your idols ye shall bear, and
ye shall know that I am the Lord Jehovah.

found those who encouraged her in her wickedness. The two sisters are again presented together to view, though Aholibah is specially singled out, being the more guilty of the two.

45. The Chaldeans are here called אֲנָשִׁים צַדִּיקִם, *righteous men*, not because they were so in comparison of the apostate subjects of the theocracy, but because in punishing them they were the executioners of the righteous judgments of God.

46–49. The Chaldeans should effect a complete termination of idolatry in the land of Judea, by the capture and destruction of Jerusalem. Though the use of stones in battle was customary, yet there may, in ver. 47, be a special reference to the fact, that stoning was a punishment inflicted for adultery among the Jews, John viii. 5. וְנִסְּרוּ, ver. 48, is construed by Gesenius as a rare instance of a Nithpael Conjugation.

CHAPTER XXIV.

Ezekiel is charged to announce to his countrymen on the Chebar, that the investment of Jerusalem had actually commenced, 1, 2. To illustrate this fact, he was to propound the allegory of a caldron which he was to set on the fire, and, having put water into it, to boil in it choice pieces of meat, 3–5. Then follows the application of the allegory to Jerusalem, showing the awful and irrevocable character of her doom, 6–14. The prophet is next apprised of the sudden death of his wife, for whom he is commanded not to exhibit any signs of mourning, 15–18: it being intimated thereby that such should be the deplorable circumstances of the Jews in Jerusalem, when deprived of the objects most dear to them. In this respect he was a prophetic sign to them, 19–27.

1 AGAIN, in the ninth year, in the tenth month, on the tenth of
2 the month, the word of Jehovah came unto me, saying: Son of
man, write thee the name of the day, this very day; the king

1. The date, as usual, is taken from the commencement of Jehoiachin's captivity.

2. The prophet is specially charged to write down the particular day on which he delivered his message, and to announce it as that on which Nebuchadnezzar had commenced his attack on Jerusalem. As he was at the time at the distance of more than three hundred miles from that city, it was not to be supposed that the intelligence could have reached him by any human means. When, therefore, the captives afterwards received the information, they had, on comparing the dates, an infallible proof

3 of Babylon lays seige against Jerusalem this very day. And propound a parable to the rebellious house, and say unto them: Thus saith the Lord Jehovah: Put on the caldron; put it on,
4 and put also water into it: Gather the pieces thereof into it, every good piece, the thigh and the shoulder; fill it with the best
5 bones. Take the choice of the flock, and lay also the pile of bones under it, make it boil well; let them also boil the bones
6 thereof in the midst of it. Wherefore thus saith the Lord Jehovah: Woe to the bloody city, the caldron in which is the rust thereof, and from which its rust hath not removed; bring it
7 out piece by piece; let no lot be cast upon it. For her blood is in the midst of her; she laid it on the sunny rock; she did not
8 pour it out upon the ground, to cover it with dust; That it might cause fury to come up, to take vengeance, I have laid her
9 blood on a sunny rock, that it may not be covered. Wherefore thus saith the Lord Jehovah: Woe to the bloody city: I will
10 enlarge the pile: Heap on the wood, kindle the fire, make ready

of the divine inspiration of the prophet. For קְרָב read קְרַב, קָרַב, *to lean or lie against anything, to bear hard upon it, to invest a city with an army*; Syr.

ܣܡܟ, *innixus fuit, discubuit, accubuit.*

3-5. The prophet was typically to perform the actions here commanded. They were propheticial transactions, the import of which is presently explained. נְתָחֶיהָ, *its pieces*, do not mean pieces of the caldron, as if it had been broken, but of the meat that was to be put into it to be boiled. "The choice of the flock" mean persons most distinguished for rank, office, or wealth in the Jewish state. הדור, and כְּדוּרָה, ver. 9, signify the round pile of fuel, from דוּר, *to be round.* The bones that had been stripped of their flesh were to be used for fuel: those to which it still adhered were to be thrown into the pot, that it might be boiled.

6. Here the prophet gives the explanation of the parable. The Jews, indeed, could be at little loss to know what was intended by it. They had already themselves bandied the metaphor about as a taunt, boasting that they should dwell securely in Jerusalem (chap. xi. 3). By חֶלְאָה is not meant scum such as that which gathers on the surface of the contents of a pot, but the rust or verdigris contracted by copper. LXX. ἰός. The moral impurity of the city is intended. Why there should be a Mappik in the pronominal affix the second time the word is used, and not the first, does not appear. As usual, the Masoretes only tell us that the ה is raphe. The pieces were to be brought out and put into the caldron without discrimination. No lot was to be cast upon them for the purpose of sparing some and not others, as was sometimes the case when persons were sentenced to be punished.

7. The bloody deeds committed in Jerusalem were so flagrant, that no pains were taken to conceal them.

8. In just retribution Jehovah declares that he would expose them with equal publicity, that the blood might call for vengeance. צְחִיחַ signifies here *sunny*, the brightest part of a bare rock exposed to the rays of the sun.

9-12. The most effectual measures were to be taken for the destruction of

11 the flesh, and spice it well, and let the bones be burned. And set it empty upon the coals thereof, that it may be hot, and its copper may glow, that its filthiness may be smelted in the midst
12 of it, and its rust consumed. Its rust is wearinesses; and its
13 much rust goes not off from it; into the fire its rust! Thine impurity was atrocious: because I would have purified thee, but thou wouldst not be purified, thou shalt no more be purified from
14 thy filthiness till I have caused my fury to rest on thee. I Jehovah have spoken; it cometh, and I will do it; I will not desist, neither have pity, nor take compassion: according to thy ways and thy doings shall they judge thee, saith the Lord Jehovah.
15 And the word of Jehovah came unto me, saying: Son of man,
16 behold, I will take away from thee the delight of thine eyes with a stroke, but thou shalt not lament, nor weep, neither shall
17 thy tears run down. Grieve in silence: make no mourning for the dead; bind thy turban about thee, and put thy sandals on thy feet; thou shalt not cover the lip, nor eat the bread of
18 men. And I spake to the people in the morning; and my wife died in the evening, and I did in the morning as I had been

Jerusalem. The destruction was to be complete. After the inhabitants had been destroyed, the city itself was to be burned to the ground. See for the fulfilment, Jer. lii. 13; Lam. iv. 11. חֶלְאָתָה תְּאֻנִים, *the rust is wearinesses*, i.e. it is so ingrained, that much labor is required in removing it, and all bestowed in vain. The process was no longer to be carried on, but justice was to effect its purpose at once.

13, 14. The impurity of the inhabitants of Jerusalem was of the most atrocious character. זִמָּה, *crime*, deliberate *wickedness*, is a term employed to denote a criminal act perpetrated on set purpose. Root זָמַם, *to think, devise, purpose*, mostly used in a bad sense. Jehovah had used a variety of means, both physical and moral, to restore them to purity, but they had produced no effect. It remained now only for the Chaldeans to do their work. The decree was irrevocable, and the execution inevitable.

15–17. With a view to affect more deeply the minds of his fellow-captives, Ezekiel has announced to him the disseverance of the tenderest of all earthly ties — the removal of her on whom he had ever been accustomed to look with affection and delight. This removal of his beloved wife was to be effected by מַגֵּפָה, *a stroke*, i.e. in so sudden and striking a manner as to show, that it was an immediate visitation of God. Distressing, however, as this event would be, the prophet is commanded to exhibit no tokens of grief on the occasion. Instead of אֶל־בְּנֵי מֵת, the construction is אֶל בְּנֵי מֵת, giving special prominence to "the dead" which is expressed in the plural with ultimate reference to those who should perish during the siege of Jerusalem, though בְּךָ, *his own dead*, was the immediate subject of discourse. He was interdicted the use of such signs of mourning as were usually manifested.

Though the High Priest was interdicted mourning for any person what-

19 commanded. And the people said unto me: Wilt thou not tell
20 us what these things which thou doest are to us? And I said
21 unto them: The word of Jehovah came unto me, saying: Say
unto the house of Israel, Thus saith the Lord Jehovah: Behold,
I will desecrate my sanctuary, the pride of your strength, the
delight of your eyes, the desire of your soul; and your sons and
22 your daughters shall fall by the sword. And ye shall do as I
have done; ye shall not cover the lip, neither shall ye eat the
23 bread of men; But your turbans shall be on your heads, and
your sandals on your feet; ye shall not lament nor weep, but ye
shall pine away in your iniquities, and mourn, a man to his

ever, Lev. xxi. 10, the ordinary priests were permitted to mourn for near relatives, ibid. vers. 2, 3. Ezekiel, therefore, though of priestly descent, would have been under no restriction in this respect. He was, however, on the present occasion, though of the most trying nature, to appear as usual, not laying aside his turban and, instead of it, casting ashes on his head, nor going barefooted, nor covering the upper lip together with its moustachio (שָׂפָם), comp. Lev. xiii. 45. Neither was he to partake of the food which it was customary for friends to bring in token of their sympathy with the mourners. This in the original is called לֶחֶם אֲנָשִׁים, *bread of men*, i.e. what men usually furnish on such occasions. Hävernick aptly compares for the idiom, חֶרֶט אֱנוֹשׁ, *a man's pen*, Isa. viii. 1, and μέτρον ἀνθρώπου, Rev. xxi. 17, ἀριθμὸς ἀνθρώπου, Rev. xiii. 18. The etymology of אֲנָשִׁים is not to be pressed, nor the word rendered, with Newcome, *wretched men*.

18. The event soon followed the communication to the people of the sorrowful event which had been pre-announced to the prophet.

19. The people perceived evidently that the strange conduct of Ezekiel under the circumstances of the case was symbolical, and asked to be informed, what bearing the symbol had upon their condition.

21. The prophet is instructed to point them to the sacred temple at Jerusalem, as the antitype of his wife. It had been the proud object of their confidence (Jer. vii. 10), and which they had regarded with feelings of delightful admiration. For the phrase גְּאוֹן עֻזְּכֶם, comp. Lev. xxvi. 19. In מַחְמַד and בַּחֲמַל is a paronomasia. They had profaned that temple with their idolatrous worship, and Jehovah would now profane it by means of the Chaldeans, who would pillage and burn it to the ground. As Hitzig observes, many parents might, when they were carried away from Jerusalem, have been under the necessity of leaving their children of tender age behind them. These the Chaldeans should mercilessly put to the sword.

23. It is predicted at the close of this verse, that while, like the prophet, the Jews should not mourn on account of the loss of their temple or their dearly beloved relatives, they should be brought to bewail their personal guilt, which had been the procuring cause of it. וּנְקֹתֶם is expressive of inward melting of spirit, the effect of vexation and grief when the mind cannot sustain its infirmities, but gives way to the pressure of calamity, and in the hopelessness of despair, gives up all for lost. The words וּנְהַמְתֶּם אִישׁ אֶל־אָחִיו are strongly expressive of the sense of national guilt which the Jewish captives should feel they had contracted, and the share which they individually had in it. Though

24 brother. And Ezekiel shall be to you for a sign; according to all that he does, ye shall do: and when it comes to pass, ye shall
25 know that I am the Lord Jehovah. And thou, son of man, shall it not be in the day when I take from them their fortress, the joy of their glory, the delight of their eyes, the desire of
26 their soul, their sons and their daughters? In that day shall he
27 who has escaped come to thee to communicate the report. In that day shall thy mouth be opened to him that has escaped; and thou shalt speak, and no longer be dumb; and thou shalt be to them for a sign, and they shall know that I am Jehovah.

prevented, by the circumstances in which they were placed in the land of their conquerors, from making any public manifestation of their sorrow, they would privately (אִישׁ אֶל אָחִיו, *one to another*) give expression to their feelings of grief. Fairbairn justly reprobates the opinion of Eichhorn, Ewald, and Hitzig, that a state of feeling the very reverse of this is intended by the language of the prophet.

24. It is not an unexampled thing for the sacred writers to introduce their own names into their productions. See Exod. ii. 11; Numb. xii. 3; Isa. xx. 3; Dan. viii. 27. Ezekiel was מוֹפֵת, *a sign* or significant typical representation, foreshadowing what was to take place in the experience of his countrymen. בְּבֹאָהּ, in *its coming to pass*; when the thing signified should happen, it would be an indubitable proof that Jehovah had revealed the event beforehand to his servant.

25-27. בַּיּוֹם, *in the day*, as occurring in verses 25 and 26, refers to that in which the temple was destroyed and the fugitive had made his escape: in ver. 27 it refers to that on which he arrived at the Chebar with the melancholy news. From the occurrence of the former event until the latter should take place, the prophet ceased from his public labors, meanwhile leaving his predictions to produce their natural effect; but then he was again to stand forth, and pointedly to appeal to the issue in proof of his divine commission. We may easily conceive of the impression which such an appeal was calculated to make on the minds of the Jews. Compare chap. xxxiii. 21, 22.

CHAPTER XXV.

Chapters xxv.-xxxii. inclusive, contain prophecies relating to foreign nations. The prophet in this chapter first directs his denunciatory discourse against the Ammonites, 1, 2; whose destruction he had anticipated, chap. xxi. 25 and 32. They were specially to be punished on account of their malicious exultation at the destruction of Jerusalem and the captivity of the Jews, 3–7. He then proceeds to denounce similar punishment against the Moabites, 8–11, the Edomites, 12–14, and the Philistines, 15–17. These prophecies were, for the most part, fulfilled by Nebuchadnezzar five years after the destruction of Jerusalem. See Joseph. Antiqq. lib. x. cap. 9. § 7.

1 AND the word of Jehovah came unto me, saying: Son of man,
2 set thy face towards the sons of Ammon, and prophesy against
3 them. And thou shalt say to the sons of Ammon: Hear ye the word of the Lord Jehovah: Thus saith the Lord Jehovah: Because thou sayest, Aha! to my sanctuary, for it is desecrated, and to the land of Israel, for it is desolate, and to the house of
4 Judah, for it is gone into captivity; Therefore, behold, I will deliver thee to the sons of the east for a possession; and they shall erect their villages in thee, and fix in thee their dwellings;
5 they shall eat thy fruit and they shall drink thy milk. And I will make Rabbah a habitation of camels, and the children of Ammon a resting-place for sheep, and ye shall know that I am

3. בְּנֵי עַמּוֹן, *the Ammonites* were the descendants of Lot, and occupied the territory to the east of the Jordan, beyond that pertaining to the tribes of Reuben and Gad. It was bounded on the south by the land of Moab, from which it was separated by the river Arnon; and on the north by the river Jabbok, which separated it from the country of the Amorites. They formed one of the most powerful of the minor neighboring states, and were frequently at war with the Hebrews. They were gross idolaters, and had for their national god Moloch or Milcom. On the fall of Jerusalem, to which as auxiliaries they contributed, and the transportation of the inhabitants of Judea to Babylon, they insolently triumphed over them, on which account the present threatening is denounced against them. The Feminine suffix in אַרְצֵךְ refers to the country.

4. Solomon Jarchi, Grotius, and others suppose that by בְּנֵי קֶדֶם, *sons of the east*, here, the Chaldeans are meant; but this is contradicted by the uniform usage of the sacred writers, who employ this phrase restrictively to designate the inhabitants of Arabia Deserta, to the east of the territories immediately bordering on the Jordan and the Dead Sea. On the destruction of the Jewish state by Nebuchadnezzar, the country was to be taken possession of by the nomadic tribes, who should there form their encampments and dwell in their tents, leading the same pastoral life to which they had been accustomed. טִירוֹת, *villages*, or *nomadic encampments* surrounded by mud-walls, as is common in the East. The word nowhere signifies palaces. The nomades had no palaces.

5. רַבָּה, *Rabbah*, literally *the great*, was the metropolis of the Ammonites, elsewhere called רַבַּת עַמּוֹן, *Rabbah of Ammon*, and, in full, רַבַּת בְּנֵי עַמּוֹן,

6   Jehovah. For thus saith the Lord Jehovah: Because thou didst
    smite with the hand, and stamp with the foot and rejoice with
7   all the despite of thy soul against the land of Israel, Therefore,
    behold I will stretch out my hand against thee, and give thee
    for a spoil to the nations, and I will cut thee off from the peoples
    and destroy thee from the lands; I will destroy thee, and thou
    shalt know that I am Jehovah.
8   Thus saith the Lord Jehovah: Because Moab and Seir say,
9   Behold, the house of Judah are like all the heathen! There-
    fore, behold, I will open the side of Moab from the cities, from
    his cities, from the extremity thereof, the glory of the land,

Rabbah of the sons of Ammon, to distinguish it from רַבָּה, a city of that name in the tribe of Judah. When afterwards restored by Ptolemy Philadelphus, it received the name of Philadelphia, and formed one of the cities of the Decapolis. By a slight corruption of the second syllable it is called امان, *Amman*, at the present day, as it was in that of Abulfeda. Tab. Syr. p. 91. Its ruins have been visited by the modern travellers, Seetzen, Burckhardt, and Irby and Mangles, who found them about nineteen English miles S.E. by E. from the town of Szalt, and situated along the banks of a stream called Moiet Amman, which flows into the Zerka or Jabbok, called according to Seetzen, *Nahhr Amman*. They exhibit remains of a palace, a mausoleum, an amphitheatre, a temple, a church, and a castle; but not a single inhabited dwelling is to be seen. See Seetzen in Zach's Monatliche Correspondenz, xviii. pp. 428, 429.

7. This desolate state of Rabbah must be referred to the three hundred years which intervened between the destruction of Jerusalem and the time of Ptolemy Philadelphus, after which it became celebrated among the Greeks and Romans, by whom, no doubt, the splendid buildings, the ruins of which still remain, were erected. בַּג occurs nowhere besides in Hebrew, except in the compound פַּתְבַּג, where it seems to be used in the sense of the Pers. پاگ, *cibus*, باج, *vectigal*. Such significations, however, ill suit the present connection; and there cannot, I should think, be a doubt that the reading is a corruption of בַּז, *spoil*, which is that of the Keri, of a great number of MSS. in the text, and is supported by that of the Complut. Bible and all the ancient versions. The letters ז and ג might easily be exchanged for one another by a copyist. Compare גֵּה for זֶה, chap. xlvii. 13.

8. Proceeding in a southerly direction, a similar threatening is denounced against *Moab* and *Seir*. These countries are here classed together, most probably on account of their close proximity to and their joint hostility against the Jews.

9. שֵׂעִיר, *Seir*, was properly a mountainous country, called by Josephus and others who wrote in Greek Γάβαλα, Γεβαλενή, Γόβαλα, and at the present day the Arabs still give it the name of جبال, *Jebal*. See Dr. Robinson's Palestine, vol. ii. p. 552. The opening up of this mountainous region from the cities of Moab expresses the clearing of the passes by which the enemy might easily enter and take possession. These were otherwise closed and fortified. The names of the cities specified are in apposition with צְבִי אֶרֶץ, *the glory of the country*, so that this is to be taken as descriptive of them, and not of קָצֵה, the frontier or extremity of Moab. They

10 Beth-yeshimoth, Baal-meon, and Kiriathaim. I will give her for a possession to the sons of the east, against the sons of Ammon, that the sons of Ammon may not be remembered among
11 the nations. And I will execute judgments in Moab, and they shall know that I am Jehovah.
12 Thus saith the Lord Jehovah: Because Edom acted revengefully towards the house of Judah, and contracted guilt by avenging
13 himself upon them, Therefore thus saith the Lord Jehovah, I will also stretch forth my hand against Edom, and cut off from it man and beast, and will make it desolate from Teman,
14 and they of Dedan shall fall by the sword. And I will inflict my vengeance upon Edom by the hand of my people Israel, and they shall execute upon Edom according to mine anger, and according to my fury, and they shall know my vengeance, saith the Lord Jehovah.
15 Thus saith the Lord Jehovah: Because the Philistines have acted revengefully, and have revenged themselves with despite of soul

are most probably so called because of their having been strongly fortified. From the significance of the name בֵּית הַיְשִׁימוֹת, *Beth-hayeshimoth, the house of desolations*, the first would appear to have sustained a siege at some previous period of its history, but from the effects of which it had afterwards recovered. It was situated on the eastern shore of the Dead Sea. בַּעַל מְעוֹן, *Baal-Meon*, in full בֵּית בַּעַל מְעוֹן, *Beth-Baal-Meon* (Josh. xiii. 17), and simply בֵּית מְעוֹן, *Beth-Meon* (Jer. xlviii. 23), lay farther inland, to the east of Mount Nebo, and appears from the name to have been celebrated on account of the worship of Baal. קִרְיָתַיִם, *Kiriathaim, the double city*, is supposed by Burckhardt to be the present ال طيم, *El-Teyim*, half-an-hour's journey to the southwest of Medeba. It was most probably on account of the strength of these cities that Moab cherished the pride so emphatically ascribed to her (Isa. xvi. 6; Jer. xlviii. 29; Zeph. ii. 8–10).

12–14. Though Seir, which strictly is the northern part of Idumea, is coupled with Moab, ver. 8, yet considering the enmity which the Edomites had uniformly manifested against the Hebrews, it was proper that they should specially share in the judgments to be executed upon the foes of the covenant people. The country of אֱדוֹם, *Edom*, properly so called, stretches from the southeast corner of the Dead Sea to Elath or Akabah on the Elanitic Gulf of the Red Sea. The two cities or districts, תֵּימָן, *Teman*, and דְּדָן, *Dedan*, being placed in antithesis, embrace the whole length of the country from north to south. They are placed in the same order (Jer. xlix. 7, 8). The former is placed by Jerome in his Onomasticon at the distance of five miles from Petra, but where the latter lay is uncertain. It is scarcely to be supposed that the trading city of this name in the bosom of the Persian Gulf can be meant. Whatever the Idumeans may have suffered from the passage of Chaldean troops through the country, it was reserved for the Jews themselves to execute the divine vengeance upon them. This was specially done at an after period by Judas Maccabeus, and they were finally conquered and incorporated with the

16 to destroy in the old enmity, Therefore thus saith the Lord Jehovah: Behold, I will stretch forth my hand against the Philistines, and cut off the Crethites, and I will destroy the
17 remnant on the sea-coast. And I will execute upon them great avengings in punishments of fury; and they shall know that I am Jehovah, when I inflict my vengeance upon them.

Jewish state by John Hyrcanus. See on Isa. xxxiv. 5.

15–17. Having taken its course through the countries to the east and south of the Dead Sea, the threatening now crosses over along the south of Judea to the country of the Philistines, situated along the coast of the Mediterranean. The inhabitants of this region, being the near neighbors of the Jews, had been their indomitable enemies from the time they entered Canaan. Hence the reference to אֵיבַת עוֹלָם, *the ancient hatred*. Mark the paronomasia in הִכְרַתִּי and כְּרֵתִים. The Philistines were called *Cherethim*, or Cretans (LXX. τοὺς Κρῆτας), because they came originally from the island of Crete, elsewhere called כַּפְתּוֹר, Caphtor. The army of Nebuchadnezzar overran and destroyed the cities on the sea-coast on his way to Egypt, after the siege of Tyre. See on Jer. xlvii.

CHAPTER XXVI.

This and the two following chapters are directed against the Phoenicians, whose country lay next in order along the coast, to the north of Philistia. It consisted of a small slip of country, not exceeding twelve miles in width, but extending about one hundred in length from north to south, between Mount Lebanon and the sea. Its inhabitants were the celebrated merchants and able navigators of antiquity, and resided in numerous cities with which the country was studded, the chief of which were Tyre and Sidon; and against these especially the prophecies before us are pronounced.

In the present chapter Tyre is introduced exulting at the downfall of Jerusalem, and congratulating herself on the accession to her commerce which she anticipated would result from that event, 1, 2. Hereupon, Jehovah declares in general terms that he would effect her destruction, and that of the lesser cities dependent upon her, 3–6. Then follows a more special prediction, descriptive of Nebuchadnezzar as the instrument divinely appointed to fulfil the purpose of the Most High; the formidable military array which that monarch should employ in the attack; his total annihilation of that celebrated city, and the capture of all her commercial treasures, 7–14. The effect produced by the intelligence of her fall on the merchant-princes of the islands and coasts of the Mediterranean is next most graphically set forth, and a funereal dirge is introduced which, in the posture and attire of mourners, they are supposed to chant, 15–18; and the prophecy winds up with a declaration on the part of Jehovah, that the desolate condition to which Tyre should be reduced would be complete and perpetual, 19–21.

1 And it came to pass in the eleventh year, on the first of the month
2 that the word of Jehovah came unto me, saying: Son of man, Because Tyre saith concerning Jerusalem, Aha! the gates of the people are broken, it is turned unto me, I shall be filled, she

1. Contrary to his usual practice, the prophet omits to specify the date of the month. Some interpreters suppose it was the fourth, others the fifth, etc.,

3   is laid waste. Therefore thus saith the Lord Jehovah: Behold, I am against thee, O Tyre! and I will cause many nations to come up against thee, as the sea causeth its waves to come up.

but nothing beyond conjecture has been advanced, nor is it a matter of much importance.

2. צֹר, a form differing little from צוּר, which signifies *a Rock*; on Phœnician monuments צר without the Vau, as also on Tyrian coins לצר, לצר אם, צדנם; Arab. صور, Greek Τύρος. This city was the most opulent and powerful emporium in the ancient world, carrying on her commerce not only in fleets down the Mediterranean as far as the western coasts of Spain and Britain and round into the Baltic, mooring them in every accessible port; but likewise in large caravans into Central and Eastern Asia. She was of high antiquity. According to Justin (Urbem ante annum Troianæ cladis condiderunt) it must have been founded B.C. 1155. Yet it was originally only a colony of Zidon, which boasted a still higher antiquity. See on chap. xxviii. 21.

Properly speaking there was a double Tyre—that proper, on the continent, called Palætyrus, ἡ πάλαι Τύρος, supposed to have been צֹר הַבֶּצֶר, *the fortress-city of Tyre*, mentioned Josh. xix. 29; 2 Sam. xxiv. 7; and the insular Tyre, built upon a rock in the sea, at the distance, according to Pliny, of seven hundred paces from the shore, which in all probability served as an outpost or station for warehouses wherein were deposited the principal articles of Phœnician traffic. According to Strabo, old Tyre lay thirty stadia south of the insular city, near the present راس العين, *Ras-elain*, or 'fountain-head,' which supplied the aqueducts with water. Μετὰ δὲ τὴν Τύρον ἡ Παλαίτυρος ἐν τριάκοντα σταδίοις. Lib. xvi. cap. 2. It was obviously this city that the army of Nebuchadnezzar first attacked, for it is said, ver. 11, that with the hoofs of his horses he should tread down all her streets. It has been maintained indeed by some that the two parts of the city were connected by an artificial isthmus; but such an idea, suggested no doubt by the fact that Alexander afterwards constructed a passage from the one to the other, would ill accord with what we may conceive to have been the sagacity of the Tyrian merchants, who, for the security of their goods, would leave the island approachable only by water. See this subject ably discussed by Vitringa on Isa. xxiii. and Prideaux's Connections. The siege lasted thirteen years, and, though we have no positive testimony from profane authors to prove that it was successful, yet there remains no ground for reasonable doubt on the subject. When it is said, chap. xxix. 18, that the king of Babylon and his army had no wages for the service they had performed, the meaning is, they had no adequate remuneration for the hardships and losses which they had sustained, and the immense expense to which he had been put on the occasion. That no mention is made by the profane authors of Greece and Rome of the successful result of the siege is rather an argument in its favor than the contrary; for we can hardly suppose it possible for them not to have adverted to so remarkable a circumstance as that the mighty king of Babylon should have been baffled in his attempt, if such had actually been the fact. Nor must it be forgotten that Jerome expressly declares that he had read in Assyrian histories of the successful conquest of the city by Nebuchadnezzar. See Hävernick's Commentary, pp. 427–442, in which the objections of Gesenius, Von Heeren, Dahlmann, Hitzig, and other modern writers are satisfactorily refuted, and compare Hengstenberg, De Rebus Tyriorum, p. 31 and

4   And they shall destroy the walls of Tyre, and raze her towers, and I will sweep away her dust from her, and I will make her
5   a dry rock. She shall be a place for spreading nets in the midst of the sea: surely I have spoken it, saith the Lord Jehovah;
6   and she shall become a spoil for the nations. And her daughters which are in the field shall be slain with the sword; and following. הֶאָח, *heach, aha!* an interjection strongly expressive of exultation over a fallen enemy. See Ps. xxxv. 21, 25. As an exception to the general grammatical rule, and an instance of *constructio ad sensum*, נִשְׁבָּרָה the predicate in the singular agrees with דַּלְתוֹת the subject in the plural. נָסַבָּה should be pointed נָסְבָה. The nominative to this verb is not Jerusalem, understood, as our translators have taken it, but what is most easily supplied by the connection, and that on which the minds of the Tyrians were most set, their merchandize, or mercantile gain. The rendering, therefore, should be "*it*," and not *she*, "is turned unto me." דַּלְתוֹת הָעַמִּים, the doors or *gates of the people*. Jerusalem was so called not only on account of her having been the great place of concourse to the Hebrews when they went up to the sacred feasts, but because it lay in the routes which the caravans with merchandize took that proceeded to Tyre from Petra, Eziongeber, Palmyra, and other places in the East, and consequently must have intercepted many of the articles of traffic before they reached their destination. On this account she must have been an object of great jealousy to the Tyrians, who now exult at the removal of this monopoly, and congratulate themselves on the commercial advantages which they would derive from her fall.

3, 4. In striking contrast with the self-congratulatory language of Tyre, Jehovah here announces her destruction. The comparison of crowds of people to the tumultuous waves of the sea is common in Scripture. It is peculiarly appropriate here, in consideration of the maritime position of Tyre. As the Mediterranean dashed against her shores with resistless fury, so should the troops of the king of Babylon, collected from the many different nations subject to his sway, attack and destroy her strongholds. לְ prefixed to צֹר is the sign of the accusative, according to Aramaic usage, as לְכָרְמִי, (Jer. xl. 2). That Tyre was strongly fortified is borne out by the testimony of Dius, as quoted by Josephus, Antiqq. viii. 5, who says that Hiram king of Tyre ἐπειδὴ ἑώρα τὰ τῶν Ἱεροσολύμων τείχη, πύργων πρὸς ἀσφάλειαν δεόμενα καὶ τῆς ἄλλης ὀχυρότητος, πρὸς γὰρ τὸ ἀξίωμα τῆς πόλεως ἡγεῖτο δεῖν καὶ τοὺς περιβόλους εἶναι, ταυτά τε προσεπεσκεύαζε καὶ πύργοις αὐτὰ μεγάλοις προσεξῆρεν. Comp. Isa. xxiii. 4, 11, 13. Hitzig indeed contends that the language of Dius only applies to Jerusalem, but it appears obvious to me that the passage concludes with a statement of what Hiram did to his own city in imitation of what he had witnessed at the capital of Judea. שָׂחִית and פָּרַיִךְ form a paronomasia. עֲפָרָהּ, *her dust.* The destruction here referred to was that of the towers, walls, and other edifices, destroyed by the besiegers. Not a vestige was to remain. In place of splendid edifices and impregnable bulwarks nothing was to be seen but bare rocks, fit only for fishermen to spread their nets on.

5. בְּתוֹךְ הַיָּם, *in the midst of the sea,* may, without straining, be applied to Continental Tyre, though the greater part of the city lay not within the sea-mark, but back in the plain in the direction of the rocky hill, المشوق, El-Mashuk, which probably formed its בְּנֹתָיהָ, castle or fortress. See Robinson, iii. 390.

7 they shall know that I am Jehovah. For thus saith the Lord Jehovah: Behold, I will bring against Tyre Nebuchadnezzar the king of Babylon, from the north, a king of kings, with horses and chariot, and with horsemen, and an assembly of much
8 people. Thy daughters in the field he shall slay with the sword; and he shall construct a circumvallation around thee, and pour out a mound against thee, and raise the buckler against thee.
9 The stroke of his battering-ram he will direct against thy walls;
10 and thy towers he will cut down with his hatchets. The multitude of his horses shall cover thee with their dust; by the noise of horsemen, and wheels, and chariots, thy walls shall shake, when he entereth into thy gates, as into the entrances of a city

6. וּבְנוֹתֶיהָ אֲשֶׁר בַּשָּׂדֶה, *And her daughters which were in the open country,* i.e. the towns and villages dependent upon her, and lying back from and along the coast. These were to be involved in the same catastrophe with the mother-city; their fate was bound up in hers.

7. מִצָּפוֹן, *from the North*, the quarter from which the Chaldeans originally came from their native mountains, and that which is always specified when their entering Palestine is referred to, because they took the route by Riblah and Hamath on the Orontes in preference to that across the desert to the southwest of Babylon. Nebuchadnezzar is dignified with the title מֶלֶךְ מְלָכִים, KING OF KINGS, Chaldean מֶלֶךְ שַׁלִּיט, Arabic ملك اطلركي, because he had conquered many kingdoms, and had under him a number of royal personages governing, as satraps and viceroys, the different countries that were subject to his sway. Thus the Turks have their سلطان سلاطين, *Sultani sulatin*; the Persians their شاهينشاه, *Shahin-shah*, and the Ethiopians their ד֗וֵשׁ שׁוֵדּ, of the same import. See for more, Gesen. Thesaur. p. 794. דָּיֵק, *the tower*, which, as employed in a siege, was moveable, and pushed forward against the city. These were stored with instruments of attack, and contained a considerable number of men. סֹלְלָה, the *agger* or mound of earth raised before a besieged city. שָׁפַךְ is appropriately used to express the formation of it from the emptying or pouring out of the earth conveyed in baskets. צִנָּה, *the buckler,* here obviously denotes the *testudo,* or vaulted roof of large united shields employed by an attacking enemy for protection in siege-operations.

9. By מְחִי קָבָל is meant the battering-ram, which was employed in making breaches in the walls; and which, in the absence of artillery, must have proved a very effective instrument of attack. Winer renders the words, *percussio oppositionis,* i.e. the hostile stroke or blow given by the instrument. מְחִי is derived from מָחָה, *to strike,* or *smite*, קָבָל from קָבַל, *to be over against, opposite to.* Compare the Arab. قبل علي, in the hostile sense of *irruit in aliquem, aggressus est rem*; Chal. פגיזותי, *tormenta bellica.* Among other warlike instruments described as employed in the destruction of Tyre חֲרָבוֹת are specified. As *swords,* which is the common acceptation of the term, however, appropriate when a battle is spoken of, is unsuitable when applied, as here to the cutting down of towers, it is now generally allowed that it is used with the signification of *axes* or *hatchets.* The assertion of Hävernick,

11 broken in upon. With the hoofs of his horses he shall tread down all thy streets; he shall slay thy people with the sword; the monuments of thy strength shall come down to the ground.
12 And they shall spoil thy riches, and plunder thy merchandise, and raze thy walls, and break down thy pleasure-houses, and shall place thy stones and thy wood and thy dust in the midst
13 of the waters. And I will cause the noise of thy songs to cease,
14 and the sound of thy lyres shall no more be heard. And I will make thee a dry rock; thou shalt be a place for the spreading of nets; thou shalt never be built any more: for I Jehovah
15 have spoken, saith the Lord Jehovah. Thus saith the Lord Jehovah concerning Tyre: Shall not the islands shake at the sound of thy fall when the wounded groan, when the slaughter

that חֶרֶב never signifies anything else than sword, is indefensible; for it also signifies a *knife* (Josh. v. 2, 3); a *razor*, (Ezek. v. 1); and is to be translated according as the exigency of the passage may require.

10, 11, A graphic description of the tremendous character of the siege. The dust, raised by the horses, filling the air, the noise made by their prancing, the rattling of the chariots, the quaking of the walls, the shrieks of the wounded, the fall of the idolatrous objects of confidence — all must have combined to inspire the inhabitants with terror and dismay. מַצְּבוֹת עֻזֵּךְ, Vulg. *statuæ tuæ nobiles*, obelisks or statues, erected in honor of their idol-gods. Comp. מַצְּבוֹת בֵּית־שֶׁמֶשׁ, *the obelisks of the temple of the sun*, Jer. xliii. 13. When the idols of the heathen are taken or destroyed in war, the courage of their votaries totally fails. The great god of the Phœnicians was Melcarte, whose fabulous history in the main agrees with that of the Grecian Hercules. He claimed as his birth-place Thebes, a Phœnician colony; and had his temple in Palætyrus, to which Alexander was referred by the Insular Tyrians, when he wished to sacrifice to him: Esse templum Herculis extra urbem, in eam sedem quam Palætyron ipsi vocant: ibi regem Deo sacrum rite facturum. — Q. Curtius, iv. 2. (4.)

מַצְּבוֹת עֻזֵּךְ in the plural agrees with עֻזֵּךְ in the singular, on the principle, that the former is taken distributively.

12. That the riches here specified must have been those found in Palætyrus and not those stored up on the island, would appear from what is stated, chap. xxix., that "neither he nor his army had wages from Tyre for the service which he had served against it." See on that passage. The throwing of the ruins of Tyre into the midst of the sea, will apply to the continental city, and is descriptive of its consignment to utter destruction.

13. In striking contrast with the former joyousness of the merchant-city, a death-like silence was to ensue. The prophet in this and the following verse reaches the climax of his description, concluding with an almost verbal repetition of verses 4 and 5.

14. לֹא תִבָּנֶה עוֹד, *thou shalt be built no more*. This was literally fulfilled with respect to the continental city. That part which lay on the island recovered itself after the lapse of seventy years, as predicted by the prophet Isaiah, chap. xxiii. 17, 18, and was in a very flourishing condition in the time of Alexander, by whom a causeway was constructed between the shore and it, by means of which he reached the city, and took it by storm after a siege of seven months.

16 slayeth in the midst of thee? And all the princes of the sea shall descend from their thrones, and lay aside their mantles, and put off their embroidered garments; they shall be clothed with trembling; they shall sit on the ground, and tremble every
17 moment, and be confounded on account of thee. And they shall take up a lamentation for thee, and shall say to thee: How art thou destroyed, that didst dwell by the seas, the celebrated city which was strong at sea, she and her inhabitants, who inspired
18 all its inhabitants with their terror. Now shall the islands tremble in the day of thy fall; the islands which are in the sea
19 shall be troubled at thy departure. For thus saith the Lord Jehovah: When I make thee a desolate city, as the cities which are not inhabited, by bringing up the deep upon thee, and the
20 mighty waters shall cover thee; Then I will bring thee down with those who go down to the pit, to the ancient people, and will make thee dwell in the land of the lowest regions, in the desolations which have been of old, with those who go down to the pit, that thou mayest not be inhabited; but I will set glory

15-18. The effects of the siege of Tyre were not to be confined to her inhabitants, but were to extend to her colonies. Of these she had many along the coasts and on the islands of the Mediterranean, in Greece, Italy, and Spain, of which the principal were Utica, Carthage, and Tartessus. Like her they were rich and powerful, and for a time were dependent upon her as the mother city. These maritime colonies are represented as struck with consternation on hearing what had befallen her; their chief magistrates, here called נְשִׂיאֵי הַיָּם, *princes of the sea*, are said to have come down from their thrones; and, exchanging their princely robes for those of mourning, to have sat down on the ground, trembling with amazement. Comp. Isa. xxiii. 8, 9. To express the greatness of their distress, they are said to have "clothed themselves with trembling"; Heb. חֲרָדוֹת, *tremblings*, i.e. great trembling. For אִיִּם, ver. 18, the Chaldee for אִיִּים, *islands* or *sea-coasts*, which reading is found in several MSS., the Vulg. has *naves*, as if the original were אֳנִיּוֹת, *ships*. Some would make a distinction between the two forms as here used, supposing that by אִי, *islands* properly so called are meant, and by אִיִּים, *maritime coasts*; but the distinction is altogether imaginary. The same localities are intended in both members of the parallelism. The feature of the description חֲזָקָה בַיָּם, *strong in the sea*, must be referred to the insular part of the city, which had, been strongly fortified as the port for the protection of the warehouses and the shipping. The concluding clause of ver. 17 is descriptive of the despotic rule which the merchant-princes of Tyre exercised over the inhabitants, whether regular citizens or those who were there temporarily on business. צֵאת, the *departure* of Tyre, signifies her disappearance as a celebrated emporium.

19. The "deep," and the "great (or many) waters," metaphors borrowed from the relative position of Tyre, figuratively describe the army of the king of Babylon.

20. The disappearance of Tyre is compared to that of the dead, who, placed in their sepulchre, are no more seen among the living. While this was

21   in the land of the living; I will fill thee with terrors, and thou
shalt not be; and thou shalt be sought for, but shalt not be found
any more for ever, saith the Lord Jehovah.

to be the fate of that renowned city, Jehovah promises to set צְבִי, *glory* in the land of the living. This Grotius and others refer to the restoration of the Jewish polity, which, considering the frequent application of this term to the land of Judea, may seem a not unnatural interpretation, and, if meant to include the Messiah and his spiritual kingdom, for whose introduction that restoration was designed to be preparatory, may readily be admitted. Comp. Isa. iv. 2: "And the Branch of Jehovah shall be לִצְבִי." Thus interpreted, the passage may be considered as Messianic. Nor is it an unusual thing with the Hebrew prophets thus abruptly to introduce a reference to the Redeemer. I cannot admit the propriety of supplying לֹא before נָתַתִּי, or carrying forward the force of that negative as Havernick, after the LXX. and Syr., has done, and so rendering, "I will not set glory in the land of the living," i.e. I will not restore thee to thy former splendor. The construction thus brought out is tame and unnatural.

21. The desolation of Tyre was to be so complete that it should be an object of terror to all who approached the spot where it had stood. Not a vestige of it was to remain: a prophecy which was literally fulfilled, for though insular Tyre afterwards rose into notice, the ancient continental city never recovered from her ruin.

CHAPTER XXVII.

The prophet proceeds in this chapter to give a detailed specification of the splendor, riches, and commerce of Tyre in the days of her prosperity, 1-11; the principal nations with which she traded, and the articles of merchandise which they respectively furnished, 12-25; thence to the end we have a beautiful allegorical description of her downfall.

1   AND the word of Jehovah came unto me, saying; And thou, son
2   of man, take up a lamentation concerning Tyre: and say to
3   Tyre: O thou that dwellest beside the entrances of the sea,
thou trader of the peoples to many sea-coasts, thus saith the
Lord Jehovah; O Tyre! thou sayest, I am perfect in beauty.

2. The prophet is commanded to commence קִינָה, a *funereal dirge* over Tyre, consisting, agreeably to the nature of such ditties, of an eulogium in praise of her splendid qualities.

3. Instead of הַיֹּשַׁבְתִּי the Keri omits the Yod, and exhibits the regular form of the participle הַיֹּשֶׁבֶת. מְבוֹאֹת יָם, *entrances of the sea*. The plural may have been adopted with reference to the double port of Tyre, at which vessels entered round the northern and southern ends of the island. These ports or harbors are thus described by Strabo, (lib. xvi. cap. 2): δύο δ' ἔχει λιμένας, τὸν μὲν κλειστόν, τὸν δ' ἀνειμένον, ὃν Αἰγύπτιον καλοῦσιν. רֹכֶלֶת הָעַמִּים, *the emporium of the peoples*, LXX. τῷ ἐμπορίῳ τῶν λαῶν, i.e. the great emporium to which the merchants of various nations

4   In the midst of the seas were thy borders; those who built thee
5   perfected thy beauty. With cypresses from Senir they built for
    thee all thy boards; they took cedar from Lebanon to make
6   masts for thee. Of oaks of Bashan they made thine oars. Thy
    deck they made of ivory inlaid in cedars, from the isles of
7   Chittim. Thy sails were of fine cotton with embroidered work
    from Egypt. Purple and blue from the coasts of Elishah were
8   thy awning. The inhabitants of Zidon and Arvad were thy
    rowers; thy wise men, O Tyre, were in the midst of thee; they

resorted, and where they bartered or bought and sold their wares. To it were brought, in heavily laden caravans, the rich productions of India and other countries of the East, which passed through it on their way to Europe. Tyre was likewise celebrated for the commerce which she carried on with foreign parts by means of her fleets and colonies. As affluence and magnificence naturally engender pride, she is here represented as boasting of her splendor.

4. Nothing could more admirably or more appropriately have set forth the magnificence of this maritime city than the figure of a gallant ship constructed with the best materials, and manned with the most skilful mariners of the age. This exquisitely beautiful figure here introduced is broken in upon at verse 9, where the prophet resumes his description of the emporium, and proceeds with great minuteness to specify the principal articles in which she traded, and the different countries with which her commerce was carried on. It is, however, very fitly again taken up, ver. 26, when the prophet would describe the wreck to which the city should be reduced. For בֹּנָיִךְ, *thy builders*, some few of De Rossi's MSS. read בָּנַיִךְ, *thy sons*, which reading the LXX. have adopted: *viol sou*: but the former, which has the suffrages of the Chaldean and Jerome, better suits the connection.

5–8. שְׂנִיר, *Senir*, a name given by the Amorites to Hermon or the high southern point of Anti-Libanus, Deut. iii. 9. Like the rest of those mountain-ranges it abounded with a variety of choice and stately trees. לֻחֹתָיִם, *boards, decks*, which appear to have been constructed double. Tabulata duplicia: Sic vocat propheta naves quod duo habeant latera aut duas extremitates, puppim et proram. (Munster.) *Bashan* was celebrated for its oaks, as Lebanon was for its cedars. Of the words בַּת־אֲשֻׁרִים it is impossible to make any tolerable sense. I therefore prefer joining them together as one word. We thus read בתאשירים in one of De Rossi's MSS., which is approved of by Solomon Jarchi, Bochart, and Celsius. In this case הָאֲשֻׁרִים will simply be the plural of הָאֲשׁוּר, a species of cedar called by the Arabs شربين, *Sherbin*; *ivory inlaid in cedars*, would thus be descriptive of the costly materials of which the קֶרֶשׁ, *deck*, was composed. That בִּפְרָשׂ designates the *sail*, seems most naturally suggested by the etymology — פָּרָשׂ, the root, signifying *to spread out, expand*. The Egyptians went to great expense in decorating the sails of their vessels with all kinds of embroidery. Witness the splendid barge of Cleopatra, in which she went to meet Anthony. כְּסֵּה denotes the *covering* or *awning*. אֱלִישָׁה, *Elishah*, is so called, according to Gesenius, from *Elis*, a district of the Peloponnesus, and so put for the whole of Greece. Michaëlis prefers *Hellas*, with a like extended signification. צִירוֹן, *Zidon*, see on chap. xxviii. 20. אַרְוַד, *Arvad*, a small island near the coast of Phœnicia, now called *Ruad*. It occupied a very high rocky situation, and

9 were thy mariners. The elders of Gebal and her wise men were in thee thy caulkers; all ships of the sea and their sailors
10 were in thee to exchange thy barter. Persia and Lud and Put were in thy force, thy men of war; the shield and helmet
11 they hung up in thee. They furnished thy splendor. The sons of Arvad and thy force were upon thy walls around, and the Gammadim were in thy towers. They hung up their shields upon thy walls around; they perfected thy beauty. Tar-
12 shish was thy trader because of the abundance of all wealth; in silver, in iron, in tin, and lead they supplied thy markets.

was about two hundred paces from the continent. Its inhabitants are still noted for their seafaring habits. Προσέθεσαν δὲ τῇ εὐτυχίᾳ ταύτῃ, καὶ πρόνοιαν, καὶ φιλοπονίαν πρὸς τὴν θαλαττουργίαν. (Strabo.) In our prophet they are classed with those of Zidon as furnishing mariners to Tyre.

9. גְּבַל, *Gebal*, the name of a Phœnician city situated on a rising ground near the sea, between Beirut and Tripolis, and inhabited by ship-builders, who, according to Strabo, were originally fugitives from Zidon. It was called Byblos by the Greeks, who celebrated it as the birthplace of Adonis. מַחֲזִיקֵי בִּדְקֵךְ, literally: *the repairers of thy breaches*, which our translators, supposing the repairing of ships to be meant, have rendered, *thy caulkers*, and their translation seems perfectly justifiable from the connection. The word is elsewhere used of the breaches or chinks in a building (2 Kings xii. 6). עָרַב, *to mix, intermix*, as in trade: hence מַעֲרָב עִזְבוֹנֵךְ, lit. *to mix thy mixing*, to carry on trade with thee; to exchange commodities.

10. פָּרַס, *Persia*, i.e. the Persians; לוּד, *Lud*, the Lydians of Mauritania in Africa, a people expert as archers; and פוּט, *Put*, the Putians, a people whose land was conterminous with that of Libya in the same direction west of Egypt. Warriors from the distant east, and likewise from the distant west, are represented as forming the military prowess of Tyre. The former might have been engaged by Tyrian colonists on the Persian Gulf where they had settlements; and the latter at Carthage and other seaports in Africa, to which the Phœnicians resorted. See my Commentary on Jer. xlvi. 9; Nah. iii. 9. Ancient warriors were in the habit of hanging their accoutrements on the walls, not only for the sake of convenience, but also for display as ornaments.

11. The Tyrians employed the inhabitants of Arvad both in their naval service (ver. 8), and in the defence of their city, which was surrounded by walls and ramparts. Who the גַּמָּדִים, *Gammadim* were, who were employed for the same purpose, it is difficult to determine. Various conjectures, both ethnographical and philological, have been advanced; but most of them are unsatisfactory; especially that of Michaelis, who, after the Rabbins, supposing the word to be allied to גֹּמֶד, *Gomed*, which signifies a cubit, imagined that it denoted men, who from their elevated position on the towers appeared like dwarfs to the people below. I should rather be disposed to consider the term as allied to the Arabic جمد, *duro animo ac immiti fuit*, warriors of a fierce, intrepid, and cruel character, not improbably from Chaldea, who were hired by the Tyrians to serve in their army. Comp. Hab. i. 6.

12-25. The prophet now enters upon an enumeration of the different nations that traded with Tyre, beginning and ending with תַּרְשִׁישׁ, *Tarshish*, Tartessus,

13 Javan, Tubal, and Meshech, they were thy traders in persons of men, and implements of copper they supplied in thy market.
14 From the house of Togarmah, horses and horsemen and mules
15 they supplied in thy market. The sons of Dedan were thy traders: many coasts were the merchandise of thy hand; horns
16 of ivory and ebony they returned as thy present. Edom was thy trader for the multitude of thy works; with carbuncle, purple, and embroidery, and cotton, and corals, and ruby, they

the celebrated Phœnician emporium in the west of Spain. From the extreme west, he returns by the countries bordering on Asia Minor to the regions on the Persian Gulf in the distant east, and thence back through Palestine to Tyre.

12. Spain has long been celebrated for the exuberant riches of the mineral kingdom. It is to be noticed, however, as a fact, that while she abounded in most of the metals, especially in silver, gold mines appear to have been only partially wrought, and they have long ceased to attract notice. Mines of iron and lead abounded, as they still do, in that country; but בְּדִיל, *stannum*, tin, was a foreign article, conveyed from the tin-mines in Cornwall to Tartessus by the Phœnicians, and thence to Tyre and other parts of the east.

13. יָוָן, *Javan*, a general term comprehending the whole of Greece, with which Tyre had much maritime intercourse. That there should here be reference to a place of that name in Arabia Felix, which Gesenius thinks probable, is not borne out by the position of the name in Ezekiel, who first introduces Arabia at ver. 21. תּוּבַל וָמֶשֶׁךְ, *Tubal and Meshech*, occur in the same connection with יָוָן, *Javan*, in the ethnographical table Gen. x. 2, and again offer themselves to our view, chaps. xxxii. 26; xxxviii. 2, 3; xxxix. 1, which see. They are now almost universally allowed to designate peoples known to Greek writers under the names of *Moschi* and *Tibareni*, who inhabited the mountainous regions between the Black and Caspian seas. They were, according to our prophet, addicted to the slave-trade; and it is worthy of remark, that till very lately the Turkish harems have been supplied with slaves imported from Circassia and Georgia, the females of which are celebrated for their beauty. By כְּלִי are meant not merely vessels for containing articles, but instruments of all kinds, among others, weapons of war, arms, etc. These are still manufactured in abundance, and of excellent quality, by the inhabitants of Derbend and other parts of the Caucasus. Their swords are celebrated as equal, if not superior, to those of Damascus.

14. תּוֹגַרְמָה, *Togarmah*, the northern Armenians, who call themselves the house of *Torgom*, and claim Torgom or Togarmah, the son of Gomer, as their founder. Compare Gen. x. 3; 1 Chron, i. 6. They inhabit the rough mountainous regions on the south side of the Caucasus. The country was celebrated for its breed of horses, which were in great request with the Persian kings: Οὕτω δ' ἐστὶν ἱπποβότος σφόδρα ἡ χώρα, Strabo, lib. xi. פָּרָשִׁים, *steeds*, horses used for riding, as distinguished from סוּסִים, chariot-horses.

15. דְּדָן, *Dedan*, an island or commercial town in the Persian Gulf, established by the Tyrians to secure the trade of India. שֵׁן, *tooth*, that of the elephant, i.e. ivory, with which India abounded. The tusks resembling horns will account for the term קַרְנוֹת, *horns*, being here employed. That by הָבְנִים we are to understand *ebony* scarcely admits of a doubt. The name is retained in the Greek ἔβενος and the Latin *ebenum*.

17 furnished thy markets. As for Judah and the land of Israel, they were thy traders; with wheat of Minnith and Pannag,
18 and honey and oil and balsam, they furnished thy mart. Damascus was thy trader in the multitude of thy works, because of the multitude of all wealth. in wine of Helbon and white
19 wool. Vedan and Javan, from Uzal, furnished in thy markets polished steel, cassia, and calamus: they were in thy
20 market. Dedan was thy trader in tapestry for riding. Arabia

Gesenius thinks the reason why it occurs in the plural is, that it was obtained only in planks split into pieces for transportation. Its great hardness made it an article of value.

16. From the circumstances that Syria may be viewed as included under Damascus in verse 18, and that no mention is made in the enumeration of Idumea, whose capital Petra formed a centre of traffic in ancient times, I am inclined to adopt the reading אֲרָם, *Edom*, which is found in fifteen codices, has been in eleven more originally, and is confirmed by the reading אֱדוֹם of the LXX., the Hexaplar-Syriac and Arabic versions. The gems here specified are rather to be referred to the Indian Ocean, than to any places in connection with Syria. מַעֲשֵׂה בְרֹשׁ here, and ver. 18, is not to be understood of articles made or manufactured in Tyre, but of articles conveyed thither for traffic. LXX. 'Ἀπὸ πλήθους τοῦ συμμίκτου σου. נֹפֶךְ the LXX., in other places, render Ἄνθραξ; but here omit it. It was one of the precious stones in the breastplate of the Jewish high-priest, but of what kind cannot absolutely be determined, though it is generally supposed to have been the emerald. כַּרְכֹּר, the *ruby.* רָאמֹת, though here reckoned among gems, was in all probability, as asserted by the Rabbins, the *red coral,* from its red, shining appearance.

17. מִנִּית, *Minnith,* is mentioned as a city of the Ammonites, Judges xi. 33. Of פַּנַּג, *Pannag,* nothing is known, but from the connection we should suppose it to be the name of a place.

18. חֶלְבּוֹן, *Helbon,* Aleppo, the wines of which were held in such high estimation that the Persian monarchs would drink no other. Τὸν Χαλυβώνιον, Strabo, lib. xv.

19. Besides the fact that no other word in the enumeration of places in this chapter commences with the copulative ו, the name of *Dan* would seem to be so entirely out of place here, that there is certainly room for the conjecture that the Vau in וְדָן, *Vedan,* is not to be read as a conjunction, but forms an integral part of the word. Whether it may still be traced in Aden, a place famous for trade near the straits of Babelmandeb, may be queried. That אוּזָל, *Uzal,* probably so called from a descendant of Joktan (Gen. x. 27), was the original name of Sanaa, the ancient metropolis of Arabia Felix, was ascertained by Niebuhr when he visited that country. It was famous for its sword blades, to which no doubt, as made from the בַּרְזֶל, iron or steel here mentioned, reference is had. It is probable that the *Javan* here mentioned along with it, and described as having its origin from it, was founded by Greek colonists who had settled there. Instead of מְאוּזָּל thirteen codices read מֵאוּזָל with a different pointing of the preposition. קִדָּה, *cassia,* an aromatic shrub resembling cinnamon, but less fragrant and valuable. By קָנֶה is meant *calamus aromaticus,* sweet cane or flag, growing in marshy ground, and used in the East for perfumes. It abounds in Arabia and Africa.

20. The Dedan here mentioned is to

21 and all the princes of Kedar, they were thy traders in lambs,
22 and rams, and he-goats; in them they were thy traders. The merchants of Sheba and Ramah, they were thy traders; with the chief of all spices and with all precious stones and gold they
23 furnished thy markets. Haran, and Calneh, and Eden, the
24 merchants of Sheba, Asshur, Chilmad, were thy traders. They were thy traders in splendid articles, in mantles, purple cloths, and embroidery, and damask stuffs bound together with cords,

be distinguished from that which occurs ver. 15, and lay in northern Arabia. The inhabitants were descended from Keturah (Gen. xxv. 3), and were celebrated for their pastoral habits. Hence the articles with which they are described as supplying Tyre, were such as their nomadic country and habits furnished.

21. סֹחֲרֵי יָדֵךְ, *thy merchants:* יָד denoting possession, or occupation.

22. שְׁבָא וְרַעְמָה, *Sheba* and *Raemah*, countries in Arabia abounding in spices, gold, and precious stones. These articles the inhabitants obtained in part from India, and transported them in caravans to Tyre. בְּרֹאשׁ, *with the chief* or *best* spices. Comp. Deut. xxxiii. 15. It was from that region that the queen came to behold the magnificence of Solomon. עִזְבוֹנָיִךְ, *thy deliverings,* i.e. in traffic, one party handing over to another. The word is also used to denote the profits or gains obtained by trading.

23. חָרָן, LXX. Χαρρά, Arab. حران ,

a city of Mesopotamia, once the dwelling-place of Abraham, and afterwards celebrated for the defeat of Crassus. כַּנֵּה, *Canneh,* otherwise spelt *Calneh,* an Assyrian city situated on the eastern bank of the Tigris, opposite Seleucia, and identical with Ctesiphon of the Greeks. עֶדֶן, *Eden,* was the name of a beautiful valley near Damascus, but occurring here in connection with *Haran* and *Calneh,* is in this case to be referred to the same country with them. Whether it is to be identified with the original abode of our first parents may be questioned. We are not authorized by the simple circumstance that the merchants of *Sheba* are here coupled with those of Haran, Canneh and Eden, to conclude with some expositors that a country in southern Arabia is intended; since, if we consider the term as including Arabia Deserta, they will be brought into a conterminous position in reference to those countries, and regarded as, jointly with the inhabitants of those lands, carrying on trade with Tyre. אַשּׁוּר, *Assyria,* as denoting the countries to the east of the Tigris, comes into its proper place. כִּלְמַד still remains in obscurity. The LXX. Χαρμάν. Scholz thinks it was probably the northern part of Media bordering on the Caspian sea; but the name would seem to have been retained in the Καρμάνδη of Xenophon, which he describes as lying beyond the Euphrates, a large and flourishing city πόλις εὐδαίμων καὶ μεγάλη. The connection of the name with that of Assyria favors this conjecture.

24. From these eastern quarters Tyre derived supplies of all kinds of costly and beautiful garments. מִכְלֻלִים, *perfections,* the most exquisite articles of finery. גְּלוֹמִים, *mantles,* wide, hanging garments, pallia. Compare the Greek Χλαμύς. Root, גָּלַם, *to wrap* or *fold.* גְּנָזִים, LXX. θησαυροὺς ἐκλεκτούς. The word is originally Persic, and signifies *treasures,* or chests in which they are deposited (Esth. iii. 9). From the connection we should infer that precious cloths are here meant. בְּרוֹמִים, *damask stuffs,* consisting of threads of various

25 and cedars, in thy market. Ships of Tarshish were thy walls, thy trade: thou wast replenished, thou wast greatly honored, in the heart of the seas.

26 Thy rowers brought thee into great waters: the east wind broke
27 thee in pieces in the heart of the seas. Thy riches and thy markets, thy exchange, thy mariners and thy pilots, thy caulkers, and those who bartered thy barter, and all thy warriors who were in thee, even with all thy collected multitude which was in the midst of thee, shall fall in the heart of the seas in the day
28 of thy fall. At the sound of the cry of thy pilots the suburbs
29 shall shake. And all who handle the oar, seamen, and all the the pilots of the sea, shall come down from their ships; they
30 shall stand on the land. And cause their voice to be heard respecting thee, and shall cry bitterly, and throw dust upon
31 their heads, and wallow in ashes, And make themselves bald for thee with great baldness, and gird on sackcloth, and weep for
32 thee in bitterness of soul, with bitter mourning; And take up a lamentation for thee in their wailing, and lament for thee: Who was like Tyre, like the destroyed in the midst of the sea?
33 When thy wares went forth from the seas, thou didst glut many peoples; with the multitude of thy riches and thy merchandise thou
34 didst enrich the kings of the earth. Now thyself art broken by the seas in the depths of the waters; thy merchandise and all thy
35 company are fallen in the midst of thee. All the inhabitants of the coasts shall be astonished at thee, and their kings shall

colors woven together in figures. Arab. مبر, *restis ex utroque filo contexta.*

25. The prophet now returns from his enumeration of the various articles of commerce with which Tyre enriched herself, and the various countries with which she traded, to commemorate her fall. But just before entering upon that part of his subject, he stops for a moment to advert to her navy, by which her wares were conveyed to Spain and other coasts of the Mediterranean. אֲנִיּוֹת תַּרְשִׁישׁ, *ships of Tarshish*, were comparatively speaking what our Indiamen are in the present day. They are called שָׁרוֹת, the *walls* of Tyre, for the same reason that we speak of our ships of war as the wooden walls of Old England. They were the glory and defence of the merchant-city.

26. All of a sudden Tyre is metaphorically introduced as a ship foundered at sea. The instrument employed in effecting her destruction was רוּחַ הַקָּדִים, *the east wind*, which blowing in a violent storm from Lebanon, is the most vehement of all in the Mediterranean. Comp. Ps. xlviii. 8. Of course the reference is to Nebuchadnezzar, who is represented under this figure.

27. This specification has the finest effect. The destruction was to be utter and irrecoverable.

28-36. Nothing can be more graphic than the description here given of the universal consternation and mourning produced by the fall of Tyre.

36 greatly shudder at thee, their faces shall tremble. The merchants among the peoples shall hiss at thee: thou shalt be an object of extreme terror, and shalt not be any more forever.

CHAPTER XXVIII.

In this chapter we have a sublime threnody on the prince of Tyre, couched in language of the keenest irony. His fall is first of all traced to his insufferable pride, which is described in the most glowing terms, verses 2–6. His merited punishment is next announced, 7–10. The prophet, in obedience to the divine command, then proceeds to deliver the funeral dirge, exaggerating the dignity and magnificence of the fallen monarch, with which he contrasts his utter degradation, 11–19. Then follows a prediction announcing the fall of the mother-city, Zidon, 20–23. And the chapter concludes with promises of deliverance to the Jews, and their restoration to prosperity in their own land, 24–26.

1 And the word of Jehovah came unto me, saying: Son of man, say
2 to the prince of Tyre: Thus saith the Lord Jehovah: Forasmuch as thy heart was lifted up, and thou hast said: I am a god; I sit in the throne of God, in the heart of the seas: (whereas thou art a man, and no god), and hast set thy heart as the heart
3 of God: Behold, thou art wiser than Daniel, nothing secret is
4 hid from thee. By thy wisdom and thine understanding thou hast procured for thyself wealth, and hast gotten gold and silver
5 in thy treasuries. By the greatness of thy wisdom and thy merchandise thou hast increased thy riches, and thy heart was
6 lifted up because of thy riches. Therefore thus saith the Lord Jehovah: Because thou hast set thy heart as the heart of God,

1. The monarch of Tyre, at the time when Ezekiel delivered his prophecy, was Ithbaal II., whose name has been preserved in the Phœnician annals. Josephus, contra Apion, § 21, calls him Ἰθόβαλος. The name is of frequent occurrence in compound proper names of Phœnician and Carthaginian men, and indicates that the prince was specially addicted to the worship of Baal, the tutelary god of the Tyrians. He is here designated נָגִיד, prince, for which name we have מֶלֶךְ, king (ver. 12). Considering the vast extent of riches possessed by the Phœnician merchants, it is not surprising that they should have emulated the state and dignity of Oriental empires, having not only petty or subordinate kings, but one supreme monarch, in whom concentrated the administration of the affairs of state. The king is, in the present instance, in language of the keenest irony, represented as impiously arrogating to himself equality with the Deity; as did the king of Babylon (Isa. xiv. 13). The contrast וַאֲנִי אָדָם וְלֹא־אֵל, but thou art a man, and not God, is inimitable. Thus was the pride of his heart checked.

3–6. Ezekiel ironically ascribes to Ithbaal a higher degree of wisdom than that displayed by Daniel, whose fame

7 Therefore, behold, I will bring against thee barbarians, the terrible of the nations, and they shall unsheathe their swords against the beauty of thy wisdom, and shall obscure thy splendor.
8 They shall bring thee down to the pit, and thou shalt
9 die the deaths of the slain in the midst of the seas. Wilt thou still say, I am God, before him that slayeth thee? seeing thou art a man, and no god, in the hand of him that smiteth thee.
10 Thou shalt die the deaths of the uncircumcised by the hand of barbarians; for I have spoken it, saith the Lord Jehovah.
11 And the word of Jehovah came unto me, saying: Son of man,
12 take up a lamentation for the king of Tyre, and say to him: Thus saith the Lord Jehovah: Thou model seal, full of wisdom
13 and of perfect beauty: Thou wast in Eden, the garden of God; every precious stone was thy covering; the sardius, the topaz, and the onyx, the chrysolite, the sardonyx, and the jasper, the sapphire, the carbuncle, and the smaragd, and gold: the work of thy tabrets and thy pipes was in thee; they were prepared in

---

had reached the Tyrian court. Instead of acknowledging him in whose hand is the power to get wealth, he arrogated his vast prosperity entirely to himself, and thereby provoked the indignation of the Most High.

7. גּוֹיִם עָרִיצֵי זָרִים, *foreigners, barbarians, the terrible ones of the nations,* i.e. the Chaldeans, noted for their barbarity. Comp. Isa. i. 7; xxv. 2; Ezek. xxx. 11; xxxi. 12.

8, 9. Ithbaal should be reduced to a state of the deepest degradation and infamy: his utter helplessness is strongly asserted. מְמוֹתֵי, *deaths*, a peculiar form of the plural, to indicate emphatically the most violent death. The death of the king of Tyre is compared to that of those slain in a sea-engagement, and cast into the deep.

10. The uncircumcised are uniformly spoken of by the Jews as objects of contempt and abhorrence: hence the force of the threatening here employed.

12. For the explanation of קִינָה, see the custom referred to in my Comment. on Jer. ix. 16; Amos v. 16. Such a doleful ditty the prophet was now to pronounce over the king of Tyre. As it was customary on such occasions to reckon up the qualities for which the deceased was distinguished, in order thereby to enhance the greatness of the loss sustained, so Ezekiel begins by lavishing his praise of the kingly state of the Tyrian monarch as one of unequalled magnificence. אַתָּה חֹתֵם תָּכְנִית, *thou art the seal of perfection.* I prefer the pointing חֹתֵם, *a seal* or *signet*, which is that of some codices and printed editions. We have thus the substantive instead of the participle. LXX. ἀποσφράγισμα. Seals were used for the purpose of authenticating or securing anything. When it is said, therefore, that the king was the seal of perfection, the meaning is that he could not be surpassed in riches, splendor, or power. The sum-total of all that was illustrious concentrated in him. He vindicated to himself all that mortal could pretend to. תָּכַן signifies *to measure,* take an accurate and perfect account of anything; hence the noun came to signify, in the highest sense, absolute perfection.

13. Not content with a simple declara-

14   the day when thou wast created. Thou wast an anointed cherub which coveredst; and I placed thee on the sacred mount of God: there thou wast; in the midst of the stones of fire thou
15   walkedst. Thou wast perfect in thy ways from the day in which thou wast created until wickedness was found in thee.
16   By the greatness of thy merchandise they filled thy midst with violence, and thou didst sin; then, from the mount of God, I treated thee as profane, yea, I destroyed thee from the midst of
17   the stones of fire, O cherub which coveredst. Thy heart lifted itself up in thy beauty, thou spoiledst thy wisdom by reason of thy splendor; I threw thee down on the earth, I placed thee

tion to this effect, the prophet enters into particulars, and commences by placing the monarch in the primitive abode of man, with which was associated every idea of pleasure and delight. It is quite a lowering of the subject to suggest with Michaelis that he might have had a summer residence in the beautiful valley of the cedars of Lebanon, whither he retired during the hot season of the year. Eden was called the garden of God, because it was of his plantation, and formed the delightful scene of his divine manifestations to the first pair. To have been there, conveys the idea of the most distinguished honor and felicity. Taking occasion from his reference to Eden, with which the Bible history connects the existence of bdellium and onyx-stones, Ezekiel, with his usual minuteness, gives a detailed account of the precious gems which adorned the regal state. The nine precious stones here specified correspond to those with the same names in the description of the high priest's breastplate (Exod. xxxix. 10–13). Those composing the third row are omitted in the Hebrew text, which Michaelis ascribes to an error of the copyist; but they are expressed in that of the LXX. The day of the creation of the king was that of his accession to the throne. It was celebrated, as such occasions usually are, with outbursts of popular rejoicing.

14. The fact of Ezekiel's mind having

been led to dwell upon the scene in the Jewish temple, furnishes the key to the words כְּרוּב הַסּוֹכֵךְ, *the cherub that covereth*. As the cherubim overshadowed the mercy-seat with their outspread wings, so the king of Tyre is represented as extending his protection to the city and all its interests. His regal position Jehovah vindicates to himself. Comp. Prov. viii. 16; Rom. xiii. 1. He was consecrated to this dignity, as everything connected with the temple was, and was so bespangled with gems that he might be said to walk in the midst of them. הַר־קֹדֶשׁ אֱלֹהִים, *the holy mountain of God.* To this his illimitable ambition aspired. In imagination he occupied Mount Zion, the dwelling-place of the Most High

15–17. The rectitude with which the monarch commenced his reign may be illustrated by a reference to the history of Hiram (1 Kings v. 7); but having in process of time become corrupt through the uninterrupted commercial prosperity of the Tyrian state, he indulged in unscrupulous acts of injustice and cruelty, on account of which merited punishment is here denounced. There is a palpable paronomasia in יִפְעָתֶךָ and יָפְיֶךָ. Both roots from which the verbs are derived have the signification in common, *to be bright, shine*, etc. Pride of heart arising from a consciousness of beauty has a strong tendency to corrupt the understanding. The royal personage was to

18 before kings that they might look at thee. By reason of the multitude of thine iniquities, through the wickedness of thy merchandise thou hast profaned thy sanctuaries; therefore I will cause fire to come forth out of thy midst, which shall consume thee; and I will reduce thee to ashes upon the ground in
19 the sight of all who behold thee. All who knew thee among the peoples shall be astounded on thine account; thou shalt be an object of extreme terror, and shalt not be any more forever.
20 And the word of Jehovah came unto me, saying: Son of man, set
21 thy face against Zidon, and prophesy against her, and say:
22 Thus saith the Lord Jehovah, Behold, I am against thee, O Zidon, and I will be glorified in the midst of thee, and they shall know that I am Jehovah, when I execute judgments in her, and
23 am sanctified in her. And I will send on her pestilence, and blood in her streets, and the slain shall fall in the midst of her by the sword against her round about, and they shall know that

be hurled from the summit of his elevation, from which he had looked down with disdain on others, and to be made an example to the great ones of the earth of the nothingness of all earthly grandeur, and the guilt contracted by violence and oppression. For לִרְאָיָה read with one of Kennicott's codices לִרְאִי.

18. Instead of מִקְדָּשֶׁיךָ, *thy sanctuaries*, forty of Kennicott's and De Rossi's codices read מִקְדָּשְׁךָ, *thy sanctuary*, in the singular. The sanctuaries of Tyre were the temples erected for the worship of the gods severally acknowledged by the different nations whose merchants frequented her port, and especially Hercules, the celebrated hero of Grecian mythology.

20–23. The prophet is now commanded to turn for a moment from Tyre, and denounce the divine judgments against the neighboring city of Zidon. Having entered with so much particularity into his description of the fall of the former city, in which that of Zidon might be regarded as virtually implied, it was not necessary to do more than generally to predict the certainty of the divine inflictions. צִידוֹן, *Zidon*, was a very ancient Phoenician city, otherwise famous for its fishery (hence its name from צוּד, *to hunt fish*, etc.), and afterwards for its extended and flourishing commerce both by sea and land. It became so noted for the manufacture of glass and other articles of luxury, that the epithet *Sidonia ars* was used by the ancients to denote whatever was elegant or magnificent. According to Strabo, the Zidonians were celebrated for their skill in astronomy, philosophy, navigation, and all the liberal arts. Zidon was founded by the first-born of Canaan (Gen. x. 15); and was situated, according to Strabo, two hundred stadia to the north of Tyre. Favored by its position on the coast of the Mediterranean, it early became celebrated for its commerce. In the time of Jacob, it is mentioned in connection with shipping (Gen. xlix. 13); and in that of Joshua, it is celebrated as a "great" city, (Josh. xi. 8; xix. 28). It lay within the boundary of the land assigned to the tribe of Asher; but was never conquered by the Israelites, (Judg. i. 31). Its proximity to Lebanon procured it many advantages. At the present day, the town of Saida, صيدا, a little to the west, occupies its site. It

24 I am Jehovah. And there shall no more be a pricking thorn or a nettle occasioning pain to the house of Israel of all who are around them, who treated them with despite, and they shall know that I am the Lord Jehovah. Thus saith the Lord Jeho-
25 vah: When I collect the house of Israel from the peoples among whom I have scattered them, and am sanctified in them in the sight of the nations, and they shall dwell in their own land
26 which I did give to my servant Jacob: Then shall they dwell in it securely, and build houses, and plant vineyards; and dwell securely, when I execute judgments upon all who treated them with despite around them; and they shall know that I am Jehovah their God.

has a fine old ruined tower projecting far into the sea, with a bridge of many arches that was built to reach it. See Robinson's Palestine, iii. 415–428. In Matt. xi. 22, Tyre and Zidon are coupled together.

We have no authentic historical information relative to the destruction of Zidon, but there can be little doubt that it was effected by the same Chaldean power which overthrew Tyre. In fact, as we have just observed, the destruction of the one virtually involved that of the other. נָפְלָל, an emphatic form of Niphal, adopted for the purpose of more forcibly expressing the completeness of the destruction which should overtake the Zidonians. Some trace of a paronomasia may be detected in נֶחֱלָל נִפְלָל.

24–26. These cities, which had been a constant source of annoyance to their neighbors, and to none more than to the Jews, being rendered powerless, the people of God, restored from Babylon to their own land, should enjoy all their ancient privileges, and all around them be compelled to ascribe to Jehovah, as their covenant God, the glory due to his name.

CHAPTER XXIX.

This forms the first of four chapters directed against Egypt. Pharaoh, a monarch with whom the Hebrews were frequently in contact, is represented as vaunting in the security of his position, when the prophet is commissioned to announce the divine interposition to effect the desolation of his country throughout its whole extent, 1–12. Though after the lapse of forty years the Egyptian people were to be restored to their country, the kingdom was never to emerge from that state of degradation to which it should be reduced, 13–16. The following verses 17–20, distinctly announce the conquest of the country by Nebuchadnezzar; and the chapter concludes with a promise of future prosperity to the Jews, 21.

1 IN the tenth year, in the tenth month, on the twelfth day of the
2 month, the word of Jehovah came unto me, saying: Son of man, set thy face against Pharaoh king of Egypt, yea, prophesy
3 against him, and against all Egypt. Speak, and say: Thus saith

3. פַּרְעֹה, *Pharaoh*, was a general name of the kings of Egypt down to the time of the Persian conquest. A more appropriate emblem of these kings could

the Lord Jehovah: Behold, I am against thee, O Pharaoh, king of Egypt, the great sea-monster that croucheth in the midst of his rivers, who saith: My river is mine, and I made it for my-
4 self. But I will put hooks in thy jaws, and will cause the fish of thy rivers to cleave to thy scales, and will bring thee up from the midst of thy rivers, and all the fish of thy rivers shall cleave
5 to thy scales; And I will thrust thee forth into the desert, both thee and all the fish of thy rivers; upon the surface of the field thou shalt fall, thou shalt not be gathered up nor collected; I have given thee to the wild beast of the earth and to the birds
6 of heaven for food. And all the inhabitants of Egypt shall know that I am Jehovah, because they were a staff of reed to
7 lean upon to the house of Israel. When they laid hold of thee by thy hand, thou wast broken, and thou didst cleave for them the entire shoulder; and when they leaned upon thee, thou wast
8 broken, and all their loins were put out of joint. Therefore thus saith the Lord Jehovah: Behold, I will bring a sword
9 upon thee, and will cut off from thee man and beast. And the land of Egypt shall become desolate and waste; and they shall know that I am Jehovah; because he said: the river is mine,
10 and I made it. Therefore, behold, I am against thee, and against thy rivers, and I will make the land of Egypt most desolate and waste from Migdol unto Syene, and unto the border of Cush.
11 No foot of man shall pass through her, neither shall foot of beast pass through her, and she shall not be dwelt in for forty
12 years. And I will make the land of Egypt desolate in the midst of desolate countries; and her cities in the midst of desolate cities; they shall be desolate forty years. And I will scatter the Egyptians among the nations, and disperse them
13 among the countries. Yet thus saith the Lord Jehovah: At the end of forty years, I will gather the Egyptians from the

not have been selected than that of פְּנִים, by which we are to understand the crocodile, the terrible sea-monster inhabiting the Nile, whose usual size is about eighteen or twenty feet in length, but sometimes from thirty to forty. This animal occurs on Roman coins as emblematical of Egypt. The יְאֹרִים, *rivers*, were the branches into which the Nile was divided, and to which the country was indebted for its fertility. קַשְׂקְשִׂים are appropriately descriptive of the *scales* of the crocodile, resembling as they do the plates of a coat of mail. Continuing his emblematical allusion, the prophet represents Jehovah as dragging up the monster with a hook, while attendant shoals adhere to his scales for shelter.

6, 7. All the alliances which the Jews formed with Egypt proved fruitless and noxious. Comp. Isa. xxx. 1–5; 2 Kings xviii. 21.

8–13. The sword which God threatens to bring upon the king of Egypt was

14 peoples whither they were scattered. And I will reverse the captivity of the Egyptians, and restore them to the land of Pathros, to the land of their nativity; and they shall be there a
15 base kingdom. It shall be the basest of the kingdoms, and shall not exalt itself any more over the nations. And I will diminish
16 them, that they may not have dominion among the nations. And they shall no more be an object of confidence to the house of Israel, causing iniquity to be remembered, while they turn after them; and they shall know that I am the Lord Jehovah.
17 And it came to pass in the seven and twentieth year, in the first month, on the first of the month, that the word of Jehovah

that of Nebuchadnezzar. Comp. verses 18-20. מִגְדֹּל, *Migdol*, and סְוֵנֵה, *Sevene*, Strabo Συήνη, were cities at the two extremities of Egypt; the former a few miles to the north of Suez in Lower Egypt; and the latter near the modern city of Asevan, towards Nubia, celebrated for its ruins of temples and palaces.

The period of forty years is supposed to include that from the conquest of Egypt by Nebuchadnezzar till she shook off the Babylonian yoke in the time of Cyrus. Some interpreters are of opinion that the years are not to be taken literally, but consider the language as hyperbolical. Fairbairn thinks that the prophecy is to be taken in a historico-ideal sense, and illustrates it by reference to the explanation he gives of chap. iv. Whatever there may be in this argument, or in the absence of strict chronological data in support of a simply literal sense, there is nothing in the circumstances of the case to warrant our absolute rejection of the latter. History so nearly quadrates with the language of the prophet, that little account is to be made of a few years more or less.

14, 15. For *Pathros* see Comment. on Isa. xi. 11. On the conquest of Babylon by Cyrus, the Egyptians who with others were captives in that country, were set at liberty. The prediction that Egypt was to be the basest of kingdoms is not to be pressed so as to make it clash with the present condition of that country.

It was sufficiently fulfilled in its continuance for so many centuries in such depressed circumstances as not to entitle it to be ranked with the ancient monarchies of the earth. It was never again to become a basis of confidence to the Jews. They should no longer hanker after protection from it, and thereby enhance the guilt anciently contracted by their fathers. Under Amasis, it was greatly reduced. It was still more humbled under Cambyses, by whom it was conquered; and none of its attempts to recover itself under the Persian monarchy succeeded. Nor has it, amid all the changes to which its affairs have since been subject, ever acquired anything in the shape of supremacy over other nations of the earth. Even in the present day, notwithstanding all that has been done for it by the Pashas, it still retains marks of inferiority.

A period of nearly seventeen years intervened between the delivery of the preceding prophecy and that which follows, but they are thrown together in the canon as relating to the same subject.

17-20. It is not to be inferred from these verses that Nebuchadnezzar was unsuccessful in his attack upon Tyre. All that can fairly be inferred from them is, that the spoils which he gained on that occasion were considered a very inadequate remuneration to him and his army for the vast expenditure of time and strength which it had cost him.

18 came unto me, saying: Son of man, Nebuchadrezzar, king of Babylon, caused his army to serve with great service against Tyre: every head was bald, and every shoulder made bare, while there was no pay to him and his army from Tyre, for the
19 service which he served against her. Therefore thus saith the Lord Jehovah: Behold, I will give to Nebuchadrezzar, king of Babylon, the land of Egypt; and he shall take away her multitude, and her spoil, and her prey, and she shall be pay for his
20 army. As his wages for what he served against her. I have given him the land of Egypt, because they wrought for me,
21 saith the Lord Jehovah. In that day I will cause the horn of the house of Israel to bud; and I will give thee an opening of the mouth in the midst of them; and they shall know that I am Jehovah.

Jehovah, whose work he had performed, here promises to recompense him with the conquest of Egypt. On breaking up from Tyre he proceeded to that country, which he found so distracted by internal commotions, that he easily devastated and made himself master of the whole land.

21. While Egypt was subject to eastern rule, the Jews were to be restored to their own land, and full liberty was to be given to the prophet to exercise his ministry among them. Sacred history is silent relative to the last days of Ezekiel, but there is nothing that militates against the supposition that he returned with his fellow-countrymen from Babylon.

CHAPTER XXX.

A second prophecy against Egypt, consisting of two parts, the first, verses 1-19, containing detailed predictions relative to the desolations which should overtake different parts of the country. The second part, 20-26, contains a repetition of the prophetic announcements of the coming judgments in more general terms.

1 AND the word of Jehovah came unto me, saying: Son of man,
2 prophesy and say: Thus saith the Lord Jehovah: Howl ye!
3 alas, for the day! For the day is near, even the day of Jehovah is near, a day of clouds: it shall be the time of the nations.
4 For the sword shall come against Egypt, and great pangs shall be in Cush, when the slain fall in Egypt, and they take away

1-3. The judgments to be inflicted should be so tremendous in their character, that they were calculated to produce feelings of the greatest alarm, not in the minds of the Egyptians only, but in other heathen nations. They were to overtake all the enemies of God and of his people.

4. חַלְחָלָה is rendered doubly emphatic by the repetition of the syllable. The word is derived from חוּל, which signifies to be in pangs as in childbirth.

5 her multitude, and her foundations are torn up. Cush, and Put, and Lud, and all the mixed people, and Chub, and the sons of the land of the covenant, with them they shall fall by
6 the sword. Thus saith Jehovah: The supports of Egypt shall fall, and the pride of her strength shall come down; from Migdol unto Syene they shall fall in her by the sword, saith the
7 Lord Jehovah. And they shall be desolate, in the midst of the countries that are desolate, and its cities shall be in the midst
8 of wasted cities. And they shall know that I am Jehovah, when I set a fire in Egypt, and all her helpers are destroyed.
9 At that day shall messengers go forth from me in ships to terrify secure Cush, and great pain shall be upon them, as in the day
10 of Egypt; for, behold, it cometh. Thus saith the Lord Jehovah: Then I will make the multitude of Egypt to cease by the hand
11 of Nebuchadrezzar the king of Babylon. He and his people with him, the terrible of the nations, shall be brought to destroy the land; and they shall unsheathe their swords against Egypt,
12 and fill the land with slain. And I will make the rivers dry, and sell the country into the hand of the wicked, and will make desolate the land and her fulness by the hand of barbarians: I

5. For כּוּשׁ, *Cush*, see Comment. on Isa. xi. 11. For פוּט, *Put*, on Jer. xlvi. 9. For לוּד, *Lydia*, on Isa. lxvi. 19. By עֶרֶב we are to understand a mixed mass of foreigners, most probably from the interior of Africa, who served in the Egyptian army. Comp. Exod. xii. 38; Jer. xxv. 20, 24. Where כּוּב, *Chub*, lay, has been much disputed. It appears to have been unknown to the translators of the LXX., for they have nothing corresponding to the word in their version. Michaelis is of opinion, that the name is to be found in *Kube*, a mercantile city on the Indian Ocean, described by ancient geographers as lying on the eighth degree of north latitude. The Arabic version reads اهل النوبة, *the inhabitants of Nubia*, which has been thought to be supported by כּנִיב, the primary reading of one of De Rossi's MSS.; but Nubia is always expressed in Hebrew by כּוּשׁ, *Cush*. בְּנֵי אֶרֶץ הַבְּרִית, *the sons of the land of the cove-* nant, cannot well be otherwise explained than as signifying the Jews, who carried Jeremiah the prophet into Egypt, and who had taken up their abode there. Even they were not to escape.

6–8. Egypt was to share the fate of the other countries that had been conquered by Nebuchadnezzar. She and her auxiliaries were to be involved in one common destruction.

9. The Ethiopians, lying beyond the cataracts of the Nile, might deem themselves secure from the attack of the invader, but they also should not escape. Messengers were to be despatched by skiffs on the Nile as far as navigable, to announce the irruption of the Chaldeans. Comp. Isa. xviii. 2. כְּיוֹם מִצְרָיִם, *as the day of Egypt*. A similar judgment should overtake the Ethiopians to that which was to be inflicted on the Egyptians.

10. *The multitude*, refers to the then existing population, which, according to

13 Jehovah have spoken it. Thus saith the Lord Jehovah: I will also destroy the idols, and cause the gods of nought to cease from Noph, and there shall be no more a prince of the land of
14 Egypt; and I will set fear in the land of Egypt. And I will devastate Pathros. and set fire in Zoan. and will execute judg-
15 ments in No. And I will pour out my fury upon Sin, the
16 fortress of Egypt, and cut off Haman No. And when I set fire in Egypt. Sin shall be in great pain, and No shall be broken in
17 upon. and Noph shall be in daily distress. The youths of Aven and Pi-beseth shall fall by the sword, and the women shall go
18 into captivity. And in Tahpenhes the day shall become dark, when I break there the sceptres of Egypt; and the pride of her strength shall cease in her; as for herself a cloud shall cover
19 her, and her daughters shall go into captivity. And I will execute my judgments on Egypt, and they shall know that I am Jehovah.
20 And it came to pass in the eleventh year, in the first month, on the seventh of the month, that the word of Jehovah came unto
21 me, saying: Son of man, I have broken the arm of Pharaoh. king of Egypt; and. behold, it shall not be bound up by giving medicines. laying on a bandage to bind it and strengthen it, that it may handle the sword.

all the accounts of the ancients, must have been very great.

12. Comp. Isa. xix. 5-10. The drying up of the canals of the Nile would greatly facilitate the conquest of the country by the invading army.

13. נֹף, *Noph*, i.e. Memphis, the ancient capital of Middle Egypt, and the chief city of her gods. See Comment. on Isa. xix. 13.

14, 15. צֹעַן, *Zoan*, one of the principal cities of Lower Egypt, and a royal residence of the Pharaohs. See Comment. on Isa. xix. 11. It would be one of the first places attacked by Nebuchadnezzar נֹא, *No*, Diospolis, or Thebes, the ancient metropolis of Upper Egypt, the splendid ruins of which, as exhibited by Wilkinson, are such as to excite the greatest astonishment. סִין, *Sin*, i.e. Pelusium, situated on the north-eastern frontier of Egypt, which having been strongly fortified, and surrounded by marshes, was regarded as the key to the country.

16. צָרֵי יוֹמָם, *enemies daily*, i.e. day after day, perpetually, till the city, however obstinate might be her resistance, should be taken.

17. אָוֶן, *Aven, On*, or *Heliopolis*, celebrated for its temple of the sun, hence called *Bethshemesh* by the Hebrews. Comp. Jer. xliii. 13. It lay a few miles north of Memphis on the eastern bank of the Nile. פִּי־בֶסֶת, *Pi-beseth*, the principal city of the region of Bubastis, whose temple attracted vast numbers of people to its festivals. Though entirely destroyed, the fine granite stones which mark its site confirm the account given by Herodotus of its ancient magnificence.

18. תַּחְפַּנְחֵס, *Tahpenhes*, a strongly fortified frontier-city, near Pelusium. See Comment. on Isa. xxx. 4; Jer. ii. 16. LXX. Τάφνη, Daphne. מֹטוֹת, if pointed מַטּוֹת, will signify *sceptres;* if מֹטוֹת, *yokes*. Either meaning will well suit

22 Wherefore thus saith the Lord Jehovah: Behold, I am against Pharaoh, king of Egypt, and I will break his arms, the strong one, and the broken one, and will cause the sword to fall out of
23 his hand. And I will scatter the Egyptians among the nations,
24 and disperse them through the countries: And I will strengthen the arms of the king of Babylon, and put my sword into his hand; and I will break the arms of Pharaoh, and he shall groan before him with the groanings of one who is deadly wounded.
25 And I will strengthen the arms of the king of Babylon, and the arms of Pharaoh shall fall; and they shall know that I am Jehovah, when I give my sword into the hand of the king of
26 Babylon, and he shall stretch it over the land of Egypt. And I will scatter the Egyptians among the nations, and disperse them in the countries, that they may know that I am Jehovah.

the connection, but the former would seem the preferable.

22-26. In addition to the victories gained by Nebuchadnezzar over Pharaoh-Necho, by which the conquests of the latter from the river of Egypt to the Euphrates were taken from the Egyptians, his strength was now to be completely broken. His armies were to be so totally annihilated as to be unable to engage any more in war against the conqueror.

CHAPTER XXXI.

In this chapter, which was delivered two months later than the prophecy contained in the concluding part of that which precedes, we have one of the most finished and beautiful specimens of Ezekiel's composition. In order to furnish a palpable exhibition of the awful catastrophe which awaited the Egyptian monarchy, the prophet gives a striking parabolic description of the Assyrian empire in its most flourishing state, comparing it to one of the majestic trees of Lebanon, on the glory of which he expatiates with the richest luxuriance, 1-9. He then by a sudden transition depicts the precipitation of the king of Nineveh from the proud position which he had held among the monarchs of the earth, and thereby foreshadows the fate of Pharaoh, who was to be delivered into the hands of Nebuchadnezzar, 10-18.

1 AND it came to pass in the eleventh year, in the third month, on the first of the month, that the word of Jehovah came unto me,
2 saying: Son of man, say to Pharaoh, king of Egypt, and to his

2. The prophet was to commence with a direct address to Pharaoh, which he accordingly does by introducing his beautiful parable. From the circumstance that the address is changed at the tenth verse into the second person, some have concluded that Ezekiel speaks throughout of Egypt, but such an opinion is not in keeping with the tenor of the parable. It is merely a momentary divarication indicative of the application on which it was to be made to tell. That by אֶרֶז, ver. 3, we are to understand the *cedar*, and not the pine or the

3 multitude: Whom art thou like in thy greatness? Behold, Assyria was a cedar in Lebanon, of beautiful branches, and giving thick shade, and lofty of stature, and his top was among
4 thick boughs. The waters made him great, the abyss made him high, flowing with its streams around his plantation, and
5 sent forth its rivulets to all the trees of the field. Therefore his height was greater than all the trees of the field, and his boughs were multiplied, and his branches became long because
6 of the many waters which he sent forth. In his boughs all the fowls of heaven made their nests, and under his branches all the beasts of the field brought forth their young, and in his shadow
7 dwelt all great nations. And he was beautiful in his greatness, in the length of his branches, because his root was towards
8 many waters. The cedars in the garden of God did not hide him, the cypresses were not comparable to his boughs, and the plane-trees were not as his branches; no tree in the garden of
9 God was comparable to him in his beauty. I made him beautiful in the largeness of his branches, and all the trees of Eden
10 envied him, which were in the garden of God. Therefore thus saith the Lord Jehovah: Because thou wast so high in stature, and he set his top among the thick boughs, and his heart was

juniper, the nature of the case before us absolutely requires. No tree is more remarkable for the magnificence of its appearance, and no object could have been more appropriately selected to set forth the surpassing glory of the king of Assyria, than the cedar of Lebanon. It is generally from fifty to eighty feet high, and the diameter of the space covered by its branches is much greater than its height. No tree equals it in tallness, symmetry, and bulk. Such had been the mighty monarch of the Assyrian empire, that none of the great ones of the earth could for a moment compare with him.

3–7. The reference being to Assyria, there is no necessity, with Michaëlis, to cast about in search of rivers on mount Lebanon corresponding to the description here given. Assuredly there is nothing deserving the name of תְּהוֹם, *abyss*, to be found there. The language is appropriately descriptive of the waters of the Tigris with its branches and canals, which irrigated the Assyrian empire. They are parabolically represented as supplying nourishment to its roots, since they afforded protection to all the surrounding countries.

8, 9. As in his portraiture of Tyre, the prophet had recourse to the garden of Eden, than which nothing surpassing was to be conceived, so he represents the monarch of Nineveh as so greatly excelling the goodliest of its trees, that they might be said to have envied him. The irony here is the keenest imaginable.

10. Ezekiel would seem here to have fallen out of his parable, and by anticipation to have applied it to the king of Egypt; but the change of person may be accounted for by his having mentioned him at verse 2, and his keeping him prominently in his eye, though the direct application of the parable was reserved for verse 18.

11   lifted up in his height: Therefore I have delivered him into the hand of a mighty one of the nations; he shall assuredly deal
12   with him; according to his wickedness I drove him out: And strangers, the terrible ones of the nations, shall cut him off, and thrust him forth; on the mountains and in all the valleys his branches shall fall, and his boughs shall be broken in all the channels of the earth; and all the peoples of the earth shall
13   come down from his shadow, when they thrust him forth. On his fallen mass all the fowls of heaven shall dwell, and upon his
14   branches shall be all the beasts of the field. In order that none of all the trees by the waters may exalt themselves in their growth, nor shoot up their top among the thick boughs, and that none that drink water may remain beside them in their height, for all of them are delivered over to death beneath the earth, among the sons of men who have gone down to the pit.
15   Thus saith the Lord Jehovah: On the day of his descent into Sheol, I will cause mourning: on his account, I will cover the abyss, and withhold its rivers, and great waters shall be restrained; and I will cause Lebanon to mourn for him, and all
16   the trees of the field shall be covered with darkness. At the sound of his fall I made the nations to shake, when I brought him down into Sheol, with them that go down to the pit, and all the trees of Eden, the choicest and best of Lebanon, all that drink water shall console themselves in the nether parts of the
17   earth. They also shall descend with him into Sheol, to the slain with the sword; and his arm that dwelt in his shadow in
18   the midst of the nations. Whom art thou thus like in glory, and in greatness, among the trees of Eden? yet shalt thou be

11–17. It makes no difference as to the sense, whether we read אֵל or אֵיל: both signify a *mighty* or *strong one*. For בְּרָשָׁיו upwards of fifty-eight codices and several of the older and many other editions read כְּרָזָיו, which has the support of the Syriac and Vulgate versions. The Assyrian monarch, whose fall is here so graphically described, was Sardanapalus. The subversion of his mighty empire was so complete, that it might well be appealed to as an example from which all other nations might take warning. It should occasion universal lamentation. The crash produced by the fall of Nineveh is represented as so tremendous that the nations shook to their centre; and all the chief princes of the earth that had been her auxiliaries, together with those in inferior stations who had enjoyed her protection, are presented to our view as descending into Hades, the common receptacle of the dead. Comp. Isa. xiv. 9–11.

18. Ezekiel now directly applies his sublime parable, showing that though the figurative description set forth the magnificence and ruin of the king of Assyria, the prophet had in his eye the Egyptian monarch, whom a similar fate awaited.

brought down with the trees of Eden to the nether parts of the earth: in the midst of the uncircumcised thou shalt lie with the slain by the sword: this is Pharaoh and all his multitude, saith the Lord Jehovah.

CHAPTER XXXII.

The prophet, not satisfied with depicting in language of surpassing force and elegance the pride and downfall of Egypt, as shadowed forth by those of the Assyrian empire, now presents the same subject in a different form. The chapter consists of two parts: the first, comprising verses 1-16, contains another prophetic ode, in which, under the bold images of a lion and a crocodile that had committed awful devastation among the nations, but which had been taken and slain, the prowess and downfall of the monarch of the Nile are strikingly exhibited. In the remainder of the chapter, verses 17-32, Pharaoh and the mighty heads of the nations that had fallen in war are presented to view in the unseen world, each in his gloomy mansion, all combining to augment the terror which the fate of Pharaoh was calculated to inspire.

1 And it came to pass in the twelfth year, in the twelfth month, on the first of the month, that the word of Jehovah came unto me,
2 saying: Son of man, take up a lamentation for Pharaoh, king of Egypt, and say to him: Thou art like a young lion of the nations, and as a sea-monster in the seas, and thou didst break forth in thy rivers, and puddle the waters with thy feet, and
3 trample their rivers. Thus saith the Lord Jehovah: I will spread my net over thee in the collection of many peoples, and
4 they shall draw thee up in my net. And I will dash thee on the ground, and cast thee headlong in the open field, and will make all the fowls of heaven to settle upon thee, and will
5 satiate the wild beasts of the whole earth with thee. And I will lay thy flesh upon the mountains, and fill the valleys with
6 thy height. And I will saturate the land to the mountains with the inundation of thy blood, and they shall fill the channels
7 with thee. And in extinguishing thee I will cover the heavens, and make the stars thereof dark; I will cover the sun with a

---

2. It was usual with the Orientals to compare a king to the lion; in addition to which, Pharaoh is here compared to the crocodile, the most formidable marine monster in the Nile.

3-6. The scene of the capture of the crocodile, by a multitude of people assembled on the bank of the river, graphically represents the seizure of the king of Egypt by the Chaldeans. Compare chap. xxix. 3, 4. רָמְךָ is properly rendered *height* in the common version, and is descriptive of the immense size of the crocodile, viewed as reaching up the sides of the valleys.

7, 8. Here the imagery is borrowed from the extinguishing of the luminaries of heaven. כָּבָה signifies *to go out* or *be*

8   cloud, and the moon shall not give her light. All the shining lights of the heavens I will clothe with blackness, on thy account,
9   and make it dark over thy land, saith the Lord Jehovah. And I will trouble the heart of many peoples when I bring thy breach among the nations in lands which thou knewest not.
10 And I will cause many people to be amazed at thee, and their kings shall be violently agitated at thee, when I brandish my sword in their sight, and they shall tremble every moment, each
11 for his own life in the day of thy fall. For thus saith the Lord Jehovah; The sword of the king of Babylon shall come upon
12 thee. By the swords of heroes I will cause thy multitude to fall, all of them the terrible of the nations; and they shall destroy the pride of Egypt, and all her multitude shall be
13 destroyed. And I will destroy all her cattle from the many waters, and the foot of man shall not puddle them any more,
14 neither shall the hoofs of cattle puddle them. Then I will cause their waters to subside, and make their rivers to flow like oil,
15 saith the Lord Jehovah. When I make the land of Egypt desolate, and the land is laid waste of her fulness, when I smite all the inhabitants therein, then they shall know that I am
16 Jehovah. It is a lamentation, and the daughters of the nations shall utter it, they shall utter it, for Egypt and all her multitude they shall utter it, saith the Lord Jehovah.
17 And it came to pass in the twelfth month, on the fifteenth of the
18 month, that the word of Jehovah came unto me, saying: Son of man, wail for the multitude of Egypt, and cause her and the daughters of splendid nations to descend to the nether parts of
19 the earth, with those who go down to the pit. By whom wast thou surpassed in beauty? descend, and lie with the uncir-
20 cumcised. In the midst of the slain with the sword they shall fall: she is delivered to the sword: drag her along and all her

quenched. The consequence of the disappearance of Pharaoh from the political horizon would be universal gloom.

9, 10. The report carried among the nations by the scattered Egyptians would be productive of the greatest consternation.

12. The magnificent ruins of the celebrated temples and cities of Egypt testify to this day to the fulfilment of the prophecy.

13, 14. Commerce and pasturing should entirely cease, so that there would be nothing to disturb the peaceful flow of the Nile.

16. Females were distinguished as mourners among the Egyptians, as they still are in the East. To this custom the prophet has been here supposed to allude; but by בְּנוֹת, *daughters*, I should rather suppose he means cities, as בַּת בָּבֶל, *daughter of Babel*, בַּת צִידוֹן, *daughter of Zidon*.

17-20. The number of the month is

21 multitudes. The strongest of heroes shall speak with him from the midst of Sheol, with those who helped him; they shall descend, they shall lie down, the uncircumcised, slain with the
22 sword. There is Assyria and all her company; round about him are his graves; all of them slain, the fallen by the sword;
23 Who have placed their graves in the sides of the pit, and her company is round her grave, all of them slain, fallen by the
24 sword, who caused their terror in the land of the living. There is Elam and all her multitude around her grave, all of them slain who had fallen by the sword, that have descended uncircumcised to the lowest parts of the earth, that caused their terror in the land of the living; and bear their reproach with
25 those who go down to the pit. In the midst of the slain have they placed a bed for her, with all her multitude; her graves are round about him; all of them uncircumcised, slain by the sword; though they caused their terror in the land of the living, they also bear their reproach with those who go down to the
26 pit; they are placed in the midst of the slain. There is Meshech, Tubal, and all her multitude, her graves are round about him; all of them uncircumcised, pierced by the sword, though they
27 caused their terror in the land of the living. Shall they not lie with heroes that have fallen, of the uncircumcised who have gone down to Sheol, with their weapons of war? and their swords were laid under their heads; and their iniquities on their bones, though they were the terror of heroes in the land

here omitted, but it is generally allowed to have been the twelfth, and that the command was given fourteen days after the preceding vision. Ezekiel is here charged to compose a funereal dirge, to be sung at the interment of Egypt, which in common with the most celebrated nations of antiquity was to be laid low in Sheol. The prophet is commanded to do what he was to predict should be done, ver. 18. How cutting the ironical interrogation: "By whom wast thou surpassed in beauty?" The humiliation should be complete. "Down into the region of the shades! There thou wilt find befitting companions who will address thee, not in the language of commiseration, but in that of taunt." Comp. Isa. xiv. 9, 10.

21–32. The change in the gender of the pronouns, in these and some other parts of the prophecy, has been satisfactorily accounted for on the principle that now the prophet has the monarch in his eye, and now the nation, — a circumstance which is not without its parallels in Hebrew composition. To aggravate the condition of Pharaoh in Sheol, the representatives of the principal nations of antiquity with which the Jews were brought into contact are enumerated as each occupying his appropriate niche, but principally Assyria surrounded by the slain of his people. For him is allotted the remotest corner of the dark abode. Elam, which formed part of the ancient Persian empire, follows next in succession, that people having

28 of the living. Thou also shalt be broken in the midst of the uncircumcised, and thou shalt lie with the slain by the sword.
29 There is Edom, her kings, and all her princes, who notwithstanding their might are laid with the slain by the sword: they lie with the uncircumcised and with those who descend to the pit.
30 There are the anointed of the north, all of them, and all the Zidonians, who have descended with the slain notwithstanding their terror, ashamed of their might; they also shall lie uncircumcised with the slain by the sword; and they shall bear their reproach with those who go down to the pit.
31 Then shall Pharaoh behold; he shall be comforted for all his multitude, slain with the sword, Pharaoh and all his host, saith the Lord Jehovah.
32 Surely I set my terror in the land of the living, and he shall be laid in the midst of the uncircumcised, with the slain by the sword, Pharaoh and all his multitude, saith the Lord Jehovah.

been mighty warriors, and specially distinguished as bowmen, Isa. xxii. 6. Their destruction by Nebuchadnezzar was predicted by Jeremiah, xlix. 34–38.

26, 28. The northern Asiatic nations are introduced, to show that they were not to be exempted from the general destruction. With Hävernick and Fairbairn I understand the negative at the beginning of ver. 27, interrogatively — "shall they not lie?" otherwise there would be no consistency between this and the following verses. There is here an allusion to the custom of the ancients, whereby they interred along with distinguished warriors, the armor they had worn (Diod. Sic. lib. 18). Though honored in Sheol with their swords under their heads, it told to their disgrace, because of the terror which they had spread by their savage incursions into more southern regions.

29. Idumea was governed not only by kings, but also by נְשִׂיאֵי, *princes*, who exercised a subordinate authority in separate provinces. They were the indomitable enemies of the Jews. For specific prophecies against that country, see Isa. xxxiv. 5, 10–17; Jer. xlix. 13–18. בִּגְבוּרָתָם, *notwithstanding their might*. בְּ, *nonobstante*. See Isa. xlvii. 9.

30. The נְסִיכֵי צָפוֹן, *princes of the north*, as distinguished from the other potentates, and occurring as they here do in connection with the Zidonians, must be taken as signifying those of Damascus, Syria, Hamath, etc. شَام,

Sham, the name by which Syria is still known among the Arabs, properly signifies the country on the left hand, or the north, as *Yemen* does the south. These were also to be destroyed by Nebuchadnezzar, previous to his conquest of Egypt. The prophet beholds them in Sheol, ashamed of their heroism which had spread terror among their contemporaries.

31, 32. Finally, Pharaoh himself is introduced into the scene as consoling himself over his own destruction and that of his vast populatiom with the thought, that they were not the only sufferers, but had merely shared the fate of many other kings and nations. This of course is the language of irony. He should experience, that however great might have been the terror inspired by their murderous deeds of war, that which was to be expected from the inflictions of Jehovah would far exceed it. For חִתִּיתוֹ, *his terror*, the Keri has the reading, חִתִּיתִי, *my terror*, which better suits the connection.

CHAPTER XXXIII.

Ezekiel, having reviewed the hostile nations around and predicted their downfall, returns now to his own people. The first nine verses contain little else than a repetition of chap. iii. 17-21. They set forth in solemn and awful language the duty of a watchman, and are highly deserving of the serious and constant consideration of all Christian teachers. The prophet is then instructed what reply to give to the impious cavils of his unbelieving countrymen, and how to vindicate the impartiality of the divine conduct in punishing them, 10-20. This he gives in language for the most part parallel to that employed chap. xviii., where the same subject is treated of. The prophet, having received information of the destruction of Jerusalem, proceeds to announce that the whole country of Israel should be involved in the calamity, 21-29. Before closing he is charged to deliver a solemn message to such Jews as professedly took delight in listening to his words, but refused to comply with their requirements, 30-33.

1 Again the word of Jehovah came unto me, saying: Son of man,
2 speak to the children of thy people, and say unto them: When I bring a sword upon a land, and the people of the land take a
3 man of their coasts, and appoint him for their watchman; And he seeth the sword coming against the land, and bloweth the
4 trumpet, and warneth the people: Then whosoever heareth the sound of the trumpet, and taketh not warning, and the sword shall come and take him away, his blood shall be on his own
5 head. He heard the sound of the trumpet, but took not warning; his blood shall be upon him; but he that taketh warning
6 delivereth his soul. But the watchman who shall see the sword come, and shall not blow the trumpet, and the people is not warned, and the sword shall come and shall take away a person from them, he shall be taken away in his iniquity; but his blood
7 will I require at the watchman's hand. So thou, Son of man, I have set thee a watchman to the house of Israel; hear therefore
8 the word from my mouth and warn them from me. When I say to the wicked: O wicked man, thou shalt surely die; and thou speakest not to warn the wicked from his way, that wicked one shall die in his iniquity; but his blood will I require at thy
9 hand. And thou, when thou warnest the wicked of his way to turn him from it, and he turneth not from his way, he shall die

---

1-6. It was customary to have a watchman stationed on a tower or a mountain, whence he could command an extensive view, so that, when the country was threatened with invasion, he might by blowing a trumpet or lighting a beacon give timely warning. Compare Isa. xxi. 6-10; Hab. ii. 1.

2. קְצֵיהֶם. This form is only apparently plural, there being no such absolute as קָצִים to which to refer the word.

7-20. An application of the reference to the watchman to the prophet's own case. His appointment, however, was much more solemn, since it had not

10 in his iniquity, but thou hast delivered thy soul. And thou, son of man, speak to the house of Israel: Thus ye speak, saying: Surely our transgressions and our sins are upon us, and we pine
11 away in them: how then should we live? Say unto them: As I live, saith the Lord Jehovah, I have no pleasure in the death of the wicked, but rather that the wicked turn from his way and live; turn ye, turn ye from your wicked ways, for why will ye
12 die, O house of Israel? And thou, son of man, say unto the children of thy people: The righteousness of the righteous shall not deliver him in the day of his sin; and as for the wickedness of the wicked, he shall not fall by it in the day of his turning from his wickedness; and as for the righteous, he shall not be
13 able to live by it in the day when he sinneth. When I say unto the righteous, he shall surely live, and he trusteth in his righteousness, and committeth iniquity, all his righteousness shall not be remembered, but he shall die for his iniquity which he hath
14 committed. And when I say to the wicked, Thou shalt surely die, and he turneth from his sin, and doeth that which is just
15 and right: If the wicked restore the pledge, make good that which he hath robbed, walk in the statutes of life without com-
16 mitting iniquity, he shall surely live, he shall not die. None of all his sins which he hath committed shall be mentioned against him: he hath done that which is just and right; he shall surely
17 live. Yet the children of thy people say: The way of the Lord
18 is not equal; but as for them, their way is not equal. When the righteous turneth from his righteousness, and committeth iniquity,
19 he shall die thereby. And when the wicked turneth from his wickedness, and doeth that which is just and right, he shall live
20 thereby. Yet ye say: The way of the Lord is not equal: I will judge you, every man according to his ways, O house of Israel!
21 And it came to pass in the twelfth year of our captivity, in the tenth month, on the fifth of the month, that one who had escaped

been derived from the people, but from God. To him he was responsible for the fidelity with which he discharged the duties of his prophetical office.

21. Strange as it may at first sight appear, that the intelligence relative to the capture of Jerusalem should not have reached the banks of the Chebar till a year and a half after the event had taken place (comp. Jer. xxxix. 2; lii. 5,6), it must be remembered that the person who conveyed it, may not have been specially delegated for that purpose, or he may have tarried at different places on the road, afraid to advance into the enemy's country. If, with eight codices, and the Syriac, we read בְּעַשְׁתֵּי עֶשְׂרֵה, *in the eleventh*, the communication would

22 from Jerusalem came to me, saying: The city is smitten. And the hand of Jehovah was upon me in the evening before he that had escaped came; and he opened my mouth until he came to me in the morning; yea, he opened my mouth, and I was no no longer dumb.

23 And the word of Jehovah came unto me, saying: Son of man, the
24 inhabitants of those wastes of the land of Israel speak, saying: Abraham was one, and he inherited the land, but we are many,
25 the land is given to us for an inheritance. Wherefore speak unto them: Thus saith the Lord Jehovah: Ye eat with the blood, and lift up your eyes to your idols, and shed blood; and
26 ye would inherit the land! Ye stand upon your sword, ye commit abomination, and each defileth the wife of his neighbor;
27 yet ye would inherit the land! Thus shalt thou say unto them: Thus saith the Lord Jehovah: As I live, those who fall by the sword in the wastes, and those who are in the open field, I will give to the wild beast for food, and those who are in the strong-
28 holds and in the caves shall die of pestilence. And I will make the land desolate and waste, and the pride of her strength shall cease, and the mountains of Israel shall be desolate without any
29 one passing through. And they shall know that I am Jehovah, when I make the land desolate and waste for all the abominations

have reached Ezekiel in less than six months after the event happened. This change in the text, however, may have originated in a desire to lessen the difficulty. At all events we may notice, that we have no recorded prophecy of Ezekiel dating at any period within the year and a half intervening between the end of the siege and the period assigned in the common version for the announcement of it to the exiles.

22. The prophet is particular in specifying the time when he received the following communication, thereby intimating that he was not indebted for it to the arrival of him who had escaped from Jerusalem, but that it had been made to him directly from heaven. הַפָּלִיט marks definitely the individual who had brought the intelligence.

23, 24. The Israelites who had been left amid the desolations of the land, are introduced as laying claim to it as their inheritance in virtue of their relation to Abraham. They maintain that the grant was not made for his sole use, but for that of his numerous posterity, and that therefore they, as left behind in the country, had a right to the enjoyment of it.

25–29. On the ground of their wicked character, Ezekiel utterly repudiates the legitimacy of their claim. אָכַל עַל־הַדָּם, to eat with the blood, means to eat flesh that had not been separated from the blood, which was contrary to the law (Levit. xix. 26). The preposition has here the idea of accompaniment, as אֵם עַל־בָּנִים, the mother with the children, (Gen. xxxii. 12). Michaelis is of opinion that there is here a reference to the drinking of blood as an act of idolatrous worship, a custom very common in Asia. The construction put upon the phrase by Spencer (De Legg. Heb. ii. 11), making it to refer to the eating of the

30 they have committed. But thou, son of man, the children of thy people are talking of thee by the walls and in the porches of the houses, and speak one to another, and each to his brother, saying:
Come now, and hear what is the word that cometh forth from
31 Jehovah. Yea, they come to thee as the people come, and sit before thee as my people, and they hear thy words, but will not do them; for they make loves with their mouth, but their heart
32 goeth after their covetousness. And, behold, thou art to them as a song of loves of one who has a sweet voice, and playeth well upon an instrument. But they hear thy words, but do
33 them not. And when it cometh, behold it cometh, then shall they know that a prophet hath been among them.

blood of animals slain in connection with magical rites, is entirely groundless.

26. עַל דָּבָר, *to stand upon*, is a phrase signifying here to depend upon the sword as a means of defence. It is declared in the following verse, that the very object of their confidence should become the instrument of their destruction.

30–33. Instead of seriously laying to heart the words of the Lord, delivered by his servant the prophet, the Jews on the Chebar made him the object of merriment and derision. While pretending to be deeply affected by his messages, and encouraging each other to listen to them, their hearts were as completely as ever estranged from their covenant God. דָּבַּר בְּ, signifies here to speak *concerning*, and not *against*, as it is rendered in the common version. שִׁיר עֲגָבִים, a *song of loves*, i.e. as Gesenius rightly interprets, an erotic song, pleasing to the people. They professed to be highly delighted with the prophetic discourses both as to matter and delivery, but it was all hypocrisy. יָדַע, *to know*, ver. 33, means here to know experimentally. Ezekiel finally assures the Jews, that the event would fully prove the legitimacy of his prophetic claims. His predictions should be realized in their woful experience. When the fugitive arrived the following morning with the intelligence that Jerusalem had been taken, there remained no hope of the escape of the captive Jews from the power of the conqueror.

15*

CHAPTER XXXIV.

This chapter contains a severe reprehension of the rulers of Israel, to whose selfish and cruel conduct the destruction of the state was ultimately to be traced, 1-10; a promise of divine interposition in behalf of the people, 11-19; the rejection and punishment of their oppressors, 20-22; a renewal of the promise of the Messiah, and the happy security of the subjects of his reign, 23-31.

1 And the word of Jehovah came unto me, saying: Son of man,
2 prophesy against the shepherds of Israel, prophesy and say unto them: For the shepherds, thus saith the Lord Jehovah. Woe to the shepherds of Israel, who are feeding themselves.
3 Should not the shepherds feed the sheep? Ye partake of the milk, and ye put on the wool; ye kill the fatlings; ye feed not
4 the sheep: The weak ye have not strengthened, neither have ye healed the sick, nor bound up that which was broken, and that which was driven away ye have not brought back, and that which was lost ye have not sought for; but with harshness and
5 with rigor ye have ruled them. And they have been scattered without a shepherd, and have become food for all the wild
6 beasts of the field, when they were scattered. My sheep have wandered through all the mountains, and on every high hill; yea, my sheep were scattered over the whole face of the earth, and no one sought them or searched them out.

7 Wherefore, ye shepherds, hear the word of Jehovah. As I live,
8 saith the Lord Jehovah, surely because my sheep have become

---

2. רֹעֶה, properly denotes a *shepherd*, one who guards and provides for his flock, and tropically a *prince* or *king*. The language here is not, therefore, to be interpreted of ecclesiastical rulers or teachers, but of the civil governors of the Jewish state, who, regardless of the welfare and prosperity of their people, only acted from respect to their own selfish interests, forming alliances with foreign powers, or provoking their ire, according as they were prompted by ambitious or mercenary motives. Comp. 2 Sam. v. 2; Isa. xliv. 28; Jer. ii. 8; iii. 15; x. 21; xxiii. 1, 2. Xenoph. Cyropæd. viii. 2, 13.

3. חֵלֶב, *the fat*, for which some would point חָלָב, *the milk*, as more suitable to the connection. Compare the Arab.

حَلَب, Eth. ሐሊብ, Both readings are appropriate; but the latter seems preferable. LXX., τὸ γάλα. Compare 1 Cor. ix. 7.

4. Careful shepherds treat with tenderness the sickly and diseased of their flock, but these Jewish rulers treated their subjects with neglect and cruelty. הַנַּחְלוֹת, a plural feminine participle in Niphal, from חָלָה, *to be sick, wounded*. Comp. Isa. xvii. 11, and the synonyme הַחוֹלָה, in the text before us.

5, 6. These verses describe the miserable condition of the Jews under their wicked kings previous to the captivity.

7-10. However these kings might flatter themselves that their misdeeds might pass with impunity, Jehovah here

a prey and my sheep have become food to every wild beast of the field, without a shepherd, and my shepherds inquire not after my sheep, but the shepherds feed themselves, and feed not
9 my sheep: Therefore hear, O ye shepherds, the word of Jeho-
10 vah. Thus saith the Lord Jehovah: Behold, I am against the shepherds, and will require my sheep at their hand, and will make them to cease from feeding the sheep; and the shepherds shall not feed themselves any more, for I will deliver my sheep from their mouth, and they shall not become food for them.
11 For thus saith the Lord Jehovah: Behold I, even I, will both
12 search for my sheep and seek them out, As a shepherd seeketh out his flock in the day when he is among his sheep that are scattered, so will I seek out my sheep, and deliver them from all places whither they have been scattered in the cloudy and
13 dark day. And will bring them out from the peoples, and gather them from the countries, and bring them unto their own land, and feed them upon the mountains of Israel, by the brooks,
14 and in all the inhabited places of the land. In a good pasture I will feed them, and upon the high mountains of Israel shall be their fold, there shall they lie down in a good fold, and shall
15 feed in a fat pasture on the mountains of Israel. I will feed my sheep, and I will cause them to lie down, saith the Lord
16 Jehovah. I will search out that which is lost, and I will bring back that which is driven away, and will bind up that which is broken, and will strengthen that which is weak; but the fat and the strong I will destroy, and will feed them with judgment.
17 And as for you, O my sheep, thus saith the Lord Jehovah: Behold, I will judge between sheep and sheep, between the
18 rams and the he-goats. Is it a small matter unto you, that ye have eaten up the good pasture, but ye must tread under your feet what remained of your pastures? and that ye have drunk of the deep waters, but ye must trample what remains with

declares that he would call them to account for their wickedness. The judgments denounced against them took full effect when Jerusalem was captured.

16. For אַשְׁמִיד, *I will destroy*, two of De Rossi's MSS., the LXX., Syr., Arab., and Vulg., read אֶשְׁמֹר, *I will preserve*, which Luther has adopted in his German version, and Michaelis explains to mean, for the purpose of securing an excellent breed. The same construction is adopted by Newcome; but it does not suit the connection so well as the textual reading. The clause is obviously adversative, containing a declaration of the punishment to be inflicted on the harsh and selfish rulers of the Jews.

17. בֵּין־שֶׂה לָשֶׂה, *between sheep and sheep*, means between one class of citizens and another. שָׁפַט, *to judge*, here is to

19 your feet? And my sheep eat that which ye have trodden with
your feet, and have drunk that which ye have trodden with your
20 feet. Wherefore thus saith the Lord Jehovah unto them:
Behold I, even I, will judge between the fat sheep and the lean
21 sheep. Because ye have thrust with side and with shoulder,
and have pushed with your horns all the diseased, till you have
22 scattered them abroad: Therefore I will save my sheep, and
they shall no more be for a prey, and I will judge between
23 sheep and sheep. And I will set one shepherd over them, and
he shall feed them, my servant David: he shall feed them, and
24 he shall be their shepherd. And I Jehovah will be their God,
and my servant David shall be a prince among them, I Jehovah
25 have spoken. And I will make for them a covenant of peace,
and will cause the evil beast to cease from the land, and they
shall dwell in the wilderness securely, and sleep in the woods.
26 And I will make them and the places around my hill a blessing;
and will cause the shower to come down in its season; there

discriminate and punish according to desert.

18, 19. Not content with consuming the best of the possessions of their subjects, the wicked rulers wantonly spoiled what might have been of use to them, and left them only the refuse.

22. The salvation of the better part of the Jewish nation was primarily to be effected by the sifting process to which they were to be subjected in Babylon. At their restoration, they should be delivered at once from the power of the heathen, and from the tyrannical rule of their own kings.

23, 24. עַבְדִּי דָוִד, *my servant David*. This can be no other than the often-promised Messiah. Compare Ps. lxxxix. 3; Isa. lv. 3; Jer. xxx. 9; Hos. iii. 5. The idea adopted by Grotius, that Zerubbabel is intended, cannot be entertained for a moment. That prince was merely a stadtholder of the king of Persia, who did not even rule alone, but had Joshua the high-priest at his side. Neither can any of the later Jewish kings be meant, for they were not of the family of David. The shepherd here promised was to be רֹעֶה אֶחָד, *one* shepherd, sin-

gularly and distinguishingly *one*; the only one of his kind. Comp. the Arab. وَاحَد, *unicus et incomparabilis*; one whose person and character should stand out in broad distinction from all others. There cannot be a doubt that our Lord had this prophecy in his eye, John x. 14 : *I am the good shepherd.* רֹעֶה, in the language of Ezekiel, is equivalent to *king.* See chap. xxxii. 29. The Messiah was הֵקִים, *set up*, constituted king by divine appointment (Ps. ii. 6; Acts ii. 36); and had the Jews received him, and submitted to his laws, their civil polity would have been preserved, and they would have enjoyed every necessary blessing under his gracious protection and care. Rejecting him, they forfeited all title to the promises here made to them.

25-31. An amplification of the promises just made, under the images of outward prosperity, exemption from all annoyance from the heathen, and from wild beasts, and the rich enjoyment of every blessing in their own land, of which Mount Zion was the capital and centre. The Jews as thus restored are

27 shall be showers of blessing. And the tree of the field shall yield its fruit, and the earth shall yield her increase; and they shall be secure in their land, and shall know that I am Jehovah, when I break the bands of their yoke, and deliver them from
28 the hand of those who serve themselves of them. And they shall no more be a prey to the nations, neither shall the wild beast of the land devour them; but they shall dwell securely,
29 and none shall make them afraid. And I will raise up for them a plant of renown, and they shall no more be consumed with hunger in the land, neither shall they any more bear the
30 reproach of the nations. And they shall know that I, Jehovah their God, am with them, and that they, the house of Israel, are
31 my people, saith the Lord Jehovah. And ye my sheep, the sheep of my pasture, are men; I am your God, saith the Lord Jehovah.

represented as enjoying the blessings connected with and flowing from the sacred spot, but which were not to be confined to that locality, but were to be extended to other parts of the land. Comp. verses 13, 14.

29. לְשֵׁם נֶטַע, *a plant of renown*. This passage has generally been interpreted of the Messiah, and viewed as parallel to those in which he is promised under the image of a branch; and to this interpretation I adhere, notwithstanding all that Rosenmüller, Hävernick, Ewald, and Fairbairn have alleged to the contrary. If the Jews themselves were to be the plant or plantation, there would be no propriety in the promise that it should be raised up *for them*.

31. These words contain an explanation of the figurative language employed in reference to the Jewish people and their rulers. It was not to be understood literally of shepherds and their flock, but of the people of Israel and those who exercised authority over them. Jehovah vindicates to himself his right of propriety in them, and renews the declaration of his gracious relation to them as their covenant God. The strong contrast asserted was designed to convey the idea, that, weak as the Israelites were in themselves, and utterly inadequate to the task of effecting their own deliverance, they were warranted to exercise strong faith in the Most High.

CHAPTER XXXV.

This chapter contains an episode relative to the Edomites, naturally arising out of the preceding promises of blessings to the Israelites. The Idumeans had been the inveterate foes of the covenant people, and had exulted with fiendish malignity at the breaking up of their polity by the Chaldeans. Jehovah had already declared by the prophet, chap. xxv. 12-14, that he would execute vengeance upon the neighboring people. This threatening he here repeats at greater length, declaring that he would utterly destroy them, and thus disappoint them of their anticipated possession of the land of Israel.

1 And the word of Jehovah came unto me, saying: Son of man, set
2 thy face against Mount Seir, and prophesy against it. And say
3 to it: Thus saith the Lord Jehovah: Behold, I am against thee, O Mount Seir! and I will stretch out my hand against thee,
4 and I will make thee desolate and waste. I will make thy cities a desolation, and thou shalt be desolate, and thou shalt
5 know that I am Jehovah. Because thou hast the old enmity, and didst deliver over the children of Israel to the power of the sword in the day of their calamity, in the time of the iniquity
6 of the end; Therefore, as I live, saith the Lord Jehovah, surely I will turn thee to blood, and blood shall pursue thee; since
7 thou didst not hate blood, therefore blood shall pursue thee. I will even make Mount Seir desolate and waste, and will cut off

---

2. שֵׂעִיר, *Seir*, the country of the Edomites; according to the etymology, *the Shaggy*, from the rough and bristling character of its mountains and forests. The northern division of the country is still called الشراة, *Essherat*. The capital was סֶלַע, *Sela*, the Rock, Petra, the remarkable ruins of which have been visited and described by several modern travellers. See especially Dr. Robinson in his Biblical Researches, vol. ii. pp. 514-538.

3. The stretching forth of the hand indicates, in such connection, threatening and punishment. שְׁמָמָה וּמְשַׁמָּה an emphatic paronomasia: lit. *desolation and desolateness*; i.e. completely desolate.

4. The country was to become an arid waste.

5. The enmity of the Edomites to the Jews dated from the earliest period of their history. They harassed and injured them in every possible way. Ps. cxxxvii. 7; Amos i. 11; Obad. 10-16. For עֵת קֵץ, *the iniquity of the end*, compare chap. xxi. 30.

6. There is singular force in the repetition of the term דָּם, *dam, blood*, in this verse, taken in connection with the fact of its relation in sound to אֱדֹם, *Edom*, the name of the country. It forms a paronomasia which it is impossible to imitate in our language. In the second and fourth instances, the word is used in the sense of *blood-shedding*. Since the Edomites had not hated shedding the blood of others, but on the contrary affected it, the guilt thereof should be avenged in the shedding of their own blood. The position of לֹא before דָּם gives greater force to the sentence. The supposition of some that blood is here to be taken in the sense of consanguinity, is utterly to be rejected, as unwarranted by Hebrew usage.

8 from it him that passeth, and him that returneth, And I will fill his mountains with his slain, thy high places and thy valleys; and as for all thy channels, the slain by the sword shall fall in
9 them. I will make thee perpetual desolations, and thy cities shall not be inhabited; and ye shall know that I am Jehovah.
10 Because thou saidst: The two nations and the two countries shall be mine, and we shall possess them; whereas Jehovah is
11 there: Therefore, as I live, saith the Lord Jehovah, I will act according to thine anger and according to thine envy which thou hast used out of thy hatred against them; and I will be
12 known among them, when I have judged thee. And thou shalt know that I Jehovah have heard all thy contempt which thou hast uttered against the mountains of Israel, saying: They are
13 laid waste, they are given to us for consumption. And ye have spoken proudly against me with your mouth, and multiplied
14 your words against me: I have heard *them*. Thus saith the Lord Jehovah: When the whole earth rejoiceth, I will make
15 thee desolate. As thou didst rejoice at the inheritance of the house of Israel because it was desolate, so will I do to thee: thou shalt be desolate, O Mount Seir, and the whole of Edom; and they shall know that I am Jehovah.

7–9. The country of the Edomites was to be depopulated and laid entirely waste, a prediction which has been literally fulfilled, as even infidel travellers have borne testimony. See Savary's Letters.

10. The Idumeans are here abruptly introduced as exulting at the thought of possessing the land of Canaan, which the Jews and Israelites had vacated, but are suddenly checked by the declaration, that Jehovah still claimed his propriety in it. He was still there. The Chaldeans could not remove him, as they did the idols of the nations.

11–15. They did not confine their contumely and hatred to the Jewish people, but treated their covenant God in the same manner. They represented him as not having been sufficiently powerful to protect the people whom he had adopted as peculiarly his own.

CHAPTER XXXVI.

In this chapter Ezekiel is charged to personify the mountains of Israel, and to assure them that, notwithstanding the proud boastings of the Idumeans, they should be restored to their pristine prosperity, 1-15. The causes of their desolation are then specifically set forth, 16-20. And the rest of the chapter comprehends gracious promises of the restoration of the captive people, and their participation in the blessings of the new covenant, 21-38.

1 AND thou, son of man, prophesy unto the mountains of Israel, and
2 say: Ye mountains of Israel, hear the word of Jehovah: Thus saith the Lord Jehovah: Because the enemy hath said concerning you, Aha! behold, the ancient heights are become our
3 possession: Therefore prophesy and say: Thus saith the Lord Jehovah: Because, even because they have made you desolate, and have swallowed you up round about, that ye might become an inheritance to the residue of the nations, and ye are taken up on the lips of talkers, and are a reproach to the people.
4 Therefore, O mountains of Israel, hear ye the word of the Lord Jehovah: Thus saith the Lord Jehovah to the mountains, and to the hills, to the streams, and to the valleys, and to the desolate wastes, and to the cities that are deserted, which had become a prey and a derision to the residue of the nations
5 which are round about. Therefore thus saith the Lord Jehovah: Surely I have spoken in the fire of my jealousy against the residue of the nations, and against the whole of Edom, which have appointed my land to themselves for a possession with the joy of all their heart, with despite of soul, that its pasture might

1, 2. Mountains being the most conspicuous part of a country, Canaan is thus introduced to view, the object of avaricious hope on the part of the Idumeans as expressed in the foregoing chapter, and of happy anticipation on the part of their lawful inheritors. These are denominated בָּמוֹת עוֹלָם, *ancient heights*, in reference to the remote antiquity from which their fertility had been celebrated. See Gen. xlix. 26; Deut. xxxiii. 15. The term Israel is here used irrespective of the division of the two kingdoms, and includes the whole of the tribes that returned from captivity.

3. There is much emphasis in the reduplication: יַעַן בְּיַעַן, which is equivalent to the same with the copula: יַעַן וּבְיַעַן, *because, even because*, or *yea, because*. Jehovah here singles out the cupidity and haughty conduct of the enemies of his people as the objects of his righteous displeasure. They had slandered the Jews because of their connection with Jehovah. הֵעָלוֹת עַל־שְׂפַת לָשׁוֹן, lit. *to cause to go up upon the lip of a tongue*, i.e. as Gesenius explains, of the slanderer.

4-12. In retribution for all the evils to which they had been subjected on the part of the neighboring nations, especially the Edomites, Jehovah promises to restore the prosperity of his people to

6 become a prey. Therefore prophesy concerning the land of Israel, and say to the mountains and to the hills, to the channels and to the valleys: Thus saith the Lord Jehovah: Behold, I have spoken in my jealousy and in my fury, because ye have
7 borne the reproach of the nations. Therefore thus saith the Lord Jehovah: I have lifted up my hand; assuredly the nations
8 that are round about you, they shall bear their reproach. But as for you, O ye mountains of Israel, ye shall shoot forth your branches, and bear your fruit to my people Israel; for they are
9 near to come. For, behold, I am for you, and will turn unto
10 you, and ye shall be tilled and sown. And I will multiply men upon you, the whole house of Israel, all of it; and the cities
11 shall be inhabited, and the waste places shall be builded. And I will multiply upon you man and beast; and they shall increase and be fruitful, and I will cause you to dwell according to your former circumstances, and will do you good more than at your
12 beginnings; and ye shall know that I am Jehovah. And I will cause men to walk upon you, even my people Israel; and they shall possess thee, and thou shalt be to them for an inheritance,
13 and thou shalt no more bereave them. Thus saith the Lord Jehovah: Because they say to you: Thou wast a devourer of
14 men, and hast bereaved thy nations, Therefore thou shalt no more devour men, neither shalt thou bereave thy nations any more,
15 saith the Lord Jehovah. And I will not cause thee to hear the reproach of the nations any more, neither shalt thou bear the insult of the nations any more, and thou shalt not bereave thy
16 nations any more, saith the Lord Jehovah. And the word of
17 Jehovah came unto me, saying: Son, of man, the house of Israel dwelt in their own land, but they defiled it by their way, and by their doings: their way was before me as the uncleanness of

a higher degree than had ever before been experienced. All the localities are specified which could suggest the ideas of convenience and enjoyment. Instead of the country being any longer bereaved of its inhabitants in punishment of their wickedness, it should again be filled with a flourishing population.

For תְּשַׁכְּלִי, upwards of twenty-eight codices read with the Keri, two ancient editions, the LXX., Arab., Syr., and Targ. תְּשַׁכְּלִי. A similar transposition occurs in the following verse, both of which are more in accordance with the exigency of the passage.

13–15. The heathen reproached the Israelites because of their rejection by their God, whom they represented as unable to deliver them. This reproach should cease on the restoration of the covenant people.

16–20. The prophet here depicts the abominable character of his countrymen, which was the cause of their removal. Even among the heathen at first their practices were so far from conciliating

18 a removed woman. And I poured out my fury upon them, because of the blood which they had shed in the land, and be-
19 cause of their idolatries with which they had defiled it. And I scattered them among the nations, and they were dispersed through the countries: according to their way, and according to
20 their doings I judged them. And when they came to the nations whither they went, then they profaned my holy name by saying of them: These are the people of Jehovah, and are
21 gone forth out of his land. But I had pity for my holy name which the house of Israel had defiled among the nations whither
22 they had come. Therefore say unto the house of Israel: Thus saith the Lord Jehovah: Not for your sakes do I it, O house of Israel, but for my holy name, which ye have profaned among
23 the nations whither ye are come. And I will sanctify my great name which hath been profaned among the nations, which ye have profaned in the midst of them; and the nations shall know that I am Jehovah, saith the Lord Jehovah, when I am sancti-
24 fied in you in their sight. Then I will take you from the nations, and collect you from all the countries, and will bring
25 you into your own land. And I will sprinkle clean water upon you, and you shall be clean: from all your filthiness, and from
26 all your idols will I cleanse you. And I will give you a new heart, and a new spirit will I put within you, and I will take away the heart of stone out of your flesh, and will give you a
27 heart of flesh. And I will put my Spirit within you, and make that ye shall walk in my statutes, and observe my judgments

their good opinion, that they tended rather to prejudice them.

21–24. There was nothing in Israel to induce Jehovah to interpose on their behalf. They richly merited the punishment inflicted upon them. It was, therefore, to be impressed upon them that their restoration would be owing to his own free grace, and his determination to recover for his glorious character that lustre which they had obscured in the sight of the heathen. He is represented as moved with sympathy for the glory of his name.

25–27. Compare on chap. xi. 18–20. To qualify the Hebrews for the enjoyment of the blessings connected with their restoration, it was necessary that they should have wrought in them a complete change of moral character. Such a change God here promises to effect in their experience. In the fullest sense the promise was fulfilled in the blessed experience of all who were truly converted to God, and returned in a spiritually regenerated state to Canaan, just as it is still in that of all who are the subjects of the saving influences of the Holy Spirit, whether Jews or Gentiles. It would be too much, however, to suppose that the great bulk of the nation experienced any such total change; as the accounts which we have in their subsequent history too abundantly show. Still, by the divine blessing on the means employed in Babylon for recover-

28 and do them. And ye shall dwell in the land which I gave unto your fathers; and ye shall be my people, and I will be
29 your God. And I will save you from all your uncleannesses, and will call for the corn, and increase it, and lay no famine
30 upon you. And I will increase the fruit of the tree and the growth of the field, that ye may no more receive the reproach
31 of famine among the heathen. And ye shall remember your wicked ways, and your treacherous doings which were not good, and ye shall be disgusted with yourselves because of your
32 iniquities and because of your abominations. Not for your sakes do I this, saith the Lord Jehovah, be it known to you:
33 blush and be ashamed of your ways, O house of Israel! Thus saith the Lord Jehovah: In the day when I cleanse you from all your iniquities, I will also cause your cities to be inhabited,
34 and your wastes to be rebuilt. And the land which had been desolate shall be cultivated, instead of its being desolate in the
35 sight of all that passed by. And they shall say: This land which had been desolate is as the garden of Eden; and the cities that had been desolate, and the waste places, and the

ing them from idolatry, they appear to have been thoroughly cured of that evil, and returned, outwardly at least, to the pure worship of Jehovah, the God of their fathers. Instead of the hard and obstinate heart which had led them to reject all the divine counsels, and persist in a course of disobedience, they were to have imparted to them a heart easily impressible by the truth of God, a disposition to love him, and walk in his ways. This is ascribed to the inhabitation and operations of the Holy Spirit, the author of all that is good in man. The whole is represented symbolically under the idea of purification — an idea borrowed from the lustrations of the Mosaic law, by which the Jews were cleansed from any pollutions which they might have contracted, especially the ceremonies connected with the water of separation made of the ashes of a red heifer (Numb. xix.). A remarkable fulfilment of this prophecy in the outpouring of the Spirit, is recorded Ezra chapters ix. x. The people generally made a great mourning, confessed their sins, renewed their covenant with God, and set themselves in right earnest to observe the law. The sacred historian observes, that they kept the feast of tabernacles in such a manner as it had not been observed since the days of Joshua the son of Nun. The Jews separated themselves from all strangers, and reformed many abuses which had crept in among them.

28-32. It is manifest from the whole tenor of the language employed by the prophet, that temporal and spiritual blessings are beautifully intermixed with each other. The Israelites are again reminded that it was not for any good thing in them meriting the divine favor, that such blessings were to be conferred upon them. Looking back on their rebellious conduct, they should discover nothing but what was calculated to fill them with shame and confusion of face. Merit, therefore, was entirely out of the question.

33-36. So great should be the change

36 ruins are fortified and inhabited. And the nations that are left around you shall know that I Jehovah build up the ruined places, and plant that which had been desolate: I Jehovah
37 have said it, and will do it. Thus saith the Lord Jehovah: Yet for this will I be inquired of by the house of Israel, to do
38 it for them; I will increase them with men as a flock. As the holy flock, as the flock of Jerusalem in her festivals, so shall the waste cities be filled with flocks of men; and they shall know that I am Jehovah.

that would take place in their outward circumstances, that it could not fail to attract the attention of by-passers. The transformation could only be compared to such a change as must take place were the land to be converted into the garden of Eden.

37. However absolute the gracious promises made to Israel, they were not to be realized independently of application on their part for their fulfilment.

Such application would show that it was fit and proper in God to accomplish his promises in their happy experience.

38. Multitudinous as were the assemblages of animals for sacrifice at Jerusalem on occasion of the annual festivals, when all the males in the nation were required to appear before the Lord, they were only a fit emblem of the restored people in all parts of the country; so great was to be their number.

CHAPTER XXXVII.

This chapter contains a parabolic vision in which was represented to the prophet the restoration of his hopelessly depressed countrymen, under the emblem of the resurrection of a multitude of dry bones which are suddenly invested with life, flesh, and beauty, 1-10. This is followed by a brief exposition of the parable, 11-14; and then, to show that the restoration was to embrace the ten tribes, as well as the two tribes and a half, two united sticks are emblematically employed, the one representing the southern or Jewish kingdom, and the other the northern or Israelitish, 15-22. The chapter concludes with renewed promises of Messiah and his kingdom, 23-28.

1 THE hand of Jehovah was upon me, and he carried me forth in the Spirit of Jehovah, and set me down in the midst of the
2 valley, and it was full of bones. And caused me to pass by them round about; and, behold, they were very many, in the
3 face of the valley; and, behold, they were very dry. And he said unto me: Son of man, can these bones live? and I said,

1, 2. That the matters narrated in this chapter were transacted in vision, we are here expressly told. Whether the בִּקְעָה, valley, specified was that in which Ezekiel had already had visions by the river Chebar, chaps. i. 1; iii. 22-24, we are not informed: but it most likely

was, as he must in that case have had literally presented to his view his captive countrymen in their condition of utter hopelessness.

3-6. To excite his attention and put his faith to the test, he is asked: Can these bones live? The only answer he

4 O Lord Jehovah, thou knowest. And he said unto me, Prophecy over these bones, and say unto them: O ye dry bones, hear
5 ye the word of Jehovah. Thus saith the Lord Jehovah unto
these bones: Behold, I will cause breath to enter into you, and
6 ye shall live. And I will put sinews upon you, and bring up
flesh upon you, and cover you with skin, and I will put breath
into you, and ye shall live; and ye shall know that I am Je-
7 hovah. And I prophesied as I was commanded; and there was
a voice as I prophesied; and, behold, a noise! and the bones
8 came together, bone to its bone. And I looked; and, behold,
there were sinews upon them; and flesh came up, and skin
covered them from above; but there was no breath in them.
9 Then he said unto me: Prophesy to the wind, prophesy, son of
man, and say to the wind, Thus saith the Lord Jehovah: Come
from the four winds, O breath, and breathe upon these slain,
10 that they may live. And I prophesied as I was commanded,
and the spirit came into them, and they lived, and stood upon
11 their feet, an exceeding great army. And he said unto me:
Son of man, these bones are the whole house of Israel: behold,
they are saying: Our bones are dried up, and our hope hath
12 perished; we are altogether cut off. Therefore prophesy, and
say unto them: Thus saith the Lord Jehovah: Behold, I will
open your graves, and will cause you to come up from your
graves, O my people! and will bring you to the land of Israel.

could give, was an appeal to divine omniscience. Upon this, he received a charge to prophesy to them, commanding them to listen to the word of Jehovah, which was followed by assurances that God would take the process of restoration into his own hand.

7–10. As Ezekiel fulfilled his commission, a commotion took place among the bones. They cohered each to its fellow in regular order; but all continued in a state of inanimation, mere motionless skeletons. The next step in the process was that of covering them with sinews, skin, and flesh. Their hideous appearance now assumed one of beauty; but still they were without life. On this the prophet was charged to invoke the wind to breathe into them; and, to convey the idea of complete reviviscence, the breath was commanded to come from all quarters of the heavens. The scene closes with a resurrection of the bones in the shape of living men.

However striking the analogy between this scene and that which will be presented to view in the general resurrection at the last day, there is no reason to believe that the doctrine of the latter was intended distinctly to be taught by it, any more than that it was intended to adumbrate the quickening of the spiritually dead by means of the gospel. The passage may be used in illustration of both, but further than this we are not warranted to go in our interpretation.

11–14. We are here expressly informed what was the object of the allegory: viz. to set forth the restoration of the Jewish state. The captives had given

13 And ye shall know that I am Jehovah, when I open your graves, and cause you to come up from your graves, O my
14 people. And I will put my Spirit within you, and ye shall live, and I will place you in your own land; and ye shall know that I Jehovah have spoken it, and will do it, saith Jehovah.
15 And the word of Jehovah came unto me, saying: Moreover, thou
16 son of man, take to thee one stick and write upon it: For Judah, and for the house of Israel, his companions: then take another stick, and write upon it: For Joseph, the stick of
17 Ephraim, and all the house of Israel, his companions. And join them one to another, one stick for thee, and they shall
18 become one in thine hand. And when the children of thy people shall speak unto thee, saying, wilt thou not show us
19 what these are to thee? Say unto them: Thus saith the Lord Jehovah: Behold, I will take the stick of Joseph which is in the hand of Ephraim, and the tribes of Israel his companions, and will put them with the house of Judah, and make them one
20 stick, and they shall be one in my hand. And the sticks on
21 which thou writest shall be in thy hand in their sight. And say unto them: Thus saith the Lord Jehovah: Behold, I will take the children of Israel from among the nations whither they have gone, and gather them from every side, and bring them
22 into their own land. And I will make them one nation in the land upon the mountains of Israel; and one king shall be king to them all: and they shall no more be two nations, neither
23 shall they be divided into two kingdoms any more. And they shall no more defile themselves with their idols, and with their abominations, and with all their transgressions; for I will save them out of all their dwellings in which they have sinned, and will cleanse them, and they shall be my people, and I will be

up all for lost. They are by this allegory taught that there is nothing impossible with God; and that, therefore, how desperate their circumstances in Chaldea might appear, there was hope for them in their covenant God. They were to be restored to a state of political independence in their own land. לָנוּ, ver. 11, rendered in the common version *for our parts*, is the reflexive dative, and is equivalent to *so far as we are concerned*.

15–22. From the time of Jeroboam the Hebrew people had been divided into two separate kingdoms, Samaria being the capital of the one, and Jerusalem that of the other. This division, which had been productive of many evils, especially that of the maintenance of idolatry, was not to exist on their return to their own land. They were to be united in one corporate body, the jealousy between them ceasing, and all joining in the worship of the true God. Compare my notes on Jeremiah xxxi. This happy state of things Ezekiel was commanded to exhibit by a striking symbolical action,

24   their God. And my servant David shall be king over them, and there shall be one shepherd to them all; and they shall walk in my judgments, and keep my statutes, and do them.

25   And they shall dwell in the land which I gave to my servant Jacob, in which your fathers dwelt: they shall even dwell in it, they and their children, and their children's children forever;

26   and David my servant shall be a prince to them forever. And I will make for them a covenant of peace; an everlasting covenant shall be to them: and I will place them, and increase

27   them, and set my sanctuary in the midst of them forever. And my tabernacle shall be over them, and I will be their God, and

28   they shall be my people. And they shall know that I am Jehovah, the Sanctifier of Israel, when my sanctuary is in the midst of them forever.

highly calculated to excite the curiosity of his countrymen. This prophecy was fulfilled in the reign of Cyrus; for not only did the Jews return and take possession of the southern parts of the country, but the Israelites also were restored to their ancient possessions.

23-25. In this state of restored harmony, and purification from all their idolatries and other sins of which they had been guilty before the captivity, they should live in conformity to the theocratic laws under the rule of Messiah. To this rule he was predestined, and if they failed to enjoy as a people the benefits of his government in the blessings of the new covenant, it was because they rejected his great salvation. The reign here and elsewhere predicted was not to be earthly and temporal, but spiritual, on the throne of David in the spiritual world. Compare 2 Sam. vii. 16;

Ps. cx. 1; Acts iii. 21 (where ἄχρι is to be rendered not *until*, but *during*) v. 31; John xviii. 36. מוֹשְׁבֵיהֶם, *their dwellings*, ver. 23, should, according to some, be read שׁוֹבְבֵיהֶם, *their defections*; but it is without any authority from Hebrew MSS. One of De Rossi's codices has פְּשָׁעֵיהֶם, *their sins*.

26-28. The covenant promised to be made with recovered Israel was the new and better dispensation (Isa. lv. 3; Jer. xxxi. 31-34), established in the mediation of Messiah (Heb. viii. 7-13). If they had complied with the conditions of this covenant, they should have remained in their land, and not been again dispersed among the nations. Their temple should have no more been destroyed, but should have been appropriated for the purposes of Christian worship.

CHAPTERS XXXVIII. XXXIX.

There cannot, I think, be a doubt that the whole subject of these chapters is to be viewed as an allegory. Under names of persons and countries, then but little known, or known only on account of their barbarous and all-conquering propensities, Antiochus Epiphanes and his armies are represented as invading Palestine, and spreading universal terror and devastation through the country.

The materials for the history of that cruel persecutor are indeed scanty, the writings which treat of his period having been all lost except what Porphyry has introduced in his fifteenth book against the Christians, of which fragments have been preserved by Jerome in his Commentary on Daniel. This much, however, may be gathered from these, from Josephus, and from the First Book of Maccabees, — that the persecutions which Antiochus carried on in Palestine were the most severe of any that the inhabitants experienced during the period which intervened between the destruction of Jerusalem by the Chaldeans, and that effected by the Romans.

Receiving information that the Jews were rejoicing at the report of his supposed death in Egypt, Antiochus returned hastily to Palestine, took Jerusalem by storm, plundered the city, slew eighty thousand persons, men, women, and children, took forty thousand prisoners, and sold as many into slavery. And, as if this were not enough, he went, under the guidance of the wicked high priest Menelaus, into the temple, profaned it by uttering blasphemous language, and removed thence all the gold he could lay his hand on, amounting to eighteen hundred talents, besides quantities of silver, all of which he carried away. To crown this wickedness, he sacrificed swine upon the altar of Jehovah, boiled pieces of the flesh, and sprinkled the whole temple with the broth.

Two years afterwards, being disappointed in his designs against Egypt, and returning from that country in disgrace, he sent Apollonius his chief collector of tribute with a division of twenty-two thousand men, with orders to cut down all the men whom he met with, and to make slaves of the women and children. The consequence was that the streets of Jerusalem flowed with blood, the houses were plundered and demolished, the city walls were thrown down, and the public services of religion ceased. In place of the altar of Jehovah, he caused an altar to be raised to be used in sacrificing to Jupiter Olympius. Every attempt to observe the law of Moses was made a capital offence; and the most cruel punishments were inflicted on such of the inhabitants as remained, and refused to comply with the impious commands of the infuriated monarch. In fact the Jews had never before been subject to such furious persecution. Compare Dan. viii. 10-26; xi. 21-45; xii. 1; and see Jahn's Hebrew Commonwealth, xciv., xcv.

This allegorical description of the apparently desperate case of the Jews is the prototype which John had in his eye when predicting the overthrow of the final antichristian confederacy, Rev. xx. 7-9.

CHAPTER XXXVIII.

To set forth a formidable attack that would be made upon the Jews after their re-settlement in Canaan, the prophet introduces an assemblage of savage people under a distinguishingly formidable leader, who should leave no method untried by which he might hope to effect their utter extermination, 1-13. Hereupon it is predicted, that by a signal interposition of Divine Providence, this enemy should be completely overthrown; that a long time should be occupied in burying the dead bodies of his army; and that their weapons should long be used as fuel by the Jews, 14-23 and chapter xxxix.

1 And the word of Jehovah came unto me, saying: Son of man, set
2 thy face against Gog. of the land of Magog, the prince of Rosh,

2, 3. The only other parts of Scripture in which these names occur are Gen. x. 2; 1 Chron. i. 5; v. 4; Ezek. xxvii. 13; xxxii. 26; Rev. xx. 8. The first of these passages is important to our present inquiry, as pointing us to the direction

3 Meshech, and Tubal, and prophesy against him; and say: Thus saith the Lord Jehovah: Behold, I am against thee, O Gog,

in which to look for the people and countries here specified. It is generally admitted that the descendants of Japhet are to be sought for in the west of Europe and the north of Asia. Tracing them back to their original abodes, we discover them about the Black and Caspian Seas, the regions of the Caucasus, part of Armenia, Asia Minor, Parthia, Persia, and the countries beyond. They were generally known to the Greeks under the name of Scythians, with which was associated the idea of whatever was rude, uncivilized, and barbarous; just as, in after times, the same idea was attached to the Tatars and other northern nations. Owing to their inroads into Southern Asia, they were partially known by the reports of their numbers and ferocity, and the devastations which they spread wherever they came.

Gog, the first name here occurring, is said to be אֶרֶץ הַמָּגוֹג, *of the land of Magog*, thereby intimating, not that the king belonged to it as his origin, but that it was the country over which he reigned, and most probably that this was the common title of the kings of the country, just as Pharaoh was of those of Egypt. There has been much speculation relative to the etymology of this name, and few have bestowed more pains upon it than the learned Bochart, in his Phaleg. lib. i. cap. ii. p. 13; lib. iii. cap. xiii. p. 212, seqq.: to which add Michaëlis, Supplementa ad Lxx. Hebraica, Nos. 341, 1352. The only probable conclusion, in which most modern interpreters seem inclined to rest, is, that the term is merely a contraction of خاقان, *Chakan*, a name generally given by the northern Asiatics to their king, and retained by the Turks as one of the titles of the Grand Sultan to this day. It may be remarked, however, that Bochart advances too preca-

rious a position when he would derive the word *Caucasus* from גּוֹג־חָסָן, *Gog-hasan*, the *fortress of Gog*. That the מ in *Magog* is local, and denotes the country, is allowed on all sides. The Asiatic nations, which have retained the Hebrew name, designate thereby the regions of the remote north, which were for the most part immersed in Cimmerian darkness. Jerome, in his Commentary on Ezekiel, says: Magog esse gentes Scythicas, immanes et innumerabiles, qui trans Caucasum montem et Mæotidem paludem et prope Caspium mare ad Indiam usque tendantur. For Gog and Magog, the Arabs employ the kindred terms یاجوج وماجوج, *Yajuj wa Majuj*, just as a similar form چین وماچین, *chin wa matchin*, is used of China.

It has been matter of dispute whether רֹאשׁ, *Rosh* is to be considered as an appellative or as a proper name. The LXX. take the latter view, and render, Γώγ, ἄρχοντα Ῥώς, Μεσόχ, καὶ Θοβέλ, *Gog, prince of Ros. Mesoch, and Thobel*. Jerome, indeed, not finding any such name in Genesis or elsewhere in Scripture, rashly concluded that it must necessarily be an appellative, not adverting to the fact, that there are other names of nations mentioned by Ezekiel, for which no authority can be found either in Moses or any other Old Testament writer.

That the Tauri inhabiting the Crimea were a Scythian people known by the name of *Ros*, is remarked by the Greek Grammarian, John Tzetzes, Chiliad ii. Hist. 393; and the same name has been traced by Ibn Fozzlan, an Arabian writer of the same period, to the Russians as dwelling on the river Volga. Constantin. Porphyr., in his work *De Administr. Imper.* p. ii. c. 13, refers to them in like manner: εἴτε Χάζαροι, εἴτε Τοῦρκοι, εἴτε καὶ Ῥώς, ἢ ἕτερόν τι ἔθνος τῶν Βορείων

4 prince of Rosh, Meshech, and Tubal. And I will cause thee to turn back, and put hooks in thy jaws, and cause thee to go out, thee and all thy host, horses and horsemen, all of them clothed in perfection, a great company with shield and buckler, all of
5 them handling swords. Persia, Cush, and Put with them, all
6 of them with buckler and helmet. Gomer and all his armies;
the house of Togarmah from the furthest north, and all his
7 armies; many people with thee. Be fully prepared, thou and all thy company that are collected to thee, and be to them for a

καὶ Σκυθικῶν: and Bochart places them in the vicinity of the river Araxes, in which word, as pronounced by the Arabians, he finds the etymology of the term.

That מֶשֶׁךְ וְתֻבָל, *Meshech and Thubal*, whatever affinity in sound there may be between the words, have any reference to *Moscovy* and *Tobolsk*, is contested with much show of reason by Michaelis, who observes that the name of the Russians is not of any antiquity in history with application to the present occupants of the empire; the ancient name of that people being *Slavi* or *Wends*. That of Moscovites is still more recent, and was given to the people because the Czars chose Moscow as their place of residence. That city was first built in the twelfth century, and takes its name from the river Moscow on which it lies. Tobolsk is of still more recent date. Nothing would therefore be more precarious than to found any theory on the present prophecy of Ezekiel relative to some future attack of the Russians upon the Jews in Palestine.

The opinion is now generally acquiesced in, that, by Meshech and Tubal, we are to understand the Moschi and Tibareni, who occupied regions about the Caucasus in the neighborhood of the Araxes.

4, 5. The simple meaning of שֹׁבַבְתִּיךָ is, *I will cause thee to turn back*, and would seem to be here used simply in reference to inducing the power spoken of to change his position, and return to some point which he had left. Compare 2 Kings xix. 28. It is not expressive of any judgment to be inflicted upon him, but simply of the influence exerted in the providence of God in order to prompt him to action. According to our hypothesis it will describe the means employed to induce Antiochus to return from Egypt to Palestine. The putting a hook in his jaws conveys the idea that it was as easy for God to control the movements of that monarch, as it is for fishermen to curb the impetuosity of a marine animal. The description of his army which follows shows that it would be of the most formidable character. It was to consist of troops collected from the most distant parts, and accoutred in the most complete manner. Auxiliaries from all quarters should swell its ranks.

6. גֹּמֶר, the ancestor of the Cimmerians or Celts who originally settled in the Crimea, whence they spread themselves across the regions to the north and east of the Taurian Chersonesus, and crossing over the Bosphorus took possession of Phrygia and Galatia. בֵּית־תּוֹגַרְמָה, *the house*, i.e. the descendants *of Togarmah* (Gen. x. 3). These were the Armenians of the Caucasus south of Iberia; see on chap. xxvii. 14. They are here mentioned along with the Cimmerians because they were only separated from them by the Euxine.

7. הִכֹּן יָחָבֵן, a variety of form for the sake of emphasis, *be prepared and prepare*, i.e. be fully prepared. The commander is ironically charged to take special care of his troops, that they might be fit

8 guard. After many days thou wilt make thy attack, in the last of the years thou wilt enter the land that is brought back from the sword, collected from many people, on the mountains of Israel which had been continually desolate; which hath been brought out from the peoples, and dwell all of them securely.
9 And thou wilt go up; as a storm thou wilt come; as a cloud to cover the land thou shalt be, thou and all thy armies, and
10 many people with thee. Thus saith the Lord Jehovah: It shall also come to pass in that day, that things shall come into
11 thy mind, and thou wilt devise a wicked device: And thou wilt say: I will go up to the land of villages, I will invade those who are at ease, that dwell securely, all of them dwelling
12 without walls, and to whom are neither bars nor doors: To take spoil and to seize booty, to turn thy hand against the inhabited wastes, and against a people gathered from the nations, acquiring cattle and substance, dwelling in the height of

for action, and disposable in whatever quarters he might see fit to employ them.

8. הִפָּקֵד, *thou shalt make thy attack*. Various interpretations have been given of this word; but all that are founded on the strictly passive signification of the verb have failed to give satisfaction. I consider it to be taken in a reflexive sense, referring the action back to the agent, and thereby rendering him more prominent.

The period of the attack is first specified very indefinitely: מִיָּמִים רַבִּים, *after many days*, which may be either longer or shorter, according to circumstances. Thus in Hos. iii. 4, the phrase denotes the period of upwards of eighteen centuries that have elapsed since the present dispersion of the Jews; but in 1 Kings ii. 38, 39, it is limited to a period not exceeding three years. The specification in our prophet, however, is rendered more definite by the following statement that the attack was to be made בְּאַחֲרִית הַשָּׁנִים, in *the last of the years*, which, in prophetic designations of time, denotes that which immediately preceded the coming of the Messiah. This again is equivalent to בְּאַחֲרִית הַיָּמִים, *the last of the days*, ver. 16. A period of upwards of three hundred years elapsed after the return of the Jews to their own land, during which they enjoyed uninterrupted tranquillity, before they were persecuted by Antiochus; which is quite sufficient to meet the claims of the prophecy. The mountains of Israel are said to have been הָרִיד, *always*, i.e. continuously waste, in reference to the protracted period of the captivity, during which they had been stripped of their inhabitants.

9. The invasion by Gog and his armies is compared to a storm, to express the impetuosity, noise, and confusion by which it should be marked. The immense number of his troops is aptly compared to a cloud sweeping over the land, and involving it in darkness — a figure of common occurrence in ancient writers. See the Iliad, xvi. 243.

11. אֶרֶץ פְּרָזוֹת, *a land of villages*, i.e. mere villages. Our translators have added *unwalled*, but quite unnecessarily, since this idea is sufficiently expressed afterwards in the verse. The word פְּרָזָה properly signifies *open country*, in contradistinction to towns and cities. Compare Esther ix. 19. The unsuspecting

13 the land. Sheba and Dedan, and the merchants of Tarshish, and all her young lions, shall say to thee: Art thou come to take spoil? hast thou collected an assembly to seize booty? to carry away silver and gold? to take cattle and substance? to
14 gain much spoil? Therefore prophesy, son of man, and say unto Gog: Thus saith the Lord Jehovah: Shalt thou not know
15 it in the day when my people Israel dwell securely? And thou wilt come from thy place, from the most distant north, thou and many people with thee; riders on horses, all of them,
16 a great company and a great army. And thou wilt come up against my people Israel, as a cloud to cover the land; in the last of the days it shall be; and I will bring thee against my land that the nations may know me, when I am sanctified in
17 thee, O Gog, in their sight. Thus saith the Lord Jehovah: Art thou he of which I spake in ancient days by the hand of my servants the prophets of Israel, who prophesied in those
18 days, years ago, to bring thee against them? And it shall be in that day, in the day of the coming of Gog against the land of Israel, saith the Lord Jehovah, my fury shall come up

confidence of the restored Hebrews is here graphically described. What is stated may have literally been the case, or the language may be expressive of the contempt with which Antiochus regarded them, conceiving that they would fall an easy prey into his hands.

12. A forcible description of the insatiable rapacity of the invader. The Hebrews are represented as dwelling in the most elevated parts of the country. טַבּוּר הָאָרֶץ, *the height of the land.* The idea of *navel*, which signification טַבּוּר has in the Talmud, and which the Vulgate expresses by *umbilicus*, is not biblical, but is derived from the Greeks, who regarded Parnassus as the highest part of their country — ὀμφαλὸς τῆς γῆς. The same word occurs Judges ix. 37, where it is used in the same acceptation, and not in that of middle, as rendered in the common version. Ewald, however, renders *Nabel*, and Hitzig attempts to defend it. חָרְבוֹת נוֹשָׁבוֹת, Rosenmüller renders: *ruinosa prius et nunc reædificata.*

13. The object of the address here made to the invader seems to have been to enter into negotiations with him for the disposal of the prey. Jahn states that more than one thousand merchants joined the army, having come for the purpose of purchasing such Jews as might be taken prisoners, p. 272. כְּפִירִים, *young lions,* i.e. taking the term as used tropically, robust princes or warriors. Compare xix. 3; xxxii. 2.

14-16. The object of Jehovah in bringing Gog into Palestine was signally to illustrate his own divine power in his destruction. It should be made manifest to the nations that there was still a God in Israel able to interpose and save. For אַחֲרִית הַיָּמִים see on verse 8.

17. Newcome supposes reference to be made here to unrecorded prophecies, but there appears no good ground for such supposition. Though no prophecy may be found in which Gog is specified by name, yet there are many which depict signal enemies of the church of God who should be subdued and destroyed. See Numb. xxiv. 17-19; Ps. lxxii. 4; lxxxix. 23; Isa. xiv. 29-32; lix. 19; Joel ii. 2. שָׁנִים, *years,* is to be

19 into my nose. And in my jealousy, in the fire of my indignation, I speak; Surely in that day there shall be a great quaking
20 in the land of Israel. And the fishes of the sea, and the fowls of heaven, and the beast of the field, and every creeping thing that creepeth upon the ground, and all men that are upon the face of the earth, shall tremble at my presence; and the mountains shall be thrown down, and the precipices shall fall, and all
21 walls shall fall to the ground. And I will call against him to all my mountains a sword, saith the Lord Jehovah; the sword
22 of each man shall be against his brother. And I will punish him with pestilence and with blood, and I will rain upon him and upon his armies, and upon the many people that are with him, heavy overflowing showers, and great hailstones, fire and
23 brimstone. And I will magnify myself and sanctify myself, and become known in the sight of many nations, and they shall know that I am Jehovah.

connected with הַנְּבִאִים, who prophesied *years ago.*

18–20. Earthquakes, which have been of frequent occurrence in Palestine, are employed by the prophets as symbols of political revolutions, in which everything is shaken and convulsed. Compare Rev. xvi. 18. Such should be the tremendous force of the concussion which should accompany the invasion of Gog, that universal nature is represented as affected by it. By a strong anthropopathy, Jehovah declares his holy displeasure with the expedition.

20. הַמַּדְרֵגוֹת, *the precipices* or steep terraces which were raised on the sides of the mountains, to prevent the earth from being washed down by the rains, and on which the vines were cultivated. The root is preserved in the Arabic درج, *to ascend by steps.*

21–23. The slaughter of the army of Gog should be immense. His military should be so desperate, that they should cut right and left, irrespective of friend or foe. Fairbairn is mistaken in supposing that the language is not expressive of mutual slaughter. His interpretation, that God would meet sword with sword in the hand of his people, however ingenious, is not borne out by Hebrew usage; whereas אִישׁ בְּאָחִיו is a common phrase for *one another*. Jehovah is represented as overthrowing the enemy by the most fearful combination of the elements. אַבְנֵי אֶלְגָּבִישׁ, *hail,* stones of ice. Arab. الجمش. Compare Rev. xvi. 21. The language being figurative, it is not so evident as Rosenmüller would have it (clarissime patet) that the reference cannot be to Antiochus Epiphanes.

CHAPTER XXXIX.

A continuation of the prophecy against Gog. The awful judgments of God are further denounced against the furious enemy of his people, 1-7. So complete would be his overthrow, that the weapons left in the field should long supply the Israelites with fuel, 8-10; and a long period should be required for burying the dead bodies of the slain, 11-16. An invitation is then given to the birds of prey and the wild beasts to come and partake of the sacrificial feast prepared for them by the slaughter of the enemy, 17-22. The chapter concludes with promises of future good to chastised and repentant Israel, 23-29.

1 AND thou, son of man, prophesy against Gog, and say: Thus saith the Lord Jehovah: Behold, I am against thee, O Gog,
2 prince of Rosh, Meshech, and Tubal: And will turn thee back, and lead thee about, and cause thee to come up from the farthest
3 north, and bring thee against the mountains of Israel. And I will smite thy bow from thy left hand, and make thine arrows
4 to fall out of thy right hand. Upon the mountains of Israel thou shalt fall, thou and all thy armies, and the people that are with thee; I will give thee for food to the bird of prey of
5 every wing, and to the beast of the field. Thou shalt fall in the open field, for I have spoken it, saith the Lord Jehovah.
6 And I will send fire on Magog, and on those dwelling securely
7 in the isles, and they shall know that I am Jehovah. And I will make my holy name known in the midst of my people Israel; and I will profane my holy name no more; and the nations shall know that I Jehovah am the Holy One of Israel.

2. וְשֹׁבַבְתִּיךָ. See on chap. xxxviii. 4. שִׁשֵּׁאתִיךָ, a ἅπαξ λεγ. Whatever apparent connection there may at first sight appear to be between this verb, and the numeral שֵׁשׁ, *six*, the signification thus suggested affords nothing suitable to the context. I do not scruple, therefore, to adopt the derivation proposed by Ludovic de Dieu, from the Ethiopic ሖወሰ, *to go about*, with the Piel signification, *to cause to wander*. This derivation is approved by Gesenius, Winer, and Rosenmüller, and is supported by the LXX. Καθοδηγήσω σε, or as the Complutensian reading has it κατάξω σε, and the Targum אַשְׁגֵא, *errare te faciam*. Compare the Arabic سا, *sa, instigatur*; Turkish ساسات, *sasat, asinum vocare ad potum*. The declaration bears that Jehovah would induce Gog to leave his position, and undertake his expedition against Palestine.

3. קַשְׁתְּךָ, *thy bow*. The Scythians were renowned as archers.

4, 5. See on verses 17-20.

6. By the inhabitants אִיִּים, *of the isles*, are meant those dwelling in Greece and the coasts of the Euxine, who took part with Gog, and helped to swell his armies. They were to be involved in intestine wars, and thus destroyed. War is frequently compared to fire, on account of its all-devouring action.

7. When the Jews obtained the mastery over their ferocious and formidable

8   Behold, it cometh, and taketh place, saith the Lord Jehovah: it
9   is the day of which I have spoken. Then shall the inhabitants
    of the cities of Israel go forth, and burn, and set on fire the
    weapons, both the buckler and the helmet, with the bows and
    arrows, the hand-spear and the lance; and make fire with them
10 seven years. And they shall not take wood from the field, nor
    hew it from the forests; for they shall kindle fire with the
    weapons; and they shall spoil those who spoiled them, and
    plunder those who plundered them, saith the Lord Jehovah.
11 And it shall come to pass in that day I will give to Gog a burying-
    place there in Israel, the valley of the passengers, on the east
    of the sea; and it shall stop the passengers; and there shall they
    bury Gog, and all his multitude, and shall call it: THE VALLEY
12 OF THE MULTITUDE OF GOG. And the house of Israel shall bury
13 them, in order to purify the country, seven months. And all·
    the people of the land shall bury them, and it shall be to them
    for a name in the day when I shall be glorified, saith the Lord

enemy, it would be manifest to the world that Jehovah, whose people they were, was a God able to deliver them and alone entitled to worship and obedience. When God is said to pollute his name, the meaning is that he permits it to be polluted.

8. הִנֵּה בָאָה וְנִהְיָתָה is very expressive, denoting the absolute certainty of the event.

9, 10. On the discomfiture of the Gogites, they would leave their armor on the field of battle, which the Hebrews observing, would make a bonfire of it, and have such a quantity left, that they would be under no necessity for a long time to repair to the woods for fuel. *Seven years* is a hyperbolical term, derived from the intensive significancy of the number in Hebrew usage, and designed to express a very long time. Scholz quotes here from Mariana, a Spanish historian, who states that after the Spaniards had gained a victory over the Saracens A.D. 1212, they found such a quantity of arms that they served them four years for fuel.

11. מְקוֹם־שָׁם קֶבֶר, *a place there of burial*, by hypallage for מְקוֹם קֶבֶר שָׁם, *a place of burial there*, in order to give prominence to the locality. Instead of obtaining Palestine as a conquest, as Gog had expected, all that he should find would be a grave. The place is denominated גֵּי הָעֹבְרִים, *the valley of the passengers*, in reference to its position on the east side of the Dead Sea, along which lay the high road for traffic to Petra and Eziongeber. It would thus be notoriously public, and, arresting travellers in their progress, would compel them to reflect on the signal judgment inflicted on the enemies of the covenant people. וְחֹסֶמֶת refers to the stopping of the passengers by the multitude of graves; and not of their noses by the stench, as has erroneously been supposed.

Compare the Arabic حسم, *impedire aliquem ab aliqua re.*

The proximity of the place to the desolated cities of the plain would remind men of the vengeance taken on the flagitious sinners who had perished there. The appropriate name of the valley should be גֵּיא הֲמוֹן גּוֹג, *the valley of the multitude of Gog.*

12–14. *Seven months* are again used

14 Jehovah. And they shall select men of continuance who shall go through the land, burying, with those who pass through, them that remain upon the face of the land, to purify it: at the
15 end of seven months they shall search. And the passengers passing through the land, when one seeth the bone of a man, he shall set up a sign beside it, until those who are burying bury it
16 in the valley of the multitude of Gog. And the name of the
17 city shall be HAMONAH; and they shall purify the land. And thou, son of man, thus saith the Lord Jehovah: Say unto birds of every wing, and to every beast of the field: Assemble yourselves and come, gather yourselves on every side to my sacrifice which I sacrifice for you, a great sacrifice upon the mountains
18 of Israel, and eat flesh, and drink blood. Ye shall eat the flesh of heroes, and drink the blood of the princes of the earth, of rams, of lambs, and of he-goats, of bullocks, all of them fatlings

hyperbolically for a long time, to denote that the number of dead bodies would be such that a considerable length of time would be required for burying them. Not only would the atmosphere be polluted with the stench, but the land was to be regarded as morally defiled, so that the most prompt and effective measures were adopted to have the very skeletons removed. אַנְשֵׁי תָכִיד, *men of continuance*: i.e. men whose constant employment it should be to collect and bury whatever remains they might find. The meaning of verse 14, at which some interpreters have greatly stumbled, seems to be simply this, that those who were uninterruptedly occupied with the removal of the dead corpses were to be assisted by such as were occasionally passing through the country, that by their united exertions a speedy riddance might be effected. All the inhabitants were to combine their efforts for this object. The computation of Fairbairn, that a million of men would be daily employed, exclusive of the Sabbaths, and that if each buried but two a day, we should have an aggregate of three hundred and sixty million corpses, is merely conjured up as a bugbear to frighten the reader out of all disposition to admit the literal interpretation.

15. Should any one accidentally discover a bone, he was not to touch it, lest he should be defiled, but was to set a mark by it, that it might be removed by the proper person appointed for the purpose.

16. Some city in the neighborhood was to receive the name עִיר הֲמוֹנָה, *the city of Hamonah*, i.e. *of the multitude*, to perpetuate the memory of the signal defeat which the enemy had sustained.

17–22. Not satisfied with having described the burial of the Gogites, the prophet takes a view of them as still lying on the battle-field, and invites the birds of prey and the wild beasts to come to a sacrificial repast on their dead bodies. To enhance the description, the guests are represented as being filled not only with the flesh of the victims in general, but with that of the horses and the charioteers. רֶכֶב, *a rider* or charioteer. See on Isa. xxi. 7, 9. The amplification which follows is quite in the style of Ezekiel. The entire passage is strikingly parallel with Rev. xix. 17–19. Compare Isa. xviii. 6; xxxiv. 6, 8; which are evidently founded on the ancient custom of feasting on sacrifices.

18. Though פָּרִים, *bulls*, which Houbigant and Newcome adopt after the LXX. and Arabic versions, may seem

19 of Bashan. And ye shall eat fat to satiety, and drink blood to
20 inebriation, of my sacrifice which I sacrifice for you. And ye shall satiate yourselves at my table with horses and charioteers,
21 heroes and all the men of war, saith the Lord Jehovah. And I will set my glory among the nations, and all the nations shall see my judgments which I have executed, and my hand
22 which I have laid upon them. And the house of Israel shall know that I Jehovah am their God from that day and forward.
23 And the nations shall know that the house of Israel went into captivity through their iniquity, because they rebelled against me, and I hid my face from them, and delivered them into the hand of their adversaries, and they fell all of them by the sword.
24 According to their impurity and according to their sins have I
25 done unto them, and I hid my face from them. Nevertheless, thus saith the Lord Jehovah: Now I will reverse the captivity of Jacob, and will have mercy upon the whole house of Israel,
26 and will be jealous for my holy name: After they shall have borne their shame and all their iniquity by which they have rebelled against me, when they dwelt securely in their own
27 land and none made them afraid. When I have brought them back from the people, and gathered them from the countries of their enemies, and am sanctified in them in the sight of many
28 nations: Then they shall know that I Jehovah am their God, in that I caused them to be taken into captivity among the heathen, but have gathered them into their own land, and have
29 left none of them there any more. And I will no more hide my face from them, when I have poured out my Spirit upon the house of Israel, saith the Lord Jehovah.

more appropriate in such connection than פָּרִים, *lambs*, yet it in all probability originated in the want of attention to the fact that פָּרִים occurs immediately after. The guests were to be amply supplied. Nothing should be wanting that could enhance the sumptuousness of the banquet.

26–29. וְנָשָׂא. There is no necessity for changing the punctuation into וְנָשְׂאוּ. Indeed it would introduce an idea contradictory of such passages as xliii. 10, 11; xxxvi. 31. The meaning is, that when the Hebrews had suffered sufficient punishment for all their acts of rebellion, Jehovah would restore them to the enjoyment of their ancient privileges, and prove himself to be their covenant God. The crowning mercy of all would be the outpouring of his Holy Spirit, by which they would be prepared to serve him acceptably and devotedly for the future.

The deliverance of the Hebrews was wrought out in a most remarkable manner. Mattathias, raising the standard of patriotism, called around him the pious portion of his countrymen. His party increased rapidly, till they became a considerable army. He appointed his third and bravest son, Judas, military commander, by whom the Syrian generals that were sent against him were defeated. In battle after battle he proved victorious. Even the army which Lysias sent into Judea could not stand before him. Though composed of forty thousand foot and seven thousand cavalry, and increased by auxiliaries from the provinces, it proved powerless before him. Putting the enemy to flight, he secured immense booty. The like success attended him the following year, when he defeated an army of sixty thousand men, made himself master of several strong cities; and, retaking Jerusalem, purified the temple and restored its solemn services. His brothers Simon and Jonathan proved themselves worthy successors of this devoted patriot; the independence of the Jews was finally secured, and the royal dignity vested in the Asmonæan family, in which it continued till the time of Herod the Great.

CHAPTERS XL.–XLVIII.

The last nine chapters of this Book contain a remarkable vision, in which Ezekiel was furnished with an ideal representation of the Jewish state as about to be restored after the captivity. The principal subjects connected with that state having been the temple and the temple-worship, the prophet presents these to view with all the minuteness and circumstantiality of detail which form so marked a characteristic of his style.

That it was the restoration of the material temple, then in ruins, that the prophet had in his eye, is the only hypothesis which fully meets the exigency of the case; the hopes of such a restoration having been rendered prominent in the minds of his captive countrymen by the preceding prophecies which he had delivered to them. It supersedes the necessity of having recourse to fanciful and arbitrary interpretations, removes all contrariety between the delineation in the vision relating to the priests, sacrifices, etc., and the doctrine of the New Testament respecting the complete abolition of the Levitical worship by the institution of the priesthood and sacrifice of Christ; and renders nugatory all expectations of a literal fulfilment in the yet distant future. What was wanted was a sanctuary that should be serviceable during what might still remain of the period destined for the existence of the old economy. When that economy should wax old and vanish away, there was to be an end of all merely external circumstances. Temple-worship, priesthood, and sacrifices should cease; and a spiritual temple, a spiritual priesthood, and spiritual sacrifices were alone to be acceptable to the Most High (John iv. 21–24; 1 Cor. vi. 19; 1 Pet. ii. 5).

The import of the vision, in the main, is this: that God would in due time accomplish the restoration of his exiled people to the land of their fathers; effect the reconstruction of their ruined temple, and the reorganization of its religious services; and bless them with manifest tokens of his favor. At the time it was granted, the Hebrews were in a state of the lowest depression in Babylon. Fourteen years had elapsed since the destruction of their sacred edifice; and nothing could have been better calculated to revive their drooping hopes, re-invigorate their confidence in their covenant God, and encourage them to return to Palestine when the hour of their liberation should arrive, than the brilliant prospect of the restoration of their civil and religious privileges which the prophet here holds out to their view.

The circumstance that in many points the city, temple, and services do not exactly accord with the state of things as existing before the captivity, forms no valid objection against the literal interpretation. The differences may have been intended to a certain extent to wean the Jews from the idea of the immutability of their ancient constitution, and thus prepare them for the complete change that was to be effected by the introduction of the new dispensation which was speedily to follow.

The statement made by Hävernick, that the post-exilian temple and its ordinances were not restored according to the pattern furnished by Ezekiel, is altogether a gratuitous assumption. It is a point on which we have no positive historical data to enable us to decide. The discrepancies, however, that have been detected between the ancient temple and that described by Ezekiel, are non-essential; all the leading points connected with the sacred theocracy being carefully preserved and prominently brought out.

The vision is not to be regarded as merely a description of what the prophet remembered of Solomon's temple; nor are the discrepancies existing between the two edifices to be attributed to defectiveness of memory on his part. It was altogether a disclosure to his view of something new, symbolizing, as it was eminently calculated to do, the renovated condition of the Jewish state. The Holy Spirit doubtless availed himself of the reminiscences of Ezekiel, which must have been very vivid in their character, for the purpose of furnishing an ideal model of the new temple, and imparted to him such additional particulars as were necessary to render it complete. His imagination was so controlled and regulated in its creative and combining operations by the superintending Spirit of inspiration, that he should present no ideas but those which it was the will of God should be exhibited to the people.

The sacred associations which the prophet had carried with him into the land of his captivity would be especially dear to him, from the interest which he must have taken in them, as a priest, he ministered in his official capacity in the temple. What more natural than that he should have spoken of the different objects as if he had seen them but yesterday? They must have continually floated in his mind's eye during his absence from Jerusalem, so that when he was mentally transported thither they could not but rush into his mind with all the freshness of pre-existing reality. With what enthusiasm may we conceive him to have caught the first glance of the magnificent structure presented in vision to his view! With what interest he must have entered the eastern porch, and recognized the altar and other parts of the sacred building! How familiar to him must have been every object that met his mental eye! With what attention he must have listened to the communications made by his celestial conductor while detailing to him the various particulars relating to the measures, the parts, and the ordinances of the temple!

Let now any reader of ordinary intelligence turn up the description of the vision, and let him be asked what is the impression which it naturally makes upon him, and which he finds it impossible to dismiss from his mind, and he will candidly own that it is that of a literal temple. The more he studies it, and the more he enters into the minutiae, with the greater force does the conviction rivet itself in his mind. Talk to him about spiritual and mystical meanings, you puzzle and bewilder him. He may admire your ingenuity, and be brought to be half-inclined to embrace your theory, but he cannot, after all, rid himself of the notion of a material building and literal ordinances. Turn the subject in which way soever he may, it always comes back upon him in this shape. A temple the Jews had possessed. It had been the glory of Jerusalem. A restoration of it had been promised. It was what was wanted to re-constitute their polity, which had been interrupted, but not abrogated. The essential parts of that polity are all minutely delineated. Could they have been intended to remain purely ideal? Were the captives on their return not to set about attempting to realize them in the outward world? Would they have been justified if they had not? And is it not a fact that on their return to their metropolis, they did, with the divine approval, adopt such measures as lay in their power for carrying the design into effect? See Ezra iii. That they carried out the plan here furnished them to its full extent, is a point which, as already stated, we have no means of positively determining. If they failed in doing so, it may have been attributable to circumstances over which they had no control. In neither case does the circumstance affect the divine authority of the prophet.

So far, then, as the temple and its ordinances are concerned, the vision is to be interpreted literally. With respect to the waters, etc. (chap. xlvii.), it is altogether different. Here there was nothing left for the Jews to do in bringing about the realization of the vision. Having left the temple, the seat of the divine residence and the source whence blessings were to flow to the restored Hebrew nation, the prophet is carried in vision southward into the regions of the Dead Sea, which had been noted for everything that was forbidden and noxious in its aspect — the very embodiment of barrenness and desolation. These were now to be converted into fertility and beauty. As in their previous condition they were strikingly symbolical of the spiritually unproductive and abhorrent character of idolatrous Israel, so they were now to serve as images of the renewed state of things when God should bring back his people, and, according to his promises, bless them by conferring upon them abundantly the rich tokens of his regard. Instead of a barren wilderness, they should now become as the garden of Eden. By the copious effusions of the influences of his Holy Spirit, he would restore his church to spiritual life, and render her instrumental in diffusing blessings to the world around. The chapter thus contains, in the garb of the usual figurative language of prophecy, representations in exact keeping with what we read, Isa. xii. 3; xliii. 18-21; xliv. 3, 4; Joel iii. 18; Zech. xiv. 8. The abundance and beneficial qualities of the waters are strongly marked, and form the most prominent feature in the picture.

The only apparently plausible objection that can be taken to the literal interpretation of the temple, is founded on the dimensions assigned to it (chap. xlii. 16-20). It remains, however, to be settled whether *reeds* be the measure there intended; and whether, supposing this to be the case, the language be not susceptible of another construction. (See note on the passage.) Nor is there any inconsistency in interpreting one part of the vision literally and the other symbolically. The cases are perfectly different. In the one, a literal temple was required to meet the circumstances of the exiled Hebrews; in the other, though outwardly restored, the temple and temple-worship would still have left them in a state of spiritual destitution, if they had not received the blessing from on high. The rich and abundant communication of this blessing we conceive to be beautifully set forth under the image of a river issuing forth from the divine presence in the new temple; and, increasing as it flows in the direction of the Dead Sea, spreading life and fertility wherever it comes. (See on chapter xlvii.)

CHAPTER XL.

Ezekiel, conducted in vision within sight of Jerusalem, then lying in ruins, is to be conceived of as set down on the north side of Moriah, whence he has exhibited to his view the structure of a city on the south, with its temple, gates, porches, chambers, windows, arches, tables, etc.

I do not deem it necessary to occupy the time of my readers by entering minutely into matters of architectural detail; for whatever interest they might have for those who study this portion of the sacred writings merely for professional purposes, they would contribute but little to the edification of the general reader. Nor, for the same reason, shall I dwell upon the etymological import of all the terms which occur in these chapters. The curious in such matters I refer to Bötcher's Proben Alt-Testamentlicher Schrifterklärung, Leipzig, 1833.

1 In the five and twentieth year of our captivity, at the beginning of the year, on the tenth of the month, in the fourteenth year after the city had been smitten, on that very day the hand of
2 Jehovah was upon me, and he brought me thither. In visions of God he brought me into the land of Israel, and set me upon a very high mountain, and upon it was, as it were, the frame of

1. Some difficulty has been found in determining what is meant by רֹאשׁ הַשָּׁנָה, *the beginning of the year*, in which the vision was granted. In all probability, however, it was that of the Jewish ecclesiastical year, the first of the month Nisan, or Abib. Ewald and Fairbairn very rationally conclude that the term שָׁמָּה, *thither*, originated in the thoughts and feelings of the prophet being directed towards Jerusalem as their centre. See the epexegesis ver. 3. By יַד יְהוָֹה, *the hand of Jehovah*, we are to understand the impulse by which the prophet was mentally transported from the Chebar to the land of his fathers. Compare chap. iii. 14.

2. For, מַרְאוֹת אֱלֹהִים, *visions of God*, compare chapters viii. 3; xliii. 3. Both these substantives are strictly plural, comprehending the various parts of the scenic representation, and are not to be interpreted of a plural of excellency, sublimity, or the like, as proposed by some. The objects were presented to the mental view of Ezekiel in a waking state, and are thus distinguishable from those which were communicated in dreams. The images exhibited possessed all the vividness and distinctness of outward objects. Gesenius renders, *visions from God*, but this is unnecessary, since it must at once be obvious that the word is designed to express, not visions of which God was the object, but those of which he was the author. הַר גָּבֹהַּ מְאֹד, *an exceeding high mountain*. Compare for the phraseology ὄρος ὑψηλὸν λίαν, Matt. iv. 8. Michaelis and some other commentators consider the term mountain to be here used metaphorically, as in Isa. ii. 2, to denote the superiority of Jerusalem in a moral point of view. The specification of the height of the mountain is not to be pressed, otherwise we cannot suppose the prophet to have been mentally located at Jerusalem. Neither Mount Zion, Mount Moriah, nor even Mount Olivet can lay claim to such a distinction. Mayer observes that, in comparison with the mountains of Switzerland, Moriah would be regarded as an inconsiderable height. Still its altitude is more than two thousand feet above the level of the

3   a city southward. And he brought me thither, and behold, a
     man whose appearance was as the appearance of brass, with a
     a line of flax in his hand, and a measuring reed; and he stood
4   in the gate. And the man spake unto me: Son of man, see
     with thine eyes, and hear with thine ears, and set thy heart to
     all that I will show thee; for in order that I might show it to
     thee art thou brought hither: declare all that thou seest to the
5   house of Israel. And, behold, a wall without the house round
     about, and in the hand of the man a measuring reed, six cubits
     by a cubit and a handbreadth; and he measured the breadth of

Mediterranean, and must have appeared very high to the prophet, situated as he had been on the plains of Babylon. אֶל occasions no difficulty, and requires no conjectural emendation into עַל. The preposition is sometimes used in a less accurate sense, to denote proximity in reference to any place, without defining whether the subject was *on*, *at*, or *by* it. It is therefore to be rendered as best suits the tenor of the discourse. Here the idea of *on* or *upon* would seem the most suitable.

Looking southward from Moriah, Ezekiel discovered the structure of a city, which he immediately proceeds to describe as a temple — that being the most prominent object in the vision — with all its different buildings and compartments. Precisely in this direction must the former city and temple have appeared to one who approached them from the north. Strictly speaking, the עִיר or citadel of Zion lay to the west of the temple on Moriah; but viewed from the north, they both lay in a southerly direction. The description gives no countenance whatever to the notion entertained by some, that a space stretching altogether to the south of Jerusalem was intended by the locality here specified.

3. Who this אִישׁ, *man*, was, we are not informed. Nor is it necessary to conjecture. Suffice it that he was prepared to execute the task committed to him of taking the dimensions of the temple, and holding converse with the prophet relative to its several appurtenances. To convey the idea of his celestial commission, the splendor of his appearance is compared to that of brightly polished metal. The messenger had in his hand two measuring instruments: the one פְּתִיל פִּשְׁתִּים, *a tape* or *line* made of flax, used in taking the longer measurements; the other, קָנֶה, the *reed*, *rod*, or *cane* employed in taking that of houses. Considerable difficulty has been found in exactly determining the length of the Hebrew measures. Michaelis enters at much length into the subject in his German Notes, which I would recommend to the perusal of the reader. Suffice it here to say, that measures of length were for the most part taken from the human body. Thus אַמָּה, ulna, *a cubit*, so called from its signifying that part of the arm which extends from the elbow to the extremity of the middle finger. To this was given the name of the greater cubit. It is described by Ezekiel as consisting of an ordinary cubit and an hand-breadth, xliii. 13, compared with xl. 1, 5. The smaller cubit reached from the elbow to the wrist or root of the hand. The טֶפַח, or *palm*, was the space occupied by the full breadth of the palm or hand.

4. Compare chapter xliv. 5. The prophet is charged to contemplate with the utmost attention and exactitude the objects presented to his view, that he might give a true representation of them to his countrymen, by whom they might

6 the building, one reed; and the height, one reed. And he came to the gate whose face was towards the east, and went up by its steps; and he measured the threshold of the gate, one
7 reed broad, and there was another threshold one reed broad. And the chamber was one reed long, and one reed broad; and between the chambers were five cubits, and the threshold of the gate beside the porch of the gate within, one reed.
8 And he measured the porch of the gate within, one reed. And
9 he measured the porch of the gate, eight cubits; and the posts thereof, two cubits; and the porch of the gate was inwards.
10 And the chambers of the gate eastward were three on this side, and three on that side; to them three was one measure; and
11 the posts had one measure on this side and on that side. And he measured the breadth of the opening of the gate, ten cubits;
12 and the length of the gate, thirteen cubits. And the boundary before the chambers, one cubit; and one cubit the boundary on that side, and the chambers were six cubits on this side, and six
13 cubits on that side. And he measured the gate from the roof of the one chamber to the roof of another: the breadth five-and-
14 twenty cubits, opening against opening. And he made the posts, sixty cubits, even unto the post of the court round about the
15 gate. And before the gate of the entrance, before the porch of
16 the inner gate, fifty cubits. And latticed windows to the chambers, and to their posts within the gate round about; and so to

be available in constructing anew the house of the Lord on their return from Babylon.

6. The mountains on which the temple had been and was again to be built not being level, access to it was by steps, בְּמַעֲלוֹת, or stairs, of which according to the LXX. there were seven (ἑπτὰ ἀναβαθμοῖς), which is confirmed by verses 25 and 26.

7. תָּא, a room or chamber. This word, of infrequent occurrence, is derived from היה, to dwell. Lee, comparing the Arabic ثَوَى, substitit divertitque, takes the same view of its meaning. These rooms appear to have been for the use of the Levites who kept watch at the gates of the temple, and for depositing utensils, musical instruments, and the like.

8. This verse is omitted in sixteen Hebrew MSS., has originally been wanting in seven, as it is in the Soncin. and Brixian editions, the LXX., Syr., and Vulg. Newcome conjectures that the porch of the inner gate may possibly be meant here. אֻלָם, LXX., πρόναος, the large vestibule or porch before the gate of the temple. Derivation, אִיל, to be first, i.e. in point of position, presenting itself to view as persons were about to enter the sacred edifice.

9. אֵיל. This word, which the LXX., the Targum, and the Syriac version leave untranslated, is an architectural term, supposed by Gesenius to denote a projection in the form of a pilaster or column which served at once for ornament, and as a bulwark for security.

16. The ancients not having glass,

the porches; and windows were round about inward; and upon
17 the posts were palm-trees. And he brought me into the outer
court; and, behold, cells and a tesselated pavement made for
18 the court round about; thirty cells upon the pavement. And
the pavement at the side of the gates, along the length of the
19 gates, was the lower pavement. And he measured the breadth
from before the lower gate before the inner court without, an
20 hundred cubits, on the east and on the north. And as to the
gate of the outward court which looketh towards the north,
21 he measured its length and its breadth. And its chambers,
three on the one side, and three on the other side; and the
posts thereof and the porches thereof were according to the
measurement of the former gate; fifty cubits the length thereof,
22 and its breadth five-and-twenty cubits. And its windows and
its porches and its palm-trees, according to the measure of the
gate which was before it, towards the east; and by seven stairs
23 they went up into it, and its porches were before them. And
the gate of the inner court was over against the gate to the
north and to the east; and he measured from gate to gate an
24 hundred cubits. And he brought me by the way of the south;
and, behold, a gate by the way of the south; and he measured its
25 posts, and its porches, according to these measures. And there
were windows to it, and to its porches round about, according to
these windows, fifty cubits in length, and the breadth five-and-
26 twenty cubits. And there were seven steps to go up by; and
its porches were before them; and it had palm-trees, one on the
27 one side, and one on the other side, upon its posts. And there
was a gate to the inner court towards the south; and he
measured from gate to gate towards the south, a hundred cubits.
28 And he brought me to the inner court in the gate of the south;
and he measured the gate of the south according to these
29 measures. And its chambers, and its porches, and posts, were

their windows were אֲטֻמִים, *latticed.*
They were let into the walls, widening
as they receded from them. That the
אֵילִים were partly for ornament would
appear from the statement that they had
representations of תִּמֹרִים, *palm branches,*
attached to them.

17. The pavement, רִצְפָה, in the East
is generally made of mosaic. Root רָצָף,
to inlay or *tesselate.* Comp. Esther i. 6.

The לְשָׁכוֹת, *cells* or *chambers,* were for
containing the tithes of salt, wine, and
oil, and served also as lodgings for the
priests while they were on duty in the
temple.

18. There were two pavements, a
higher and a lower, the former of which
was level with the entrance at the gate:
the latter on either side of the entrance
thus formed.

according to these measures; and there were windows to it, and to its posts round about, fifty cubits in length, and the
30 breadth twenty-five cubits. And the columns thereof round
31 about were twenty-five cubits long, and five cubits broad. And its columns were towards the outer court; and palm-trees were upon the posts thereof; and its ascent consisted of eight steps.
32 And he brought me into the inner court toward the east; and
33 he measured the gate according to these measures. And its chambers, and its posts, and its columns, were according to these measures; and it, and its columns, had windows round
34 about, fifty cubits long, and five-and-twenty cubits broad. And its columns were towards the outer court; and palm-trees were upon its posts, on the one side and on the other; and its ascent
35 consisted of eight steps. And he brought me to the north gate,
36 and measured according to these measures. The chambers thereof, and its columns, and its windows round about, fifty
37 cubits long, and five-and-twenty cubits wide. And the posts thereof were towards the outer court; and palm-trees were upon its posts, on this side, and on that side; and its ascent
38 consisted of eight steps. And the cells, and their entrances, were by the columns of the gates, where they should wash the
39 burnt-offering. And in the vestibule of the gate were two tables on this side, and two tables on that side, on which to slay the burnt-offering, and the sin-offering, and the trespass-offering.
40 And on the side without, by the ascent of the entrance of the gate northward, were two tables; and by the other side which
41 was in the vestibule of the gate, were two tables. Four tables on this side, and four tables on that side, by the side of the
42 gate; eight tables, on which they should slay. And four tables for the burnt-offering, of hewn stones, the length one cubit and a half, and the breadth one cubit and a half, and the height one cubit, on which they should lay the instruments with which
43 they should slay the burnt-offering and the sacrifice. And the double stalls, one hand-breadth, fixed within round about; and
44 upon the tables the flesh of the offering. And without the inner gate were cells for the singers in the inner court, which was at the side of the north gate; and their prospect was toward the south; one at the side of the east gate, having the
45 prospect toward the north. And he said unto me: This cell, whose prospect is toward the south, is for the priests, the keepers
46 of the charge of the house. And the cell whose prospect is

47 towards the north is for the priests, the keepers of the charge of the altar; they are the sons of Zadok; who, of the sons of Levi, approach to Jehovah to serve him. So he measured the
48 court, a hundred cubits long, and a hundred cubits broad, four square; and the altar was before the house. And he brought me to the perch of the house; and he measured the porch, five cubits on the one side, and five cubits on the other side; and the breadth of the gate was three cubits on the one side, and
49 three cubits on the other side. The length of the porch was twenty cubits, and the breadth eleven cubits; and there were steps by which they went up to it; and there were pillars in the vestibule, one on the one side, and one on the other side.

46. Zadok was lineally descended from Aaron, and had the high priesthood conferred upon him by Solomon, who had set aside the family of Ithamar in consequence of the part which Abiathar had taken in the rebellion of Absalom. 1 Kings ii. 26, 27.

CHAPTER XLI.

The conductor now introduces Ezekiel into the sacred edifice, which is specially distinguished by the name of הַהֵיכָל, *the palace* or *residence* of Jehovah, which is described with its divisions, galleries, posts, doors, windows, cherubim, ornamental palm-trees, etc.

1 He then brought me to the temple, and measured the vestibules, six cubits broad on this side, and six cubits broad on that side,
2 the breadth of the tabernacle. And the breadth of the door was ten cubits; and the sides of the door were five cubits on the one side, and five cubits on the other side; and he measured the length thereof forty cubits, and the breadth twenty cubits.
3 Then he went inward, and measured the post of the door, two cubits; and the door, six cubits; and the breadth of the door,
4 seven cubits. And he measured the length thereof, twenty cubits, and the breadth twenty cubits, before the temple; and he said
5 unto me: This is the holy of holies. He then measured the wall of the house, six cubits; and the breadth of the side, four cubits;
6 round about the house on every side. And the side-chambers side to side were three-and-thirty measures; and they entered into the wall which belonged to the house for the side-chambers round about, that they might be fastened; but they were not
7 fastened in the wall of the house. And there was an enlarging, and it winded still upward, to the side-chambers; for the winding about of the house was still upward round about the house;

therefore the breadth of the house was still upward, and so the
8 lowest went up to the highest by the middle. And I saw the
height of the house round about; the foundations of the side-
chambers were a full reed, six cubits to the root of the hand.
9 The breadth of the wall which was for the side-chamber without,
was five cubits; and what was allotted for the house was for
10 the side-chambers belonging to the house. And between the
cells was a width of twenty cubits about the house all around.
11 And the doors of the side-chambers were towards the allotted
space, one door towards the north, and another door towards
the south; and the breadth of the allotted space was five cubits
12 round about. And the building which was before the separate
place on the west side was seventy cubits broad; and the wall
of the building was five cubits broad round about, and its length
13 was ninety cubits. So he measured the house, the length a
hundred cubits; and the separate place, and the building toward
14 the east, a hundred cubits. And the breadth of the face of the
house, and of the separate place toward the east, a hundred
15 cubits. And he measured the length of the building over against
the separate place which was behind it, and the galleries thereof
from one side to another, one hundred cubits, with the inner
16 temple and the porches of the court; the door-posts, and the
latticed windows, and the galleries round about on their three
sides, opposite to the door-posts, boarded with wood round
about; and from the ground up to the windows, and the windows
17 were covered; Over above the door, even to the inner house,
and without, and to all the wall round about, within and without
18 the house, by measures. And there were made cherubim and
palm-trees; and there was a palm-tree between each cherub;
19 and the cherub had two faces. And the face of a man was
toward the palm-tree on the one side, and the face of a young
lion toward the palm-tree on the other side; it was made
20 through all the house round about. From the ground to up
above the door the cherubim and the palm-trees were made in
21 the wall of the temple. As for the temple, the door-posts were
square, and before the holy place; the appearance of the one
22 was as the appearance of the other. The altar of wood was
three cubits high, and its length two cubits, and its corners and

20. הַהֵיכָל. This word, which is repeated at the beginning of the following verse, is one of fifteen which the Masoretes have marked with extraordinary points, to indicate that they did not belong to the original text.

its length and its walls were of wood. And he said unto me:
23 This is the table which is before Jehovah. And the temple and
24 the sanctuary had two doors. And the doors had two leaves,
two turning leaves, two for the one door, and two leaves for the
25 other. And there were made for them, for the doors of the
temple, cherubim and palm-trees, as had been made for the
walls; and there was a thick plank-work before the porch from
26 without. And latticed windows and palm-trees, on the one side
and on the other side, at the sides of the porch; and on the
side-chambers of the house, and the thick planks.

CHAPTER XLII.

Having surveyed the sanctuary, our prophet has his attention drawn to the chambers for the use of the priests, which are described in succession. Certain regulations are then prescribed, relating to the table of the priests, and their official dress; and the chapter concludes with a specification of the measurements of the sacred building.

1 AND he brought me out into the outer court, the way toward the
north, and brought me into the cell that was opposite the
separate place, and which was opposite the building toward the
2 north. Before the length of an hundred cubits was the north
3 door, and the breadth was fifty cubits. Opposite the twenty
cubits which were for the inner court, and opposite the pavement which was for the outer court, was one terrace before
4 another in three stories. And before the cells was a walk of
ten cubits breadth inward, a way of one cubit; and their doors
5 were toward the north. And the upper chambers were shorter,
for the galleries contained more than these, more than the
6 lower and the middlemost of the building. For they were in
three stories, but they had no pillars as the pillars of the courts,
therefore it was contracted from the lower and from the middle-
7 most from the ground. And the wall which was without over
against the cells by the way of the outer court before the cells
8 was as to its length fifty cubits. For the length of the cells
which belonged to the outer court was fifty cubits; and, behold,
9 before the temple were an hundred cubits. And below these
cells was the entrance from the east, as one went into them
10 from the outer court. In the breadth of the wall of the court
towards the east before the separate place, and before the build-

11   ing, were cells. And there was a way before them, like the appearance of the cells which were toward the north, as long as they, and as broad as they; and all their outgoings, according
12   to their fashions, and according to their doors. And according to the doors of the cells which were toward the south, a door at the beginning of the way, the way before the separate place,
13   by the way of the east, to the entrance into the same. And he said unto me, The cells toward the north, and the cells toward the south, which are before the separate place, are cells of the holy place, where the priests who draw near to Jehovah shall eat the most holy things; there they shall place the most holy things, both the meat-offering, and the sin-offering, and the tres-
14   pass offering, for the place is holy. When the priests enter in, they shall not go forth from the holy place into the outer court, but they shall leave there their garments in which they have officiated, for they are holy, and put on other garments, and shall approach the place that belongeth to the people.
15 And he finished the measurements of the inner house, and brought me out by way of the gate which looketh toward the east, and
16   measured it round about. He measured the east side with the measuring reed, five hundred reeds with the measuring reed

16–20. The prophet, having specified the different measurements of the sacred edifice, here sums up in a gross estimate the extent of the whole. The reading קָנִים, reeds, in these verses, has been much disputed. From the circumstance that almost throughout the description of the temple, אַמּוֹת, cubits, are used as the measure, it has been inferred that Ezekiel must have meant the same here; and because the plural form קָנִים is elsewhere in Hebrew usage employed only to designate the branches of the candlestick, it has been maintained that it cannot be taken in the sense of a measure. But this reasoning is altogether fallacious, for it does not appear, if it was necessary to express the plural at all, why it should not be employed to convey the idea of measure as well as of anything else.

The textual reading of verse 16, חָמֵשׁ אַמּוֹת, five cubits, being altogether unsuitable to the connection, the Keri, transposing the order of the letters from אָמֹית into מֵאוֹת, prescribes that five hundred is to be regarded as the true reading; and this is adopted here in a great number of Heb. MSS.; in the Soncin. and Brixian editions, and is supported by the ancient versions.

The LXX., omitting the number entirely ver. 16, simply read καὶ διεμέτρησε πεντακοσίους, and measured five hundred; but in verses 17 and 20 they supply πήχεις, cubits. In this they are followed by Capellus, J. D. Michaelis, Newcome, Ewald, Hitzig, and other moderns, who unceremoniously strike קָנִים out of the Hebrew text, in violation of one of the first principles of Hebrew criticism, since the word is found in all the MSS. that have yet been collated.

The objection urged by Lightfoot, and repeated by Fairbairn, that the number would furnish a compass of ground incomparably larger than that of Mount Moriah several times over, may be ob-

17, 18, 19, 20 round about. He measured the north side five hundred reeds, with the measuring reed round about. He measured the south side five hundred reeds, with the measuring reed. Turning to the west side, he measured five hundred reeds with the measuring reed. He measured it by its four sides; it had a wall round about, five hundred long, and five hundred broad, to make a division between the holy place and the profane.

viated by supposing that the prophet here employs an architectural hyperbole with the view of conveying the idea of sufficient amplitude, just as he specifies *four thousand cubits* as the gross length of the river, to express that of great abundance, (chap. xlii. 1–5). Viewed in this light, the notion of a natural impossibility vanishes, and leaves the literal interpretation intact.

CHAPTER XLIII.

This chapter contains a vision of the return of the visible symbol of the divine presence to the temple, which had been withdrawn, when Jerusalem was taken by the Chaldeans, 1–3; a resumption of his throne by Jehovah, as King of the Jews, 4–6; the sacredness of the temple contrasted with its former desecration, 7–12; together with a particular specification of the measures of the altar, and of the propitiatory sacrifices that were to be offered upon it, 13–27.

1 And he conducted me to the gate, the gate which faceth the east.
2 And, behold, the glory of the God of Israel came from the way of the east, and the sound thereof was as the sound of many
3 waters, and the earth shined with his glory. And the appearance was as the appearance which I saw, as the appearance which I saw when I came to destroy the city, and appearances as the appearance which I saw by the river Chebar; and I fell
4 upon my face. And the glory of Jehovah entered the house by
5 the way of the gate whose aspect is towards the east. And the Spirit lifted me up, and brought me into the inner court; and, behold, the house was filled with the glory of Jehovah.

1–5. What is here described took place in vision, just as we are to understand what is said of the removal of the visible symbol of the divine presence, (chap. xi. 23). It is not necessary therefore to suppose that this token was actually restored; and indeed the Jews themselves allow that it was one of those things in which the second temple was deficient. What we are taught in the passage is, that Jehovah would renew the manifestation of his favor to the covenant people, which he did pre-eminently when he dwelt among them in the person of his incarnate Son.

6 And I heard one speaking to me from the house, and a man stood
7 beside me. And he said unto me, Son of man, this is the place of my throne, even the place of the soles of my feet, where I will dwell among the children of Israel forever; and the children of Israel shall not defile my holy name any more, they, nor their kings, with their whoredoms, and with the carcasses of
8 their kings on their death: While they set their threshold beside my threshold, and their door-post beside my door-post, and the wall betwixt me and them, they even defiled my holy name with their abominations which they committed, wherefore
9 I consumed them in mine anger. Now let them remove their whoredom, and the carcases of their kings far from me; and I will dwell in the midst of them forever.
10 Thou, O son of man, show the house of Israel the house, that they may be ashamed of their iniquities, and let them measure the
11 pattern. And if they are ashamed of all that they have done, show them the form of the house, and the pattern thereof, and the goings out thereof, and the comings in thereof, and all the forms thereof, and all the statutes thereof, and all the forms thereof, and all the laws thereof; and write it in their sight, that they may observe all the forms thereof, and all the ordi-
12 nances thereof, and do them. This is the law of the house upon the summit of the mount; the whole boundary thereof round about shall be most holy; behold, this is the law of the

7-9. The particle אֵת here possesses a peculiarly demonstrative and emphatic power, and requires the substantive verb *is*, or as Maurer gives it, *behold* to be supplied. The whole of the precincts of the temple being considered sacred, it was a profanation to inter the dead bodies even of the kings in any part of them. בְּמוֹתָם, with fifteen of De Rossi's MSS. and the Soncin. edition, I would point בְּמוֹתָם, and render *when they are dead*. Ewald: *die Leichen ihrer verstorbene Könige.* See my Comment. on Isa. liii. p. 385. The construction put upon this verse by Hävernick and Fairbairn, that by their kings we are to understand their Molochs or idol gods, I cannot but consider forced and inept. Not content with bringing their abominations into immediate contact in point of proximity with the temple by burying the dead bodies of their kings within its sacred precincts, the idolatrous princes built altars to idols in the temple itself, doing the utmost despite to its glorious inhabitant (2 Kings xxi. 4-7; xxiii. 12).

10-12. By exhibiting to the view of the Hebrews an exact pattern of the temple and its ordinances, they were to be reminded of what they had forfeited by their apostasy, and thus to be led to repentance and deep humiliation before their God, who, notwithstanding, was willing to receive them back again into favor. It seems scarcely possible to conceive of the propriety of the language here employed on any other principle than that of admitting its reference to a material temple and its ordinances. The repetitious forms convey the idea

13 house. And these are the measurements of the altar by cubits: the cubit is a cubit and a palm: and the hollow a cubit, and the breadth a cubit, and the border thereof to the edge thereof round about shall be a span; and this is the back of the altar.
14 And from the hollow of the ground to the lower settle two cubits, and the breadth a cubit; and from the smaller settle to
15 the greater settle four cubits, and the breadth a cubit. And the altar shall be four cubits; and from the altar and upward, shall
16 be four horns. And the altar shall be twelve cubits long, by
17 twelve broad, square on the four sides thereof. And the settle shall be fourteen cubits long, and fourteen broad, square on the four sides thereof; and the border round it shall be half a cubit, and the settle thereof one cubit round about; and the ascent to it shall face the east.
18 And he said unto me: Son of man, thus saith the Lord Jehovah: These are the ordinances of the altar in the day when they shall make it to offer burnt-offerings thereon, and to sprinkle blood
19 thereon. And thou shalt give to the priests the Levites, who are of the seed of Zadok, who draw near unto me, saith the Lord Jehovah, to serve me, a young bullock for a sin-offering.
20 And thou shalt take of the blood thereof, and put it upon the four horns of *the altar*, and upon the four corners of the settle, and upon the border round about: thus shalt thou cleanse it,
21 and expiate it. And thou shalt take the bullock of the sin-offering, and he shall burn it in the appointed place of the
22 house, without the sanctuary. And on the second day thou shalt offer a kid of the goats without blemish for a sin-offering; and they shall expiate the altar, as they expiated it with the

of intensity, indicating the care which was to be taken that everything was effected with the utmost exactitude. The whole was to be stamped with the character of peculiar sanctity. The temple and the whole of its precincts were to be קֹדֶשׁ קָדָשִׁים, *holy of holies*, i.e. most holy, a phrase which in this superlative form is used exclusively of the adytum (Exod. xxvi. 34), was now to characterize the entire edifice and its precincts.

13. In elucidation of the term אֲרִיאֵל, *Ariel*, some refer to אֲרִיאֵל, Isa. xxix. 1, viewed as signifying *lion of God*, and thereby denoting the invincible strength of Jerusalem; but even when occurring there, the word much more appropriately characterizes that city as the centre of the Jewish worship, of which the offering of burnt sacrifices formed so prominent a part. See my note on that passage. The idea of *altar*, therefore, is that distinctly conveyed.

18–27. Here the sacrificial ordinances of the Levitical law are distinctly recognized, a clear proof that respect is had to a time when these ordinances were still in force. Yet upon this portion of the vision has been constructed the

23 bullock. When thou hast made an end of cleansing it, thou
shalt offer a young bullock without blemish, and a ram out of
24 the flock without blemish. And thou shalt offer them before
Jehovah: and the priests shall cast salt upon them, and offer
25 them up for a burnt-offering to Jehovah. Seven days thou
shalt prepare, each day, a goat for a sin-offering, and a young
26 bullock, and a ram out of the flock without blemish. Seven
days shall they purge the altar and purify it, and fill their
27 hands. And when the days are expired, it shall be upon the
eighth day and forward, that the priests shall prepare your
burnt-offerings and your peace-offerings upon the altar, and I
will accept you, saith the Lord Jehovah.

hypothesis of commemorative sacrifices under the Christian dispensation, which is nothing better than a pure invention, unsupported by any authority in the New Testament. The only rite commemorative of the death of Christ sanctioned by divine authority is the ordinance of the Lord's Supper. The re-institution of literal sacrifices would be to fly directly in the face of the doctrine expressly taught, Heb. x. 1-18. It would imply that sin was still unatoned for, and consequently that the guilt of believers remained untaken away. That the sacrifices described by Ezekiel were strictly piacular or propitiatory, and not merely commemorative and eucharistical, is evident from the terms employed in describing them. They were to be זִבְחֵי דָם, *bloody sacrifices*, specifically offered כִּפֶּר, *to make expiation, to placate*, or remove contracted guilt. The bullock and the kid of the goats were to be offered לְחַטָּאת, *for a sin-offering*, which conveys the same idea. To *fill the hand*, ver. 26, implies to fill it with offerings, to take a full supply of them. The reference is to the mode of sacerdotal consecration, Exod. xxix. 24, 35.

CHAPTER XLIV.

We have here regulations relating to the prince or civil ruler of the Hebrews when he drew near to worship before the Lord, 1-3; together with reproofs of the people, and especially of the Levites, who, for their breach of the divine covenant, were to be excluded from the priesthood, 4-14. This high office was now to be restricted to the sons of Zadok, in reward of their fidelity during the general defection, 15-31. (Comp. chap. xl. 46).

1 THEN he brought me back by the way of the gate of the outer
2 sanctuary which faceth the east; and it was shut. Then said
Jehovah unto me: This gate shall be shut: it shall not be
opened, and no man shall enter by it, because Jehovah the

3 God of Israel hath entered in by it: it shall be shut. The prince, indeed, the prince shall sit in it to eat bread before Jehovah; by the way of the porch of the gate he shall enter in,
4 and he shall go out by the way of the same. And he brought me by the way of the north gate before the house; and I looked; and, behold, the glory of Jehovah filled the house of Jehovah;
5 and I fell upon my face. And Jehovah said unto me: Son of man, set thy heart, and behold with thine eyes, and hear with thine ears all that I say unto thee concerning all the ordinances of the house of Jehovah, and concerning all the laws thereof; and set thine heart to the entrance of the house with all the goings
6 out of the sanctuary. And thou shalt say to the rebellious house of Israel: Thus saith the Lord Jehovah: Let it suffice you for
7 all your abominations, O house of Israel, In that you have brought strangers into my sanctuary, uncircumcised in heart, and uncircumcised in flesh, to be in my sanctuary, to pollute my house, when ye offer my bread, the fat and the blood; and they have broken my covenant, because of all your abominations.
8 And ye have not kept the charge of my holy things, but have
9 set keepers of my charge in my sanctuary for yourselves. Thus saith the Lord Jehovah: No stranger, uncircumcised in heart, nor uncircumcised in flesh, shall enter into my sanctuary, of
10 any stranger that is among the children of Israel. And the Levites, who departed away from me when Israel went astray, who went astray from me after their idols, even they shall bear
11 their iniquity. Yet they shall be ministers in my sanctuary, having charge at the gates of the house, and ministering to the house; they shall kill the burnt-offering and the sacrifice for the people, and they shall stand before them to serve them.
12 Because they served them before their idols, and were a stumbling-block of iniquity to the children of Israel, therefore I lifted up my hand against them, saith the Lord Jehovah, and
13 they shall bear their iniquity. And they shall not come near to me to do the office of priest unto me, to come near to any of my holy things in the most holy place, but they shall bear their shame, and their abominations which they have committed.

---

3. It cannot but appear strange that any should suppose that the prince here referred to is any other than the civil ruler, for the time being, of the Jewish state. With our Saviour he cannot be identified, since the simple fact of his offering animal sacrifices for himself (chap. xlvi. 4) would in such case flatly contradict what we are taught, Heb. x. 18. See on chap. xliii. 18–27.

14 Yet I will make them keepers of the charge of the house, and all the service thereof, and for all that shall be done therein.
15 But the priests, the sons of Zadok, the Levites who have kept the charge of my sanctuary, when the children of Israel went astray from me, they shall come near unto me to serve me, and they shall stand before me to offer unto me the fat and the blood,
16 saith the Lord Jehovah. They shall enter into my sanctuary, and they shall come near unto my table to serve me, and they
17 shall keep my charge. And it shall be when they enter in at the gates of the inner court, that they shall be clothed with linen garments; and wool shall not come upon them while they
18 serve in the gates of the inner court, and within. They shall have linen bonnets on their heads, and they shall have linen drawers upon their loins: they shall not gird themselves with
19 anything that causeth sweat. And when they go out into the outer court, even into the outer court unto the people, they shall put off their garments in which they have ministered, and lay them in the holy cells, and put on other garments; and they shall not sanctify the people with their garments. Neither shall they shave their heads, nor allow their hair to grow long; they
21 shall only poll their heads. Neither shall any priest drink wine,
22 when they go in to the inner court. Neither shall they take for them for wives a widow, or her that hath been put away, but maidens of the seed of the house of Israel; but they may
23 take a widow who hath been the widow of a priest. And they shall teach my people the difference between the holy and the profane, and cause them to discern between the unclean and the
24 clean. And in matter of litigation they shall stand in judgment; they shall judge it according to my judgments, and they shall keep my laws and my statutes in all mine assemblies; and they
25 shall hallow my Sabbaths. And they shall not go in to a dead man to defile themselves; but for father, or for mother, or for son, or for daughter, for brother, or for sister who hath had no
26 husband, they may defile themselves. And after he is cleansed,
27 they shall reckon unto him seven days. And in the day that he goeth into the sanctuary, into the inner court, to minister in the sanctuary, he shall offer his sin-offering, saith the Lord
28 Jehovah. And it shall be to them for an inheritance: I am their inheritance; and ye shall give them no possession in Israel:
29 I am their possession. They shall eat the meat-offering, and the sin-offering, and the trespass-offering; and every devoted

30 thing in Israel shall be theirs. And the first of all the firstlings of all, and every oblation, every one of all your oblations, shall be the priests'; and ye shall give unto the priest the first of
31 your dough, to cause a blessing to rest upon your house. The priests shall not eat anything that hath died of itself, or is torn, whether it be of fowl or of beast.

CHAPTER XLV.

Everything connected with the temple having been settled, the division of the land is naturally next adverted to, with special reference to the provision for the sacred services, and for the city, the priests, and the prince; and particular instructions are given bearing against oppression and acts of injustice.

The special territorial division of the country among the tribes is reserved for chap. xlviii.; only the portion devoted to the Lord is here subdivided into three parts; that which was to be specially appointed for the uses of the sanctuary, 2, 3; a portion for the priests who were attached to the service of the temple, 4; and a separate portion for the Levites to occupy as dwellings while discharging the functions of their office, 5. (Comp. chap. xlviii. 8–13).

1 AND when ye divide the land by lot for inheritance, ye shall heave a heave-offering unto Jehovah, a holy portion of the land; the length shall be the length of five-and-twenty thousand, and the breadth ten thousand: it shall be holy in all the border
2 thereof round about. Of this shall be for the sanctuary five hundred by five hundred, square round about; and fifty cubits
3 an open place for it round about. And of this measure thou shalt measure the length of five-and-twenty thousand, and the breadth of ten thousand: and in it shall be the sanctuary, the
4 holy of holies. The holy portion of the land shall be for the priests the ministers of the sanctuary, who draw near to serve Jehovah; and it shall be to them a place for houses, and a holy

---

1. A portion of the land of Canaan, called the תְּרוּמָה, *Terumah* or *Oblation*, was to be reserved for Jehovah, as proprietor of the soil. It is so called, because usually when anything was offered to the Lord, the action was accompanied by lifting up the hand; root הָרִים, *to raise*. The dimensions specified in this chapter have been much disputed. Reeds have been introduced in italics into the text by our translators, and are defended by Hävernick and Fairbairn; but I think inconsistently with the natural import of the statement, ver. 3, for הַמִּדָּה הַזֹּאת, *this measure*, can be no other than that of *cubits* just specified in the preceding verse. It is quite unnecessary to assume the larger measure, since the dimensions according to cubits must have been amply sufficient to meet the demands of the different parties here referred to.

5 place for the sanctuary. And the five-and-twenty thousand in length, and the ten thousand in breadth, shall be for the Levites serving the house, for themselves, for a possession, twenty cells.
6 And ye shall appoint the possession of the city five thousand broad, and five-and-twenty thousand long, over against the holy
7 oblation; it shall be for the whole house of Israel. And for the prince shall be on one side and the other of the oblation of the holy place, and of the possession of the city, before the oblation of the holy place, and before the possession of the city, on the west side westward, and on the east side eastward, and the length over against one of the portions from the west border unto the
8 east border. As to the land, it shall be to him for a possession in Israel; and my princes shall no more oppress my people; and *the rest of* the land they shall give to the house of Israel
9 according to their tribes. Thus saith the Lord Jehovah: Let it suffice you, ye princes of Israel; remove violence and spoil, and execute judgment and justice; take away your exactions
10 from my people, saith the Lord Jehovah. Ye shall have just
11 balances, and a just ephah, and a just bath. The ephah and the bath shall be of one measure, that the bath may contain the tenth part of an homer, and the ephah the tenth part of an
12 homer; the measure thereof shall be after the homer. And the shekel shall be twenty gerahs; twenty shekels, five-and-twenty
13 shekels, fifteen shekels, shall be your maneh. This is the oblation that ye shall offer, the sixth part of an ephah of an homer of wheat; and ye shall give a sixth part of an ephah of
14 an homer of barley. And as for the appointed quantity of oil, the bath of oil, the tenth part of a bath out of the cor, which is
15 an homer of ten baths: for ten baths are an homer. And one lamb out of the flock, out of two hundred, from the well-watered pastures of Israel, for a meat-offering, and for a burnt-offering, and for peace-offerings, to make atonement for them, saith the
16 Lord Jehovah. All the people of the land shall give this
17 oblation for the prince in Israel. And it shall be for the prince to give the burnt-offerings, and the meat-offerings, and the drink-offerings, on the festivals, and on the new moons, and on

---

12. The standard weights and measures having perished when the temple was destroyed by the Chaldeans, it was necessary there should be a fresh specification of them. The three orders of shekel here referred to were probably coins differing in value. No importance is to be attached to the order in which they occur, twenty, twenty-five, fifteen, instead of fifteen, twenty, twenty-five.

the Sabbaths, on all the appointed feasts of the house of Israel: he shall prepare the sin-offering, and the meat-offering, and the burnt-offering, and the peace-offerings, to make an atonement
18 for the house of Israel. Thus saith the Lord Jehovah: In the first month, on the first of the month, thou shalt take a young
19 bullock without blemish, and cleanse the sanctuary. And the priest shall take of the blood of the sin-offering and put it upon the posts of the house, and upon the four corners of the settle of the altar, and upon the posts of the gate of the inner court.
20 And thus shalt thou do on the seventh of the month for every one that erreth, and for him that is simple; and ye shall make
21 atonement for the house. In the first month, on the fourteenth day of the month, ye shall have the passover, the feast of seven
22 days; unleavened bread shall be eaten. And the prince shall on the same day prepare for himself, and for all the people of
23 the land, a bullock as a sin-offering. And on the seven days of the feast he shall prepare a burnt-offering for Jehovah, seven bullocks and seven rams without blemish daily, the seven days;
24 and for a sin-offering, a kid of the goats, daily. And he shall prepare a meat-offering of an ephah for a bullock, and an ephah
25 for a ram, and a hin of oil for an ephah. In the seventh month, on the fifteenth day of the month, he shall prepare on the festival, as on these seven days, according to the sin-offering, according to the burnt-offering, and according to the meat offering, and according to the oil.

CHAPTER XLVI.

A continuation of ordinances relating to the worship performed by the prince, 1-8, and likewise by the people, 9-15, at their annual festivals, as well as in relation to the daily ministrations.

1 THUS saith the Lord Jehovah: The gate of the inner court that looketh towards the east shall be shut the six work-days, but on the Sabbath it shall be opened, and on the day of the new
2 moon it shall be opened. And the prince shall enter by the way of the porch of that gate without, and shall stand by the post of the gate, and the priests shall prepare his burnt-offering, and his peace-offerings, and he shall worship at the threshold of the gate; and he shall go forth; and the gate shall not be

3 shut until the evening. And the people of the land shall worship at the door of this gate on the Sabbaths, and on the
4 new moons, before Jehovah. And the burnt-offering, which the prince shall bring near to Jehovah on the Sabbath, shall be
5 six lambs without blemish, and a ram without blemish: And a meat-offering, an ephah for a ram, and a meat-offering for the lambs, according as his hand shall attain to, and a hin of oil to
6 an ephah. And on the day of the new moon, a young bullock without blemish, and six lambs, and a ram; without blemish
7 they shall be. And he shall prepare a meat-offering, an ephah for a bullock, and an ephah for a ram, and for the lambs according
8 as his hand shall attain to, and a hin of oil to an ephah. And when the prince entereth, he shall enter by the way of the porch
9 of the gate, and by the way thereof he shall go forth. And when the people of the land enter before Jehovah in the appointed feasts, he that entereth by the way of the north gate to worship, shall go out by the way of the south gate; and he that entereth by the way of the south gate shall go out by the way of the north gate; he shall not return by the way of the gate
10 by which he entered, but shall go out over against it. And the prince shall be among them; when they enter in, he shall enter
11 in; and when they go out, he shall go out. And on the festivals, and in the solemn assemblies, shall be the meat-offering, an ephah for a bullock, and an ephah for a ram, and for the lambs as much as his hand shall attain to, and of oil a hin to the ephah.
12 And when the prince shall prepare a voluntary burnt-offering, or voluntary peace-offerings unto Jehovah, they shall open to him the gate that looketh toward the east, and he shall prepare his burnt-offering and his peace-offerings, according as he prepareth on the Sabbath-day; and he shall go forth, and the door
13 shall be shut after he hath gone forth. And thou shalt prepare daily a burnt-offering unto Jehovah, a lamb of a year old without
14 blemish; every morning thou shalt prepare it. And thou shalt prepare for it a meat-offering every morning, the sixth part of

---

4. It is noticeable that *six* lambs are here specified as the number to be offered on the Sabbath, whereas only *two* are prescribed by the Mosaic law, (Numb. xxviii. 9). The difference may be accounted for on the ground, that in the one case respect is had to the offerings of the people in general, but in the other to those of the prince in particular; and that in consequence of the liberal provision made for the establishment of the latter, it was assumed that he would set a proportionately bountiful example to the people.

an ephah, and the third part of a hin of oil with which to moisten the fine flour, a meat-offering to Jehovah, continually by a
15 perpetual statute. And they shall prepare the lamb, and the meat-offering, and the oil, every morning, a continual burnt-offering.
16 Thus saith the Lord Jehovah: When the prince shall give a gift to any of his sons, the inheritance of it shall be for his sons;
17 it shall be their possession by inheritance. But when he shall give a gift of his inheritance to one of his servants, it shall be his to the year of liberty; then shall it return to the prince;
18 but his inheritance shall be for his sons. And the prince shall not take of the inheritance of the people to thrust them out of their inheritance by oppression; he shall give his sons inheritance out of his own possession, that my people may not be scattered every one from his possession.
19 Then he brought me through the entrance, which was by the side of the gate, into the holy cells of the priests which looked toward the north; and, behold, there was a place at the two ends toward
20 the west. And he said unto me: This is the place where the priests shall boil the trespass-offering and the sin-offering, where they shall bake the meat-offering, that they may not bring them
21 out into the outer court to sanctify the people. Then he brought me forth into the outer court, and caused me to pass over to the four corners of the court; and, behold, there was a court in
22 every corner of the court. In the four corners of the court were smaller courts, of forty in length, and thirty in breadth, one
23 measure to the four corners. And there was a row round about in them, round about them four, and boiling places were made
24 underneath the rows round about. And he said unto me: These are the place for boiling, where the servants of the house shall boil the sacrifice of the people.

17. The mention in this verse of the jubilee year, or year of release, as that when alienated land should revert to its original occupier, is a strong confirmation that the prophet intended a literal reference to events that were to transpire during the continuance of the Mosaic economy. That the Sabbatic year was restored after the captivity is sufficiently proved by the testimony of Josephus, *Antiqq.* xiv. 10, 6. See also 1 Macc. vi. 49.

CHAPTER XLVII.

This chapter contains a sublime prophetical vision, emblematical of the rich abundance of blessings which Jehovah was prepared to confer upon his restored people. The imagery is taken from the scenery about the south of Judea, and forcibly depicts the contrasted condition of the Jews as apostate under the curse, and as restored to their privileges as the people of God, together with the abundant communication of divine blessings both to them and to the Gentile world. The vision bears on the very face of it such palpable incongruities if taken literally, that no room is left to doubt of its symbolical import. The localities specified are to be regarded as the sources whence the imagery is borrowed; but, in explaining them, care must be taken not to strain the language so as to obscure the more sublime objects which they were intended to adumbrate.

The vision, though connected with, is to be regarded as distinct from, that of the temple. It naturally springs out of the view given in the previous chapter of the worship to be performed by the prince and the people, under the superintendence of the priests. While that worship should be acceptable to God, if offered in a proper spirit, the manifestations of his loving-kindness were not to be confined to the sacred locality, but were to extend to the whole land, and ultimately to the whole world. To set forth this extension of the divine blessing, a series of beautiful images is introduced into the scene. From under the eastern wall of the temple, the prophet is shown a collection of waters which gush forth, and, increasing as they flow towards the Dead Sea, convey viridity, life, and beauty, wherever they come.

The existence of fountains and aqueducts in the vicinity of Moriah has long been known, and they are particularly described by Dr. Robinson and other travellers in the East; but they throw little or no light upon the passage before us. The waters here described are represented as flowing in an easterly direction, קָדִימָה, consequently towards the Kedron, having reached which they must be supposed to have taken their course in the direction of the Jordan, and so down the Ghor towards the Dead Sea. The main point in the picture is the rapid augmentation of the river, not by the influx of any side streams, but by its own self-supply from the sacred source in the temple. It is evidently not to be explained on any principles of natural philosophy, but is to be resolved into the miraculous, so undeniably held forth to our view in the text.

1 Then he conducted me back unto the door of the house; and, behold, waters issued from under the threshold of the house eastward; for the front of the house was toward the east; and the waters flowed down from under the right side of the house,
2 at the south side of the altar. And he conducted me by the way of the gate northward, and led me about the way without to the outer gate by the way which looketh eastward; and,
3 behold, waters ran out from the right side. When the man that had the line in his hand went forth on the east, he measured a thousand cubits, and he brought me through the waters; the
4 waters were to the ankles. Again he measured a thousand, and brought me through the waters; the waters were to the knees. Again he measured a thousand, and brought me through; the
5 waters were unto the loins. Then he measured a thousand, a river which I could not pass over; for the waters were high,

6 waters to swim in, a river that could not be passed over. Then
he said unto me: Son of man, hast thou seen this? then he
brought me and caused me to return to the bank of the river.
7 When I turned, behold, on the bank of the river very much
8 wood on the one side, and on the other. Then he said unto me:
These waters issue forth into the east circuit, and flow down
into the desert, and go into the sea. And being brought out
9 into the sea, the waters shall be healed. And it shall come to
pass that every living being that moveth, whithersoever the river
shall come, shall live; and there shall be a very great multitude
of fish, because these waters shall come thither; and they shall
be healed, and shall live wheresoever the river shall come.
10 And it shall be that fishers shall stand beside it from En-gedi
to En-eglaim; there shall be a spreading of nets; their fish
shall be according to their kind, as the fish of the great sea,

7. The numerous trees on the banks of the river are symbolical of the greatest prosperity. What had previously presented only a scene of barrenness was now to be remarkable for the abundance of fruit which it yielded.

8. The LXX., Targ., and Syriac have preposterously rendered הַגָּלִיל by *Galilee*, taking the river to the north from Jerusalem instead of along the course of the Jordan southward. הָעֲרָבָה, *the Arabah*, or great valley of the Jordan, still so called in the present day, stretching from Tiberias to the Red Sea. There is an emphasis in the repetition הַיָּמָה, *into the sea*, i.e. the sea so remarkable for historic facts. The waters that required to be healed were those of the lake, whose deadly character has long given the name to it, and has been fully established by the testimony of modern travellers. See Dr. Robinson, vol. ii. p. 222. "According," he says, "to the testimony of all antiquity, and of most modern travellers, there exists within the waters of the Dead Sea no living thing — no trace, indeed, of animal or vegetable life. Our own experience, as far as we had an opportunity to observe, goes to confirm the truth of this testimony. We perceived no sign of life within the waters."

Compare De Sauley, vol. i. p. 168, who testifies to the same effect.

9. So complete should be the moral change which the prophet has in his eye, that it could only be fitly symbolized by the conversion of the Asphaltitic lake into a collection of waters abounding in all kinds of fish, for supplying the inhabitants of the neighboring country. מַיִם is a dual, signifying *the two rivers*, but as only one river is mentioned at the end of the verse, I have no hesitation in adopting the division of the word into יָם, *the river of the sea*, i.e. the Jordan, which flows into that sea, to which it is evident reference is had, and not, as Jarchi supposes, to the Mediterranean.

10. עֵין גֶּדִי, *En-gedi*, عين جدي,
originally called Hazezon-Tamar, was discovered in modern times by Seetzen, and is described by Dr. Robinson and De Sauley as situated close to a perpendicular cliff of more than fifteen hundred feet above the Dead Sea, on its western side. Where עֵין עֶגְלַיִם, *En-eglaim*, was situated, cannot with certainty be determined; but on comparing עֶגְלַיִם, *Eglaim*, (Isa. xv. 8), it would seem probable that it lay on the confines of Moab, over against Engedi, and near the entrance

11, 12 exceeding many. But the miry places thereof, and the pools thereof, shall not be healed; they are given for salt. And by the river, there shall come up on the bank thereof, on one side and on the other, all trees for food, whose leaves shall not fade, neither shall the fruit thereof be consumed; they shall produce new fruit according to the months thereof, because the waters thereof issued forth from the sanctuary; and the fruit thereof shall be for food, and the leaves thereof for medicine.

13 Thus saith the Lord Jehovah: This is the border, according to which ye shall divide the land for an inheritance to the twelve

of the Jordan into the sea: "Engallim in principio est maris mortui ubi Jordanes ingreditur." (Jerome.)

11. This verse has generally been viewed as a drawback upon the promise of good so forcibly and repeatedly made in the preceding verses, and the expression, to give or devote to salt, if applied to land, and not to water as in the present instance, would unquestionably convey this idea. See Deut. xxix. 23; Ps. cvii. 34 (Heb.); Zeph. ii. 9; but as it is the water of the Dead Sea that is the subject spoken of, the proper interpretation is that founded on the circumstance, that, owing to the great evaporation which takes place, especially during the heat of summer, large quantities of salt are deposited on the shores, or collected by the Arabs in pits, from which they obtain abundant supplies for the use of their families and flocks. No language could more forcibly represent than the whole passage the salutary influences of the Holy Spirit in healing the corruptions of human nature, and converting what before was poisonous and destructive into elements of vitality, utility, and enjoyment. Compare Isa. xxxv. 1, 2, 6, 7; xli. 18, 19; xliii. 19, 20; John vii. 38.

12. The prophet here sums up what he had to deliver relative to the happy change which was to take place in the condition of the church, in a picture only surpassed by that of the paradise of Eden. Instead of the vine of Sodom and the grapes of Gomorrah (Deut. xxxii. 32), which were nauseous and revolting, trees of righteousness should produce fruit to the praise and glory of God. Compare Rev. xxii. 2, where the language is copied almost verbatim, and made to serve as descriptive of the state of heavenly blessedness.

13–23. The remainder of the chapter, and the greater portion of that following, are occupied with the arrangements made for the territorial division of Palestine among the tribes. It is quite evident that פֹּה, which affords no sense, must be a corrupt reading for זֶה, the Zain having been mistaken by some copyist for Gimel, a letter similar in shape. LXX. ταῦτα τὰ ὅρια. According to Kitto that country may be regarded as embracing an area of almost eleven thousand square miles; but being for the most part hilly, the sides of the mountains and the slopes of the hills greatly enlarge the available extent of the superficies. There cannot therefore be a doubt that the population might have been increased to an extent comprehending all who remained behind in the East, if they had chosen to return. All would have found ample accommodation in the land of their fathers. The literal Canaan, and the literal tribes here named, alone meet the demand of the unbiassed expositor, just as in the case of the temple, which requires to be treated literally. By the geographical marks given by Ezekiel it may easily be ascertained that the same country is intended which the Hebrews had in possession

14 tribes of Israel: Joseph shall have *two* portions. And ye shall inherit it, one as well as another, which I lifted up my hand to give it to your fathers, and this land shall fall to you for an
15 inheritance. And this shall be the boundary of the land on the north side, from the great sea by the way of Chethlon to the entering in of Zedad: Hamath, Berothah, Sebaraim, which are between the border of Damascus and the border of Hamath;
17 Hazor-hatticon, which is on the border of Hauran. And the border from the sea shall be Hazor-ainon, the border of Damascus, and the north northward, and the border of Hamath; and this
18 shall be the north side. And the east side shall be from between Hauran and Damascus and Gilead, and from between the land of Israel on the Jordan; from the boundary by the eastern sea
19 ye shall measure; and this shall be the side eastward. And the south side southward from Tamar unto the waters of Meriboth-Kadesh, the river to the great sea; this shall be the south side
20 southward. And the west side shall be the great sea, from the border over against the entrance of Hamath: this shall be the west side.
21 And ye shall divide this land to yourselves for the tribes of Israel.
22 And it shall come to pass that ye shall divide it by lot for an inheritance to yourselves and to the strangers who sojourn among you, who have begotten children among you, and they shall be to you as a native among the children of Israel: they shall have inheritance with you among the tribes of Israel.

before the captivity, exclusive of that beyond Jordan, which did not properly belong to the paternal territory (Gen. xiii. 14–18). The boundaries differ little from those fixed by Moses (Numbers xxxiv.), only the latter commences with the south, the former with the north, for what reason it is impossible to conjecture, except it was designed, with other changes, to prepare the minds of the Jews for the greater change which was to be effected by the introduction of the new economy to be established by the Messiah.

13. Joseph, as representative of the tribe of Ephraim, is here placed in the foreground, to intimate, that though that tribe had been the ringleader both in the civil revolt and in idolatry, it was not to be neglected in the new state of things, but was graciously to have restored to it the double portion which Jacob bestowed on Joseph, and which was inherited by his two sons, Ephraim and Manasseh, instead of Reuben who had forfeited his birthright. See Gen. xlviii. 5. There was now no distinction to be made that might seem to savor of partiality, but all were to have a sufficient share allotted to them.

22, 23. A joint participation in the inheritance of the land between the Hebrews and such foreigners as might sojourn among them, was something altogether new in the history of the covenant people. Its object seems to have been gradually to wean them from that exclusiveness of spirit which naturally marked their character, and thus to pave the way for the introduction of

23   And it shall come to pass that in what tribe soever the stranger sojourneth, there shall ye give him his inheritance, saith the Lord Jehovah.

the gospel dispensation, which, as it respects spiritual blessings, considers all men, without distinction, as upon a level before God, and excludes none who submit to its terms from the enjoyment of the privileges of the divine kingdom.

CHAPTER XLVIII.

Having finished his description of the boundaries of the land of Canaan generally, the prophet now takes up the several allotments of the tribes in particular, with special reference to Jerusalem, as the common centre, 1-7, 23-28. According to the locations here laid down, seven of the tribes were to have their portions in the northern division of the country, and the remaining five were to occupy the smaller division in the south. The tribes of Judah and Benjamin were to be specially honored: having their portions assigned to them in immediate contiguity to the sacred area appropriated to the temple and its officiants. The reason is obvious: they had remained faithful to the house of David amid the general defection; and would again be prepared by their military spirit to resist any attack that might be attempted upon the sacred enclosure.

1   Now these are the names of the tribes: from the north end to the coast of the way of Chethlon, to the entering in of Hamath, Hazar-ainon, the border of Damascus northward to the coast of Hamath; and these are the sides thereof east and west:
2   Dan, one. And by the border of Dan, from the east side to
3   the west side: Asher, one. And by the border of Asher, from
4   the east side even to the west side: Naphtali, one. And by the border of Naphtali, from the east side to the west side:
5   Manasseh, one. And by the border of Manasseh, from the
6   east side to the west side: Ephraim, one. And by the border of Ephraim, from the east side even to the west side: Reuben,
7   one. And by the border of Reuben, from the east side to the
8   west side: Judah, one. And by the border of Judah, from the east side to the west side, shall be the oblation which ye shall offer, five-and-twenty thousand in breadth, and in length as one of the parts from the east side to the west side; and the sanc-
9   tuary shall be in the midst of it. The oblation which ye shall offer to Jehovah shall be five-and-twenty thousand in length,

---

8. The measures here and afterwards specified I take to be *cubits*, and not *reeds*, as given in our common version. See on chapter xlv. 1.

10 and ten thousand in breadth. And for these, for the priests, the oblation shall be; toward the north, five-and-twenty thousand, and toward the west ten thousand in breadth, and toward the east ten thousand in breadth, and toward the south five-and-twenty thousand in length; and the sanctuary of Jehovah shall
11 be in the midst thereof. It shall be for the priests that are sanctified of the sons of Zadok, who have kept my charge, who went not astray when the children of Israel went astray, as the
12 Levites went astray. And the oblation of the land that is offered shall be unto them a most holy thing, by the border of
13 the Levites. And over against the border of the priests, the Levites shall have five-and-twenty thousand in length, and ten thousand in breadth: all the length five-and-twenty thousand,
14 and the breadth ten thousand. And they shall not sell of it, nor exchange, nor alienate the first-fruits of the land, for it is
15 holy to Jehovah. And the five thousand that are left in the breadth over against the five-and-twenty thousand shall be a profane place for the city, and for dwelling, and for an open
16 place: and the city shall be in the midst of it. And these shall be the measures thereof: the north side four thousand and five hundred; and the south side four thousand and five hundred; and the east side four thousand and five hundred; and the west
17 side four thousand and five hundred. And the open space for the city northward, two hundred and fifty; and toward the south, two hundred and fifty; and toward the east, two hundred and
18 fifty; and toward the west, two hundred and fifty. And the residue in length over against the oblation of the holy portion shall be ten thousand eastward, and ten thousand westward; and it shall be over against the oblation of the holy portion; and the increase thereof shall be for bread for them that serve
19 the city. And they that serve the city shall serve it out of all
20 the tribes of Israel. All the oblation shall be five-and-twenty thousand by five-and-twenty thousand: ye shall offer the holy
21 oblation four square with the possession of the city. And the residue shall be for the prince, on the one side and on the other side of the holy oblation, and the possession of the city, before

---

15. When it is said that the five thousand cubits here spoken of were to be חֹל, *profane*, it is not meant that they were to have any positive impurity either legal or moral attached to them, but that they were to be regarded and treated as *common*, not being appropriated by any particular individuals. They were to be free to the use of all.

the five-and-twenty thousand of the oblation toward the east border, and westward before the five-and-twenty thousand toward the west border, over against the portions for the prince; and it shall be the holy oblation; and the sanctuary of the house
22 shall be in the midst thereof. Moreover from the possession of the Levites, from the possession of the city, in the midst of that which belongs to the prince, between the border of Judah,
23 and the border of Benjamin, shall be for the prince. And as to the rest of the tribes; from the east side to the west side:
24 Benjamin, one. And by the border of Benjamin, from the east
25 side to the west side: Simeon, one. And by the border of Simeon, from the east side to the west side: Issachar, one.
26 And by the border of Issachar, from the east side to the west
27 side: Zebulon, one. And by the border of Zebulon, from the
28 east side to the west side: Gad, one. And by the border of Gad, on the south side southward, the border shall be from Tamar, the waters of Meriboth-Kadesh, and to the river toward
29 the great sea. This is the land which ye shall divide by lot unto the tribes of Israel for inheritance; and these are their
30 portions, saith the Lord Jehovah. And these are the goings forth of the city; on the north side four thousand and five
31 hundred measures. And the gates of the city shall be according to the names of the tribes of Israel: three gates northward, one
32 gate of Reuben, one gate of Judah, one gate of Levi. And on the east side, four thousand and five hundred; and three gates, even one gate of Joseph, one gate of Benjamin, one gate of Dan.
33 And on the south side four thousand and five hundred measures; and three gates, one gate of Simeon, one gate of Issachar, one

28. The תָּמָר, *Tamar*, here mentioned is not Jericho, as the Targumist expounds, but a locality situated at the distance of a day's journey to the south of Hebron, and a little to the west of the Dead Sea. Both, however, take their name from the *palm trees* abounding in the neighborhood. By נַחֲלָה כְּלִיתָיִם הַגָּדוֹל, *the river by the great sea*, we are to understand the *Rhinocorura* or the *Wadi el-Arish*, on the confines of Palestine and Egypt. elsewhere called, on this account, נַחַל מִצְרַיִם, *the river of Egypt*. The ה in הַחֵמָה is simply the postpositive adverb, indicating direction towards a place.

35. As there was to be a new city, it was befitting that it should have a new name. The import of that here given: יְהֹוָה שָׁמָּה, *Jehovah-shammah*, indicates that it was to be specially honored with the divine presence and protection. שָׁמָּה is not in this place to be taken strictly as an adverb of direction, as if meant to express the idea that Jehovah would be specially propense towards Jerusalem, but is simply equivalent to the local signification *there*. Compare Gen. xxiii. 13; Isa. xxxiv. 15; Ps. cxxii. 5; and as to meaning, Ps. xlviii. 1–3.

34 gate of Zebulun. And on the west side, four thousand and five hundred, with their three gates; one gate of Gad, one gate of Asher, one gate of Naphtali.

35 Round about eighteen thousand measures; and the name of the city from that day shall be: JEHOVAH IS THERE.

Here endeth this remarkable vision, which, though greatly mystified by many of the attempts that have been made to explain it, stands forth to view on the sacred page as a noble specimen of divine wisdom, admirably calculated to inspire the captive exiles in Babylonia with the cheering hope of their re-settlement in their own land, and the restoration of their beloved metropolis and temple. In contemplating it, the truly spiritually-minded Christian, with his thoughts raised above all earthly localities, will not, as the Germans express it, perplex himself with *Grübeleien*, subtle and trifling inquiries, but will grasp the grand ideas which the vision suggests, and anticipate for himself in a future world a realization of what was only dimly shadowed forth by that which is here described. May it be the happiness of the writer and each of his readers to be raised to dwell in the house not made with hands, eternal in the heavens!

CATALOGUE OF BOOKS

PUBLISHED BY

WARREN F. DRAPER,

ANDOVER, MASS.

These Books will be sent post-paid to any Address on Receipt of the price named.

Angel over the Right Shoulder, The; or the Beginning of a New Year. By the Author of " Sunnyside." 40 cents.

" It is as provokingly short as it is exquisitely beautiful." — *Boston Recorder.*
" What a blessed thing is a sunny spirit, ever cheerful and happy, and ever diffusing joy over all around it. Such a spirit is the Author of " Sunny Side." She comes to us again as a living angel — in good omen over the *right* shoulder. We commend it to all mothers, and especially to all Mrs. Jellabys." — *Independent.*

Appleton. Works of Jesse Appleton, D.D., with a Memoir of his Life and Character. 2 vols. 8vo. $3.00

" They will ever form standard volumes in American theological literature." — *Biblical Repository,* 1837, p. 249.

Augustine's Confessions. SEE SHEDD.

Augustinism and Pelagianism. By G. F. WIGGERS, D.D. Translated from the German, with Notes and Additions, by PROF. R. EMERSON, D.D. pp. 383. 8vo. $1.50

" The two theories of these distinguished men are thoroughly presented in this work, and are valuable to the theologian." — *Religious Union.*

Bascom. Political Economy. Designed as a Text-Book for Colleges. By JOHN BASCOM, A.M., Professor in Williams College. 12mo. pp. 366. $1.50

" It goes over the whole ground in a logical order. The matter is perspicuously arranged under distinct chapters and sections; it is a compendious exhibition of the principles of the science without prolonged disquisitions on particular points, and it is printed in the style for which the Andover Press has long been deservedly celebrated." — *Princeton Review.*
" This is a valuable work upon a subject of much interest. Professor Bascom writes well, and his book makes an excellent manual. His stand-point in the middle of the nineteenth century gives it a character quite unlike that of the older works upon the subject." — *Boston Recorder.*
" This work is one of value to the student. It treats of the relations and character of political economy, its advantages as a study, and its history. Almost every subject in the range of the science is here touched upon and examined in a manner calculated to interest and instruct the reader." — *Amherst Express.*
" The book is worthy a careful study, both for the views it contains and as a mental training. The author understands himself, and has evidently studied his subject well. — *Evening Express.*

Ellicott. Commentaries, Critical and Grammatical, of C. J. Ellicott, Bishop of Gloucester and Bristol, viz.: on

| Galatians, | Ephesians, |
| Thessalonians, | The Pastoral Epistles, |

Philippians, Colossians, and Philemon.

THE SET in two volumes, black cloth, bevelled edges,	$8.00
THE SET in two volumes, tinted paper, cloth extra, bevelled edges, gilt tops,	10.00
THE SET in five volumes, same style,	12.00

These Commentaries may also be had separately, in black cloth.

The Commentaries of Prof. Ellicott supply an urgent want in their sphere of criticism. Prof. Stowe says of them, in his Notice to the Commentary on the Galatians: "It is the crowning excellence of these Commentaries that they are exactly what they profess to be — *critical* and *grammatical*, and therefore in the best sense of the term, *exegetical*. ..... His results are worthy of all confidence. He is more careful than Tischendorf, slower and more steadily deliberate than Alford, and more patiently laborious than any other living New Testament critic, with the exception, perhaps, of Tregelles."

"They [Ellicott's Commentaries] have set the first example in this country [England] of a thorough and fearless examination of the grammatical and philological requirements of every word of the sacred text. I do not know of anything superior to them in their own particular line in Germany; and they add, what, alas! is so seldom found in this country, profound reverence for the matter and subjects on which the author is laboring; nor is their value lessened by Mr. Ellicott's having confined himself for the most part to one department of a commentator's work, — the grammatical and philological." — *Dean Alford.*

"His Commentaries are among the best, if not the very best, helps a student can have." — *American Presbyterian and Theological Review.*

"Ellicott is one of the best commentators of this class [grammatical interpretation]" — *Princeton Review.*

"They fill a scholar with genuine admiration. Their patient examination of the text bringing out the most delicate shades of meaning and developing the logical sequence of thought by grammatical criticism; their insight into spiritual truth; their candor and honesty and thoroughness in dealing with controverted passages; their reverence for the inspired record; their modesty and charity united with a firmness in adhering to truth; their brevity and condensed fulness make them just the guide a Christian scholar loves in studying the sacred page." — *Watchman and Reflector.*

"The Commentaries of Prof. Ellicott belong to the first class of critical writings of the New Testament. The author is an able, independent, and candid critic, his learning is full and accurate, and his judgment sound and discriminating." — *Boston Recorder.*

"We would recommend all scholars of the original scriptures who seek directness, luminous brevity, the absence of everything irrelevant to strict grammatical inquiry, with a concise and yet very complete view of the opinions of others, to possess themselves of Ellicott's Commentaries." — *American Presbyterian.*

"A scho'arly and religious earnestness, a thoroughness, candor, and moderation, in connection with their convenient shape and compendious comprehensiveness, give them a character elevated and unique among works of their class." — *The Lutheran and Missionary.*

"To Bishop Ellicott must be assigned the first rank, if not the first place in the first rank, of English biblical scholarship. The series of Commentaries on the Pauline Epistles are in the highest style of critical exegesis." — *Methodist Quarterly.*

"The best English work of this character." — *New Englander.*

"Strictly grammatical and critical, thorough and fearless, concise yet complete, worthy of all confidence." — *Evangelical Review.*

Books Published by W. F. Draper.

Ellicott. Commentaries, Critical and Grammatical, of J. C. Ellicott, Bishop of Gloucester and Bristol, viz.: on

Galatians. With an Introductory Notice by C. E. STOWE, Professor in Andover Theological Seminary, 8vo. pp. 183. $1.75

"We have never met with a learned Commentary on any book of the New Testament so nearly perfect in every respect as the 'Commentary on the Epistle to the Galatians,' by Prof. Ellicott, of King's College, London — learned, devout, and orthodox." — *Independent.*

"The grand idea of Professor Ellicott in this exegetical Commentary, is by a critical examination of the Greek text, according to the grammatical construction of the language, to ascertain the exact ideas which the inspired penmen designed to convey; and beyond all doubt the author has brought to his work an amount of learning which is not surpassed by any critical scholar of the age." — *Philadelphia Enquirer.*

"As an aid in preparation for recitations in a seminary, or as a volume to be used in connection with lectures on the New Testament, as exhibiting a true and thorough scholarship, as brought to bear upon the sacred writings, or as inciting the student to imitate the example set before him by the author, and thus to labor diligently in this department of his education, this Commentary cannot be too highly recommended." — *New Englander.*

Ephesians. 8vo. pp. 190. $1.75

"Ellicott, possessed of a deeper reverence [than de Wette] and a more thoughtful piety, has adopted the same method [grammatical analysis], and has produced Commentaries on the Pauline writings, which, for accurate analysis and clear statement, have not as yet been equalled. The superiority of this method of exegesis, is, perhaps, more strikingly evident in the Commentary on the Ephesians. Only by this method could the language of this transcendent Epistle be made to give forth its profound meaning in clearest utterance." — *Watchman and Reflector.*

"The careful critical student of Ephesians will find Ellicott a most welcome and valuable assistant." — *Christian Review.*

"A brief analysis of the Epistle is all that is needed to render this volume one of the most perfectly finished works in the department of sacred letters to which it belongs." — *North American Review.*

"The whole volume is worthy of adoption as a manual in the theological school and in the classical library." — *Lutheran and Missionary.*

"It is the best comment on the Ephesians, for students of the original, which we have yet seen — by far. Its learning is affluent, its discriminations nice, and its spirit admirable." — *Congregationalist.*

Thessalonians. 8vo. pp. 171. $1.75

"For clearness, brevity, scholar-like fidelity, appreciation of the real grammatical sense of the text, absence of all discursive disquisitions, and evidence of comprehensive and profound learning without the slightest parade, and joined with a childlike reverence for the word of God, these Commentaries are unique in the biblical literature of England. We know nothing equal to them anywhere." — *American Presbyterian.*

"A learning deep, varied, and accurate; a critical faculty strong by nature, cultivated with great diligence, and exercised with singular delicacy; and with that unfailing modesty which springs from being thoroughly grounded in the great principles of the Catholic faith; such are the qualities that give worth to these weighty pages." — *The Church Journal.*

Pastoral Epistles. 8vo. pp. 265. $2.50

"Passages which the reader may have thought incapable of any further elucidation, when submitted to his critical process, often are seen to possess a richness of meaning hitherto unsuspected." — *National Baptist.*

Philippians, Colossians, and Philemon. 8vo. pp. 278. $2.50

This set of Commentaries may also be had bound in two volumes.

Haven. Studies in Philosophy and Theology. By JOSEPH HAVEN, D.D., Professor in Chicago Theological Seminary. 8vo. pp. 502. $2.00

"This work is divided into two parts. The first part contains Essays having the following titles: Philosophy of Sir William Hamilton; Mill versus Hamilton; the Moral Faculty; Province of Imagination in Sacred Oratory; the Ideal and the Actual. The second part contains Essays on Natural Theology; the Doctrine of the Trinity; Theology as a Science — its dignity and value; Place and Value of Miracles in the Christian System; Sin as related to Human Nature and the Divine Mind; Arianism, the Natural Development of the Views held by the Early Church Fathers.

"Dr. Haven has exhibited much ability and a good spirit in discussing various controverted questions in philosophy and theology. We hope that this volume will tend to increase the interest of the religious public in these important questions. Men who differ from the author in some of his speculations, will be pleased with his distinctness of thought and perspicuity of style." — *Bibliotheca Sacra.*

"Dr. Haven writes with clearness, and with the ease of a man who has made a thorough study of the subjects which he undertakes to deal with." — *The Presbyterian.*

"The reader will find that Prof. Haven is remarkable for a very lucid explanation of abstruse matters. His style is transparent, and he constantly surprises or delights the reader by some unexpected sally of wit or play of fancy." — *Independent.*

"They grapple earnestly and clearly with the great problems now agitating the world of philosophy and theology..... The views of the writer we believe to be sound, and judiciously and clearly expressed, and we regard him as worthy of the thanks of the busy age and busy church for placing them before the public in this permanent and attractive shape." — *American Presbyterian.*

"Prof. Haven's merits as a clear, vigorous, and fresh thinker are well understood; while those who have heard or read him much, become sensible in him of a certain quaint charm of expression, which frequently lightens up what else would be some dull waste of prosaic, though very necessary thought, with a singularly pleasing glow of animation. Everybody who knows him, too, knows that he is a sturdy believer in the good old Scotch Hamiltonian philosophy, and the distinctively New England Theology, and will not think of looking for anything else here. These they will find — from different angles of vision, and in different forms of illustration; with no slavish subordination, but in the free putting forth of an honest and able disciple, who believes in them *ex animo*; who believes that they are, and must, and will be supreme among the entities and the ologies; and who seeks to use them in an honest and earnest way for the solution of the great problems which belong to the characters and relations of God and man." — *Congregationalist and Recorder.*

"Dr. Haven's views in philosophy, contravening Mill, and giving a qualified approval of Hamilton, coincide substantially with those of McCosh, Porter, and other able writers of England and America on such topics. As to the foundation of moral obligation he holds that the right is ultimate and inexplicable, and in a condensed Supplementary Note of four pages, ably replies to the criticism of his views by Pres. Hopkins in the 'Law of Love.'.... The theological essays are timely as well as able; opposing rationalizing tendencies, yet defending new school positions; maintaining evangelical doctrine, yet dealing candidly with objectors, both as regards the history and the reason of each case. This is especially true of the author's treatment of the difficult subject of the Trinity, and the development of Arianism." — *The Advance.*

"Pofessor Haven gives us in this condensed form, the fruitage of his life-thoughts upon the grandest themes that can engage the human attention..... We deem it no more than just to say, that in this volume philosophy and faith blend, each strengthening the other, to a degree unsurpassed in any work of the kind. The wavering will be confirmed by his logic, while those inclined to credulity will be quickened to thought." — *Chicago Evening Journal.*

"The propositions and the subsequent arguments are always clear and distinct, while Prof. Haven's style has enough of grace and force to relieve his topics of any dulness which naturally belongs to them." — *Springfield Republican.*

Books Published by W. F. Draper.

Henderson. Commentaries, Critical, Philological, and Exegetical, viz.: on

The Book of the Twelve Minor Prophets. Translated from the Original Hebrew. By E. HENDERSON, D.D. With a Biographical Sketch of the Author, by E. P. BARROWS, Hitchcock Professor in Andover Theological Seminary. 8vo. pp. 490. $4.00

"This Commentary on the Minor Prophets, like that on the Prophecy of Isaiah, has been highly and deservedly esteemed by professional scholars, and has been of great service to the working ministry." — *Bibliotheca Sacra.*

The work is invaluable for its philological research and critical acumen. It is published in substantial and elegant style, clear white paper and beautiful type. The notes are learned, reliable, and practical." — *American Presbyterian, etc.*

"This is probably the best commentary extant on the Minor Prophets. The work is worthy of a place in the library of every scholar and every diligent and earnest reader of the Bible." — *Christian Chronicle.*

"It is altogether the best commentary in existence on the Minor Prophets." — *Religious Union.*

"The Minor Prophets" is a valuable book. Dr. Henderson is very careful to avoid fanciful interpretations — at least this is his canon, and there is much good sense shown everywhere." — *Presbyterian Quarterly.*

"We have met with no so satisfactory a commentary on this part of the prophetic scripture." — *Watchman and Reflector.*

"Practical good sense joined to the most thorough and extensive erudition that give so great a value to all his works, and not the least so to this. The work of the American editor is well done." — *Free Press.*

"The only satisfactory commentary on the Minor Prophets we know of in the English language." — *Episcopal Recorder.*

"The volume before us gives abundant evidence of patient scholarship and clear conceptions of evangelical truth." — *Evangelical Quarterly.*

"Dr. Henderson's commentaries are rich in wholesome and true exposition." — *Presbyterian Magazine.*

"The notes are replete with the fruits of varied learning." — *The Presbyterian.*

Jeremiah and Lamentations. Translated from the original Hebrew. 8vo. pp. 315. $3.00

"Whatever surrounds the reader with the national life of the Hebrews, enables him to understand the sacred writers. In addition, the critical student needs exegetical helps in catching the sense of the author. Dr. Henderson has undertaken to meet these wants to a considerable extent, and has succeeded well. Those ministers who are in the habit of giving brief expositions of the prophetic writing, will find great assistance from this volume." — *Congregational Review.*

"The late Dr. Henderson is favorably known to the American public by his two works upon Isaiah and the Minor Prophets. His familiarity for many years with Oriental literature fitted him, in connection with his daily studies of Scripture as a theological professor, to be an expounder of the Hebrew Prophets. — *The Advance.*

"It is a scholarly and devout analysis of the saddest of the prophets. It is a valuable contribution to our biblical literature." — *Zion's Herald.*

"His work on Isaiah was first given to the world in 1840; then came his commentary on the Minor Prophets (1845, reprinted at Andover in 1859), then the present work (1851), and lastly one on Ezekiel. They are alike noted for accuracy and breadth of scholarship, patient research, and a happy commingling of a critical with a devout spirit." — *Burlington Free Press.*

"This admirable commentary meets a want long felt by biblical students. Those acquainted with Dr. Henderson's work on the Minor Prophets need scarcely be told of the ability and learning and piety which characterize this volume." *Protestant Churchman.*

"With some drawbacks of taste and judgment, and somewhat too evident theological prepossessions, we commend the volume as affording biblical students the best commentary at their command." — *Independent.*

K

Books Published by W. F. Draper.

Murphy. *Critical and Exegetical Commentaries of Prof. James G. Murphy, LL.D., T.C.D., viz.: on*

Genesis.   Exodus.

"Dr. Murphy in his commentaries has a definite plan, which he carries out. The text is explained, translated anew, and comments are added on the difficult and mooted points. He is a fair, clear, and candid interpreter. His aim is to reconcile the Scriptures with science by an impartial examination of the text." — *American Presbyterian and Theological Review.*

Genesis. With a Preface by J. P. Thompson, D.D., New York. 8vo. pp. 535. $3.50

"The most valuable contribution that has for a long time been made to the many aids for the critical study of the Old Testament is Mr. Draper's republication of Dr. Murphy on Genesis, in one octavo volume. Dr. Murphy is one of the Professors of the Assembly's College at Belfast, and adds to a thorough knowledge of the Hebrew, and of the science of interpretation, great common sense, genuine wit, and admirable power of expression. Hence his commentary is racy and readable, as well as reliable. No volume will be more useful to those who have been troubled by the Colenso criticisms; and no man has pricked the bubble of that inflated bishop with a more effectual and relieving wound than Dr. Murphy. It is a good deal to say of a commentary, but we say it in all sincerity, that this volume furnishes about as fascinating work for one's hours for reading as any volume of the day, in any department of literature; while its general influence will be salutary and effective for the truth." — *Congregationalist.*

"Dr. Thompson, in the preface, commends this work 'as a timely antidote to much of the negative and destructive criticism upon the Pentateuch.' Dr. Murphy is an Irish Presbyterian, who has prepared several books which show high scholarship and patient research; and this book proves him to be a devout and believing Christian. His handling of Colenso's difficulties shows his Irish wit, as well as his learning and logic. The translation here given is very beautiful, and in such explicit language as to be a rich commentary of itself, while the abundant and rich information given in the notes charms the reader on with more than the zest of fiction. — *Boston Recorder.*

"A Commentary on Genesis, embodying the results of the latest investigations and criticisms, and treating the record fairly and in a Christian spirit, has long been needed. We think the want is here excellently well supplied. Dr. Murphy is evidently at home in 'Hebrew criticism.' He is soundly 'orthodox' in his own doctrinal views. He rejects, with the contempt they deserve, the absurd glosses and inventions of rationalist theologians, whether German or English; and he is not afraid to stand loyally by all the demands of the original record, strictly interpreted. We do not hesitate to say that his exposition of the first chapter of Genesis satisfies our own mind better than any other we have ever seen. He holds that the days of creation were literal days; a sufficient interval of time, as he thinks, being implied between the first and second verses of the chapter for all those immense effects which Geologists claim to trace, and the work of the six days being simply the preparation of the earth's present surface for its present inhabitants. — *Christian Times and Witness.*

"This work is very timely in its appearance, and will prove a good antidote to the rationalistic publications and infidel theories respecting the history of mankind as given in the Old Testament Scriptures." — *New York Observer.*

"We confess to a peculiar satisfaction in this commentary for this thing: that the author does not feel called on to go, in his exegesis, beyond the text and the light of the times when it was written. The style of the writing is peculiarly good, being simple, clear, and quite free from scholastic words and hybrid English, such as we find in Bengel." — *Boston Review.*

"In the critical study of the Old Testament this monograph will be found an important help." — *Evangelical Review.*

"The work before us is one of great value, and meets the long-existing want better than any work on Genesis we have yet seen." — *Morning Star.*

Q

Books Published by W. F. Draper.

Murphy. Critical and Exegetical Commentaries, of Prof. James G. Murphy, LL.D., T.C.D., viz.: on Exodus. 8vo. pp. 385. $3.00

"Thus far nothing has appeared in this country for half a century on the first two books of the Pentateuch so valuable as the present two volumes." [On Genesis and Exodus]. His style is lucid, animated, and often eloquent. His pages afford golden suggestions and key-thoughts..... Some of the laws of interpretation are stated with so fresh and natural a clearness and force that they will permanently stand." — *Methodist Quarterly.*

"I feel that I am richer for having it on my shelf of Christian armory. I wish every one of my brethren in the ministry had the same joy; and few need be deprived of it, for the books are very cheap." — *Rev. H. C. Fish, D.D.*

"Prof. Murphy's Commentary on Genesis has been published long enough to have secured the highest reputation for scholarship, research, and sound judgment. This volume on Exodus takes its place in the same rank, and will increase rather than diminish its author's reputation among scholars." — *National Baptist.*

"Dr. Murphy has done a noble service to his college and church in the publication of this work." — *The Occident.*

"This is the second volume of the ablest Commentary on the Pentateuch that has yet fallen into our hands." — *The Weekly Press.*

"By its originality and critical accuracy it must command the high regard of the scholar and theologian, whilst the ease and grace of its style, the judiciousness with which it selects and unfolds its many subjects of discussion, will be sure to fix and reward the attention of the general student." — *The Lutheran.*

"This volume is a fit successor of that on the Book of Genesis, by the same author. The two ought to be in every minister's library, and they will be found valuable helps to Sabbath-school teachers and others." — *Vermont Chronicle.*

Monod's St. Paul. Five Discourses. By ADOLPHE MONOD. Translated from the French by Rev. J. H. MYERS, D.D. 12mo. pp. 191. 90 cents.

"The aim of the author is to present an estimate of the character, labors, and writings of the Apostle Paul in the light of an example, and to apply the principles which actuated him, and which he maintained, to Christians of the present day." — *Boston Journal.*

"A book unsurpassed in its department, in any language, for manly eloquence, thorough research, profound reflection, a most earnest, glowing, winning, Christian spirit, united with an exact appreciation of the great Apostle's character and work, and a wise, cautious, but bold and unflinching, application of his teachings to the times in which we live." — *The Translator.*

"This little volume we regard as a very valuable addition to what may be called the "Literature of the Apostle Paul." The number of books that have been composed upon St. Paul, is one of the many proofs of his greatness, both by nature and grace. But of them all, there is not a more vital and appreciating book than this of Monod. Original and suggestive thoughts are continually struck out upon collateral subjects, while yet the principal aim of the work is never lost sight of. The account of the physique of the Apostle, in its relations to eloquence (p. 115 seq.), will interest the preacher. The translation is faithful and elegant; reproducing, in no ordinary degree, the finer and more intangible qualities in the style of a vivid and commanding orator." — *Bibliotheca Sacra.*

"A masterly and most eloquent delineation of the inner life of the great Apostle." — *Evangelical Quarterly.*

"These Sermons are remarkable for richness of thought and expression, and for a correct application of the principles and practice of the Apostle to the events of our own time." — *Religious Union.*

"These Discourses are distinguished for genuine eloquence, thorough research, and profound thought, accompanied with a glowing, earnest spirit, adapting the lessons of the great Apostle to the spiritual wants of men." — *Christian Observer.*

"A very interesting book this is, and calculated to stir up the reader's mind and conscience." — *Banner of the Cross.*

Books Published by W. F. Draper.

Stuart. Critical and Exegetical Commentaries by Moses Stuart, late Professor in Andover Theological Seminary, viz.: on

Romans,	Hebrews,	The Apocalypse,
Proverbs,		Ecclesiastes.

Commentary on the Epistle to the Romans. Third Edition. Edited and revised by Prof. R. D. C. Robbins. 12mo. pp. 544. $2.25

"His Commentary on the Romans is the most elaborate of all his works. It has elicited more discussion than any of his other exegetical volumes. It is the result of long-continued, patient thought. It expresses in clear style his maturest conclusions. It has the animating influence of an original treatise, written on a novel plan and under a sense of personal responsibility. Regarding it in all its relations, its antecedents and consequents, we pronounce it the most important Commentary which has appeared in this country on this Epistle." — *Bibliotheca Sacra.*

"We heartily commend this work to all students of the Bible. The production of one of the first biblical scholars of our age, on the most important of all the doctrinal books of the New Testament, it deserves the careful study not only of those who agree with Prof. Stuart in his theological and exegetical principles, but of those who earnestly dissent from some of his views in both respects." — *Watchman and Reflector.*

"Not only as one of the earliest contributions of American scholarship to biblical criticism, but also as one of the best commentaries upon the most difficult of Paul's Epistles, the work of Prof. Stuart on the Romans will have a permanent place in biblical literature. Prof. Stuart's method combines the exegetical with the doctrinal and practical. His rare force and earnestness, however, are mainly expended in what may be styled critico-theological discussion. His tendency was somewhat to repetition and diffuseness — a pardonable fault in the infancy of biblical criticism in this country. Prof. Robbins has obviated this defect by carefully pruning the Commentary of redundancies, without in the least impairing the sense of the author. He has also reduced the length of some of the Excursus, which the progress of biblical science has rendered less important. On the other hand, in the Introduction, which he has almost entirely rewritten, and in brief notes scattered through the volume, Prof. Robbins has enriched the Commentary with the fruits of later criticism, and of his own researches in the same field. It now forms a neat duodecimo volume at about one half the cost of the first edition." — *Independent.*

"We are glad to see a new edition of this valuable Commentary, without which no ordinary theological library is complete. The exegetical works of Prof. Stuart have many excellences, and it will be a long time before the student of the Bible in the original will be willing to dispense with them as a part of his critical apparatus. The Commentary on the Epistle to the Romans was originally prepared with great labor by the author, and the present edition has the advantage of having passed under the supervision of Prof. Robbins, whose studies have given him a special fitness for such a service. Alterations have occasionally been made, with abridgment in some places and additions in others." — *Boston Recorder.*

"All of Prof. Stuart's works would be improved by similar editing, — cautious, reverent, skilful, sufficient, — and brought down to date in the literature of the Epistle. To all students at Andover under Prof. Stuart his commentaries have great interest, and (except, perhaps, that on the Apocalypse) no other can supersede their frequent use. The spirit of the man is so intertwined with them as to be a perpetual stimulant and benediction to the reader. — *Congregationalist.*

"In turning over its pages we recall the learning, the zeal, the acumen, and the idiosyncrasies of one of the most remarkable of the great and good men which our theological world has produced ...... This contribution by Prof. Stuart has justly taken a high place among the Commentaries on the Epistle to the Romans, and, with his other works, will always be held in high estimation by students of the Sacred Scriptures." — *New York Observer.*

W

Books Published by W. F. Draper.

Commentary on the Epistle to the Hebrews. By Prof. Moses Stuart. Third Edition. Edited and revised by Prof. R. D. C. Robbins. 12mo. pp. 575. $2.25

"The Commentaries of Prof. Stuart abide the test of time. Though somewhat diffusive in style, they contain so much thorough discussion of doctrinal points, so much valuable criticism on pregnant words, and such an earnest religious spirit, that they must live for generations as a part of the apparatus for the biblical student." — *Independent.*

"It is from the mind and heart of an eminent biblical scholar, whose labors in the cause of sacred learning will not soon be forgotten." — *Christian Observer.*

"It is a rich treasure for the student of the original. As a commentator, Prof. Stuart was especially arduous and faithful in following up the thought, and displaying the connection of a passage, and his work as a scholar will bear comparison with any that have since appeared on either side of the Atlantic." — *American Presbyterian.*

"This Commentary is classical, both as to its literary and its theological merits. The edition before us is very skilfully edited by Prof. Robbins, and gives in full Dr. Stuart's text, with additions bringing it down to the present day." — *Episcopal Recorder.*

"We have always regarded this excellent Commentary as the happiest effort of the late Andover Professor. It seems to us well-nigh to exhaust the subjects which the author comprehended in his plan." — *Boston Recorder.*

"Professor Stuart has held a large place in the eye of the church, as a man well furnished with all the learning required in a scriptural commentator; and we recognize his merit, while we do not always rely on the theology of his comments." — *Presbyterian.*

"One of the most valuable critical expositions of that master work of the Apostles that exists in our language. It is not necessary or fitting to enter here upon any extended statement of its character and value, as that is well known and properly appreciated, but only to call the attention of those who wish to possess the results of modern criticism — both with respect to the Epistle itself, and the various questions regarding its authenticity, authorship, the churches to which, and the language in which, it was written — to this, as being all that is desirable at a low price and in small compass." — *Banner of the Covenant.*

Commentary on the Apocalypse. By Prof. Moses Stuart. 2 vols. 8vo. 504, 504. $5.00

"The first volume is taken up with matters of an introductory nature, pertaining to the character of the book, its authorship, and the time when it was written, nature of its language and idiom, comparison of it with Old Testament prophecies and with contemporary apochryphal writings, history of the interpretation of it, etc. The second volume contains the Commentary and several dissertations on various topics connected with the subject. The Commentary will, doubtless, awaken general attention and earnest discussion both in this country and in Great Britain, the more so, as on some fundamental points, it is at variance with the interpretations of the Apocalypse which have had universal currency where the English language is spoken." — *Bibliotheca Sacra.*

"The first volume treats of the Apocalypse in general, noticing its peculiar form and arrangement — with other and Apocryphal Apocalypses — and proving John the beloved disciple to have been its author; while the second volume is wholly occupied with the exposition of the book in hand, and of six discourses on as many distinct topics of special interest, connected with the exposition ..... The spirit of the author — candid generous, sincere, elevated, and yet subdued by conscious imperfection, to the admission of his own incompetency to develop the meaning of the Holy Spirit, except so far as he is moved by the same Spirit, and controlled by the changeless laws of interpretation. A more copious stock of sacred learning, we say without hazard, is nowhere to be found within an equal compass. Every page, so far as we have gone with it, is full of riches drawn from the exhaustless storehouse of fact, philosophy, and revelation, duly arranged, chastely displayed, and readily pouring into any hand opened to receive them." — *Boston Recorder.*

Commentary on Ecclesiastes. By PROF. MOSES STUART. Second Edition. Edited and Revised by R. D. C. ROBBINS, Professor in Middlebury College. 12mo. pp. 316. $1.50

"A most thorough, plain, careful, faithful Commentary. It consists of a preliminary dissertation on the nature, design, method, and history of the book; a translation having the commentary after each verse, and a brief final summary of most of the chapters. The commentary is worked out in a most thorough manner, both its philosophy and exegesis." — *Independent.*

"The first characteristic of Professor Stuart as a commentator is the exhaustive thoroughness of his labors. His exegesis is in general skilful and felicitous, especially in bringing out the meaning of the obscure passages, and adding new and delicate shades of thought to the more obvious and superficial sense." — *North American Review.*

"This Commentary casts much light on this difficult portion of God's word." — *Boston Review.*

"The Commentary on Ecclesiastes was among the latest and ripest of its author's works." — *Christian Review.*

"It bears the marks of his vigorous and intuitive mind on every page." — *Boston Transcript.*

"One of the ripest and most interesting of Dr. Stuart's works." — *The Lutheran.*

Commentary on the Book of Proverbs. By PROF. MOSES STUART. 12mo. pp. 432. $1.75

"This is the last work from the pen of Prof. Stuart. Both this Commentary and the one preceding it on Ecclesiastes, exhibit a mellowness of spirit which savors of the good man ripening for heaven; and the style is more condensed, and, in that respect more agreeable, than in some of the works which were written in the unabated freshness and exuberant vigor of his mind. In learning and critical acumen they are equal to his former works. No English reader, we venture to say, can elsewhere find so complete a philological exposition of these two important books of the Old Testament." — *Bibliotheca Sacra.*

Stuart. *Works of Moses Stuart, late Professor in Andover Theological Seminary; viz.*

Critical History and Defence of the Old Testament Canon. By PROF. MOSES STUART. 12mo. pp. 450. $1.75

"The author elucidates, in their order, in series of chapters, many questions touching the writings and literature of the Jews, with a freedom and fulness that cannot fail to interest a studious inquirer in this wide field of sacred learning.

"This whole work of Stuart's is lucid and instructive." — *Christian Reflector.*

"It is a reply chiefly to Andrews Norton, and some other Unitarian writers in this country, who discard, if not the whole, yet the greater part of the Old Testament, and portions also of the New, from the canon of the inspired Scripture. The discussion is temperate and manly, and at the same time thorough and satisfactory." — *Christian Secretary.*

"The learning, the shrewdness, and force brought to bear on the grand question at issue, are unsurpassed." — *Boston Recorder.*

Miscellanies. 12mo. pp. xii and 369. $1.25

The work contains, 1. Letters of Dr. Channing on the Trinity; 2. Two Sermons on the Atonement; 3. Sacramental Sermon on the Lamb of God; 4. Dedication Sermon — Real Christianity; 5. Letter to Dr. Channing on Religious Liberty; 6. Supplemental Notes and Postscripts of new additional matter.

Hebrew Grammar of Gesenius as edited by Roediger. Translated, with Additions, and also a Hebrew Chrestomathy. 8vo. pp. viii and 360. $1.25

Books Published by W. F. Draper.

Tyler. *The Theology of the Greek Poets.* By W. S. TYLER, Williston Professor of Greek in Amherst College. 12mo. pp. 365. Cloth, bevelled. $1.75

"Professor Tyler has here produced a work which is an honor to American literature. It is well fitted to be a classic in our Colleges and Theological Seminaries. It furnishes admirable illustrations of the truth of both natural and revealed theology, and suggests original methods for the defence of these truths." — *Bibliotheca Sacra.*

"There are few better Greek scholars in the country than Professor Tyler, who has devoted himself with great earnestness and enthusiasm to the culture and teaching of Greek literature. The chapters which compose the book have all appeared in former years in different Quarterlies. In this way they have attracted the attention of many of our best scholars." Prof. Tyler has done good service to the cause of truth in showing that the Iliad and Odyssey, as well as the dramas of Aeschylus and the tragedies of Sophocles, express ideas and sentiments very much like those we find in contemporary Scriptures." — *Hours at Home.*

"The first Essay is an ingenious and powerful argument in proof that the God of the church is also the God of nature and of providence; so declared by reason in the evidence which it affords. The second essay discusses freshly and powerfully the Homeric question. The four remaining Essays develop the natural theology that is interwoven in the poems thus demonstrated to be Homer's, and in those of Aeschylus and Sophocles." — *Congregationalist.*

"The book is an important contribution to natural theology. It traces the relation of the theology of the Greek poets to that of Christ. Prof. Tyler does his work with the mind of a master." — *Zion's Herald.*

"I have been interested and instructed by reading Professor Tyler's work on the Theology of the Greek Poets. The book is worthy of a wide circulation." — *Prof. Samuel Harris.*

"This volume must be regarded as a standard in its department." — *National Baptist.*

"Prof. Tyler has a strong, plain, clear-cut style, and never writes on stilts, — though his thoughts are high enough, — delights in Anglo-Saxon words, and uses them with great power; packs his pages so full of thought that they are better to read than to listen to, — an unusual trait in these days of wishy-washy writing, — and finally does not leave his subject till it is exhausted." — *Springfield Republican.*

"The whole forms a body of interesting criticism." — *The Presbyterian.*

"Every page exhibits the erudition of the thorough scholar and the accomplished writer." — *Evangelical Quarterly.*

"The aim of the author is to detect the analogies between the myths of the Greek drama and epic, and the truths of revelation. The care of the scholar and the enthusiasm of the poet have been given to the work." — *Independent.*

Taylor. *Questions on Kühner's Grammar.* See Bateman.

Venema's Institutes of Theology. Translated by REV. A. W. BROWN, Edinburgh. 8vo. pp. 532. Fine Edition. $2.50

"It must be admitted that Venema had far more independence, both of thought and style, than belonged to many of his contemporaries. The perusal of Venema's treatise cannot fail, we think, to awaken a spirit of biblical investigation, and to illustrate the importance of an accurate and well-balanced theological system." — *Bibliotheca Sacra.*

"We always feel strong in quoting this profoundly learned writer. In all that is substantial in Oriental scholarship he was the equal of the modern Germans, while he was far before them in what may be called biblical unction, or the power of discerning profound ideas in the Scriptures." — *Prof. Tayler Lewis.*

Vinet. *History of French Literature in the Eighteenth Century.* By ALEXANDER VINET, Professor of Theology at Lausanne. Translated from the French by JAMES BRUYCE. 8vo. pp. 484. Cloth. $3.00

Winer. A Grammar of the Idiom of the New Testament: prepared as a Solid Basis for the Interpretation of the New Testament. By Dr. GEORGE BENEDICT WINER. Seventh edition, enlarged and improved. By Dr. GOTTLIEB LÜNEMANN, Professor of Theology at the University of Göttingen. Revised and Authorized Translation. 8vo. pp. 744.

Cloth, $5.00; sheep, $6.00; half goat, $6.75

"After his death a seventh edition of his Grammar was published in 1866, under the editorial care of Dr. Lünemann. This editor incorporated into this edition the numerous manuscript notes which Winer had prepared for it. 'Without altering the general distribution of matter as it appeared in the sixth edition, he [Winer] constantly improved the book in details, by additions of greater or less extent in more than three hundred and forty places, by erasures and reconstructions, by the multiplication of parallel passages from biblical and from profane literature, by a more precise definition of thoughts and expressions,' etc. Professor Lünemann has added to the seventh edition not only these improvements, but also improvements of his own; and has thus made the seventh edition more full, as well as more accurate, than either of the preceding.

"The first edition of Winer's Grammar was translated into English by Professors Stuart and Robinson in 1825; the fourth edition by Professors Agnew and Ebbeke in 1839; the sixth edition, translated by Professor Masson, was published at Edinburgh, and his translation of the sixth is the basis of Professor Thayer's translation of the seventh [Lünemann's] edition. Professor Thayer, however, has introduced numerous and important corrections of Masson's translation, and has made the present edition of the Grammar decidedly superior to any of the preceding translations. He has made it especially convenient for the uses of an English student, by noting on the outer margin of the pages the paging of the sixth and seventh German editions, and also of Professor Masson's translation. Thus the reader of a commentary which refers to the pages of either of those volumes, may easily find the reference by consulting the margin of this volume. Great care has also been bestowed on the indexes of the present volume, which are now very accurate and complete. One of the indexes, that of passages in the New Testament explained or cited occupies sixty pages, and notes distinctively not only the texts which are merely cited, but also those which are commented upon. For this, much credit is due to Professor G. W. Warren, of the Baptist Theological Seminary in Chicago. The three indexes fill eighty-five pages, and largely augment the value and richness of the volume. The typographical execution of the book also deserves praise; so far as we have examined it, we have been surprised at its correctness in places where the types are apt to err." — *Bibliotheca Sacra.*

"The work of the American editor is done in a thorough and scholarly manner." — *Congregational Quarterly.*

"While nothing has been done by either the American or German editor to alter the character and plan of the work as Winer left it after the labor of a life, nothing has been left undone to correct and complete it, and provide for its more extended usefulness." — *Princeton Review.*

"The whole appearance of the work as it now stands indicates a careful and thorough scholarship. A critical comparison of several pages with the original confirms the impression made by a general examination of the book. In its present form, this translation may now be recommended as worthy of a place in the library of every minister who desires to study the New Testament with the aid of the best critical helps." — *Theological Eclectic.*

"Great pains also have been taken to secure typographical accuracy, an extremely difficult thing in a work of this kind. We rejoice that so invaluable a work has thus been made as nearly perfect as we can hope ever to have it. It is a work that can hardly fail to facilitate and increase the reverent and accurate study of the Word of God." — *American Presbyterian Review.*

Winer's Chaldee Grammar. Translated by PROF. HORATIO B. HACKETT. 8vo. pp. 152. Half cloth. 75 cents.

www.ingramcontent.com/pod-product-compliance
Lightning Source LLC
Chambersburg PA
CBHW021802230426
43669CB00008B/603